Poverty Reduction Strategies in Action

Poverty Reduction Strategies in Action

Perspectives and Lessons from Ghana

EDITED BY
JOE AMOAKO-TUFFOUR AND
BARTHOLEMEW ARMAH

LEXINGTON BOOKS

A division of
ROWMAN & LITTLEFIELD PUBLISHERS, INC.
Lanham • Boulder • New York • Toronto • Plymouth, UK

LEXINGTON BOOKS

A division of Rowman & Littlefield Publishers, Inc.
A wholly owned subsidary of The Rowman & Littlefield Publishing Group, Inc.
4501 Forbes Boulevard, Suite 200
Lanham, MD 20706

Estover Road
Plymouth PL6 7PY
United Kingdom

British Library Cataloguing in Publication Information Available

Library of Congress Cataloging-in-Publication Data

The hardback edition of this book was previously cataloged by the Library of Congress as follows:

Poverty reduction strategies in action : perspectives and lessons from Ghana / edited by Joe Amoako-Tuffour and Bartholemew Armah.
    p. cm.
  Includes bibliographical references and index.
1. Poverty—Ghana. 2. Ghana—Economic policy. 3. Ghana—Economic conditions. I. Amoako-Tuffour, Joe. II. Armah, Bartholomew K.
  HC1060.Z9P6277 2008
  362.5'609667—dc22   2007038512

ISBN-13: 978-0-7391-1010-2 (cloth : alk. paper)
ISBN-10: 0-7391-1010-1 (cloth : alk. paper)
ISBN-13: 978-0-7391-2965-4 (pbk. : alk. paper)
ISBN-10: 0-7391-2965-1 (pbk. : alk. paper)
eISBN-13: 978-0-7391-3003-2
eISBN-10: 0-7391-3003-X

Printed in the United States of America

♾™ The paper used in this publication meets the minimum requirements of American National Standard for Information Sciences—Permanence of Paper for Printed Library Materials, ANSI/NISO Z39.48–1992.

Contents

Part 1: Poverty, Inequality, and Reform Approaches

Part 2: Designing, Implementing, Financing, and Monitoring the GPRS

Part 3: Special Topics in Poverty Reduction

    Daniel K. Twerefou and Eric Osei-Assibey

Part 4: Lessons and the Way Forward

    Bartholomew Armah and Joe Amoako-Tuffour

List of Tables

List of Figures

List of Boxes

Acronyms and Abbreviations

AEP	Alternative Employment Program
BWI	Bretton Woods Institution
CAS	Country Assistance Strategy
CBO	Community Based Organization
CDF	Comprehensive Development Framework
CEPA	Center for Policy Analysis
CSOs	Civil Society Organizations
CWIQ	Core Welfare Indicators Questionnaire
DACF	District Assembly Common Fund
DANIDA	Danish International Development Agency
DPCU	District Planning Coordinating Unit
DWAPs	District Wide Approaches
EAP	Environmental Action Plan
EIA	Environmental Impact Assessment
EPA	Environmental Protection Agency
ERP	Economic Recovery Program
ESAF	Enhanced Structural Adjustment Facility
FAO	Food and Agricultural Organization
FM	Framework Memorandum
GDP	Gross Domestic Product
GE	Generalized Entropy
GIPC	Ghana Investment Promotion Council
GLSS	Ghana Living Standard Survey
GPRS I	Ghana Poverty Reduction Strategy
GPRS II	Growth and Poverty Reduction Strategy
GSS	Ghana Statistical Service
HIPC	Heavily Indebted Poor Countries
HPI	Human Poverty Index
ICCES	Integrated Community Centers for Employable Skills
IEA	Institute of Economic Affairs
IFI	International Financial Institutions
ILO	International Labour Organization
IMF	International Monetary Fund
ISSER	Institute of Statistical, Social and Economic Research

JSA	Joint Staff Assessment
LDP	Letter of Development Policy
M&E	Monitoring and Evaluation
MDA	Ministries, Department and Agencies
MDG	Millennium Development Goals
MDBS	Multi Donor Budgetary Support
MDPI	Manpower Development and Productivity Institute
MEPRC	Ministry of Economic Planning and Regional Cooperation
MESW	Ministry of Employment and Social Welfare
MLGRD	Ministry of Local Government and Rural Development
MoFEP	Ministry of Finance and Economic Planning
MTDP	Medium Term Development Plan
MTEF	Medium-Term Expenditure Framework
MTP	Medium-Term Plan
NBSSI	National Bureau of Small Scale Industries
NDAP	National Decentralization Action Plan
NDC	National Democratic Party
NDPC	National Development Planning Commission
NED	National Economic Dialogue
NEPP	National Environmental Protection Program
NGO	Non-Governmental Organization
NPP	New Patriotic Party
NVTI	National Vocational Training Institute
OECD	Organization of Economic Cooperation and Development
OFY	Operation Feed Yourself
OIC	Opportunities Industrialization Centre
PAMSCAD	Program of Action to Mitigate the Social Costs of Adjustment
PEF	Private Enterprise Foundation
PNDC	Provisional National Defence Council
PRGF	Poverty Reduction and Growth Facility
PRS	Poverty Reduction Strategy
PRSC	Poverty Reduction Support Credit
PRSP	Poverty Reduction Strategy Paper
PSI	Presidential Special Initiative
PSRMP	Public Sector Reform Management Program
PUFMARP	Public Financial Management and Reform Program
SAL	Structural Adjustment Loan

SAF	Structural Adjustment Facility
SAP	Structural Adjustment Program
SAPRI	Structural Adjustment Participatory Review Initiative
SC	Structural Conditionality
SEA	Strategic Environmental Assessment
SECALs	Sectoral Adjustment Loans
SIP	Social Investment Program
STEP	Skills Training and Employment Program
SWAPs	Sector Wide Approaches
SWOT	Strengths, Weakness, Opportunities and Threats
SSA	Sub-Saharan Africa
UNCTAD	United Nations Conference on Trade and Development
UNDP	United Nations Development Program
UNICEF	United Nations Children Fund
USAID	United States Agency for International Development
WB	World Bank

Preface

Poverty reduction is an integral part and a fundamental goal of economic development. Nearly four decades after America embarked on a *War on Poverty*, many developing countries in the early 2000 re-focused their development efforts, more than they have ever done in the past, to tackle the problems of widespread poverty. Perhaps, nowhere was the challenge more clear than in sub-Saharan Africa. Ravaged by cold war geo-politics, bad governance and conflicts, reforms in the 1980s led by the World Bank and the International Monetary Fund brought modest development gains. But by the time the late 1990s rolled along, official data on human development and on many dimensions of economic development, brought home the desperate situation, and, with it, the need for an accelerated plan to tackling the poverty problem.

A Poverty Reduction Strategy (PRS) represents a national plan of action. It provides the poverty diagnosis of a country, defines the range of policies and programs to tackling the poverty problem, and, in the scheme of things, how to finance the poverty alleviation programs. PRS articulates a broader perspective of issues: from macroeconomic management to sector policies, from the efficiency of public spending to the capacity of revenue generation, from employment creation and income growth to income distribution, and from access to public goods to the protection of the vulnerable. The story of Ghana's Poverty Reduction Strategy (GPRS) has not been told before in the way we have attempted to do in this volume.

During the period 2000-2003, several of the contributors to the book served in a variety of roles in this poverty reduction experiment. From their vantage points, they observed the process as politicians, bureaucrats, civil society, bilateral donors, and the multilateral institutions (African Development Bank, World Bank, the International Monetary Fund, the United Nations Development Planning) debated, and collaborated, reluctantly at times, to develop a poverty reduction strategy. Many of the contributors have also seen the tragedy of poverty at first hand in their travels across the country. It is partly this confrontation with poverty that prompted us to evaluate the design, the content, and the prospects of the GPRS in tackling the poverty problem. This volume is about what was done, how it was done, some of the missing pieces, the prospects of the strategy in tackling the poverty problem, and the lessons learned.

Beginning in 2001, the GPRS became the centrepiece of policy-making. After successive structural adjustment reform programs, which begun in 1983, Ghana, on the eve of the new millennium, was highly indebted and trapped in a low growth and a high and volatile inflation path. In December 2000, the opposition party for nearly two decades was elected into office. The party manifesto

"An Agenda for Growth," and cleverly abridged in a twelve point acronym "CREATE WEALTH," sparked optimism. Three months into office, the optimism was tempered. Ghana opted to seek debt relief under the Heavily Indebted Poor Countries (HIPC) Initiative. As part of the HIPC process, Ghana had to formally prepare a Poverty Reduction Strategy Paper (PRSP) in conformity with the general principles outlined by the World Bank.

Wealth creation can be a mesmerizing undertaking. Will poverty reduction spark the same enthusiasm among state actors and the public? Will it substitute for a development strategy to create wealth? Will it provide the foundations of alternative pathways to growth and development, or will it constitute a mere re-labelling of adjustment policies? A vocal minority of the population denied that Ghana was on the brink of a fiscal catastrophe. They wondered whether the HIPC path was the right one to take. But when cynicism and hope conflict over poverty, hope often wins because there was more than just the lack of income at stake. Incomes and consumption poverty were only the beginnings of a long list of the many dimensions of poverty, which include high unemployment, under-employment, malnutrition, infant mortality, maternal mortality, the high incidence of preventable illnesses, poor sanitation, poor access to school and health facilities in the rural areas, and the lack of public attention to the aged, blind, deaf and physically disabled.

In 2002, a task force was put together. An initial framework was developed, followed by a series of town hall meetings and public consultations. These culminated in the formulation of a draft that was subsequently subjected to a wide range of discussions. Marked by moments of controversy and consensus, a revised, professedly comprehensive strategic plan, spanning the period 2003–2005, was finalized in February 2003.

Ghana has been a forerunner in sub-Saharan Africa in several respects. Its comprehensive attempt at poverty reduction was yet another step in that direction. It was not lost on the contributors that in the war on poverty there can be no conquest, only work in progress. For these reasons alone, the story of the GPRS is worth putting together in a volume to benefit future research work. Ghana's experience provides lessons for policymakers and technocrats engaged in the process of formulating and implementing the second (and possibly third) generation of poverty reduction strategies.

Joe Amoako-Tuffour
Bartholomew Armah

Acknowledgments

This volume originated from the opportunity the editors had to work in Ghana during the years 2001–2004. We are both grateful to our respective institutions—St. Francis Xavier University (Canada) and University of Wisconsin-Milwaukee (USA)—for granting us leaves of absence. Little did we know that our chance meeting will lead to this collaboration. Joe Amoako-Tuffour is also grateful to St. Francis Xavier University for a follow-up grant to conduct workshop in Ghana with the contributors to this volume.

A number of people supported our efforts. David Kuijper of the Royal Netherlands Embassy in Accra took interest in the book project and helped secure a grant for research and publication support (activity 10155). Joe Amoako-Tuffour is grateful to J. L. S. Abbey, Executive Director of Centre for Policy Analysis (CEPA), for much help and discussions. CEPA has since 1994 given me the opportunity for summer visits to Ghana. I am grateful for the opportunity to have been part of the stimulating discussions on policy issues with CEPA research colleagues Charles Jebuni, Abena Oduro, and Nii Ashong.

Bartholomew Armah wishes to thank the University of Wisconsin-Milwaukee (UWM) community, particularly faculty of the department of Africology, for granting him three consecutive years of leave despite staffing constraints. Armah is also thankful to Charles Mensa of the Institute for Economic Affairs who provided the institutional support to undertake research in Ghana.

The following people read different aspects of the manuscript, some more than once, and made valuable suggestions: Atsu Amegashie (Guelph University), Emmanuel Yiridoe (Nova Scotia Agricultural College), Santo Dodaro and Glenna Quinn (St. Francis Xavier University), John Asafu-Adjaye (University of Brisbane) and Paul Walters (DFID).

We are grateful to Paa Kwesi Ndoum, Kwame Pianim, Asenso-Okyere (former Vice Chancellor, University of Ghana), Samuel Adei (Executive Director of GIMPA), Ernest Aryeetey (Director of ISSER), Gyan Baffour (former Executive Director of the National Development Planning Commission, NDPC), Akoto Osei (Deputy Minister of Finance and Economic Planning), Angela Farhat also of NDPC, Alfred Fawundu (Resident Director of UNDP, Accra) for sharing ideas and perspectives on the poverty reduction exercise.

We wish to thank many public officials, especially those in the Ministry of Finance and Economic Planning and the NDPC, for their valuable cooperation. Anne Marie MacPherson provided help in typesetting. The final thanks go to our beloved spouses (Joe to Akosua Marfowaa and Bart to Fafa) who had to endure the inconveniences of our physical and mental absences from home for as long as it has taken to complete this volume.

1

Introduction: Poverty Reduction in Ghana

Joe Amoako-Tuffour and
Bartholomew Armah

Poverty was a medieval scourge for a good reason: the world was generally poor then.

—*Debraj Ray 1998, 249*

"In nearly all of economic history most people have been poor and a comparative few have been rich," wrote John Kenneth Galbraith.[1] It is not surprising the efforts that have gone into explaining why this is so. This inquiry into the sources of growth, why some are so rich and some so poor, fascinates the rich and the poor alike. For the rich because it seems possible that none should be poor, especially during the nineteenth and twentieth centuries when economic growth has been higher than during any other period in history. The economists' prediction that under some conditions the living standards of the poor and rich economies may converge is an exciting prospect for the poor, even if the growth experience tampers the optimism.

Since the Industrial Revolution, per capita income growth has been sustained in some countries and, as a result, became rich. For them, the basic links between economic growth, standards of living, and gains in welfare by successive generations are seen as normal course of events. But in several parts of the world, particularly in Africa, the Caribbean and Latin America, growth has been hard to come by (Easterly, 2001). So much so that the prospect of convergence in well-being remains elusive, at least for the billion or so people who in 1998 lived in extreme poverty (Besley and Burgess, 2003). Low and slow rates of growth have been all too common for many countries in sub-Saharan Africa (SSA). For some, high growth rates themselves have not been sufficient to reduce the incidence of poverty without some forms of public intervention because the growth-poverty alleviation nexus seems loose and unpredictable.

We encounter poverty in every part of the world. The causes and the depth vary. Even for industrialized countries, where concerns for inequality and deprivation may have lost some vitality, poverty is not yet a vanquished foe (Sawhill,

1

1988; Jorgenson, 1998). It remains less pervasive, however, and on a relatively smaller scale than in many other parts of the world. But the depth of poverty in some regions of the world, particularly sub-Sahara Africa (SSA), raise deep questions about the performance of economies, of political institutions, and of the global cooperation to help protect people from extreme poverty.

Although the share of the world population living in relative poverty (below the income cutoff of two dollars per day) declined from 60 percent in 1987 to 57 percent in 1998, the headcount increased by 250 million during the same period.[2] This means that globally, nearly twenty-one million people either were born into poverty every year or missed the pathway out of poverty because of disease, debilitating sickness, persistent crop failure, lack of resources, and conflict.

Across the globe, the predicament varies. The proportion of the world population living in extreme poverty (living on less than a dollar a day) fell from 29 percent to 24 percent between 1987–1998, but increased from about 47 percent to 49 percent for SSA, and is projected to decline only to 46 percent in 2015. Looking ahead, even the most optimistic reader of the evidence cannot miss the ominous picture. Between 2000 and 2015, it is predicted that income poverty in East and South Asia will decline by nearly 36 percent, but will rise in Africa by a further 14 percent.[3] For a region with the greatest number of countries with the highest fertility rates and slowest growing economies, the stakes couldn't be higher. While these numbers are not beyond controversy (Chen and Ravillion, 2001 and Deaton, 2002), the picture of poverty in SSA is clear.

The disparaging evidence on world poverty and its human effects have since the 1980s ignited a passion to tackling poverty.[4] By the 1990s, concern for inequality and human deprivation had regained vitality in public debates as it did in the 1960s in western economies. So much so that poverty alleviation would seemingly become "a moral imperative"[5] of the global community. The historian David Landes (1999) remarked poignantly that the greatest single danger facing the world in the third Millennium is "the gap in wealth and health that separates the rich and the poor." That fighting poverty would become a major development focus in recent years, is partly because the presumption that economic growth would lead to poverty reduction everywhere has proven to be less likely than many had hoped for. Predictions had gone awry. Moreover, we may have understood less than we do now about the consequences of a global society where the majority are poor, and are without social safety nets or social protection measures. Extreme poverty is an invitation to social disharmony everywhere.

Increasingly concerned about the seemingly unstoppable advances of poverty, the United Nations (UN) in the 1990s turned its attention to the increasing gap between the rich and the poor, the imminent global consequences, and the need for global partnership for poverty reduction. In the early 1990s, the World Bank President, Lewis Preston, declared that poverty is the benchmark against which we must be judged. The Organization of Economic Cooperation and Development (OECD) in its 1996 report,[6] set out its vision and acknowledged that eradicating poverty is a shared objective of the international community. The explosion of passion and commitment culminated in the Millennium Development Goals (MDGs). Agreed to in September 2000 by 149 countries at the UN Millennium Summit in New York, the central objective of the MDGs was to reduce global poverty by half by 2015. The International Financial Institutions (IFI) joined in the strides towards this central objective. For the IFI, particularly the International Monetary Fund (IMF) and the World Bank (WB), structural adjustment policies that once underpinned lending to developing countries would, at least in name, take a back seat to poverty reduction as the mantra of development finance. The WB's development financial assistance changed from Economic Reform Support Operation (ERSO) to Poverty Reduction Support Credit (PRSC). The IMF's lending supported programs changed from the Enhanced Structural Adjustment Facility (ESAF) to Poverty Reduction Growth Facility (PRGF).

The design of the Ghana Poverty Reduction Strategy (GPRS), initiated in 2001 and completed in February 2003, is part of the global attempt to seek common fronts in the fight against poverty. The GPRS represents Ghana's blueprint for poverty reduction and human development to be financed in part by debt relief resources and official development assistance. Professedly comprehensive, it represents the initial framework the government intended to adopt to support growth and poverty reduction over the medium term. As a blueprint, the GPRS would be thrust dramatically to the centre of government policy-making and serve as a lever of coordination at local, district and regional level planning.

Poverty reduction strategies also reflected somewhat a new development agenda. Poor country governments would set national priorities, ideally reflecting the choices of the people, articulate the specific measures most needed to be taken, and bring the international community on board to support implementation. The core guiding principles of country ownership, process legitimacy, accountability and global partnership had forthright appeal on two grounds. First, having in place such a development framework ideally should make unnecessary the proliferation of fragmented external-led initiatives towards the same goal of poverty alleviation. Second, for Ghana at least, the process envisaged in the preparation of the poverty reductin strategy marked a new era of making, shaping, implementing, and monitoring public policy using a multi-stakeholder process. More than any planning initiative before it, the GPRS ushered in the language of partnership and stakeholder consultation in the policy arena. There was now recognition of the importance of monitoring and evaluating policy processes, outputs, outcomes, and impacts.

Several of the contributors to this book participated in the process of developing the GPRS between the period 2000 and 2003. In their various capacities, they had the vantage points to witness the process unfold as the executive, parliament, bureaucrats, civil society, multilateral and bilateral development partners coalesced to fashion a common effort towards poverty reduction. From the perspective of the contributors, in the context of sub-Saharan Africa, Ghana has been a forerunner and an exemplar of sorts. In the late 1980s and early 1990s, reformist Ghana was a test case of adjustment lending (Easterly, 2001). In aid and debt relief for poverty reduction, Ghana, less fragmented and relatively better governed than its neighbours, will be yet another test case. For this reason alone, the story of one poverty reduction strategy in action is worth putting together in a book. The prospects, the missing pieces and the lessons learnt will be useful for informing the policy-making process and in the endless quest to improve the welfare of citizens.

The Ghana Poverty Reduction Strategy

Undoubtedly, tackling poverty as a national development goal is not new. Ghana has since the 1950s explicitly and relentlessly formulated several development plans to improve the living standards of citizens. The 1951—1956 first five-year Development Plan preceded Independence in 1957. This was followed by the Consolidated Plan of 1957—1959 and the second five-year Development Plan of 1959—1964. Most notable of the development plans was the short-lived seven-year (1963—1970) plan, following the overthrow of the Nkrumah regime in 1966. It was succeeded by a two-year plan of 1968—1970, a one-year plan of 1970—1971, and then the five-year plan of 1975—1980. None of these plans had poverty alleviation as its explicit thrust. Indeed the term *poverty alleviation* had not been coined yet, at least not in the sense that it is used in the development literature now. But the goals and objectives of the plans were articulated in programs and activities with the ultimate objective to improve standards of living. Some observers have argued that except for the 1959—1964 and the 1963—1970 development plans, several of the development plans were more reactive than proactive, responding largely to pressing crisis of the day and lacking a long-term vision or mission statement (see Adjibolosoo, 1988).

The momentum for poverty alleviation and its central role in the development dialogue steadily increased under the Heavily Indebted Poor Countries (HIPC) initiative. Begun in 1996, the HIPC initiative was intended to provide debt relief to low income countries. Debt relief and poverty alleviation subsequently became inseparable. In September 1999, the World Bank and the IMF endorsed a new framework for poverty reduction. Debt-ridden countries yearning for debt relief were expected to prepare poverty reduction programs which outlined the intended use of the debt-relief resources made available to them. As well, these poverty reduction programs were to provide the basis for concessional assistance from both institutions and other bilateral donors.

Ghana's poverty reduction strategy paper was complex in its origin and design. For the ruling party, the decision to opt for the HIPC Initiative stirred debate among political opponents. For a party with an ambitious wealth creation agenda, the emphasis on poverty reduction rather than accelerating growth created discomfort and resentment among party stalwarts. But the preparation of a poverty reduction program in Ghana, if not in name but in principle, pre-dates the debt relief initiative.

The National Development Planning Commission (NDPC), established in April 1990, was charged with coordinating a national planning effort to advise the President on development planning strategies. The NDPC was also charged with the preparation of a broad national development plan. The NDPC subsequently prepared the National Development Policy Framework which outlined the strategic direction for national development over a twenty-five year period from 1996-2020. The document that came to be known as Vision 2020 had as its main development goal to transform Ghana from a poor, underdeveloped, low-income country into a prosperous middle-income country within a generation. This vision was to be implemented through a series of five-year development policy frameworks.

The Vision 2020 was preceded by the Economic Recovery Program (ERP) and Structural Adjustment Policies (SAP) begun in 1983 in a bold attempt to reverse the era of economic decay and the attendant social consequences that had bedevilled the economy since the mid-1970s. The World Bank and the IMF played major roles in assisting the government of Ghana shape the ERP/SAP as well as underwriting its implementation. The implementation trickled through the annual budget but in a less than consistent manner. Although the stabilization measures succeeded in raising average GDP growth from 0.6 percent over the period 1970–1983 to between 4 and 5 percent from 1984–1992, there were mixed reviews. While the measures halted the decline in economic growth and in achieved some level of macroeconomic stability, the pace of growth was slower than envisaged, and the distribution experience were uneven. A weak link between economic growth and poverty reduction further exacerbated deprivations and spatial inequality even as aggregate poverty declined.

Against this background, the first five-year Medium-Term Policy Framework was completed in January 1995 as "Ghana-Vision 2020: The First Step: 1996-2000". The Accelerated Poverty Reduction Strategy presented to the tenth Consultative meeting in 1999 was particularly important if Ghana was to accelerate equitable poverty reduction and raise its average per capita income. An interim Poverty Reduction Strategy Paper (PRSP) was presented to the Bretton Woods Institutions (BWI) in July 2000. In the same month the process of preparing the broader, more consultative GPRS was launched.

As elections approached, the preparation of the GPRS, building on the Vision 2020, came to a temporary halt. The December 2000 election ushered in the new government of the National Patriotic Party (NPP). The NPP brought into office a long-term vision expressed in the party manifesto "Agenda for Positive Change". The action plan was cleverly abridged in the twelve point acronym: "CREATE WEALTH." Barely three months in office, the decision by the government to opt for debt relief under HIPC, reportedly with some persuasion from the British but to the disappointment of Japan, elevated poverty reduction to the fore of the national agenda. This was a reversal of the decision not to opt for HIPC by the previous government of the National Democratic Congress (NDC). The need for a poverty reduction focus was by many indications uncontroversial if Ghana was not to fall further behind in the indicators of growth and socio-economic development. Indeed the famous NPP party manifesto itself was a culmination of nearly two decades of thinking as an "opposition" party. The GPRS embraced well known facts: that there was a widening gap in standards of living between rural and urban Ghanaians, and between different regions of the country; child poverty was on the rise; infant and maternal mortality rates were worsening; human resource development was at risk; and labour market opportunities in the private sector were increasingly on the decline.

For Ghana, preparing a comprehensive poverty reduction strategy document and determining the multi-year costs of the relevant programs and activities had no precedent. To be successful, the spatial distribution and the hierarchies of the poor, the chronic poor, and the vulnerable had to be identified and their circumstances understood prior to defining the pathways to alleviate their poverty or vulnerability to poverty. The World Bank's *Comprehensive Development Framework* (CDF) and the companion one-thousand pages *Poverty Reduction Strategy Paper Sourcebook* provided guidelines for process and content. These documents provide a framework to gauge the adequacy of a country's efforts towards designing effective poverty alleviation strategies. The framework requires that a poverty reduction strategy be based on a proper poverty diagnosis, be country-driven, participatory, comprehensive in scope, costed, results oriented, partnership-oriented, and have a long-term perspective. Indeed, for all low income countries having capacity constraints, developing a poverty reduction strategy document that meets these minimum set of requirements in a timely fashion is not a light responsibility (CEPA, 2000).

What emerged would become the blueprint for medium-term development planning. Winning the war on poverty by the year 2020, as originally set forth in the Ghana Vision 2020, meant relying on three broad themes: growth, human development, and good governance, even if with unequal emphasis. These were covered under the five thematic goals: *macroeconomic stability, production and gainful employment, human resource development and provision of basic services, programs for the vulnerable and excluded, and governance.* The multi-layered attack included following an anti-inflation macroeconomic regime, adopting prudent budgetary policies that protected social expenditures, rationalizing and re-distributing public financial resources towards the kinds of public goods which causally influence capabilities and economic opportunities, and strengthening the institutions of governance.

Wanting to do more than reduce basic poverty, the government identified medium-term priorities. These included private sector development, good governance, enhanced social services, and modernized agriculture. The priorities also emphasized infrastructure development, particularly roads, communication technology, and energy. The latter emphasis sparked controversy because the donor community saw this direction as a departure from PRSP as conceived under the HIPC Initiative. Critics argued that poverty reduction should focus on pressing social services (basic health, primary education, water and sanitation) and the economic problems that needed fixing to meet the major poverty reducing targets, including the Millennium Development Goals (MDGs). Other matters could be pursued later when poverty reduction as envisaged under debt relief had borne sufficient fruit. Defenders of the medium-term priorities argued that infrastructure development, despite its high investment cost, was crucial for economic growth which ultimately is the best weapon against poverty.

Marked by alternating moments of controversy and consensus, and by high public expectations, the socio-economic experiment of poverty reduction began in earnest. Among other targets, consumption headcount poverty was projected to decline from 39.5 percent of the population in 1998/1999 to between 28.5-33.5 percent by 2005. Incidence of extreme poverty was projected to fall from 27 percent to 21 percent, gross primary schooling enrolment to rise from 44.6 percent to 82 percent, under age five mortality from 110 to 95 per 1000 births, infant mortality from 56 to 50 per 1000, and maternal mortality from 200 to 160 per 100,000.

What is in this Book?

The purpose of this exercise was not to assess the success or failure of the strategy. Such an undertaking would have been premature at the time the book was initiated. The data requirement for such an undertaking is extensive and will require a comprehensive national survey. But we don't have to wait for the results to speak of the process of developing the GPRS, of its content, its gaps, its potential for combating poverty, as well as lessons learned. The book is organized into three parts. Part one, chapters two to four, provides the background and the traditional approaches to economic reform in poor countries, particularly the evolution from aid and lending for economic reforms to aid and debt relief for poverty alleviation. Part two, chapters five to eight, examines processes, particularly the making of the strategy, linking the strategy to the budget for financing and implementation, and the challenges of monitoring and evaluating the strategy. Part three addresses the content of the strategy and the gaps in it. The issues tackled here are poverty reduction and decentralization, child poverty, employment creation, informal sector activities and urban unemployment, gender, and environmental sustainability.

Part I

The starting point is to examine the factors that combined to make the majority of Ghanaians poor not just in meeting daily basic needs, but also in their capability to develop and use their resources to make a living. In chapter two, Amoako-Tuffour traces the macroeconomic trends, agricultural production, especially food production capacity, population dynamics, policy regimes and institutional weakening. He reflects on how these factors combined to drive the poverty process in the four decades preceding the onset of the GPRS. In addition, he assesses why it should not be surprising that poverty reduction did not progress as quickly as many had hoped for in the era of economic reform. In chapter three, Vanderpuye-Orgle provides a snapshot of the spatial dimensions of poverty in Ghana. Despite the freedom of mobility, spatial differences in opportunities and the vulnerability to poverty evoke a sense of spatial inequality. Vanderpuye-Orgle assesses spatial inequality and polarization in Ghana using the 1991/1992 and 1998/1999 household surveys and asks: Is inequality in Ghana a spatial phenomenon and is there a disappearing middle class?

In chapter four, Armah takes a critical look at structural adjustment policies (SAPs) and poverty reduction strategies (PRSs), their historical roots, their underlying principles and the practical realities framing their implementation. He compares SAPs and PRSs lending facilities to determine whether the requirements of PRSs are consistent with the underlying principle of country ownership. Furthermore, using Ghana as a case study, he examines whether the theoretical principles underlying the Poverty Reduction and Growth Facility (PRGFs) and Poverty Reduction Support Credit (PRSCs) compare favorably with the realities in Ghana.

Part II
Part two explores the process of developing the strategy, the financing and implementation, and the challenges of monitoring and evaluating the strategy. In chapter five, Amoako-Tuffour looks at the participatory or consultative process followed in the making of the GPRS. He catalogues the experience and throws light on a number of questions: How did the process shape the content of the final document? Did the consultative efforts engage citizens in a genuinely participatory exercise, or were the consultations meant only to generate evidence in support of a policy development which was already done? Did the people consulted see themselves as passive recipients or active participants in fashioning out the strategy? The role of civil servants and the conundrum of country ownership and development partnership in the design of the poverty policy complete the chapter.

Well thought out development planning may fail to deliver on its intended goals unless the strategy is effectively translated and implemented through the national budgetary process. In chapter six, Armah examines the implementation of the poverty reduction strategy focusing on the challenges of linking the programs, projects and activities to the national budget. Of particular interest are the institutional cleavages or turf wars and the structural rigidities that bedevil the implementation of the PRSP. He reckons that progress in realizing even modest gains in the implementation of the GPRS hinges on the extent to which it is being executed through the budget and expenditure framework. He poses two fundamental questions. Did budgetary allocations reflect the priorities of the GPRS? To what extent have the sectors that received such funds used them in a manner that is consistent with the spirit of the GPRS?

In chapter seven, Amoako-Tuffour poses the question: what financing options should underpin a nation's poverty alleviation strategy? There are three options: build on the strength of domestic revenue capacity; build on the basis of expenditures needed to reach minimum social development targets but relying mostly on domestic financing; or build on the basis of expenditure needed to reach some international development targets. The GPRS was built on the basis of the third option, setting a subset of its development targets in line with the Millennium Development Goals. The scope of spending needed to achieve these targets far exceeded domestic non-inflationary finance. Even with savings from debt relief, external financing will be vital. The GPRS gave birth to a new instrument of aid delivery in the form of Multi-Donor Budgetary Support (MDBS). The objectives, the background and the drivers of this aid policy shift, its potential risks and benefits, and an ex-post assessment of the direct pooled budget support form the content of chapter seven.

Never before have the impact and outcomes of economic policies been so systematic and prominent in national development planning in Ghana. If the GPRS is to achieve its poverty reducing and social goals, its implementation must be complemented by effective monitoring and evaluation. In chapter eight, Armah assesses the performance of the monitoring and evaluation systems in Ghana. He also highlights concrete issues and problems associated with the implementation of monitoring and evaluation in developing countries in general.

Part III
Part three turns to the specific issues of content and the focus of the GPRS. In spite of its constraints and challenges, decentralization is generally seen as one of the most important and appropriate strategies leading to poverty reduction. Consequently, it is pointed out that the interaction between decentralization and poverty reduction should emphasize the importance of transfer design and the desirability of providing periodic evaluation of that design. The faith in decentralization as a strategy for poverty reduction is based on its potential to improve efficiency in mobilizing and allocating resources, in bringing service delivery closer to consumers. Against this background, Asante and Ayee in chapter nine examine poverty reduction in Ghana and the link with decentralization.

Children under age fifteen accounted for about 44 percent of the Ghanaian population according to the 1998/99 Ghana Living Standards Survey. Although many children live with families, many were thought to be poor in ways that point ominously to their future development. In chapter ten, Oduro and Osei-Akoto examine whether and how the GPRS tackles issues of child poverty. They pose a number of questions. First, did the poverty profile contained in the GPRS adequately provide a situation analysis of child poverty? Second was child poverty adequately prioritized in the GPRS? Third, did social sector spending in the GPRS address the needs of children? Finally, was the growth strategy sub-scribed to in the GPRS sufficiently pro-poor? They conclude that the GPRS did not effectively tackle child poverty because the latter was subsumed under adult poverty. If child poverty and deprivation are to be tackled, then what is needed is a comprehensive profile of children which highlights those aspects of their well-being that have registered slow progress if not deterioration.

Increasing production that generates gainful employment was one of the core themes needed to improving individual livelihoods in the framework of the GPRS. In chapter eleven, Baah-Boateng assesses the employment content of the design of the strategy and whether employment generation was sufficiently inte-grated into policymaking. Like in previous development plans, Baah observes that employment was treated as a passive outcome of sectoral and macroeco-nomic policies. The absence of a consistent human resource database posed a constraint in designing effective and monitorable employment outcomes. The GPRS also acknowledges the role of the informal sector as a source of employ-ment generation, the links particularly with youth unemployment, and the gen-eral nature of underemployment in the economy.

The informal sector makes up a considerable part of urban employment and is dominated by retail trade, manufacturing, and personal services. Amoako-Tuffour and Sackey ask whether the poverty profile contained in the GPRS ade-quately provides a situation analysis of the urban informal sector. In chapter twelve, they examine closely the nature of urban informal sector activities, the extent of poverty associated with this segment of the labour force and the impli-cations for poverty reduction policies. They observe that while the GPRS ac-knowledges the severity of the problem and the desire to do something about it, the policy effort was rather weak for two reasons: it was based on anecdotal evidence, and the poverty analysis that informed the strategy was very superfi-cial. The GPRS sees those engaged in the informal sector as a homogenous group, ignoring the range of motivations of the participants and the hierarchies or the level of informality.

The main goal of Ghana's Poverty Reduction Strategy (GPRS) is "to ensure sustainable equitable growth, accelerated poverty reduction and the protection of the vulnerable and excluded within a decentralized, democratic environment." This goal cannot be achieved if issues of gender equality are not an integral part of the strategy. Ensuring gender equity is one of the objectives to be achieved in order to attain the overarching goal of the GPRS. In chapter thirteen, Oduro as-sesses the extent to which the strategies of the poverty reduction contribute to achieving gender equity in Ghana. She evaluates the approach that was taken by the architects of the strategy and asks whether a gender in development ap-proach or women in development approach was adopted, and whether gender issues were effectively prioritized. She notes that the GPRS is not silent on gen-der. In fact, achieving gender equity is one of the objectives through which the overall goal of the poverty reduction was to be achieved. However, she argues that the GPRS approach simply targets women in specific programs without presenting a comprehensive framework which would bring out clearly the issues of gender inequality and gender equity. There is therefore a need for a transformative change if gender is to be mainstreamed into poverty reduction strategy. This, she argues, requires commitment at all political levels. She points to the lack of expertise to conduct broad gender analyses as one of the reasons for the weaknesses of the GPRS on gender issues. Effective gender analysis requires new data requirements at the individual and intra-household levels. Changes then have to be made to the format of national data collection efforts.

In chapter fourteen, Twerefou and Osei-Asibey examine the issues of environmental sustainability within the GPRS. They point out that Ghana is signatory to many international agreements on the environment. This notwithstanding, environmental problems persist largely as a result of institutional failures, and the challenges of policy implementation even where laws and regulatory measures are in place. As impressive as government's commitment may have been in the GPRS to improve standards of living, there are obvious missing pieces when it comes to the environment. There was notable absence of policies to improve natural resource management as part of the human resource development. There was notable lack of focus on liquid and solid waste management. In their view, the key setbacks include the limited analysis of the links between poverty and resource depletion, polluted rivers, air pollution, and soil and forest degradation associated with logging and mining in particular. Environmental problems were treated as cutting across different government departments and therefore were not given a specific home in the government institutional machinery. Once again, environmental issues and their effect on poverty suffered the classic problem of the commons: everyone's property is no one's property. Chapter fifteen provides a synthesis of the arguments and the findings of the preceding chapters, sets out some policy issues from these findings, and proposes an agenda for future research.

Notes

1. Economics in Perspective: A Critical History, Houghton Mifflin Company, Boston, 1987.
2. World Bank, World Development Indicators, 2000
3. World Bank, World Development Indicators, 2000
4. Amartya Sen (1992), in his book *Inequality Examined*, provides a survey of the literature on the measurement of inequality and the analytical aspects of the evaluative problems.
5. Nordstöm (1999).
6. OECD, "Shaping the Twenty-first Century: The Contribution of Development Cooperation."

References

Adjibolosoo, S. B-S. K. ed. *International Perspectives on the Human Factor Development,* Preager, Connecticut. 1998.

Besley, T. and R. Burgess, "Halving Global Poverty." *Journal of Economic Perspectives,* Vol. 17, 3 (Summer 2003):3—22.

Boateng, E. O., K Ewusi, R. Kanbur, A. McKay. *A Poverty Profile for Ghana-1987-99,* Social Dimensions of Adjustment in Sub-Sahara Africa. Working Paper No. 5. Washington. 1990.

Centre for Policy Analysis. *Towards a Stable Macroeconomic Environment,* Accra, Ghana. 2000.

Chen S. and M. Ravillion. "How Did the World's Poor Fare in the 1990s?" *Review of Income and Wealth,* Vol. 47, 3 (2001):283—300.

De Haan, A. Lipton, M, Darbellay, E., O'Brien, D., and Samman, E. "The Role of Government and Public Policy in Poverty Alleviation in sub-Sahara Africa," Collaborative Research Project, Africa Economic Research Consortium. 1997.

Deaton, A. "Is the World Poverty Falling?" *Finance and Development,* Vol. 39, 2(June 2002): 4—7.

Easterly, W. *The Elusive Quest for Growth: The Economists' Adventures and Misadventures in the Tropics,* The MIT Press, 2002.

Galbraith, J. K. *Economics in Perspective: A Critical History.* Houghton Mifflin Company. Boston. 1987

Ghana Commercial Bank. *Quarterly Economic Review,* Vol.5(1—4): January—December. 1982

———. *Quarterly Economic Review,* Vol.7 (1—4): January—December. 1984.

———. *Quarterly Economic Review,* Vol.23 (1) p.7 January—March. 2002

Ghana Statistical Service. *Ghana Living Standards Survey: Report on the Third Round (GLSS3)* Accra, Ghana (March). 1995.

———. *Ghana Living Standards Survey: Report on the Fourth Round (GLSS4)* Accra, Ghana (October). 2000.

———. *Poverty Trends in Ghana in the 1990s* Accra, Ghana (October). 2000.

Government of Ghana, *Public Expenditure Review, 1993.* Ministry of Finance. 1994

———. *Ghana-Vision 2020: The First Medium-Term Development Plan (1997—2000).* National Development Planning Commission 1997

———. *Ghana Poverty Reduction Strategy (2003—2005): Agenda for Growth and Prosperity,* National Development Planning Commission. February 2003.

———. *An Agenda for Growth and Prosperity: Monitoring and Evaluation Plan.* National Development Planning Commission 2003.

Islam, R and D. Wetzel. "Ghana: Adjustment, Reform and Growth." in *Public Sector Deficits and Macroeconomic Performance* edited by W. Easterly, C.A. Rodriguez and K. Schmidt-Hebbel, World Bank Publication. 1994.

Jorgenson, D. W. "Did We Loose the War on Poverty?" *The Journal of Economic Perspectives,* 12(1) (Winter 1998):79—96.

Landes, D. S. *The Wealth and Poverty of Nations: Why Some are so Rich and Some so Poor,* W.W. Norton & Company, New York. 1999.

Loxley, J. Ghana: *The Long Road to Recovery 1983–90*, The North-South Institute, Ottawa. 1991.

National Patriotic Party. *Agenda for Positive Change: Manifesto*, 2000.

Nordstöm, H. "Trade, Income Disparity and Poverty: An Overview." in *Trade, Income Disparity and Poverty* edited by Dan Ben-David, Nordstöm, H. and Winters, A. World Trade Organization, Special Studies. 1999.

Sawhill, I. V. "Poverty in the US: Why is it so Persistent?" *Journal of Economic Literature*, 26(3): (Sept. 1988):1073–1119.

Sen, A. K. *Choice, Welfare and Measurement*, Harvard University Press. Cambridge Mass. 1982.

———. "Well-being, Agency and Freedom: The Dewey Lectures 1984." *Journal of Philosophy*, 82. 1985.

———. *Development as Freedom*, Anchor Books, New York. 1990

———. *Inequality Reexamined*. Harvard University Press. Cambridge Mass. 1992.

UNICEF, Ghana. 1986. *Adjustment Policies and Programs to protect Children and Other Vulnerable Groups*, Accra. 1986.

Van de Walle, D. "Public Spending and the Poor: What we Know, What we need to Know." Policy Research Department, World Bank (undated).

World Bank. *Ghana: Growth, Private Sector, and Poverty Reduction: A Country Economic Memorandum.* Report No. 14111–GH. 1995a.

———. *Ghana: Poverty Past, Present and Future*, Report No. 14504–GH 1995b.

———. *World Development Report 2000/2001: Attacking Poverty*. New York. Oxford University Press, 2001a.

———. *Globalization, Growth and Poverty: Building an Inclusive World Economy*. New York. Oxford University Press, 2001b.

PART 1

Poverty, Inequality, and Reform Approaches

2

The Evolution of Poverty in Ghana: 1960–2000

Joe Amoako-Tuffour

> *One who has been touched by the accounts of life of the poor may feel that those who produce the extensive and highly technical literature on definition, measurement and incidence of poverty are insensitive to the real problems of the poor.*
>
> —*Jack L. Roach and Janet K. Roach, Poverty, 1972, p. 21*

1. Introduction

By conventional standards, the levels of welfare of Ghanaians remained low and in some cases declined during the period 1960–2000. The simple facts are compelling. First, by 1957 standards, the index of per capita output of 106.3 in 2000 was below its 1960 level of 108.3, down by 1.85 percent.[1] The annual per capita output growth of 1.5 percent between 1984 and 2000 was not enough to offset the annual growth of negative 1.6 percent between 1961 and 1983 (Easterly, 2001). Second, the index of food production fell from 139 in 1960/1961 to 119 in 1998, down by 14 percent.[2] Third, the average daily caloric intake averaged 2100 calories during 1965–1992.[3] This intake was estimated to be about 90 percent of what was deemed adequate for minimum physical work. If other characteristics of poverty are *ordinally* related to income and consumption poverty (Ray, 1998), then it is reasonable to assume that a sizeable proportion of the population could not have fared any better in their access to primary public goods of health, education, water and social services.

The explanations for the disappointing record of standard of living have run from emphasis on adverse terms of trade of the major exports (cocoa, timber and gold) to adverse weather conditions (Huq, 1989; Loxley, 1991; Alderman, 1990; Sarris, 1993). If these were the primary causes of poverty then only sub-groups of the population would have experienced periodic rise in consumption poverty without limiting their access to primary public goods or their opportunities to earn a living in other areas of the economy. Corruption is the other common explanation (Chazan, 1983; Huq, 1989; Rimmer, 1992; Killick, 2004). The view in this chapter is that the poverty process may have been driven less by these factors, but more systematically by demographic changes, systemic policy failures, and systemic deterioration in the institutions and processes of economic management.

This chapter discusses poverty trends and explains the overall level of poverty focusing on the four decades prior to the onset of the Ghana Poverty Reduction Strategy (GPRS). The remainder of this section looks briefly at the definition and measurement of poverty that form the basis of public policy in Ghana. Section two provides an overview of the poverty process in the 1960 to early 1980s era, a period marked by anecdotal evidence of the depth and severity of poverty despite all the visible signs. Section three covers the post economic recovery period between 1983 and 2000. Three household surveys conducted between 1987 and 1999 changed policy makers' awareness of the poverty problem as anecdotes gave way to facts. In section four we turn our attention to the key factors that underlie the poverty process. The concluding observations follow in section five.

Poverty Definition and Measurement
Official poverty analysis acknowledges that poverty is multi-dimensional. The Ghana Living Standards Survey (GLSS) focused on three dimensions: consumption poverty, deprivation of access to social amenities, and limited opportunities for human development. Consumption poverty lines are based on the income level needed to maintain nutritionally adequate diet adjusted for variations in the cost of living across households and the differences in household size and composition (Ghana Statistical Service, GSS, 2000).[4] From here, the proportion of the population falling below the cut-off poverty line provides the 'headcount' measure or the incidence of poverty.

In general, two approaches have been used to establish the cut-off points. First, the GLSS established poverty lines by fixing the lower (upper) income or expenditure cut off as 49.6 percent (63.7 percent) of mean per capital household expenditures in 1992.[5] The lower poverty line is defined as what is needed to maintain basic nutritional requirements of household members. The upper poverty line incorporates essential food and non-food consumption. Using the GSS working exchange rate of March 1999 of the local currency cedis (¢) 2394 to the U.S. dollar, the upper (lower) poverty lines of household income of ¢900,000 (¢700,000) was equivalent to $375 ($292) per annum. Once poverty lines are established, poverty can be measured in several ways. Based on the number of households that fall below the upper poverty line, about four in every ten households was poor in 1999, down marginally from nearly five in ten in 1992. By the lower poverty line, about three in every ten households was classified as extremely poor in 1999, down from four in ten in 1992. The second measure has more to do with inequality than with absolute poverty. Relative income poverty identifies proportions of the total population within income ranges. Those falling in the bottom fifth of the income distribution are classified as extremely poor. By this measure, about two in every ten households was extremely poor in 1999. By both measures, poverty is a relative notion, which depends on the average consumption or income measure in society. Noteworthy, Ghana's upper income cut-off of only $1.02 a day, corresponded to the $1-a-day global extreme poverty line. By this standard about 60 percent of the population in 1987/1988 and 40 percent in 1998/1999 lived below the global poverty line.

2. Poverty Trends and Income Distribution: 1960–1985

Most work on poverty and income distribution in Ghana has been limited to trends since the mid-1980s because this is when consistent nation-wide survey data became available. The evidence before that is weakly documented and much of that is anecdotal.[6] Without comprehensive household survey, the general trends in GDP growth, general price level, food production, food prices, and the minimum wage were considered as gauges of aggregate welfare. The deterioration in these indicators ultimately translates into the specific deprivations of hunger, malnutrition, undernourishment, unemployment and vulnerability to income shocks. The analysis in this section assumes this causal link.

2.1 Macroeconomic Trends

The economic performance of the 1960s and 1970s has been the subject of various studies, notably Killick (1978, 2000), Huq (1983), Chazan (1983), Loxley (1991), Rimmer (1992) and Leith and Soderling (2003). The basic facts about economic performance (Table 2.2) and the incidence of poverty over the past forty years nearly mirror the cycle of post-independence regime in Table 2.1.

Table 2. 1   Political Regimes

Period	Regime
1957–1966	First Republic: Nkrumah's Convention People's Party
1966–1969	National Liberation Council/Supreme Military Council
1969–1972	Second Republic: Progress Party
1972–1979	Succession of 3 military regimes
1979–1981	Third Republic:
1982–1991	Military: Provisional National Democratic Council (PNDC)
1992–2000	Fourth Republic: National Democratic Congress (NDC)
2001–	New Patriotic Party (NPP)

The early 1960 witnessed a range of state controls and an ambitious public investment in the hope to accelerate industrialization and growth. The development of social infrastructure and the growth of public enterprises expanded job opportunities and set the tone for rural-urban migration. In the early days of the 1960s development strategy, the adverse effects on growth and income distribution of the statutory controls on imports, foreign exchange, interest rates, bank credit, and on prices of consumer goods were less noticeable. The macroeconomic gains of the post-independence era were short-lived. The military regime following the overthrow of the First Republic in February 1966 attempted to restore economic balance through IMF-led stabilization efforts that begun in 1967/1968, but without much success. The rural development programs of the Second Republic under the Progress Party government (1969–1972) focused on alleviating rural poverty. The succession of military interventions from 1972–1979 led to lax management of fiscal and monetary policies, and sowed the seeds of economic decline and with it the descent into poverty. To many observers, the period 1972–1983 was one of prolonged economic and political crisis. The crisis manifested in reduced investment and fallen output growth. It also accelerated the deterioration in the institutions of economic governance and in the gradual emergence of rent-seeking and public sector corruption.

Figure 2. 1   Growth of Real GDP

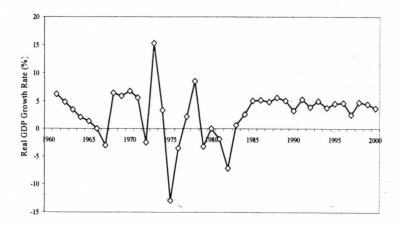

Source: World Bank data

Table 2. 2 Selected Economic Indicators

	1961–1965	1966–1970	1971–1975	1976–1980	1981–1985	1986–1990	1991–1995	1996–2000
Real GDP Growth rate (percent)	3.6	3.2	1.8	0.8	-0.1	4.8	4.5	4.0
Real GDP/capita 1957 = 100):1960 = 108.3 (1)	116.4	111.5	121.6	105.6	90.4	92.4	97.65	106.3
Growth of real per Capita GDP (percent)	0.93	1.06	-0.99	-0.86	-3.45	1.23	1.32	1.86
Average Inflation rate	10.8	4.6	17.1	70	62.3	31.6	27.5	25.6
End of period official exchange rate (¢/US$) (2)	0.71	1.02	1.15	2.75	54.4	326.3	1200	5430
Trade balance (US$, millions)	-38.1	-24.0	92.4	137.7	-77.7	-153.2	-411.0	-716.2
Current account (US$, millions)	-99.1	-55.1	25.4	34.9	-175.3	-105.9	-321.0	-695.0
Central government budget balance (percent of GDP) (3)	-6.5	-3.4	-8.5	-9.1	-3.6	0.9	-5.9	-8.5

Notes: Sources: International Financial Statistics and Bank of Ghana Bulletin, various issues
(1) Real GDP per capita data calculated from J.C. Leith and L. Solderling (2003) Appendix 1 p. 90. (2) Exchange rate data is taken as at end of the 5-year period.
(3) Central government budget balances are Narrow Budget from 1960-1989 and Broad Budget balance from 1990–2000.

[Handwritten annotations: "when Ghana crashed and then policy shifted at end of 5 yrs", "pop. growing very fast so econ. is growing very fast", "things Ghana imports (oil) cost a lot but what it exports (cocoa) costs a little"]

The macroeconomic history is quite marked by the trends in real GDP growth in Figure 2.1 and the summary economic indicators in Table 2.2. The path of real output alternated between growth and decline beginning from the late 1960s to the early 1980s. Real per capita output increased by 8.4 percent in the immediate post independence era (1957—1960). The persistent decline in growth begun in the early 1970s and by the mid-1970s progress had stalled. With the population growing between 2—3 percent, this meant that average growth of real per capita output turned negative. It averaged minus one percent in the 1970s and decelerated further to negative 3.4 percent in 1981—1985. Easterly (2001) estimated that per capita growth averaged minus 1.6 percent between 1961 and 1983.

The inflation effect on the poverty process is explored later. It is sufficient to note that as the average inflation rate reached double digits in the early 1970s and triple digits in 1977 and again later in 1983, the cost of living progressively worsened. Most observers of the Ghanaian economy point to 1972—1974 as the beginning of the institutional collapse and the descent into poverty.

2.2 Sectoral Trends

Table 2. 3   Sectoral Sources and Growth Rates of National Output

	1970—1975	1976—1982	1983—1986	1987—1990	1991—1995
Agriculture	52	51	52	46	42
Industry	19	17	12	14	14
Services	29	32	36	40	44

Sectoral Growth Rates

	1972—1975	1976—1982	1983—1986	1987—1990	1991—1995
Agriculture	-2.3	1.4	1.5	1.3	2.7
Industry	1.9	-7.3	5.6	7.0	4.3
Services	0.2	1.2	5.7	7.9	6.1

Source: Calculations are based on data from World Bank and Ghana Statistical Service (Quarterly Digest of Statistics). Data is derived from Aryeetey and Harrigan (2000) Tables 1.6 and 1.7.

Table 2.3 and the three panels in Figure 2.2 show the trends in sectoral composition of GDP and the extent of the collapse in the production of the major food items that took place from the early 1960s to early 1980s. Agriculture contributed about 52 percent of GDP in the mid 1970s, and about 44 percent between

Figure 2. 2   Index of Production of Selected Food Crops

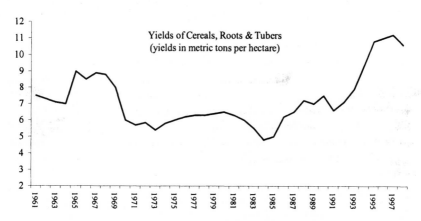

Yields of Cereals, Roots & Tubers
(yields in metric tons per hectare)

Data Source: Food and Agriculture Organization of the United Nations: Earth Trends, 2003

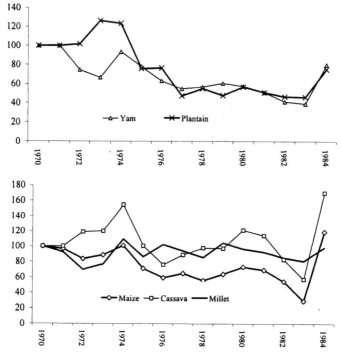

Data are computed by author from Ministry of Food and Agriculture as reported in Alderman (1990)

the mid-1980s and early 1990s. Annual growth rate averaged 3.1 percent in the 1960s, deteriorated to negative 2.3 percent in the early 1970s, and averaged only 1.4 percent annually between 1976 and 1985, barely enough to overcome the precipitous decline in the early 1970s. With an employment capacity of about 60-70 percent of the population, predominantly rural, the trends in the agricultural sector largely map the performance of the economy in general and of the income trends in the rural economy in particular.

In addition to the decline in the production of the major exportable item, cocoa, by 22 percent in 1974/1980 and 42 percent in 1980/1983, the decline in the major staple food crops—cassava, cocoyam, yam, plantain, and grains, including maize, millet, rice and sorghum are evident in Figure 2.2.[7] Two episodes of drought first in 1975–1977 and again in 1981–1982 worsened living conditions, as food crop production plunged. Between 1974 and 1980, maize, cassava and yam production declined by about 21, 35, and 24 percent respectively while rice production stagnated. The yields of most staple food crops (cereals, roots and tubers) in 1970–1980 fell short of the 1965–1970 level resulting in a 1.44 percent decline in average calorie intake between 1961–1965 and 1976 (FAO, 1980). But outside of the drought period the general decline continued throughout the 1970s. Understanding the cumulative effects of these trends provides the beginnings of the answer to the question what drives the poverty process. Noteworthy, the decline in food production particularly throughout the 1970s also coincided with the decline in food aid to Ghana largely in response to the succession of three military regimes during the period 1972–1979.

The decline in food production adds to urban poverty in two ways: first, it puts upward pressure on food prices, and second, as rural income opportunities dwindle, the rural poor migrate to swell the ranks of the urban underclass. Urban poverty is also tied to the public and the private industrial sectors. In the aftermath of the collapse of the 1960 development strategy, industrial capacity use fell from 36 percent in 1978 to 25 percent in 1980 and declined further in 1982. In certain industries production virtually ceased and workers sent home on indefinite leave.[8] Two things happened as a result of the decline in industrial production. First, public sector employment expanded at a rate of about 14 percent annually between 1972 and 1985 (Alderman, 1990). Second, the decline in public sector real wages prompted an exodus of the professional labour force to neighboring countries.

What inference can we make about poverty trends in the 1970s and early 1980s? The proportion of the population that may have drifted into poverty depends on the net natural population increase, the net migration, and on the availability of income support as real incomes plummeted. Apart from pension payments to retired wage employees, who form a small minority of the elderly, there is no public safety net to the elderly, handicapped, or those who suffer seasonalities in income flows. For the majority of Ghanaians, including the disabled and orphans and the nearly half of the labor force who are self-employed, it is not hard to contemplate their vulnerabilities to poverty because they are excluded from the formal social welfare provisioning system (Gayi, 1995). If we focus on demographic changes alone, the point can be made that the proportion of the population that drifted into poverty, especially children, the elderly, the weak and handicapped is likely to be more than the net out-migration. In any event, those who migrated must have done so in order to escape imminent individual or household poverty.

2.3 Early Literature

As mentioned earlier, the pre-1980 is restricted to ordinal rather than cardinal comparisons of poverty trends. Appiah *et. al.* (2000) used minimum wage data to provide a crude baseline of standard of living trends. They noted that although wage levels and standard of living were generally low for the largest proportion of low income workers, mostly those in the agriculture and construction sectors, the general incidence of poverty did not worsen in the 1950s and in the immediate post independence years.[9] Leith and Söderling (2003) put together growth accounting data to suggest that even by their rough estimates, output per worker grew on average by nearly 5 percent per annum between 1960 and 1965. Earlier, Ewusi (1971) estimated that the number of households who earned minimum wage dropped from 48 percent in 1957 to 25 percent in 1966. This suggests that either there was an increase in real incomes or that some people simply moved into the informal sector. Even if there was an increase in the minimum wage, the effect on living standards very likely would have been limited to the small urban wage earners.

It is difficult to judge the trends in general living standards from this evidence alone. Hart (1973) citing a 1970 study by Douglas Rimmer presented anecdotal evidence of declining incomes for urban wage earners. Based on three separate indices, Rimmer reported that real earnings decreased in the range of 36—55 percent during the period 1960/1961 to 1965/1966 but also showed a slight upturn in 1967—1968 following an 8 percent increase in the minimum wage.[10] Analyzing what appears to have been the first comprehensive household budget survey of 1974/1975, Ewusi (1984) reported that about 75 percent of the sample fell below the poverty line in the early years of the contraction that lasted into the early 1980s.[11]

The only data available on the deprivation suffered by children and other vulnerable groups was reported in a UNICEF (1986) study. Infant mortality was reported to have risen by 32 percent from the 86 per 1000 live births in the late 1970s to the mid-1980s. Social deprivations were noted to have been more severe in the northern parts of the country. Using time series data on prices and wages, Sarris (1993) noted that all income groups suffered serious losses in welfare between 1977/1978 and again in 1983/1984.

2.4 Institutional Decline

There is another part of the poverty story which has its origins partly in instabilities in political administration and partly in the general economic decline. A major observation by the National Capacity Building Assessment Group (1996), put together by the World Bank, was the major deterioration of public sector institutions that had occurred in Ghana in its post-independence history. The major reasons according to the Group's findings were dwindling budgets in many institutions, the lack of consistent direction in dealing with economic, political and social issues, the massive over-staffing at the junior levels, the lack of well-qualified and motivated technical and managerial staff, the overall inadequate pay levels and the gradual compression of the pay scale, and the exodus of professionals out of the country.

Indeed, if people suffered consumption poverty only as a result of crop failure and poor pricing, then the eradication of poverty would have been straightforward. Government could provide temporary financial assistance and subsidies to help overcome the adverse shocks. Donors have often helped through aid, yet the goal of reducing the overall level of poverty proved elusive. Institutional weakening often accentuates government failure. The exodus of technical and professional personnel weakened the various technical and managerial activities in most sectors of the economy. For example, in the health and education sectors, the exodus led to the slow destruction of the institutions and processes that build capacity for national development. The deteriorating state of the administrative, technical, and the overall organizational capacity of the state, slowly but surely, manifested in the diminished ability of the government to maintain the physical infrastructure for development—roads, utilities, sanitation—as well as the capacity to provide technical support to the agricultural sector. The lack of focus and consistency in public administration also meant that governments were unable to redefine the functions and responsibilities of public institutions to deal with or to adapt to changes in the environment. At the end of the 1970s, prolonged effects of drought, inertia in real wage adjustments, political instability, massive economic policy failures, and the deteriorating institutions of economic management were the major culprits of the emerging poverty.

3. Poverty Trends in the mid-1980s to 2000

The post 1983—1985 period saw marked contrast in the direction of all macroeconomic indicators (Table 2.2) and real sector growth rates (Table 2.3). Real GDP growth averaged 4.5 percent between 1985 and 2000. The five-year average growth of per capita income ranged between 1.2 and 1.9 percent between 1986 and 2000. Inflation rate dropped from 62 percent in 1981—1985 to 25.6

percent in 1996—2000. Most important, the Ghana Living Standards Survey (GLSS1) initiated in 1987 provided the first comprehensive data on the depth and incidence of poverty. The intermediate survey of 1988/1989 (GLSS2) was followed by the more comprehensive surveys of 1991/1992 (GLSS3) and 1998/1999 (GLSS4).[12] The GLSS1 survey set the baseline. The GLSS3 and GLSS4 provided detailed assessments of the composition of the poor, the evolution of poverty in the 1990s and the possible impact of public policy on poverty.

Table 2. 4   Income Poverty Statistics

	Upper Poverty line (¢900,000)		Lower Poverty line (¢700,000)	
	Poverty Incidence (percent)	Contribution to Total Poverty (percent)	Poverty Incidence (percent)	Contribution to Total Poverty (percent)
GLSS3 (1991/1992)				
National	51.7		36.5	
Urban	27.7	17.8	15.1	13.7
Rural	63.6	82.8	47.2	86.3
GLSS4 (1998/1999)				
National	39.5		26.8	
Urban	19.4	16.3	11.6	14.4
Rural	49.5	83.7	34.4	85.6

Source: Poverty Trends in Ghana in the 1990s: Ghana Statistical Service, October, 2000, Table 2. Using the GSS working exchange rate of March 1999 of ¢2394 to the U.S. dollar, the upper (lower) poverty line is equivalent to $375 ($292) annually or $1.029 ($0.80) daily.

The results from the GLSS1, comprehensively analyzed by Boateng *et. al.* (1992), confirmed the anecdotes and the previous case studies' evidence of the depth and incidence of poverty. Briefly, nearly over a third (36 percent) of the population was below the upper poverty line in 1987/1988 and nearly 7 percent was below the lower or extreme poverty line.[13] Poverty among rural households accounted for nearly 84 percent of the national incidence of extreme poverty. Although the surveys which followed later were not strictly comparable in design and scope to the GLSS1, the general picture of the poverty process was becoming clearer than before.

The GLSS3 conducted between October 1991 and September 1992, when adjusted for comparability with the 1998/1999 survey, revealed that 51.7 percent of the population lived below the upper poverty line of $375 and 36.5 percent lived under the lower poverty line of $292 (Table 2.4). The survey also confirmed that poverty is prevalent in households headed by someone engaged in agriculture, and/or is illiterate, and that farmers were the most poor among socio-economic groups. The incidence of extreme poverty in the rural areas in 1998/1999 was nearly three times the incidence in the urban areas. Moreover, although about 66 percent of the population was rural, rural poverty accounted for about 83 percent of the national poverty. As a result of the rural-urban migration, a disproportionate number of the rural poor were the elderly, female and children.

Spatially, about 38 percent of the people living in the rural savannah covering much of the northern and upper regions of the country were under the upper poverty line. More worrying, children of the poor were less likely to attend school than their non-poor counterparts. Infant mortality rate had fallen from 77/1,000 live births in 1988 to 66/1,000 in 1991/92. And even then this ratio was unacceptably high, so was child mortality which had also fallen from 155 to 119 per 1,000 births during the same period. These findings startled policymakers and raised questions about the effectiveness of past policy efforts. In-depth analysis of the surveys uncovered systemic failings of public policy where it mattered most as a weapon of anti-poverty. The most surprising finding was that the poor benefited least from public spending in the areas of education and health. The poorest 20 percent of the population gained just under 12 percent and 16 percent of government spending on health and education, respectively. This outcome had a lot to do with policy targeting, a point to be taken up later in the chapter.

The lack of consistent comprehensive living standards data makes decades' long comparisons impossible. But the profile of poverty which emerged from the baseline survey in 1987 hinted that living standards may have been worse than what was discernible from the anecdotal evidence. So much so that even after sustaining annual real GDP growth rates of 4–5 percent between 1986–1993, Alderman (1994)'s prognosis for the future was that it would take up to the year 2000 for living standards to return to their 1965 level. Alderman's prediction was conditional on maintaining the 5 percent growth rate and, most importantly, maintaining the disinflation course. The latter, however, was not to be because fiscal-induced inflationary pressures re-emerged in 1996.

It is small wonder that the GLSS4 conducted between April 1998 and March 1999 revealed only limited improvements in the fight against poverty. The overall poverty incidence declined between 1991/1992 and 1998/1999 from 52 percent to 40 percent (Table 2.4). The percentage of the population at the extreme poverty also declined from 37 percent to 27 percent. As for the spatial dimension of poverty little had changed for the better. The modest decline in poverty varied substantially by region, but some had gotten poorer. Five out of the ten regions had more than 40 percent of their population living in poverty in 1999. More alarming, nine out of ten people in Upper East (UE) region, eight out of ten in Upper West (UW), seven out of ten in Northern region, and five out of ten in the Central and Eastern regions were classified as poor.

Using the first three rounds of the GLSS survey,[14] Canagarajah *et. al* (1998) found that inequality increased during the 1990s on the basis of per capita expenditures and that the increase was greatest at the lower end of the income distribution. As Vanderpuye-Orgle's work in chapter three will show, the degree of inequality in the distribution of expenditures moved in different directions in different regions and among different socioeconomic groups.

Table 2. 5 Income Share by Quintile Groups

Income Quintiles	Income Share		Expenditure share	
	GLSS3	GLSS4	GLSS3	GLSS4
Lowest 20 percent	3.8	1.5	7.3	5.1
Second Lowest 20 percent	8.7	5.7	11.7	9.5
Middle 20 percent	13.6	11.3	15.9	14.5
Second Highest 20 percent	21.3	20.9	21.8	22.6
Highest 20 percent	52.7	60.6	43.3	47.3
Total	100.0	100.0	100.0	100.0
Gini Coefficient	0.48	0.60	0.35	0.43

Source: Ghana Living Standards Survey (1991/1992 and 1998/1999)

The rising Gini coefficient in Table 2.5 suggests that income distribution remained less egalitarian at the close of the 1990s than it did at the beginning. Noteworthy, the largest losses in income and expenditure share occurred in the lowest quintiles. On income basis, the share of the lowest 40 percent income recipients dropped from 12.5 percent in 1991/1992 to 7.2 percent in 1998/1999, compared to the 15 percent gain in income share of the highest income group from 52.7 percent to 60.6 percent respectively. Killick (2004) remarked that it is extremely difficult to rely on official data alone to assess the extent of poverty in Ghana. While official data recorded a drop in headcount poverty during the 1990s, there was no reduction in inequality. If income information base is anything to go by, the picture presented above suggests, even if tentatively, that the success of the nation's poverty reduction strategy should be gauged not just by a rise in per capital income, but also by how much of the rise in incomes translate into increases in household consumption and the reductions in inequality.

4. Drivers of the Trends in Poverty

Transient droughts, the decline in food production, political instabilities and weakening of the public institutions combined to accelerate the descent into poverty. There were other factors which are less obvious yet interacted powerfuly with the above listed factors to drive the poverty process. Here I will focus the role of population growth and government policy failures.

4.1 Demographic Changes and Consumption Poverty

Food insecurity and the terrible problems of hunger, malnutrition, and under-nourishment are critical dimensions of poverty. If these conditions persist, they increase and predispose large segments of the population to chronic poverty. But food insufficiency is relative to the population growth. Detailed analysis of demographic changes in Ghana has not been available since 1984, and before that, the 1970 census. For that reason, it is difficult to capture at reasonable time intervals the trends in demographic changes and what those changes mean for the supply and distribution of primary public goods.

Figure 2. 3   Index of Per Capita Food Production: 1961-1998

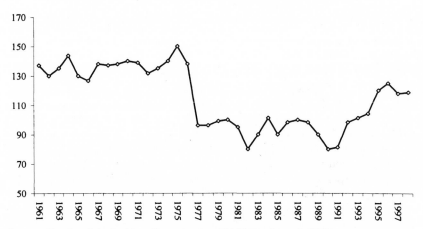

Source: Food and Agriculture Organization (FAO) Earthtrends 2003

If the projections of growth are to be believed, then the population is re-ported to have increased by 60 percent between 1960 and 1980 (Killick, 2000), by 32 percent during 1972–1983 (Loxley, 1991), and, by another estimate, to have doubled between 1960 and 1990.[15] Projections by Ghana Statistical Service put the increase at 115 percent from 1970 to 2000. We can infer that the popula-tion more than doubled between 1960 and 2000. What does this mean?

A high rate of population growth relative to the capacity to provide for basic needs exacerbates the poverty problem in many ways. At face value, the average annual decline in agricultural output of about negative 0.2 percent between 1970 and 1983 may be small. But the cumulative effects relative to the annual popula-tion growth of 2.6 percent[16] are large and consequential.

Assume for simplicity that all agricultural output go to meet domestic food consumption. A crude estimate is that by 1983 there would have been a shortfall of nearly 40 percent in the output that was needed to maintain consumption per head at its 1970 level. Figure 2.3 shows the decline in per capita food production, most noticeably, beginning in the mid 1970s. While the accuracy of these numbers is not beyond controversy, the numbers nevertheless are indicative of the general trend. The 1998 index of 119 remained below the 1960–1965 average of 135. As we saw earlier for the major food crops (Figure 2.2), maize production dropped four-fold between 1970 and 1983, yam and plantain by nearly two-fold, cassava by nearly a half and millet by nearly one-fifth of the 1970 output. Although there were noticeable improvements in the production of all major food crops in the mid 1980s, the effects of mal-nutrition and under-nutrition as a result of persistent food inadequacies in the past, particularly among children and the elderly, are not easily remedied. Indeed the issue of remedy doesn't even arise if public policy fails to recognize these problems from the past.

The launch of "Operation Feed Yourself" (OFY) program in 1974 was an euphoric public policy attempt to tackle the imminent food crisis. The program, however, proved unsuccessful. The rise in local food prices persisted because the increase in supply fell short of the effective demand (Aryeetey and Harrigan, 2000). Poor planning, poor targeting, and infrastructural bottlenecks contributed to the failure of the grandiose political scheme (Chazan, 1983). The secondary objective to attract the youth into agriculture failed because the scheme relied heavily on student voluntarism in providing labor. It also failed to provide incentive schemes that will induce the youth to commit to a career in agriculture.

It is not only food inadequacy that became a problem. The additional population also meant that so much more must be provided in the form of schools, health facilities and basic social amenities. According to 1986 UNICEF report, real education expenditures per head declined from 77.3 in 1969/1970 to 28.7 in 1981/1982. The corresponding expenditures for health fell from 71.6 to 22.6 (UNICEF, 1986). Between 1970 and 1982, development expenditures intended for the expansion of public amenities declined from 3.5 percent to 1.1 percent of GDP.

On the employment side, Killick (2000) remarked that although the country's population increased by 60 percent during 1960–1980, total recorded formal sector employment remained the same. As population increased and as economic conditions worsened, migration, whether it was from the rural to urban areas, or out of the country, played the role of reducing the vulnerability of households to the correlates of income poverty. The combination of economic decline, out-migration and the population drift into the urban informal sector diminished further the revenue raising capacity of government through conventional tax measures.

At the household level demographic change provided its own momentum to poverty. Households that fall below the poverty line also tend to be large relative to the average family size and tend to have a high ratio of dependent members, often children. Poor household comprised, on average, 6.3 members in 1992 compared with a mean of 3.6 for the non-poor (GSS,[17] 1995). In the absence of institutional safety nets and in an environment where infant mortality still remains a hurdle, the incentives to have larger families may not have diminished yet for the majority of the rural population. Surviving children provide valuable safety nets for the elderly. But larger family size may both be the effects of poverty as the cause (Ray, 1998). Larger families are likely to have diminished per capita consumption, diminished private savings, which in turn increase their vulnerability to adverse shocks to income earning opportunities.

Table 2. 6   Total Population and Economically Active Population (1998/1999)

Age Group	Estimates of total population			Economically active population*		
	Male	Female *(millions)*	All	Male	Female *(percent)*	All
7-14	2.21	2.19	4.4	32.6	33.8	33.2
15-24	1.62	1.55	3.17	71.0	65.8	68.5
25-44	1.69	2.33	4.02	87.6	82.4	84.6
45-64	1.01	1.15	2.16	89.1	87.8	88.4
65+	0.41	0.51	0.92	78.0	80.4	79.3
All	6.94	7.73	14.67	65.9	66.0	65.9

Source: Ghana Living Standards Survey (GLSS4), Ghana Statistical Service, 2000
* The economically active is that part of the population which at the time of the survey is actually engaged or is available and willing to engage in the production of goods and services.

Table 2.6 points to the legacy of high population growth rate and the imminent trend in the age-gender mix of the poor. At the close of the decade of the 90s, about a third of underage children (7—14) and about 80 percent of those over sixty-five years were working or willing to work, most of them likely hard pressed for nutrition and basic needs. One of the drawbacks of having children working or willing to work is that they are likely to miss schooling. Heintz (2000) estimated that 18 percent of children (7—14 years) and 35 percent of the youth (15—24 years) who were employed had never been to school. Of the elderly (sixty-five years and over), there were proportionately more females (80.4 percent) than males (78 percent) who remained active in the labour force.

While any inference about the facts in Table 2.6 on poverty dynamics will be mechanical, the data nevertheless point to the striking facts of population growth and poverty that many analyses of poverty in Ghana have overlooked. What is of concern is not the population growth per se, but rather the relative institutional and production capacity of the economy to meet the demographic needs of the growing population. Otherwise, a faster growing population only means greater consumption poverty and limited per capita access to education, health and other public amenities needed for human development. Equally noteworthy is the grim picture that poverty among the elderly could be severe, or becoming.

4.2 Role of Public Policy

What does public policy have to do with the poverty process? The link runs in many ways. The direct links are through policy-measures that affect enterprise, production incentives, employment, earnings, relative prices, and access to social amenities and to markets. The indirect links are through policy measures that ignite inflation, induce serious price misalignments, and distort incentives in the allocation of resources. This section looks at the impact of inflation, wage and exchange rate policies on the poverty process.

Inflation and Poverty

The experiences of price inflation, real interest rates and inflation tax are depicted in Figures 2.4 and 2.5. Strong inflationary pressures started to develop in the Ghanaian economy in 1973. The inflation rate jumped from 10 percent in 1972 to 18 percent in 1973, rapidly to 116 percent in 1977, before falling to 50 percent in 1980. The latter drop however was short-lived. Annual inflation surged again to triple-digits to 123 percent in 1983.

Although supply factors including supply rigidities and oil price shocks combined to exert upward pressure on prices, sustained pressures could only have come from the persistent food supply shortfalls and the persistent monetary financing of government spending. The contention here is that, in a large measure, both forces that fuelled the inflationary process trace their origins to the same causes: domestic policy failures; most notably, an over-valued foreign exchange policy and the bad export pricing policy.

And both policy measures were largely the result of political instincts. The ensuing inflationary dynamics made both individuals and successive governments poorer in income capabilities. Revenue from conventional tax bases dwindled from 20 percent of GDP in 1970/1971 to 5.5 percent in 1983 (Islam and Wetzel, 1984). Current accounts deficits grew from $81 million to $238 million in 1983 (Loxley, 1991). The reliance on the inflation tax[18] to finance deficits increased steadily. It peaked at 10 percent of GDP in 1977 and remained relatively high prior to the mid-1980s (Figure 2.5). But government recourse to inflation tax proved counterproductive. Except for 1972 and 1975 when the old cedi was demonetized to the new cedi, the actual seigniorage[19] revenue (Figure 2.5) from money creation remained negative from 1970 to 1985. Islam and Wetzel (1994) remarked that seigniorage revenue would have been considerably higher had the inflation rate been about 30 percent; nearly half the actual inflation experience between 1972 and 1985.

Figure 2. 4   Average Inflation and Real Interest Rates

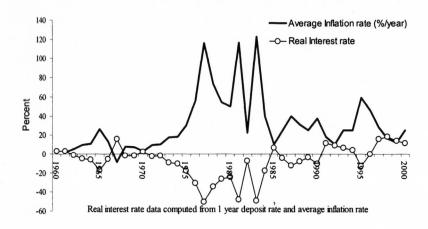

Real interest rate data computed from 1 year deposit rate and average inflation rate

Figure 2. 5   Seigniorage Revenue and Inflation Tax

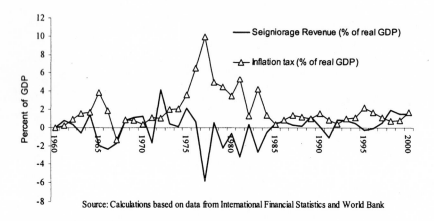

Source: Calculations based on data from International Financial Statistics and World Bank

The decline in government revenue from money creation matched the rise in inflation tax on private holdings of financial assets. Moreover, the policy to maintain interest rate ceilings and heavy reserve requirements on banks meant that the economy operated with negative real interest rates (Figure 2.4) for much of the period between 1960 and 1980. This coupled with government's strong demand for bank credit meant that the financial system was massively repressed with adverse impact on savings and credit flows. In the view of Mckinnon and

Shaw (1973), any form of financial repression rather than helping the non-rich, actually hurts them.

Wage policy and poverty

The history of real wages from the early 1970s to the late 1980s is shown in Figure 2.6. The trend is indicative of the decline in disposable income and consequently of private consumption for formal sectors workers. In the formal sector, public sector wage can be expected to have ripple effects on the private sub-sector (Canagarajah and Mazumdar, 1997). What is crucial here is that the public sector wage bill has persistently made fiscal policy more difficult in Ghana. Faced with the choice of reducing the size of the public sector, compressing the salary structure, or reducing the real wage, successive governments relied more on the latter options. So much so that the real wage in 1983 was barely 12 percent of its 1974 level. Sen (2000, p. 161) remarked: "[a] person may be forced into starvation even when there is plenty of food if he loses his ability to buy food in the market, through a loss of income." The majority of public sector employees suffered this fate. UNICEF in its 1986 report remarked that for many employees of the formal sector the real wages in 1983 could not support the food requirements of a single adult, let alone the family plus housing requirements. The populist policy of compressing the wage structure in the early

Figure 2. 6   Index of Minimum Wage (1977=100)

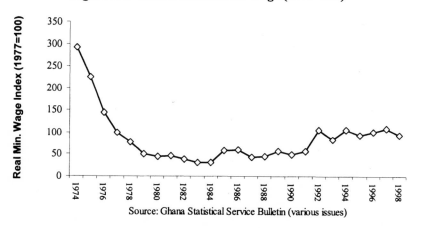

Source: Ghana Statistical Service Bulletin (various issues)

1980s was yet another form of policy-induced deprivation, which precipitated a further exodus of professionals and a further weakening of government administrative machinery.

Exchange rate misalignment, producer price policies and poverty
Perhaps the most pernicious policy-induced descent into poverty was the exchange rate and producer price policies pursued for nearly two-and half decades
beginning in the 1960s. According to Bateman *et. al* (1990), the long decline in
Ghana's cocoa production from nearly 50 percent of world output in 1965 to
nearly 10 percent in 1990, is in large measure associated with policies that over-
valued the domestic currency and lowered domestic producer prices.

For much of its history since the 1960s, the local currency was grossly over-
valued against the major currencies. This not only represented a macro-level
distortion but also a source of sectoral price distortion which had implications
for sectoral performance, employment, income and the standard of living.[20] The
exchange rate remained fixed with only three devaluations between 1957 and
1982 (Jebuni, 2004). Devaluation occurred in 1967, 1972 then in 1978. The
value of the domestic currency was held at cedis (¢) 2.75 to the dollar till the
end of the first quarter of 1983.[21] Until 1984, the export duty on cocoa averaged
60 percent of the country's export revenue (Loxley, 1994) and typically provided between 25 and 50 percent of government revenues (Islam and Wetzel,
1994). For a government that relies on export duties, the persistent over-valued
exchange rate meant a fall in the export tax base and therefore a decline in export revenues from the traditional foreign exchange earners——cocoa, timber,
mining (Kusi, 1998).

Shrinking government revenue impaired the governments' ability to carry
out even the most elementary functions of governing (Leith and Söderling,
2003) and forced cutbacks in real expenditures on non-wage essential services,
maintenance and investment. Not least affected was the government's ability to
deliver public services to remote parts of the country. As governments became
poorer, roads, schools, health, water and sanitation facilities in many parts of the
country deteriorated. And for many in the rural areas, especially those who relied on rail services, this meant diminished access to markets to sell what is produced in order to better own lives.

Besides the problem of access, the relatively lower producer prices of exports meant lower income to farmers and a weakened multiplier effects on the
rural economy as the demand for labor in the cocoa and forest sectors declined.[21]
Although there were attempts to evade the pernicious tax through smuggling, the
transaction costs of smuggling reduced the impact of the tax on producer incomes without eliminating it.[22]

The over-valued exchange rate affected the major foreign exchange earners——mining, timber and cocoa——differently. First, unlike cocoa, exports of
timber and mining products are not under a marketing board scheme. Exporters
are not compelled to sell to government at domestic controlled prices. Second,
timber and mining companies, largely foreign-owned, could retain part of their
earnings offshore for the purchase of machinery and for investment recovery.

Figure 2. 7   Index of Cocoa Purchase and Wood Exports

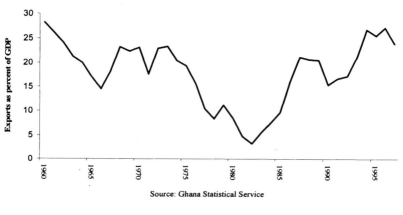

Source: Ghana Statistical Service

Source: Data from Leith and Soderling (2003)

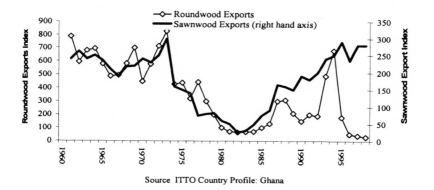

Source ITTO Country Profile: Ghana

They, unlike cocoa farmers, control the timing and the means of repatriation of their earnings. Third, when it comes to coping with the pernicious effects of government policies, miners and timber merchants have the option to postpone extraction and harvesting because both products are storable in their natural state. The yield value of cocoa tress is "non-storable." Worse, farmers must re-habilitate cocoa tress continuously to maintain yield.

Clearly, the burden of exchange rate misalignment and bad pricing policies on cocoa farmers can be severe and long-lasting. What is common though among the three traditional exports is that bad policies encouraged smuggling, discouraged investment, precipitated the loss of rural employment and incomes and collapsed government revenue. The extraordinary collapse of exports of cocoa and timber products is evident in Figure 2.7.

Another consequence of the trend in the cocoa, forestry and mining sectors was the gradual migration of labor away from these rural based activities to more urban-based trading, real estate, transportation and to a lesser extent to food crop production. Aryeetey and Harrigan (2000) observed that the service sector with its low demand for fixed investment, its rapid turnover rate, and very amenable to smuggling activities became the sector of last resort for the migrating labor.

A less recognized but important impact of the decline in cocoa production was on food production. Food crops play multiple roles in cocoa farming. They provide shade for cocoa seedlings in the early years of planting, provide household food security, and, in the short-term, serve as the main income source to support livelihoods and general well-being. In the farm enterprise, the one time cost of land acquisition and the preparation for planting is amortized over the twenty to thirty year life of the cocoa farm. The decline in investment in cocoa farming therefore translates into considerably higher average cost of producing food crops alone.

Inefficient policies have a habit of reinforcing themselves. The introduction of import licensing and price controls on an array of imported foods were yet further distortionary measures to compensate for the misaligned exchange rate effects (Jebuni, 2000). With diminished foreign exchange, the lack of imported capital and raw material inputs further inhibited industrial production, causing "extremely low capacity utilization,"[23] and lower urban employment.

The general misunderstanding of the poverty problem by governments is exemplified by the events that took place in 1979—1982 in the succession of military regimes. There is always the real danger that societies steep in high levels of poverty may be prone to social strife and disorder because of the perceptions of inequalities. Looking back, it is not difficult to argue that the Rawlings' revolutions in 1979 and again in 1981 must have confused perceived inequalities with the trend in the overall level of poverty. This fundamental misunderstanding manifested in several ill-conceived policy measures: including, the withdrawal of the ¢50 notes (the highest denomination of the local currency) in early 1982, the recall of all loans and advances to the internal trade sector within one month, the freezing of bank accounts in excess of ¢50,000,[24] and the vetting of individuals and business enterprises under the pretext of tax evasion.

The literature on risk and vulnerability (Dercon, 2002) suggest that it is not hard to anticipate people's coping responses to such extra-judiciary measures. People lose confidence in the banking and monetary system. They redirect savings away from the formal sector into less productive ventures with serious repercussions on savings and private investment. Others will resort to capital flight. All these responses destroy or reduce the physical, financial and social capital of households. In short, when an economy is in a decline and the incidence of poverty rising, any form of re-distribution could not have been the best pathway to alleviate poverty. The testimonies of market women and small businesses in the course of the National Reconciliation Hearings of 2002—2003 attest to the long-lasting and damaging impact of the revolutionary misadventures on livelihoods.

In short, bad policies can perpetuate mass poverty even when they are not the immediate cause of poverty. Bawumia (2004, p. 46) wrote "1972—1983 was a decade of consistent application of bad economic policies with attendant poor performance."[25] Against this background, it should not be surprising that any measure of recovery, within, say, three to five years after the onset of the Economic Recovery Program (ERP) in 1983, could only have been recovery from acute into less acute poverty. Any meaningful progress will take time. Alderman (1990) put it well. "Such poverty is not a product of current policies, but is, nevertheless, its challenge" (p. 5).

4.3 The Persistence of Poverty in the 1990s

The absence of national household surveys prior to the mid-1980s meant that it was difficult tracking the poverty dynamics in any systematic way. The GLSS1 completed in 1987, barely three years into the ERP, arguably had limited comparative meaning. It was only to be understood properly as establishing a baseline—which proved to be spectacularly surprisingly to policymakers. Against the background of policy failures, political instability, a general deterioration in the institutions of economic management, and an economy which by all indications had literally broken down by the early 1980s, it remains an interesting but largely an unanswered question how some commentators[26] could uniquely establish causal links between economic reform and the evolution of poverty in Ghana.

The 1986 UNICEF study on *Adjustment Policies and Programs to protect Children and other Vulnerable Groups* deserves mention. The study focused on those believed not to be benefiting from the reform and raised concerns about the social dimensions of the recovery program. The study provided quick images of the poverty problem without identifying causes, and counted on the donor community to finding solutions to the problem. The response was swift but worrisome. Without proper diagnosis of the problem it was all too easy for policy responses to be driven by political instincts and for donors to focus on visible short-run triumphs. The timing of the report also made it all too easy, especially for those who believed that the recovery program was "cold blooded" and uncaring to people's well-being, to attribute the state of welfare indicators to reform measures.

Concerned with the extent of social indicators of poverty, the World Bank initiated and with the donor community funded the Program of Action to Mitigate the Social Costs of Adjustment (PAMSCAD). PAMSCAD was intended to focus on the rehabilitation of rural and urban infrastructure, improving water supply, sanitation, primary education and health. But for all its well-intended goals, the program had several weaknesses and Gayi (1995) had written comprehensively about them. First, the program assumed that there was an identifiable group of a "new poor." Second, the poverty of this "new poor" was assumed to have come about only as a result of structural adjustment measures. The program failed to recognize that there was a fundamental problem of preadjustment poverty, chronic poverty, deprivation and vulnerability of a wider segment of the population. While PAMSCAD may have been intended to benefit all these groups, there was no database to identify them and therefore to target the assistance. Guided by a muddled through framework, PAMSCAD's only virtue was to show that the living standards of the least well-off members of society concerns public policy and the ethical interest of the donor community. Loxley (1991, p. 43) rightly remarked that PAMSCAD addressed "mainly a social pathology which has its origins in the economic crisis itself rather than in the ERP per se."

This, of course, is not to deny that the ERP and the structural adjustment era did add to the pool of the unemployed. The point here is simply to emphasize that the deterioration in all the correlates of poverty——consumption poverty, child malnutrition, maternal mortality, urban street vending by the army of youth and so forth——did not suddenly emerge. They evolved steadily and reached more acute stages in the 1980s. While public sector retrenchment in the mid-1980s added to the pool of the unemployed, there is no reason to believe that the policy of overstaffing associated with the growth of the public sector between 1972 and 1985 (Alderman, 1990) necessarily guaranteed improvements and less hardships in people's standard of living. This is especially so since real wages had fallen, and the public sector deficits had sown the seeds of an inflationary spiral. The low labor absorptive capacity of the declining private sector coupled with wage and labor policies resulted in a large underpaid public sector. The question then arises, could the ERP have delivered instant relief?

Economic Recovery Program and Poverty
How were reform measures intended to influence poverty? Making better the conditions for the functioning of a market economy was the starting point for

reform measures. The first generation of reform (under ERP1: 1983–1986) came in the form of liberalization measures——exchange rate deregulation, removal of price controls, financial sector improvements, privatization of state enterprises—— the strengthening of tax administration, rationalizing government expenditures, and encouraging private sector development.

Several of these measures did not require fundamental institutional changes. These were simply stroke-of-the-pen liberalization measures. And they did not fundamentally curtail the power of the state machinery in the allocation and distribution of resources. The measures sought to address a wide range of disincentives and obstacles which limited production capacity, especially in the agricultural sector. The program assumed that private sector response to the incentives of liberalization would be instantaneous. Growth would follow. The benefits of growth would be distributed widely among the population through increased employment and earnings, even without social intervention policies.

The program succeeded in removing price distortions and in moving economic management to rely on market based instruments (Jebuni, 1995). As the data in Tables 2.2 and 2.3 suggest, the program also succeeded in halting the economic decline. It failed, however, to move the economy rapidly beyond recovery to the kind of growth that would have been needed to overcome the depth of deprivations of the past for the majority of the population.

The poverty reducing impact of the first stage reforms rested on the successful implementation of the second wave of reform measures (ERP2: 1987–1989). These measures, however, were more complex and challenging. ERP2 required reforming dysfunctional institutions, re-shaping government administrative machinery, as well as streamlining the process of economic management. The package also included reforms in education, the health sector, public utilities and the civil service machinery.

Fundamentally, ERP2 had two broad objectives: (1) to re-shape government at the micro-level by curtailing government involvement in the financial sector, in the energy and utilities sectors, and (2) to change the delivery of and access to social services. These were intended to bring public resources and public spending into line, and to curb the latter as a means of curtailing budgetary pressures at the macro level.

The speed of pursuit of these measures and the multiplicity of structural conditionalities that were needed to accomplish these goals would, however, be seen in some quarters as an attempt to undermine the legitimate role of the state, and with it the ownership of domestic policy-making. Certainly, the perception that reform measures were externally dictated without domestic consultations did not help with the program implementation. For example, for a country that had suffered significant decline in food production in the preceding two decades, the insistence that the government eliminates fertilizer subsidies as a precondition of U.S. food aid support for reform was ill-conceived.[27] No less counter-productive were the removal of subsidies on pesticides and the premature retrenchment of social services sector. However sound the economic arguments, the government's moral strength in pursuing reforms was weakened especially by the imposition of user fees and charges for the use of services in education, health clinics and access to clean drinking water.

For failing to seek adequate local input in policy design, for failing to balance reforms on economic ideological grounds against the social and political imperatives, for failing to sequence the implementation of reforms in a gradualist approach, and for the rush to show visible short-term triumphs, the ERP soon came to be seen as part of the poverty problem, not the solution. Despite the overall positive trends in the macroeconomic indicators that followed in the late 1980s and early 1990s, the optimism that reform could solve the poverty problems gradually turned to pessimism.

Why did this happen? With hindsight, the answer is partly in the premise of the reform design and partly in what may have been taken for granted. From the perceived necessity of achieving macro stability in the shortest possible time and doing something about public finances emerged a new problem. Much was subsumed in what liberalization and privatization alone could do. The private sector's momentum for growth, as a source of job creation and government revenue, however, lagged considerably behind the re-shaping of government. Moreover, the institutional innovations that were needed to improve microeconomic efficiency in both the private and public sectors failed to materialize or at best moved very slowly. The rapid succession of nine adjustment loans by the World Bank and the IMF between 1984 and 1994, not to mention bilateral loans and grants, may have diminished the incentives for the hard reforms necessary for rapid growth to occur (Easterly, 2001).

Finally, the failure of PAMSCAD demonstrated that well-intentioned antipoverty measures will fail to work under poor policy environment. Historically, governments had attempted to help the poor in many different ways. Antipoverty programs arguably have included subsidies on water, electricity, petroleum and subsidies in education and health. In these areas, governments in principle have always professed to be pro-poor. A major problem though is that government efforts in this direction typically relied more on the advice of multilateral and bilateral institutions and less on local inputs. Coupled with the weak organizational capacity of the state, the consequences of this approach to policy-making have been poor program design, poor targeting and the associated errors of program implementation. PAMSCAD was no exception.

Benefit incidence analysis in the health and education sectors by Canagarajah and Ye (2001) and Canagarajah and Portner (2003) revealed that actual spending has not always been pro-poor. For example, for primary education subsidies to the very poor and the poor declined from 43.3 percent in 1989 to 41.2 percent in 1998, while the percentage of subsidies captured by the top quintile rose from 14 percent to 17 percent. This observation underscores both the ex post regressive nature of public spending, the difficulties in targeting, and the leakages in spending.

Poor program design and poor targeting are not the only problems, so is weak institutional coordination, especially at the local level where targeted spending is most needed. Without adequate institutional mechanisms that coordinate the development, implementation, and monitoring of social programs, the ability to carry forward poverty alleviation programs will be severely inhibited. To this end, since the majority of the poor are in rural communities in different socio-economic groupings, with different levels of need for public services, it is also hard to think of how to improve on the delivery of social programs and national initiatives to alleviate poverty without moving forward meaningfully on decentralization.

5. Conclusion

This chapter has reviewed the basic facts about trends in the incidence of poverty since the 1960s. The lack of comprehensive living standards data prior to the late 1980s makes long-term comparison of trends impossible. If we rely on output growth, food production and population growth as predictors of poverty incidence, we deduce that the standard of living of the majority of the population declined about 40 percent between 1961 and 1983. For the period when data is available, poverty declined somewhat in the late 1980s and throughout the 1990s. Progress was slow and uneven and inequality increased in the 1990s.

Periodic drought and crop failure only tell part of the story. I have highlighted the cumulative effects of demographic changes, government policy failures and institutional decay as key drivers of the poverty process. Poverty is about people and their numbers relative to the capacity of the economy to provide for their primary needs matter. The cumulative effects of even modest declines in food production in the 1970s and early 1980s had a telling effect on the basic needs of nutrition and primary goods for a growing population. The sporadic growth of the economy, particularly during 1965–1985, meant that population growth also outstripped the growth of labour market opportunities.

What is at stake is not just an awareness of the demographic changes. Just as important are the basic capabilities of government and the list of policy failures which historically have had a habit of adversely reinforcing themselves, pushing both individuals and government into poverty. Shrinking government revenue and weak organizational capacity of the state combined to weaken the government's ability to maintain, let alone add to, public capital goods even as population more than doubled between 1960 and 2000.

From the poverty policy perspective, perhaps the greatest credit of the Economic Recovery Program of the mid 1980s is that it succeeded in halting the economic decline and the associated deprivations. It also succeeded in curtailing price distortions which undermined production incentives. But the poverty fighting impact was limited. Reformers understated the extent of the depth of poverty, and overstated the causal links from reforms to growth and from growth to poverty reduction. Perhaps, most important, the Fund and the Bank also overstated the response of the private sector to reforms, the readiness of government, and their own capacity to leverage and accelerate the needed institutional reforms. Those who looked to reform as a quick fix to rural poverty must have overestimated the short-run real price elasticity of supply. Years of deterioration in physical infrastructure in the rural economy, the decline in farm investment, the ageing population, and the out-migration of the active rural labor force suggest that the loss in agricultural production capacity could not have been resolved so soon to produce visible poverty fighting impact. On the eve of the millennium and after four comprehensive surveys, the depth and incidence of poverty in Ghana were no longer anecdotal. The case for taking a many sided approach to poverty alleviation had become clearer. The course of poverty reduction was set.

Notes

1. Source: International Financial Statistics and cited in Leith and Söderling (2003) p. 90. The link of poverty and changes in living standards to some income measure as Sen (1992) put it "is often hard to avoid given the comparatively greater availability of income statistics rather than other types of data." (p. 105).

2. Earthtrends, Food and Agricultural Organization (FAO). 2003.

3. United State Agency for International Development (USAID) Centre for Development Information and Evaluation (1997).

4. The nutritionally adequate diet definition of poverty, developed for North America, has subsequently been adopted for many countries with adjustments for needs standards or poverty thresholds in different environments.

5. The conventional World Bank absolute income cut-off for the lower bound (extremely poor) is if consumption is less than a (U.S.) dollar per day. For the upper bound, one is identified as poor if consumption per day is less than two dollars.

6. A national household survey was conducted in 1961/62 and was reported by Golding (1962). However, the data for this are not in the public domain. A second survey conducted in 1974 by the Central Bureau of Statistics was analyzed by Ewusi (1984). His findings and some remarks follow later in the chapter.

7. Ghana Commercial Bank, *Quarterly Economic Review*, Jan-Dec. 1982, Vol. 5 (1-4).

8. Ghana Commercial Bank (1982) Table 2.

9. Moreover, with a GDP growth of 6 percent, Ghana's per capita income of £70 was higher than that of Egypt of £56, Nigeria £26 and India £25 (Ghana Commercial Bank, Quarterly Economic Review, Jan-March 2002, Vol. 23 (1),7.

10. Rimmer's study is cited in Hart (1973, 64).

11. The poverty line was defined as per capita annual household income of less than a hundred (U.S.) dollars. For the urban (rural) area the incidence of poverty was estimated at 53 percent (85 percent). Regional disparities ranged from 92.4 percent in the Volta region to 49.5 percent in Greater Accra.

12. The fifth comprehensive survey (GLSS5) was expected to be underway at the time of writing.

13. The lower and upper poverty lines were defined as one-half and two-thirds, respectively of the mean per capital household expenditures.

14. The time periods for the surveys are as follows: GLSS 1 September 1987-August 1988; GLSS2 October 1988–September 1989; and GLSS3 October 1991-September 1992.

15. Ghana Commercial Bank, "Family Planning in Ghana." *Monthly Economic Bulletin*, Vol.8 98) October 1977.

16. Ghana Living Standards Survey (GLSS4), Ghana Statistical Service, 2000.

17. Ghana Statistical Service, "The Pattern of Poverty in Ghana, 1988-92." mimeo (Jan 1995).

18. The inflation tax is calculated as the product of the average annual inflation rate and the real value of the monetary base.

19. The traditional definition of seigniorage revenue used here is the change in the monetary base (currency plus reserves) divided by GDP.

20. Regulated nominal interest rates in the face of inflation had similar detrimental sectoral effects as real interest rates turned negative.

21. The National Liberation government which took over from Nkrumah in February 1966 devalued the currency on 8 July 1976. The par value of the cedi was set at a dollar to cedis (¢) 1.02. The Busia government devalued the currency in December 1971 to US$ to ¢1.82. The military government that toppled the second Republic revalued the currency at a dollar to ¢1.28. The rate will remain fixed until June 1978 when Ghana introduced a flexible exchange rate system. This was short-lived as the rate was fixed again in August 1978 at a dollar to ¢2.75. Based on the parallel market exchange rate, the over-valuation with respect to the US dollar ranged from 121 percent in 1972 to 577 percent in 1980, 955 percent in 1981 and 2788 percent by the first quarter of 1983.

22. As Loxley (1991) put it, cocoa farmers were unable to pay labor to maintain and harvest their crop, and often it did not pay them to rehabilitate or replant trees or harvest all their crop. An example of the effect of exchange rate over-valuation and the effect on the cocoa industry was played out in 1981. The government tripled the producer price of cocoa from ¢120 to ¢360 per 30 kilos. At the prevailing average price per ton of £1,247 and the exchange rate of ¢5.18, the Ghana Cocoa Marketing Board (GCMB) could only earn export revenues of ¢6,459 per ton as against the new legislated producer price to farmers of ¢12,000 per ton. The inability of GCMB to pay this producer price provided further incentive for smuggling and exit from the industry (Ghana Commercial Bank, *Quarterly Economic Review*, Jan-Dec. 1982 Vol. 5).

23. Aryeetey and Harrigan (2000, 8).

24. Bank of Ghana Annual Report 1982/83 (unpublished)

25. The period 1972 to 1982 was also under five different military governments and the third parliamentary government.

26. See the collection of papers in Konadu-Agyeman (2001).

27. USAID's Centre for Development Information and Evaluation (1997), Number 3.

References

Alderman, H. "Downturn and Economic Recovery in Ghana: Impacts on the Poor." Paper prepared for United States agency for International Development, African Bureau. April 1990.

————. "Ghana: Adjustment Star Pupil?" in *Adjusting to Policy Failures in African Economies*, edited by D. Dahn et. al., Cornell University Press, Ithaca. 1994.

Appiah K., L. Demery and S. G. Laryea-Adjei. "Poverty in a Changing Environment." Pp. 304-320 in *Economic Reforms in Ghana: The Miracle and the Mirage*, edited by E. Aryeetey, J. Harrigan, and M Nissanke, Oxford University Press, 2000.

Aryeetey E. and J. Harrigan. "Macroeconomic and Sectoral Developments Since 1970." in *Economic Reforms in Ghana: The Miracle and the Mirage*, edited by E. Aryeetey, J. Harrigan, and M Nissanke, Oxford University Press, 2000.

Aryeetey, E and R.S. Kanbur. eds. *Macroeconomic Stability, Growth and Poverty Reduction in Ghana.*(Paragon Printing Press, 2004.

Bateman M.J., A Meeraus, D. M. Newbery, W. Asenso-Okyere and G.T O'Mara. "Ghana's Cocoa Pricing Policy." The World Bank (WPS 429), June 1990.

Bawumia, M. "Aid, Debt Management, Macro Economic Stability and Medium-Term Growth." Pp. 42-58 in Aryeetey, E and R. S. Kanbur, 2004.

Boateng, E. O. K. Ewusi, R. Kanbur, & A. Mckay. "A Poverty Profile for Ghana: 1987-88." *Social Dimensions of Adjustment in Sub-Saharan Africa,* Working Paper No.5 World Bank, 1990.

Burtless, G and T. M. Smeeding. "The Level, Trend and Composition of Poverty," Pp. 27-68 in *Understanding Poverty* edited by S.H. Danziger and R.H. Haveman, Harvard University Press, 2001.

Canagarajah, S. and Xiao Ye. "Public Health and Education Spending in Ghana in 1992-98." *Policy Research Working Paper* 2579, The World Bank. April 2001.

Canagarajah, S. and C.C Pörtner. "Evolution of Poverty and Welfare in Ghana in the 1990s: Achievements and Challenges." *African Region Working Paper Series* No. 61, World Bank, October 2003.

Canagarajah, S and D. Mazumdar. "Employment, Labour Markets, and Poverty in Ghana: A Study of changes during Economic Decline and Recovery." *Policy Research Working Paper* 1845, World Bank. Nov. 1997.

Chazan, N. *An Anatomy of Ghanaian Politics: Managing Political Recession 1969-82.* Westview Special Studies in Africa. Boulder, Co: Westview Press, 1983.

Dercon, S. "Income Risk, Coping Strategies and Safety Nets." World Bank Research Observer, 17 (2002): 141-166.

Dornbusch, R. *Stabilization, Debt, and Reform: Policy Analysis for Developing Countries,* Prentice Hall, Englewood Cliffs, NJ. 1993.

Easterly, W. *The Elusive Quest for Growth*, M. I. T. Press. Cambridge, Mass. 2001.

Ewusi, K. *The Distribution of Monetary Incomes in Ghana*, ISSER Technical Publications Series. No. 14, ISSER, University of Ghana, Legon. 1971.

————. "The Dimensions and Characteristics of Rural Poverty in Ghana." ISSER Technical Publication No. 43 April 1984.

Gayi, S. K. "Adjusting to the Social Costs of Adjustment in Ghana: Problems and Prospects." Pp.77-100 in *Adjustment and Social Sector Restructuring*, edited by Jessica Vivian. United Nations Research Institute for Social Development, London. 1975.

Ghana Commercial Bank. "Family Planning in Ghana." *Monthly Economic Bulletin*, Vol. 8, 98 October 1977.
———. *Quarterly Economic Review*, Jan-Dec. 1982, Vol. 5 (1-4).
———. *Quarterly Economic Review* "Interest Rates and Savings in Ghana," January-December Vol. 14 1991.
Ghana Statistical Service. "The Pattern of poverty in Ghana, 1988-92." Accra, Ghana mimeo (January 1995)
———. *Core Welfare Indicators Questionnaire (CWIQ) Survey*, Main Report, 1997.
———. *Poverty Trends in Ghana in the 1990s*, Ghana, October 2000.
———. Report of the Fourth Round (GLSS 4), October. 2000.
Goldstein M. and R. Bhavnani. "From Independence to Economic Reform: Rural Poverty in Ghana from 1967-1997." Paper presented at Ghana's Economy at the Half Century, July 18-20, Accra Ghana. 2004.
Hart, Keith. "Informal Income Opportunities and Urban Employment in Ghana." *The Journal of Modern African Studies*, Vol. 11. No. 1 1973. Pp 61-89.
Heintz, J. "Elements of an Employment Framework for Poverty Reduction in Ghana," Report of Joint ILO/UNDP Mission, 2004.
Huq, M. M. *The Economy of Ghana: The First 25 Years Since Independence.* London: Macmillan, 1989.
Hutchful, E. "Military Policy and Reform in Ghana." *The Journal of Modern African Studies*, 35(2). (1997): 251-278.
Islam, R. and D. Wetzel. "Ghana: Adjustment, Reform, and Growth," Pp. 310-367 in *Public Sector Deficits and Macroeconomic Performance*, edited by Easterly, W. A. C Rodriguez., and K Schmidt-Hebbel, Oxford University Press. 1994.
Jebuni, C. "Governance and Structural Adjustment in Ghana." *Working Paper Series* No. 15260, The World Bank. 1995
———. "Monetary Policy, Exchange rate Policy, Macroeconomic stability and Medium term Growth." Pp. 29-41. in *Macroeconomic Stability, Growth and Poverty Reduction in Ghana*, edited by E. Aryeetey and R.S. Kanbur. (Paragon Printing Press, 2004).
Killick, T. *Development Economics in Action: A Study of Contemporary Policies in Ghana.* London: Heinemann, 1978.
———. "Fragile Still? The Structure of Ghana's Economy 1960-94." Pp. 51-67 in *Economic Reforms in Ghana: The Miracle and the Mirage*, edited by Aryeetey et. al.: African World Press, Trenton N.J. 2000.
———. "What Drives Change in Ghana?" Paper presented at *Ghana Half Century Conference*, Accra, Ghana July 2004.
Konadu-Agyeman, K. ed. *IMF and World Bank Sponsored Structural Adjustment Programs in Africa. Ghana's experience, 1983-1999.* Ashgate, USA. 2001.
Kusi, N. K. *Tax Reform and Revenue Productivity in Ghana*, AERC Research Paper 74. African Economic Research Consortium, Naroibi, Kenya. March 1998.
Leith, J. C. and L. Söderling. *Ghana-Long Term Growth, Atrophy and Stunted Recovery*, The Nordic African Institute. Research Report No. 125. 2003.
Loxley, J. *Ghana: The Long Road to Recovery 1983-90.* Ottawa: The North-South Institute, 1991.
McKinnon, R. J. *Money and Capital in Economic Development*, Washington DC. Brookings Institution, 1973.

Mencher, S. "The Problem of Measuring Poverty." *British Journal of Sociology*, Vol.18, 1 (1967): 1-12.

National Capacity Building Assessment Group. *An Assessment of National Capacity Building in Ghana*, Report, August 1996. Accra

Ray. D. *Development Economics*, Princeton University Press, Princeton, 1998.

Rimmer, D. *Staying Poor: Ghana's Political Economy 1950-1990*. Oxford: Pergamon Press, 1992.

Roach, J. L. and J. K. Roach. eds., *Poverty: Selected Readings*. Harmondsworth, England, Penguin Books, 1972.

Rockman, B. A. "The Changing Role of the State." Pp. 20-44 in *Taking Stock: Assessing Public Sector Reforms, edited by B. G. Peters and D. J. Savoie*. McGill University Press, 1988.

Sandbrook R. and J. Olebaum. "Reforming Dysfunctional Institutions Through Democratisation? Reflections on Ghana." *The Journal of Modern African Studies*, Vol. 35, 4 (1997): 603-646.

Sarris, A. H. "Household Welfare during Crisis and Adjustment in Ghana." *Journal of African Economies*, Vol. 2 No. 2. (1993): 195-237.

Sen, A. *Inequality Reexamined*, Harvard University Press, Cambridge Mass. 1992
———. *Development as Freedom*, Anchor Books, New York, 1999.

UNICEF. *Adjustment Policies and Programme to Protect Children and Other Vulnerabile Groups*, Accra, Ghana. 1986.

USAID. "Food Aid in Ghana: An Elusive Road to Self-Reliance." Center for Development Information and Evaluation, Number 3, 1997.

World Bank. *Ghana Growth, Private Sector, and Poverty Reduction*, Report No. 14111-GH, May 1995.

3

The North-South Divide and the Disappearing Middle Class: An Analysis of Spatial Inequality and Polarization in Ghana

Jacqueline Vanderpuye-Orgle

1. Introduction

Ghana is often touted as the success story of economic reform. The reform process of the 1980s and 1990s may be categorized into three phases: successful stabilization phase marked by the introduction of the Economic Recovery Program (1983—1986), structural adjustment phase also known as Economic Recovery Program II (1987—1991) and the oscillating policy reform phase set off by fiscal dislocation in the wake of multiparty elections (1992—2000).[1] The first two phases involved economic liberalization with the removal of import controls, price controls on goods, interest rates deregulation, currency devaluation, and the rehabilitation of deteriorated infrastructure. Indeed, growth rates moved from negative to positive, inflation rates fell significantly, the deficit to GDP ratio declined, and the macroeconomy was reasonably stable during this period.

Stabilization and adjustment were partially derailed in 1992 largely due to an 80 percent election-related wage increase (Tsikata, 2001). Public sector wage bill rose by 38.7 percent. Election pressures drove up rural development expenditures. The fall in tax revenues as a result of the poor 1991/1992 cocoa harvest and the interruption of lending by the multilateral institutions added to the fiscal deterioration. The oscillating phase was thus marked by macroeconomic instability including higher inflation, a reversal from fiscal surplus in 1991 to a deficit of about 5 percent of GDP as well as increasing money supply. The government reigned in the fiscal pressure by 1994 only for it to resurface in the run-up to the 1996 and 1999 elections.

The reform process generated considerable interest, especially with respect to its social impact. For instance, the downsizing of the public sector as part of civil service reforms was decried by the general public. Nyantenteng and Seini

(2000) observed that the "philosophy that continuous growth following liberal policies would eventually lead to a more equitable social distribution ensured that (at least initially) no special efforts were made to reach the poor." The Program of Actions to Mitigate the Social Costs of Adjustment (PAMSCAD) received mixed reviews. Debates centered on whether the policies exacerbated the circumstances of the poor and the vulnerable in Ghana (Gayi, 1995).

Although there was a net reduction in poverty at the national level in the 1990s, the decline was not evenly distributed spatially. Whilst Accra and the forest areas saw marked reductions, poverty increased in the urban savannah (and in the rural savannah using a lower poverty line).[2] Even in the areas which experienced a decline, the evidence was that "the gains . . . have been smaller for the poorest" (GSS, 2000). The reduction seemed to be centered on those close to the poverty line; the poorest experienced very slight improvements and in some cases poverty levels increased. In short, the income distribution actually worsened in some regions of the country. Income inequality increased; the relatively well off got richer and the poor got poorer——the middle class was disappearing with the income distribution becoming clustered at the extremes.

Historically, spatial inequality in Ghana has been associated with North-South dimension. The literature identifies colonial policies and the resulting unequal infrastructural development as the root of this disparity. Another dimension often cited is the rural-urban divide. These two dimensions are central to poverty trends in Ghana. Poverty remains a rural phenomenon and is predominant in the northern half of the country.

In assessing the role of inequality in poverty dynamics, GSS (2000) noted that "growth in the average standard of living will reduce poverty other things being equal, but where it is accompanied by an increase in inequality, the reduction in poverty is reduced." Inequality is inimical to poverty reduction and economic development as a whole. In addition, the accompanying gradual disappearance of the middle class will result in the polarization of the populace. This in turn could escalate into political or civil strife, further retarding economic growth.[3]

Canagarajah *et. al.* (1998) observed a reduction in income inequality, albeit modest, from 1988—1992.[4] However, this was before the turbulence in the economy that characterized the oscillating policy phase. Hypothetically, economic growth (or more broadly improvement in a nation's macroeconomic stance) and equitable poverty reduction can and should go hand in hand. A better understanding of the distribution of income that takes into account the spatial variation in endowments and socio-economic infrastructure is important in formulating integrated regional strategies that may succeed in achieving sustainable poverty reduction whilst fostering economic growth. The present study makes a contribution to this end.

The objectives are as follows: first, to examine how spatial inequality evolved in the period 1988—1999; second, to determine how much of total inequality in Ghana can be attributed to spatial inequality; and third, to analyze trends in polarization in Ghana. The current study builds on existing studies to produce a consistent analysis of inequality in Ghana. It extends the analysis by closely examining the spatial dimension of inequality. The latter dimension of poverty has been ignored in the welfare dialogue in Ghana. Although the extant literature identifies areas where poverty is prevalent, there is a research void in examining the extent and the nature of clustering in the distribution of income. This has implications for the assessment of economic growth and the nature of poverty in Ghana.

The paper is organized as following. Section two presents a review of the literature. Section three assesses trends in spatial inequality. Section four analyses polarization in Ghana followed by a summary of the major findings of the paper. The results suggest that the Ghanaian population is clustered and that polarization is on the rise. The differences within-group specific means are considerably larger than the between-group components in explaining static levels of interpersonal inequality. However, changes in the levels of inequality are principally driven by changes in the between-group, i.e., the spatial, component of inequality.

2. Spatial Inequality and Poverty in Ghana

Generally, the dialogue on spatial economics evolved from the 1970s, when neo-Marxists viewed the world economy as made up of the "core" and the "periphery," through the rather disconcerting characterization into "temperate" and "tropical" by Karmack (1976), to the New Keynesian perspective of "North" and "South." Spatial inequality in Ghana has been treated predominantly as a "reversed" North-South phenomenon although the terminology as used in the Ghanaian literature is purely a geographic classification. The North consists of the Northern, Upper East and Upper West Regions of Ghana. The South consists of the Ashanti, Eastern, Western, Central, Brong-Ahafo, Greater Accra and Volta Regions. Of the latter group, Ashanti, Eastern, Central as well as the Western and Brong-Ahafo Regions make up the forest ecological zone of the country's South—the prime cocoa, timber and mineral producing areas and the core of the nation's spatial economy.[5] The coastal areas are also a part of the core by virtue of rapid growth in the port towns. Historically, the North has been treated as the periphery.

Researchers have identified broad disparities between the northern part of Ghana and the rest of the country. Forde (1968), using factor analysis, principal components and regression analyses, divided Ghana into relatively homogenous multivariate regions. Based on the 1960 population census he derived two main regions—the North and the South, reflecting regional inequality accompanying economic development. Songsore (1989) used principal component analysis and data from the 1970 population census to identify key variables explaining spatial inequality.[6] He concluded that the North-South divide was the main dimension of spatial inequality: the North had been left behind in the development process.

Songsore (1989) argued that dependency and capitalist penetration, under colonialism, shaped the country's internal structure to fit the needs of the colonial metropolis. He argued that this structure had not changed much even after independence. He concluded that this has led to the distortion of the internal patterns of production, and the spatial organization of economic and social activity. Chazan (1991) on the other hand pointed out that between 1983–1991, the period marking the early stages of the Economic Recovery Program (ERP), the nation was insulated from strong interest group demands. The military government, at the time, had broken ties with the post-colonial elites.

The mid-1980s saw an increasing awareness of the deprived North and a shift in policy focus to facilitate the development of the area. Given the vestiges of colonial legacy, the adjustment policies may not have bridged the North-South gap. Poverty in both 1991/1992 and 1998/1999 was disproportionately concentrated in the savannah belt which lies in the northern half of the country (GSS, 2000). It is, however, erroneous to treat the North or South as monoliths. Within these two broad areas, there is a rural-urban disparity in infrastructure and services. In the North, for instance, social and public services are concentrated in the capital Tamale and its vicinity. A similar pattern underlying rural-urban disparities is observed in the South.[7]

Trends in inequality have evolved over time. Canagarajah *et al* (1998) using the Gini coefficient, entropy class measures and stochastic dominance analysis examined changes in inequality by locality. Based on the first three rounds of the Ghana Living Standards Survey (GLSS) they defined locality as Accra, Other Cities and Rural Areas. They reported (a) the within-group inequality in these three areas, (b) the fraction of overall inequality explained by within inequality and (c) the fraction of overall inequality explained by inequality between these localities as well as the administrative regions.[8] Between the second (1988) and third (1991/1992) round surveys, they observed that inequality increased in Accra but fell in the Other Cities and Rural areas. Between the third and fourth (1998/1999) round surveys, and based on a more disaggregated definition of locality, the GSS (2000) observed that inequality decreased in Accra, the urban savannah and rural forest areas but increased in the urban forest, urban coastal as well as the rural coastal and rural savannah areas.

It is evident from the above that the pattern of inequality varies even within rural and urban areas, respectively. Spatial inequality may also be attributed to the differential resource endowment of regions. Within a given locality, there is a rural-rural divide between those rural areas more closely tied to commodity production for export and those tied to subsistence production.

Another important dimension is the administrative regions. GSS (2000) noted that "the pattern of poverty . . . by region reveals sharp differences in poverty levels even between geographically adjacent regions." Poverty was highest in the North (i.e. Upper East, Upper West and Northern Regions) in 1992 and

1999, whereas Greater Accra Region had the lowest poverty. It is worth noting that some of the regions (e.g. Central and Eastern Regions) in the South also experienced high poverty incidence in 1999. The North-South distinction becomes blurred with regard to poverty dynamics as well: the Central Region experienced an increase in poverty whilst poverty decreased for the rest of the South. On the other hand, the Upper West experienced a decrease in poverty whilst poverty increased for the rest of the North. These nuances may have implications for the conventional wisdom that the North-South is the main dimension of spatial inequality in Ghana. Canagarajah *et. al.* (1998) observed that inequality between administrative regions contributed the most to overall inequality in 1988 but this declined in 1992.

Given the fourth round survey data, what is the general trend in spatial inequality? Is inequality in Ghana essentially a spatial phenomenon? Which dimension of poverty is most germane to efforts aimed at reducing inequality? Within-group inequality increased in Accra but decreased in Other Cities and Rural Areas (Canagarajah et al, 1998). However, how does this compare to the changes in the between-locality component? Is the population becoming clustered, vis-à-vis the income distribution, such that within each locality members are very similar but between localities members are different?

3. Estimating Spatial Inequality in Ghana

This study adopts the standard procedure of using the real per capita consumption expenditure as a measure of the standard of living.[9] The Lorenz consistent (relative) measures of inequality——the Gini coefficient (Cowell 1995) and the Generalized Entropy (GE) class of measures (Shorrocks, 1980, 1984) were used as the basis for analysis.

The Gini coefficient is sensitive to changes that occur at the middle of the distribution. It is a widely used summary statistic and is thus useful for purposes of comparison. On the other hand, the GE class of measures is collectively sensitive to all parts of the distribution. The Mean Logarithm Deviation (GE with c=0) is especially sensitive to incomes at the bottom of the distribution; the Theil Index (GE with c=1) is constructed to be responsive across all ranges of the distribution; while the GE with c≠0,1 is sensitive to changes that occur at the middle part of the distribution. For exogenously given groups, the GE measure is also additively decomposable into within-group and between-group components of inequality. We used the Mean Logarithm Deviation (i.e. GE(0)) in order to adequately capture changes at the bottom of the distribution.[10]

First, we estimated the overall inequality in Ghana as a benchmark for analysis using the Ghana Living Standard Survey (GLSS) data. Both the Gini coefficient and GE(0) measures reveal that inequality increased over the 1988-

1999 period (Table 3.1).[11] The Gini coefficient increased by 9.42 percent whereas the GE(0) increased by 22.36 percent.

Table 3.1 Inequality in Ghana: 1988-1999

Year	Gini	GE(0)
1988	0.382	0.246
1989	0.405	0.276
1992	0.383	0.241
1999	0.418	0.301
percent change: 1988-1999	9.42	22.36

Source: Author's calculaton

With respect to changes between the respective survey periods: inequality in Ghana increased in 1988–1989; it then fell until 1992, reflecting the adjustment phase of the reforms. The upward turn that begun in 1992, lasting through to 1999, coincides with the derailment of the economy in the wake of the multiparty elections, *inter alia*, during the oscillating policy phase. It is noteworthy that the initial net decline in the GE(0) from 1988–1992 was consistent with that observed by Canagarajah et al (1998).

Given the trends in overall inequality, how does spatial inequality vary over time? As mentioned earlier, the GE measure can be decomposed into the within-group and between-group components. For a given spatial dimension, the former captures what happens within the respective groups in a given dimension whereas the latter reflects the level of inequality between the mean incomes of the respective groups. Thus, a measure of spatial inequality can be defined as the between-group component of the GE:[12]

$$SI = I\left(\mu_1 e_1, ..., \mu_K e_K\right) \qquad (1)$$

Our analysis looked at several dimensions of spatial inequality. The conventional dimension is the North–South divide. The Rural-Urban is also widely perceived as a prime dimension of spatial inequality. Amendments made to the Constitution of the Republic of Ghana in April of 1992, preceding multiparty democratic elections, allowed for decentralization and the formation of local governments. The appointment of Regional Ministers and District Chief Executive in each of the ten administrative regions fostered some semblance of autonomy at the regional level. Diverse policies and public expenditures may ultimately reflect in some disparities in the income distribution. In addition, differences in resource endowments as captured by the ecological zones warrant a closer look at the latter as a dimension of spatial inequality. Variants of these are also defined to capture the rural-rural, urban-urban, within-North and within-

South dynamics.[13] Precise definitions of these dimensions are given in Appendix 3.B.

Group-specific means of per capita expenditure were computed for the respective dimensions and weighted by the national mean for ease of comparison (Table 3.2). Households in rural areas consistently had lower per capita expenditure levels than those in urban areas in the respective survey periods. The per capita expenditure in the rural areas was lower than the national average. These observations are consistent with the extant literature—poverty is largely a rural phenomenon. Similarly, households in the North had lower per capita expenditures than those in the South as well as the national mean in all the survey periods. With regards to the ecological zones, the savannah areas had the least per capita expenditure values, whereas the coastal areas had the highest values. This is also consistent with the fact that "poverty is disproportionately concentrated in the savannah" (GSS, 2000). The coastal areas include the Accra-Tema metropolis which forms the business and administrative core of the country.

At the regional level, the Greater Accra Region consistently had the highest per capita expenditure level. The Upper West Region had the least per capita expenditure level in all the survey periods. The Upper West Region has been noted as the poorest region in Ghana. About 90 percent of the population was living below the upper poverty line by 1992; this number fell slightly to 84 percent in 1999 (Canagarajah and Portner, 2003). In addition, the Upper West, Northern and Upper East Regions consistently had expenditure levels below the national means. Canagarajah and Portner noted that these regions "are substantially poorer than the rest of Ghana."

It is interesting to note that using the North-South dimension all the regions in the South had expenditure levels that exceeded the national averages whereas all the regions in the North were below the respective national means. However, at the regional level of disaggregation, it is evident that the Volta and Eastern regions actually had values that were below the national means as well. Central Region was also below the national means in all survey periods except 1992 when it exceeded the mean by a 5.5 percent margin.

Examining intra-urban dynamics in Locality 3, Accra had higher per capita expenditure levels than the other urban areas. Disaggregating the rural and urban areas by ecological zones in Locality 7, the Rural Savannah had the least per capita expenditure levels. With regards to the differences between groups in a given dimension, Locality 7 had the widest difference in per capita expenditure levels in 1988. The Administrative Regions had the widest difference in 1989, 1992 and 1999. The least difference between groups in a given dimension was that of the Rural-Urban dimension in 1988, 1992 and 1999. The Ecological zones had the least difference in 1992. *Prima facie*, the widest disparity or inequality in welfare (as proxied by per capita expenditure) was between the administrative regions for all the survey periods except 1988 when Locality 7 had the widest disparity.

Table 3.2 Weighted Group-Specific Mean Per Capita Expenditures Index

Spatial Dimension/ Characteristic	1988	1989	1992	1999
a) Rural-Urban	(36.39)	(37.90)	(15.86)	(56.07)
Rural	79.20	86.28	94.47	79.45
Urban	115.59	124.18	110.33	135.51
b) North-South	(43.77)	(36.84)	(20.80)	(59.75)
North	61.67	67.77	82.14	47.62
South	105.44	104.61	102.93	107.37
c) Ecological Zones	(59.11)	(35.32)	(24.48)	(58.52)
Forest	91.09	99.20	102.53	101.61
Coastal	125.30	113.91	107.89	120.09
Savannah	66.19	78.58	83.41	61.57
d) Administrative Regions	(102.66)	(75.28)	(56.94)	(127.22)
Greater Accra	156.21	139.69	120.26	162.37
Central	84.70	93.24	105.55	78.10
Western	124.25	113.77	89.29	109.86
Eastern	95.44	89.23	97.07	84.82
Volta	75.17	76.43	94.57	76.14
Ashanti	92.93	96.38	118.52	119.26
Brong-Ahafo	87.39	120.19	81.23	102.80
Northern	64.26	69.24	86.17	58.43
Upper East	64.15	67.41	85.87	42.24
Upper West	53.55	64.40	63.32	35.15
e) Locality 7	(112.79)	(68.05)	(44.95)	(112.66)
Accra	170.19	141.05	124.44	167.22
Urban Coastal	115.44	124.44	103.54	119.19
Urban Forest	99.20	115.80	106.94	136.12
Urban Savannah	82.65	101.77	100.76	89.64
Rural Coastal	97.15	87.73	99.95	88.15
Rural Forest	81.65	93.03	100.96	87.73
Rural Savannah	57.40	73.01	79.48	54.55

Table 3.2 Continued

Spatial Dimension/ Characteristic	1988	1989	1992	1999
f) Locality 3	(90.99)	(56.03)	(29.97)	(87.77)
Accra	170.19	142.31	124.44	167.22
Other Urban	102.91	116.66	104.54	123.10
Rural	79.20	86.28	94.47	79.45
National Mean	100.00	100.00	100.00	100.00

Source: Author's calculation
Mean values were weighted with the national average as the base. The national mean per capita expenditure values were 75,461.92; 238.167.44; 273,796.17 and 1,360,451.00 Cedis in 1988, 1989, 1992 and 1999 respectively. The widest difference in per capita expenditure for each spatial classification for the respective years is given in parentheses. For example, the gap between the rural and urban expenditure index relative to the national average was 36.39 in 1988. It narrowed down to 15.56 by 1992, but widened sharply to 56.07 by 1998/1999.

For all the respective dimensions the range of disparity was least in 1992. Several reasons account for this reversal in 1992. Perhaps the most compelling is the changes made in the third round of the GLSS survey discussed in Appendix 3B and mentioned earlier as a caveat. Another reason could be the effect of the economic reform process. The evidence is not conclusive. Data limitations restrict any robust empirical tests. In addition, it is difficult to disentangle the effects of policies from the other concurrent events such as the worsening terms of trade. Even though this paper makes mention of the reform phases, we only acknowledge correlations and do not purport to establish causality of any sort.

Spatial inequality in Ghana was estimated using the six dimensions identified in Table 3.2. As mentioned earlier, the between-group component of the GE was used as the measure for spatial inequality. This reflects the mean difference between group specific distributions. In essence, it captures the static level of interpersonal inequality between individuals in respective groups in a given dimension.

All the dimensions yield the same trend (Table 3.3 and Figure 3.1). The fact that multiple alternative groupings of individuals along the dimensions all show the same trend reflects the robustness of the results. Spatial inequality in Ghana fell sharply in the period 1988–1989. It continued to decline, albeit less steeply, in 1989-92 and subsequently took an upward turn. This varies slightly from the trend in overall inequality——spatial inequality was declining in 1988-89 as overall inequality was rising.

Table 3.3 Spatial Inequality in Ghana

Year	Administrative Regions	Ecologi- cal Zones	Locality7	Locality 3	North- South	Rural- Urban
1988	0.040	0.026	0.037	0.029	0.014	0.027
1989	0.026	0.009	0.021	0.017	0.009	0.016
1992	0.012	0.005	0.008	0.004	0.003	0.003
1999	0.062	0.026	0.053	0.037	0.029	0.034

Figure 3.1 Spatial Inequality in Ghana

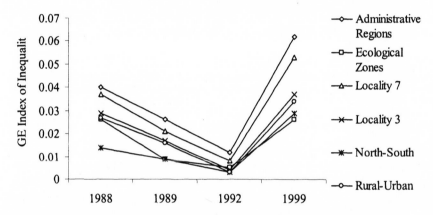

Source: Author's calculation

Even though the adjustment phase was characterized by positive macroeconomic indicators, the poor were becoming even poorer in all areas. Growth may not have offset the socioeconomic impact of reforms for the poorest subset of the population during the 1988-1989 period. This observation reflects, to some extent, the lack of synergy between policies targeted at economic growth and those aimed at poverty reduction and improving the income distribution. While the groups in the respective dimensions were growing more like each other with macroeconomic improvement, the income distribution for the entire population was worsening.

With regards to the relative magnitudes, the graph for the administrative regions was almost everywhere above those for the other dimensions. Spatial inequality was relatively higher by the administrative regions than by North-South dimensions. However, in general the magnitudes of spatial inequality were low. To further understand the dynamics in the overall versus spatial inequality, we examined the within-group component of the GE measure (Appendix 3.C). The magnitudes were consistently larger than the between-group spatial inequality estimates: the disparity in the income distribution within the groups was more than that between groups. This underscores the lack of synergy mentioned earlier. Even though reform policies reflected in overall growth or macroeconomic improvement in general and thus may have lowered the levels of inequality between spatial groups, the dearth of policies targeted at the poorest of the poor meant that within a given group only those above a certain income threshold could take advantage of any income-improving opportunities attendant with growth. As noted by the GSS (2000), poverty reduction seemed predominantly among those close to the poverty line whilst the hardcore poor became worse off in some cases—widening the income gap. Inequality was thus much higher within given groups.

Figure 3.2 Within Group Inequality

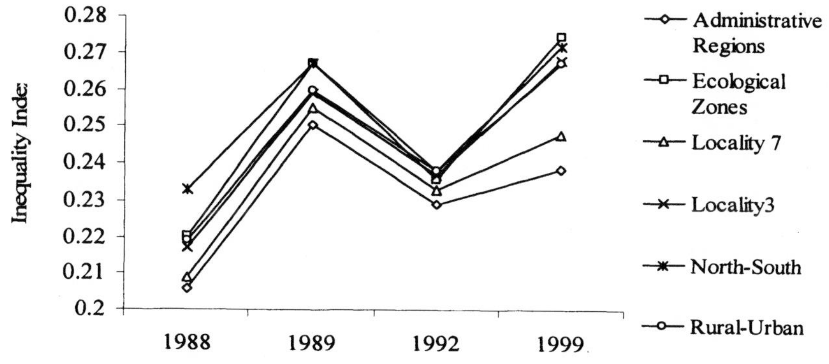

Source: Author's calculation

The respective dimensions showed the same trend in within-group inequality (Figure 3.2). Within-group inequality increased in the 1988—1989 period; declined till 1992 and then turned upward. It is interesting to note the dynamics in spatial versus within-group inequality. In 1988—1989, as the populations within the groups became more disparate (i.e. within-group inequality was rising), the group means were converging (i.e. the groups became more alike). Hence, intra-group populations were becoming equally disparate for all dimensions. Beyond 1989, both spatial inequality and within-group inequality declined till 1992 and then took an upward turn as the macroeconomy was derailed.

How much of the change in overall inequality can be attributed to changes in spatial inequality? Suppose there are K exhaustive and mutually exclusive groups in each spatial dimension.[14] The between-group inequality from the decomposable GE measure represents the distance between the group means. The change in overall inequality attributable to the change in the between component can be estimated in one of three ways, two of which will be used in the paper.[15]

First, the ratio of the change in between-group inequality to the change in total inequality may be regarded as a share of spatial variation index because it captures the proportion of variation in total inequality attributable to changing spatial variation. We estimated this index for the respective dimensions over the contiguous survey periods. The percentage values are presented in Table 3.4.

Table 3.4 Percentage Share of Spatial Variation in Change in Total Inequality

Dimension\Period	1988-1989	1989-1992	1992-1999
Administrative Regions	-49.23	40.04	84.34
Ecological Zones	-55.81	11.88	35.92
Locality 7	-54.54	37.95	75.61
Locality3	-40.55	37.55	55.21
North	-14.75	17.94	43.69
Rural	-38.48	36.70	52.50

We focus on the last two columns.[16] With a caveat regarding the faults in the dimensionality of comparison, variations in inequality in Administrative Regions, rather than the North, seemed consistently to have the most impact on overall inequality. Between 1989 and 1992, 40 percent of the change in total variation was due to the change in the inequality between administrative regions whereas in 1992–1999 this dimension accounted for 84 percent of the change in overall inequality in Ghana. This result may have implications for the current debate on policy targeting focused on the North-South dimension.

Locality 7 was the next most relevant dimension explaining changes in overall inequality. This variable captured the dynamics between ecological zones (and thus resource endowments) and urbanization. In addition, changes in spatial inequality in Locality 3 and Rural accounted for over 50 percent of the change in the overall inequality in the 1992–1999 period.

The more fitting level of comparison is that of the temporal level in a given dimension. It is evident that the changes in spatial variation accounted for increasingly larger shares of the changes in overall inequality. It accounted for almost twice as much in 1992–1999 as it did in 1989–1992. Remarkably, moving from examining the levels of inequality to the changes in the levels of inequality, the spatial dimension seemed to play a very crucial role.

One crude way of controlling for dimensionality, is to normalize the spatial variation (SV) measure by the size of the dimension (i.e. the number of groups in a given dimension). This controls for the very source of variation that one is interested in. We estimate the weighted share of spatial variation in inequality in

Table 3.5 Normalized Share of Spatial Variation of Change in Inequality

Dimension\Period	1988-1989	1989-1992	1992-1999
Administrative Regions	-4.92	4.00	8.43
Ecological Zones	-18.60	3.96	11.97
Locality5	13.09	7.29	14.30
Locality3	-13.52	12.52	18.40
North	-7.38	8.97	21.85
Rural	-19.24	18.35	26.25

Table 3.6 Change in the Share of Spatial Variation in Total Inequality (percent)

Dimension \Period	1988-1989	1989-1992	1992-1999
Administrative Regions	-7.10	-4.53	15.90
Ecological Zones	-7.18	-1.27	6.78
Locality 7	-7.80	-4.20	14.46
Locality3	-5.80	-6.07	10.71
North	-2.20	-2.16	8.54
Rural	-5.37	-4.56	10.24

Table 3.5. In this case the variation in the Rural-Urban dimension, and not the Administrative Regions, consistently accounts for most of variation in total inequality.

An alternative measure of the share of spatial variation is the change in the ratio of between to overall inequality. This measure is bounded in the interval [-1, 1]. It is also well defined over the entire interval. The values are reported in Table 3.6. The change in the share of spatial variation in total inequality was much larger in 1992-99 than in 1989–1992 for all dimensions. There is a slight difference in interpretation. For instance, the negative values for 1989–1992 imply that the share of between-group component in total inequality was much lower in 1992 than it was in 1989. However, the share of between-group component in total inequality was much larger in 1999 than in 1992. In short, the between group component is becoming increasingly important in explaining total inequality. Overall, one important conclusion can be drawn. The fact that the result from Table 3.4 was not robust to alternate measures of the share of spatial variation index suggests that the focus on the North-South dimension as the root of inequality may be overstated.

4. Polarization

Concerns about the disappearing middle class warrant a closer look at the income distribution. Polarization captures the extent to which the population is becoming clustered, such that within each cluster members are very similar, but between clusters members are very different (Fedorov, 2002). This differs from inequality, which does not impose any conditions of clustering within the distribution.

Polarization is particularly pertinent since inequality in Ghana is perceived as a spatial phenomenon. In addition, a cursory look at a map of Ghana shows that the administrative regions, the North-South divide attributed to colonial and the post-colonial policies as well as ecological zones (and thus differences in resource endowments) all run parallel to the coast. This also captures the major ethnic and religious differences as well. Polarization along spatial dimensions in Ghana could thus be very volatile. Civil strife and or ethnic conflicts that could result from this phenomenon, if unchecked, would not only inhibit further economic growth and but could result in a significant loss of infrastructure and manpower.

A number of measures have been proposed for the measurement of polarization.[17] The most widely used measures are the Esteban–Ray (1994) and Wolfson (1994) indices. These indices, however, identify the existence of clustering in a given distribution without giving any information about the dimensions along which polarization occurs. We are interested in polarization between the exogenously given dimensions discussed in Section 2. The Kanbur and Zhang (2001) index of polarization allows for *a priori* specification of a given dimension and thus, forms the basis of this analysis.[18] This measure captures the average distance between the group means in relation to the income differences within groups. As income differences within groups diminish (i.e., as the groups become more homogenous internally), the relative differences between groups are magnified and polarization is higher. The index is defined as follows:

$$KZ = \frac{I\left(\mu_1 e_1, \ldots, \mu_K e_K\right)}{\sum\limits_{g=1}^{K} w_g I_g} \tag{2}$$

Table 3.7 Kanbur-Zhang Index of Polarization

Year	Administrative Regions	Ecological Zones	Locality 7	Locality3	North	Rural
1988	0.196	0.117	0.179	0.135	0.059	0.125
1989	0.102	0.003	0.082	0.066	0.035	0.061
1992	0.050	0.020	0.032	0.016	0.012	0.012
1999	0.261	0.096	0.214	0.138	0.107	0.129

Figure 3.3 Kanbur-Zhang Index per Dimension

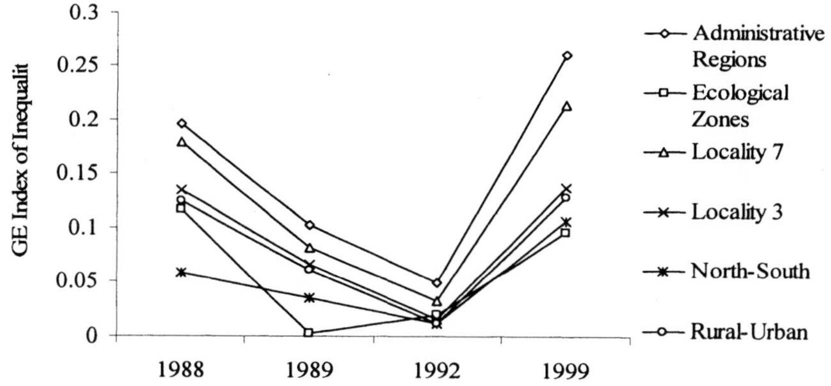

Source: Author's calculation

The index was computed for the six dimensions used thus far in the study, based on the real per capita expenditure and the GE measure with c=0.The results are presented in Table 3.7. The levels of polarization range from 0.003 for the Ecological Zones in 1988 to 0.261 for the Administrative Regions in 1999. To put these figures in perspective, Kanbur and Zhang (2001) in a similar study using per capita consumption figures in China estimated the levels of polarization in the range of 2.41–3.56 in the rural-urban dimension and 0.19–0.42 in the inland-coastal dimensions. Fedorov (2002) estimated values in the range of 0.006–0.0409 in the East-West dimension using expenditure data from Russia. With a cautionary note on the potential hazards of stylized cross-country comparisons, it is evident that in relation to Russia the Ghanaian population experienced higher levels of polarization in most dimensions, especially in 1988 and 1999. With a caveat on dimensionality, the Administrative Regions consistently had the highest level. Overall, polarization increased over the 1988–1999 period: the Administrative Regions saw the largest increase of 6.5 percent, followed by the North-South dimension with a 5.8 percent increase.

Focusing on the dynamics instead of magnitudes, Figure 3.3 shows trends in the polarization index. As in the previous cases, all the dimensions exhibit the same temporal trend in polarization. The latter was congruent to the pattern of spatial inequality. Polarization in Ghana declined during the adjustment phase (1988–1992) and took an upward turn during the 1990s.

5. Conclusion

Despite the reform process in Ghana in the 1980s and 1990s, poverty remained a pressing issue at the end of the 1990s. Poverty deepened and income distribution worsened throughout its post-independence history, particularly beginning in the mid-1970s. The spatial dimension of deprivations certainly has become a popular dimension of the poverty debate. Geography and public policy have become natural suspects of spatial inequalities in Ghana. But short of implementing policy for its own sake, there is a need to fully understand the spatial dynamics of the income distribution and the possible impact of future reform efforts in ameliorating spatial inequality.

The evidence suggests that inequality increased by nearly 22 percent over the 1988–1999 period. For its temporal trends, inequality increased in 1988-1989, fell by 1992, before rising again, reflecting the adjustment phase of the reforms. Although the magnitudes of spatial inequality were low, spatial inequality was relatively higher by administrative regions than by the North-South dimensions. The trends in the level of spatial inequality were consistent for all dimensions. It declined during the structural adjustment phase, and increased thereafter during the oscillating phase of reform in the late 1990s.

What is surprising is that regardless of administrative regions, the level of inequality within the groups in the respective dimensions was relatively high. This supports the evidence that poverty reduction was concentrated among those close to the poverty line. Even though overall poverty may have declined at the national level with macroeconomic progress, only those above a certain income threshold were able to move out of poverty in a given locality. The hardcore poor were left behind and in some cases became worse off—resulting in the widening of the income gap. This suggests that some poverty reduction policies should be targeted at improving the incomes particularly of the hardcore poor in the given spatial dimensions. Extant literature identifies this group as predominantly rural, female-headed households, with high dependency ratios, having little or no education and engaged in food crop farming.

Although spatial inequality appears to be lower than the within-group component, changes in the levels of inequality are driven largely by changes in the between-group component of inequality. This suggests that overall inequality in Ghana may be ameliorated by formulating policies directed at reducing disparities in spatial inequality. For instance, the government could use the existing local government structure to aid targeting of fiscal redistributive policy aimed at reducing the level of inequality at the administrative regional level.

The share of spatial variation in the change in total inequality revealed that spatial differences in poverty follow regional administrative boundaries. The results are not robust to normalization. Temporal trends in the Kanbur-Zhang index reveal an increase in clustering in the income distribution along almost all spatial dimensions over the 1988–1999 period. Increased polarization may provoke dissent if unchecked. Spatial inequality not only drives the increase in overall inequality, it also progressively manifests in a polarized nation: the higher the between-group component of inequality the higher the polarization index, *ceteris paribus*. Extensive poverty reduction and welfare improvement for all would be greatly enhanced by policies aimed at actively reducing spatial inequality.

Appendices

Appendix 3.A Definitions of Inequality Measures

a) *Gini Coefficient*
The Gini coefficient can be expressed as follows:

$$G = \frac{1}{\mu} \sum_{i=1}^{K} \sum_{j=1}^{K} f(y_i) f(y_j) |y_i - y_j| \qquad (3)$$

y_i is the value of the welfare index for the given spatial dimension i, μ is the average value for the whole country, $f(y_i)$ represents the population share of the dimension i in the total population and K is the number of dimensions.

b) *The Generalized Entropy Class of Measures*
The three GE classes of measures are in (4), with the variables as defined for the Gini coefficient. The GE class of entropy measures is additively decomposable into within-group and between-group components.

$$GE = \begin{cases} \sum_{i=1}^{K} f(y_i) \left[\left(\frac{y_i}{\mu} \right) - 1 \right] & c \neq 0,1 \\ \sum_{i=1}^{K} f(y_i) \left(\frac{y_i}{\mu} \right) \log \left(\frac{y_i}{\mu} \right) & c = 1 \\ \sum_{i=1}^{K} f(y_i) \log \left(\frac{y_i}{\mu} \right) & c = 0 \end{cases} \qquad (4)$$

For K exogenously given groups the GE can be decomposed as follows:

$$GE = \sum_{g=1}^{K} w_g I_g + I(\mu_1 e_1, ..., \mu_K e_K) \qquad (5)$$

The first term on the right-hand-side of the above equation is the within-group inequality and second term is the between-group inequality.

$$w_g = \begin{cases} f_g \left(\dfrac{\mu_g}{\mu} \right)^c & c \neq 0,1 \\[2ex] f_g \left(\dfrac{\mu_g}{\mu} \right) & c = 1 \\[2ex] f_g & c = 0 \end{cases} \qquad (6)$$

I_g is the inequality in the gth group, μ_g is the mean of the gth group, e_g is a vector of 1's of the length n_g, and n_g is the population of the gth group.

Appendix 3.B Definition of Variables

Variable	Definition
North-South	North=1 if: Northern, Upper East, or Upper West Region North=0 if: Western, Central, Greater Accra, Eastern, Volta, Ashanti, or Brong-Ahafo Region
Administrative Regions	The ten regions aforementioned
Ecological Zones	Coastal; Forest; Savannah
Rural-Urban	Rural =1 if: population < 1500 people or 0 otherwise
Locality 7	Accra; Urban Coastal, Urban Forest, Urban Savanna (i.e. other than Accra); Rural Coastal, Rural Forest; Rural Savanna
Locality 5	Accra; Other urban; Rural Coastal, Rural Forest, Rural Savanna
Locality 3	Accra; Other Urban; Rural

Appendix 3.C The Ghana Living Standards Survey
The Ghana Living Standards Survey (GLSS) is a nationwide household survey[19] of 3,200 households selected on the basis of the 1984 population census. The clusters were chosen such that each household had an equal probability of being selected. The survey was designed to be a rotating panel. It must be noted that the change in sample composition would not affect the spatial analysis since the definitions of the respective dimensions do not change over time.

GLSS1 and GLSS2 were based on the same set of questionnaires. Additional information was collected in GLSS2 and almost all resurveyed clusters were renumbered.[20] GLSS3 and GLSS4 differ from GLSS1 and GLSS2[21] because the former had a longer recall period and contained more detailed income, consumption and expenditure modules.[22] There are also differences in household size between GLSS1 and GLSS2. This may be adjusted for using per capita or the adult equivalence scales. The GSS adopted the per capita measure because there was no suitable equivalence scale for Ghana and it was not deemed prudent to use that of another country. This is maintained in the present study. Various measures of mean expenditure have been proposed based on correction for the errors.[23] The GSS corrected for changes in prices over time and across localities.[24] It also corrected for population growth over the survey periods.

Appendix 3.D Measures of Spatial Inequality

a) Share of Spatial Variation (SV) Index I

The ratio of the change in between-group inequality to the change in total inequality may be regarded as a share of spatial variation index because it captures the proportion of variation in total inequality attributable to changing spatial variation. To determine how much of variation in overall inequality can be attributed to variation in spatial inequality a share of spatial variation index as:

$$SV = \frac{\Delta I\left(\mu_1 e_1, ..., \mu_K e_K\right)}{\Delta GE} \qquad (7)$$

There were some ex ante concerns regarding the measure. First, given the uneven spacing of the survey, I expected that estimates of the SV over longer time periods would be systematically overestimated. The change in spatial inequality would be larger over longer time periods; however this is matched by larger changes in the overall inequality. Second, one might expect that the group size would bias the index upwards. In the limit, if you consider the individual as the unit of analysis, all of the variation in total inequality will be explained by the variation in the between component. However, the number of groups in a given dimension is a direct function of the definition of that dimension——the latter is precisely the phenomenon that the study is interested in. For example, how does the North-South divide versus the disparity in administrative regions, say, affect overall inequality? It is encouraging to note that evidence from the Table 3.4 negates the initial concerns about the SV index.

b) Share of Spatial Variation Index II

In addition to the preceding caveats the SV measure is unbounded. It is also ill-defined when the change in GE = 0. A more rigorous alternative is the change in the ratio of the between over the total:

$$SV = \Delta \left[\frac{I(\mu_1 e_1, \ldots, \mu_1 e_1)}{GE} \right] \tag{9}$$

c) *Share of Spatial Variation Index III*
An alternative measure of the share of spatial variation is the change in the ratio of the between-group to the within-group component; i.e.,

$$SV = \Delta \left[\frac{I(\mu_1 e_1, \ldots, \mu_1 e_1)}{\sum_{g=1}^{K} w_g I_g} \right]$$

However, this measure is more reflective of dynamics in the clustering of income distribution discussed in Section 4.

Notes

1. See Tsikata (2001) for details on this on this characterization of the economic reform period. The extension of the oscillating period from 1996–2000 is based on the trends in economic indicators.

2. See GSS (2000) for detailed discussions on the trends in poverty over the 1990s.

3. The perceived disenfranchised group could very likely take up arms to demand/enforce redistributive policies or broader development policies from the government if they feel the latter is not performing adequately. Indeed, this has been the source of coup d'etats in several countries.

4. The Gini coefficient fell by 4 percent. Whereas the Generalized Entropy class of measures showed reductions in the 1.32–10.5 range.

5. During the colonial era, Ghana was developed as a satellite nation to export food and raw materials to Britain and to consume manufactured products from the latter.

6. He defined the variables as general social welfare, literacy factor and the ethnic mixture—electricity factor.

7. See for instance Songsore (1989).

8. The study did not report between-group inequality. In addition, it did not fully explore the spatial dynamics in income inequality. The present study departs from this, by examining the various dimensions of the Ghanaian geographic space. It analyses inequality in the North-South dimension and on the basis of ecological zones, allowing for differential resource endowments and the interaction between these and the rural–urban dimension.

9. This measure is preferred over per capita income because of the inherent measurement problems associated with the latter. If one assumes all households have the same utility function, consumption expenditures may thus be interpreted as a money metric

measure of utility and would result in the same ranking of welfare levels. In addition, the real per capita expenditure is more stable and thus a better measure of welfare.

10. See Appendix 3.A for the formulae of these indices.

11. It must be noted that the values of the Gini and GE (0) measures are not directly comparable. In addition, the comparison made across survey periods is under the caveat that the GLSS survey structure was not the same for all 4 rounds. Adjustments made are mentioned in Appendix 3.E.

12. Recall, I is the inequality in the gth group, μ_g is the mean of the gth group, e_g is a vector of 1's of the length n_g, and n_g is the population of the gth group.

13. The within-South and within-North components were dropped since these were not exhaustive subsets of the whole population and hence yielded GE measures equal to zero.

14. For instance, in the North-South dimension there are two groups (i.e. North and South), whereas in the ecological dimension there are three groups (i.e. coastal, forest and savanna).

15. See Appendix 3.E for a discussion on the alternate definitions of the share of spatial variation index.

16. Demery and Mehra (1997) demonstrated that the GLSS2 and GLSS3 are more comparable than GLSS1 and GLSS3 for expenditure based analysis. The module for GLSS3 was maintained for GLSS4.

17. See Fedorov (2002) and Zhang and Kanbur (2001) for a detailed discussion

18. This index is based on the decomposable GE measure. For K groups in a given dimension, this measure captures the average distance between the group means in relation to the income differences within groups. As income differences within group diminish (i.e., as the groups become more homogenous internally), the relative differences between groups are magnified and polarization is higher.

19. Four rounds of the survey have been conducted: 1987-88 (GLSS1), 1988–1989 (GLSS2), 1991–1992 (GLSS3) and 1998–1999 (GLSS4). See the GLSS (1987–1988) Data User's Guide for a detailed description.

20. A panel with personal identification codes of 3,370 individuals and 741 households has also been created by the GSS based on the comparisons of age and gender.

21. See Coulombe and McKay (1995), Jones and Ye (1995) and Demery and Mehra (1997) for discussions of the comparability of the GLSS data sets.

22. The recall period for collecting food and subsistence expenditures reduced from 2 weeks in GLSS1 and GLSS2 to two days in the rural areas and 3 days in the urban areas. Both recall and coverage differences may cause food expenditure estimates in GLSS1 and GLSS2 to be biased downwards.

23. See Coulombe and McKay (1995) for a discussion of these measures.

24. Regional price indices were constructed and the household expenditure adjusted to a common base so as to account for regional variation in purchasing power. Spatial and temporal variations in the cost of living were accounted for by deflating the nominal expenditure values with a Paasche price index.

References

Agyeman-Badu, Y., and K. Osei-Hwedie, *The Political Economy of Instability, Colonial Legacy, Inequality and Political Instability in Ghana*. Virginia: Brunswick Publishing Company, 1982.

Bruno, M., M. Ravallion and L. Squire, "Equity and Growth in Developing Countries: Old and New Perspectives on the Policy Issues." Pp. 117-146 in *Income Distribution and High Quality Growth*, edited by V. Tanzi, and K. Chu. Cambridge, Massachusetts: MIT Press, 1998.

Canagarajah, S., D. Mazumdar and X. Ye, "The Structure and Determinants of Inequality and Poverty Reduction in Ghana, 1988-92." *Poverty Reduction and Social Development Division Working Paper 33*. Washington DC: The World Bank, 1998.

Chazan, N., *An Anatomy of Ghanaian Politics: Managing Political Recession, 1969-82*. Boulder, Colorado: Westview, 1983.

Cowell, F., *Measuring Inequality*. Wheatshef, London: Prentice Hall, 1995.

Coulombe, H., and A. McKay, *An Assessment of Trends in Poverty in Ghana, 1988-92*. Washington DC: The World Bank, 1995.

Demery, L., and K. Mehra, *Measuring Poverty over Time: Dealing with Uncooperative Data in Ghana*. Washington DC: The World Bank, 1997.

Dickson, K., *Urban-Rural Contrast in Ghana: Its Implications for Development*. Ghana: Ghana Academy of Arts and Sciences, 1984.

Ewusi, K., *Economic Inequality in Ghana*. Legon, Ghana: Institute of Statistical, Social and Economic Research, University of Ghana, 1977.

Fedorov, L., "Regional Inequality and Regional Polarization in Russia, 1990-99." *World Development* 30, no. 3 (March 2002): 443-456.

Forde, E. R., The Population of Ghana, *A Study of Spatial Relationships of its Sociocultural and Economic Characteristics*. Evanston, Illinois: Northwestern University, 1968.

Ghana Statistical Service, *Ghana Living Standards Survey Round Four (GLSS4) 1998/99: Data User's Guide*. Accra, Ghana: Ghana Statistical Service, 2000.

———. *Ghana Living Standards Survey - Report on the Round Three (GLSS3) 1991-92: Data User's Guide*. Accra, Ghana: Ghana Statistical Service, 1995.

Jones, C., and X. Ye, *Understanding Poverty Changes in Rural Ghana, 1988-92*. Washington DC: The World Bank, 1995.

Kanbur, R., and X. Zhang, "What Difference Do Polarization Measures Make? An Application to China." *Journal of Development Studies* 37, no. 3 (February 2001): 85-98.

Nyanteng, V. K., and A. W. Seini, "Agricultural Policy and the Impact of Growth and Productivity 1970-95". Pp. 267-283 in *Economic Reforms in Ghana -- The Miracle and the Mirage*, edited by E. Aryeetey, J. Harrigan and M. Nissanke. Oxford, England: James Currey Ltd., 2000.

Shorrocks, A., "The Class of Additively Decomposable Inequality Measures." *Econometrica* 48, no. 3 (April 1980): 613-625.

————. "Inequality Decomposition by Population Subgroup." *Econometrica* 52, no. 6 (November 1984): 1369 -1386.

Songsore, J., *Structural Crisis, Dependent Development and Regional Inequality in Ghana*. Hague, Netherlands : Institute of Social Studies, 1979.

————. "The Spatial Impress and Dynamics of Underdevelopment in Ghana." Pp. 23-41 in *Inequality and Development: Case Studies from the Third World*, edited by K. Swindell, J. M. Baba and M. J. Mortimore. London: Macmillan Publishers, 1989.

Tsikata, Y., "Ghana." Pp 45-100 in *Aid and Reform in Africa Lessons from Ten Case Studies*, edited by S. Devarajan, D. Dollar and T. Holmgren. Washington DC: The World Bank, 2001.

Watkins, K. *The Oxfam Poverty Report*. Oxford: Oxfam, 1995.

World Bank. *Ghana Living Standards Survey (GLSS), 1987-88 and 1988-89 Basic Information*. Washington DC: Poverty and Human Resources Division, The World Bank, 1999.

4

From SAPs to PRSPs: A Tale of Two Paradigms or Simply a Tale?

Bartholomew Armah

1. Introduction

The Bretton Woods Institutions—The World Bank and International Monetary Fund (IMF)—have played a dominant role in the development agenda of developing countries particularly since the oil crises of the 1970s and the subsequent debt crises of the 1980s. Indeed, by the late 1970s the IMF and World Bank, embarked on a comprehensive transformation of developing economies to adjust them to the requirements of the world market. But while the Bank and Fund have assisted developing countries by providing financing on concessional basis, a key contention among debtor governments and civil society has been the conditionalities or benchmarks associated with such loans. Developing countries have long argued that the neo-liberal policies of privatization, restrictive monetary and fiscal policies and liberalization of trade and financial markets have not been associated with rapid growth and sustainable development. On the contrary, they argue, such interventions have been linked with rising poverty. In the 1980s and early 1990s macro-stabilization and liberalization underpinned the World Bank's Structural Adjustment Programs (SAPs). However, SAPs were criticized for contributing to the structural causes of poverty by advancing reforms that deregulate labor, weaken environmental laws, reduce the state's role in social programs, and promote rapid privatization of government enterprises, allowing well-connected elites to reap the monetary benefits at the expense of the poor. Indeed, in sub-Saharan Africa, the $1 per day poverty head count index rose from 47 to 49 percent from 1990 to 2000.[1]

Funding for SAPs was provided by the World Bank and IMF through their lending instruments. The Fund financed SAPs through the Structural Adjustment Facility (SAF) which was introduced in 1986 and subsequently replaced by the Enhanced Structural Adjustment Facility (ESAF)[2] in 1987. The World Bank supported SAPs through two lending facilities: Structural Adjustment Loans

73

(SALs) and Sectoral Adjustment Loans (SECALs). Fifty one countries received one or more SALs or SECALs from the World Bank between 1980 and 1987.

In 1999 Poverty Reduction Strategies (PRS) replaced SAP largely in response to growing criticism from civil society. In support of the new development approach, the IMF and World Bank respectively introduced new lending facilities called the Poverty Reduction and Growth Facility (PRGF) and the Poverty Reduction Support Credit (PRSC). But did the change from SAPs to PRSs really constitute a fundamental shift in development thinking by the Bretton Woods institutions, or was it merely window dressing aimed at muting public outcry and frustration with the failure of SAPs to deliver on their development objectives?

This chapter takes a critical look at SAPs and PRSs by examining their historical roots, their underlying principles and the practical realities framing their implementation. It also compares SAP and PRSs lending facilities in the context of their conditionalities to determine whether the requirements of PRSs are consistent with the underlying principle of country ownership. Furthermore, using Ghana as a case study, the chapter examines whether the principles underling PRGFs and PRSCs compare favorably with the realities on the ground.

The chapter is organized as follows. The second section highlights the triggers of change, the resistance to change and the apparent capitulation by the Bretton Woods Institutions. This is followed by a detailed analysis of the new lending facilities of the BWIs (i.e., PRGF and PRSC) to assess whether they are consistent with the new development agenda of poverty reduction and country ownership. Using Ghana as a case study, we examine whether PRSs are fundamentally different from SAPs. The fourth section provides recommendations for policymakers on the way forward.

2. SAPs and PRSs

2.1 Historical Evolution of SAP

Structural Adjustment Programs or Economic Recovery Programs are policy responses by the Bretton Woods Institutions to the oil crisis of the 1970s, the concurrent worsening terms of trade and balance of payment problems, and the subsequent debt crisis of the 1980s. Both the World Bank and the IMF played different but complementary roles in addressing the economic problems of debt strapped African countries. The Fund responded to the balance of payments problems facing the world's poorest countries by providing concessional financing through an evolving range of lending facilities. From the mid 1970s to April 1986, financing was provided through the Trust Fund. The Structural Adjustment Facility (SAF) replaced the Trust Fund in March 1986. The SAF was in turn replaced by the Enhanced Structural Adjustment Facility (ESAF) in December 1987 barely a year after the SAF was introduced. In 1996, the ESAF was made a permanent facility and the primary facility for assistance to low-income countries. SAPs were generally regarded as shock treatments to an economy because of the short duration of the program and the deflationary impact of the administered policies.

Box 4.1 ESAF Eligibility

ESAF eligibility was based on a country's per capita income. Furthermore, countries had to qualify for funding under the International Development Association (IDA), the World Bank's concessional window. Countries could borrow up to a maximum of 140 percent of its IMF quota under a three year arrangement. However, funding could be extended to a maximum of 185 percent of quota. ESAF loans carried an annual interest rate of 0.5 percent with semi-annual repayments with a 5.5 year grace period. Payments ended 10 years after disbursement. ESAF operations were financed mainly by contributions by IMF member countries in the form of loans and grants to the ESAF Trust administered by the IMF.

The Bank provided adjustment loans in support of SAPs.[3] Originally intended to provide support for macro-economic policy reforms, including trade policy and agricultural reforms, adjustment loans evolved to focus more on structural, financial sector, and social policy reform and on improving public sector resource management. Adjustment operations generally aimed to improve competitive market structures (e.g. legal and regulatory reform) correct distortions in incentive regimes (taxation and trade reform) establish appropriate monitoring safeguards (financial sector reform), create an environment conducive to private sector investment (judicial reform) encourage private sector activity (privatization and private-public partnerships) promote good governance (civil service reform) and mitigate short term adverse effects of adjustment (establishment of social protection funds).

Adjustment loans are made as part of a comprehensive lending program set out in the Bank's Country Assistance Strategy (CAS)[4] which tailors assistance to each borrower's development needs. Adjustment loans were disbursed in one or more stages (tranches) into a special account. The release of tranches was contingent on the borrower's compliance with stipulated release conditions or benchmarks such as the passage of reform legislation and or privatization of stipulated parastatals. The most commonly used adjustment instruments were structural (SAL) and sectoral adjustment loans (SECAL). SALs supported reforms that were cross-sectoral, while SECALs focused on sector specific reform issues. Between 1980 and 1987, fifty-one countries received one or more SAL or SECALs from the Bank totaling fifty-one billion dollars. Almost half the number of loans and credits for adjustment went to sub-Saharan Africa, although the value of the loans were much smaller compared to Europe, Middle East, North Africa and Latin America (Avramovic D., 1989).

2.2 Structural Adjustment Programs

The key elements of SAP were privatization of state enterprises, rationalization of the public sector, trade and financial sector liberalization, fiscal austerity and tight monetary policy to achieve single digit inflation. The premise was that macro-economic stability characterized by price and exchange rate stability, market driven prices, and a lean but efficient public sector would provide a conducive environment for private sector growth and development.

Common guiding principles and features of SAP are export-led growth, privatization and liberalization, and the efficiency of the free market. Generally it requires countries to devalue their currencies against the dollar, lift import and export restrictions, balance their budgets and remove price controls and state subsidies. These preconditions for aid are what have been described as conditionalities, benchmarks and more recently "triggers."

Conditionality

According to the IMF Articles of Agreement, conditionality plays a twin role in IMF supported programs, namely (i) providing assurances to members that the committed resources would be available to them upon compliance with agreed policies; and (ii) giving the IMF confidence that the country will be able to repay—which requires that the policy program being supported is consistent with the restoration of the country's external viability.

Conditionality in IMF-supported programs has traditionally relied predominantly on quantitative targets for macroeconomic variables deemed crucial for the restoration of a country's external viability. Virtually all IMF-supported programs include quantitative targets on the fiscal deficit and/or public debt, the expansion of domestic credit, and the accumulation of international reserves. As a result, policies such as trade reform; price liberalization and privatization became important areas of structural conditionality (SC) in programs aimed at increasing efficiency and promoting investment and growth. The additional use of structural conditionality, involving changes in policy processes, legislation, and institutional reforms is a more recent development. The increase in the number of structural conditionalities since the 1990s, the widening range of areas over which they were applied and, in many instances, their very detailed nature, led to strong outside criticism.[5]

Devaluation

Devaluation of the domestic currency, relative to the dollar, increases the purchasing power of the dollar relative to the local currency. The rationale for devaluation is that by increasing the purchasing power of foreign currencies and correspondingly reducing the purchasing power of the local currency, it makes the poor country's exports cheaper relative to their imports. However, because most developing country exports are priced in foreign currencies (e.g., the dollar) devaluation does not necessarily make exports more attractive to foreigners unless it is associated with a decline in the dollar-price of the exports. Furthermore, devaluation is intended to improve the balance of payments of developing countries by increasing the domestic price of imports. However, since most imported items are intermediate inputs for local producers and have no domestic substitutes, devaluation has the effect of fuelling cost-push inflation. Ironically, this is in conflict with the SAP objective of reducing inflation. Indeed, when devaluation is combined with the removal of price controls, the effect is a dramatic hike in prices which disproportionately impacts on the poor thereby increasing the incidence of poverty. Finally, devaluation also increases the cost of debt servicing since such payments are denominated in foreign currency the price of which rises following a devaluation.

Cuts in Government Spending

Reductions in government expenditure may, in some cases, be necessary especially when such spending is inflationary and geared toward consumption activities. However, what often happens is that it is the so-called soft sectors of education, health, housing, etc., which suffer from the cuts in spending. Many governments do not reduce expenditure on the army or on other non-productive and unnecessary areas. The result is that cuts in government expenditure end up harming the welfare of the people.[6]

Privatization

Structural adjustment policies call for the sale of government-owned enterprises to private owners, often-foreign investors. The rationale is that public enterprises tend to be inefficient because they often operate as monopolies. However privatization is typically associated with layoffs and pay cuts for workers in the privatized enterprises with little systematic evidence of improved efficiency. Indeed, it is argued that privatization often results in a substitution of private monopolies for public monopolies.[7]

Imposition of User Fees

Many IMF and World Bank loans call for the imposition of "user fees" that is, charges for the use of government-provided services like schools, health clinics and clean drinking water. For very poor people, even modest charges result in the denial of access to services.

Promotion of Exports

Under structural adjustment programs, countries undertake a variety of measures to promote exports, at the expense of production for domestic needs. In the rural sector, the export orientation is often associated with the displacement of poor people who grow food for their own consumption, as their land is taken over by large plantations growing crops for foreign markets. Moreover, SAPs encourage countries to focus on the production and export of primary commodities such as cocoa and coffee to earn foreign exchange. But these commodities have notoriously erratic prices subject to the whims of global markets, which can depress prices just when countries have invested in these so-called "cash crops." [8]

Tight Monetary Policy

To reduce the rate of inflation induced by rapid growth in the money supply, SAPs encourage tight credit policies through a decline in the money supply. The result is higher interest rates. While higher rates may increase the incentive to save money, they also encourage speculative investment that brings quick paper money profits to a few people while adding nothing to productive capacity. High interest rates and tight credit also increase investment costs and undermine job creation. Small businesses, often operated by women, find it more difficult to gain access to affordable credit, and often are unable to survive. [9]

Trade Liberalization

SAPs encourage trade liberalization to increase domestic export competitiveness and promote international trade. However, trade liberalization for underdeveloped economies can have some serious side effects. In the absence of strong institutions to monitor imports, liberalization in Africa has been associated with the dumping of cheap products from outside. This has undermined existing local industries served as a barrier to new entrants into the market and contributed to mass layoffs. [10]

In addition to the above problems, SAPs were criticized for: their neglect of the social and environmental implications of their policy outcomes; focusing on narrow economic objectives; encouraging the exploitation of cheap labor, and the persistence of poverty; and being negotiated in secret with a small circle of government officials. [11]

2.3 From SAPs to PRSPs

In 1997, SAPs were subjected to joint reviews by the World Bank and a network of civil society groups in ten[12] selected countries including Ghana under the Structural Adjustment Participatory Review Initiative (SAPRI). Central to the review process was a commitment to discuss concrete changes in macroeconomic policy and policymaking based on field research and consultations carried out through public forums which provided citizens' organizations an opportunity to present their experiences with specific adjustment policies that had directly affected their lives.

Overall, the findings of SAPRI were unfavorable. Key findings included the following:

- Financial sector liberalization had failed to improve economic efficiency within the financial sector. It had also resulted in a concentration of assets among a privileged few.
- Small and medium sized enterprises and rural and indigenous producers had limited access to credit under financial sector liberalization.
- Indiscriminate trade liberalization allowed import growth to surpass exports thereby destroying the conditions necessary for sustainable growth of domestic firms.
- Labor market reforms had weakened regulations concerning labor stability and firing practices thus facilitating the use of temporary contracts.
- The concentration of growth in export-oriented production had contributed to low levels of job creation as this sector tends to have weak links with the domestic economy.
- Women had suffered the most under SAP as a result of the labor market reforms; in some cases (El Salvador) such policies eliminated special protections for women such as defense against layoffs due to pregnancy and benefits such as maternity leave.
- An increase in child employment and senior citizens in response to the decline in household income by primary wage earners;
- Utility-rate increases following privatization had created further hardships for the poor and low-income segments of society.
- Agricultural reform had not improved food security and the income of farmers in most countries.
- Reforms had allowed large scale mining to expand without effective environmental controls, thereby polluting local and regional environments and degrading sensitive biologically rich zones (e.g., in the gold rich town of Tarkwa in Ghana).
- Structural adjustment programs had led to a sharp deterioration in public spending for health care and education resulting in deterioration in quality.
- The imposition of cost-sharing and revenue generating schemes had created additional constraints to access by the poor to quality services.

2.4 Jubilee 2000 Campaign

Meanwhile, in the mid-1990s a wide coalition of aid agencies, trade unions, churches and pressure groups was raising the profile of debt issues amongst their own adherents. It was primarily this discreet activity that facilitated the creation of an informed, motivated mass movement called Jubilee 2000.[13] While focusing on the need to cancel poor country debt, the international movement raised other significant debt-related issues such as the need to ensure that debt relief is not conditioned by adherence to externally imposed economic policies such as SAPs.

In apparent response to pressure from Jubilee 2000, the World Bank and IMF launched the Heavily Indebted Poor Country Initiative (HIPC) in the spring of 1996 to cancel the debts of eligible poor countries. Eligibility was however linked to the IMF's ESAF program in the sense that participating countries were required to have achieved at least three years of favorable performance under ESAF. In an apparent effort to de-link aid from donor conditionalities HIPC eligible countries were required to formulate Poverty Reduction Strategies (PRSs) that spelled out country-owned initiatives to address poverty. These programs would be funded using savings derived from debt relief.[14] Beyond HIPC, PRSs are currently the basis for International Finance Institutions (IFI) concessional lending to low-income countries. Besides, many donors have adopted the PRSs as the framework to channel aid. Under this regime, each country receiving loans from International Finance Institutions (IFI) prepares a Poverty Reduction Strategy Paper (PRSP), which outlines its objectives with regard to poverty reduction and stipulates the policies needed to achieve these goals.

The introduction of PRSs in the context of debt relief necessitated a new lending facility couched in a framework consistent with the PRSP principle of country ownership. Indeed, it would have been inconsistent and politically unsavvy to appeal to nations to craft nationally owned development programs and then to provide financial assistance based on the old paradigm of externally imposed conditionalities. Accordingly, in September 1999 (IMF, September 2005), the IMF replaced the Enhanced Structural Adjustment Facility (ESAF), with the Poverty Reduction and Growth Facility (PRGF).[15] The link between PRSPs and PRGFs is straightforward at least in theory; the targets and policy conditions in a PRGF-supported program are to be extracted from the country's PRSP. Specifically, the Fund based its PRGF on three key features:

- Broad public participation and greater country ownership of the policies underlying the PRGF
- PRGF-supported programs must reflect each country's poverty reduction and growth priorities.
- PRGF-supported programs focus on strengthening governance with particular emphasis on improving public resource management, trans-

parency and accountability. PRGF programs also focus on the poverty and social impacts of key macro-economic policy measures.

PGRFs are designed to cover only areas within the core responsibilities of the IMF such as advising on prudent macroeconomic policies and related structural reforms such as exchange rate and tax policy, fiscal management, budget execution, fiscal transparency, and tax and customs administration. Thus, for the PRGF to reflect broad country ownership, the design of the macroeconomic framework of the PRSP must also be nationally owned.

The counterpart to the IMF's PRGF is the World Bank's Poverty Reduction Support Credit (PRSC), which was also created to support implementation of PRSs and to complement traditional adjustment loans. PRSC are also supposed to be grounded in country's PRSP following an assessment of the latter by the Bank (i.e., the Joint Staff Assessment). The assessed PRSP subsequently feeds into the Bank's Country Assistance Strategy (CAS). In principle, each PRSC is based on:

- receipt of an acceptable Letter of Development Policy (LDP);
- satisfactory macroeconomic framework;
- upfront completion of a set of specific structural reform measures;
- satisfactory progress towards the carrying out of a medium term program extracted from the PRSP.

Ultimately the PRSC supports a Medium Term Program (MTP) drawn from the PRSP and the Joint Staff Assessment (JSA). The key elements of the MTP are summarized in the government's Letter of Development Policy and a multi-year matrix of policy and institutional reforms.

Both the PRSC and PRGF provide support for the poverty reduction strategies of participating countries. It is generally understood that the Bank will normally provide support through a PRSC with the understanding that the Fund provides support through a PRGF arrangement. Furthermore, where a country is on-track with respect to PRGF arrangements, it is presumed by the Bank to be on-track with respect to its macro-economic framework. Similarly, the presence of an on-track PRSC arrangement is adequate evidence to the Fund, of an appropriate social and structural development program.

However, it is argued that the switch from SAPs to PRSP did not fundamentally alter the relationship between the BWIs and developing countries. The view is that the fundamentals of SAPs remain largely unchanged for the simple reason that, notwithstanding the principle of country ownership, the World Bank still requires countries to adopt the same types of policies as SAPs. The policy contents of PRSP, their strengths and weaknesses and the innovations introduced by the PRSP are discussed below.

3. SAPs and PRSs: Any Difference?

3.1 Elements of Poverty Reduction Strategy Papers

A Poverty Reduction Strategy Paper (PRSP) is a national plan of action. It sets out an analysis of poverty in a country and defines a national strategy for dealing with it. Since their introduction in 1999, PRSPs have been the basis for IMF and World Bank concessional lending to poor countries, and for debt relief provided under the Enhanced HIPC (Heavily Indebted Poor Countries) initiative. They are also increasingly becoming the focus for bilateral donors seeking to improve the quality of their development aid. Five principles should underlie the process of formulating, implementing and monitoring PRSPs. According to the World Bank and IMF, PRSPs must be:

Country-driven – involving broad-based participation by civil society and the private sector in all operational steps;
Results- oriented – focusing on outcomes that benefit the poor;
Comprehensive – in recognizing the multi-dimensional nature of poverty (economic and social dimensions);
Partnership-oriented – involving coordinated participation of development partners (bilateral, multilateral and non-governmental); and
Long-term – based on a long-term perspective for poverty-reduction.[16]

The PRSP document is usually the result of a process that starts with an interim PRSP (IPRSP). The aim of the IPRSP is to set out a country's existing poverty reduction policies and outline a 'road map' of the steps that will be taken towards producing a full PRSP. It also helps to address the issue of the tension between qualifying for debt relief and allowing time to develop a good PRSP. Recognizing the considerable time required to formulate a full PRSP and the need for HIPCs to receive debt relief in the short term, debt relief is permitted to begin when a country completes an Interim PRSP.[17]

In principle, PRSPs offer two important opportunities. First, poverty reduction efforts are more likely to achieve buy-in by both governments and citizens of poor countries, and therefore stand a better chance of successful implementation. Second, poverty reduction could be mainstreamed into government planning processes and used to guide expenditure not only of aid but also of the national budget as a whole. In addition to these it is argued that by encouraging broad-based participation PRSPs empower the poor and disadvantaged by leveraging their access to resources and social services. Furthermore, by switching the focus of conditionality away from specific policies and towards policy processes, PRSPs adjust the balance of power between rich and poor countries and thereby improve the effectiveness of development aid.[18]

3.2 Comparing SAP and PRS

One school of thought is that while PRSs have improved diagnostics on the various dimensions of poverty and the allocation of spending, they have not differed much from previous adjustment programs as far as the core economic policies are concerned. What is the evidence from Ghana?

National Ownership
A criticism of SAPs was that it was imposed by the Fund and Bank with little input from the recipient countries. Presumably both institutions responded to this criticism by anchoring PRSs in national ownership. But for a number of reasons discussed below, governments and their citizens do not feel a sense of ownership of their PRSPs.

Continued Leverage of the Multilaterals
Country ownership is compromised by the economic leverage that donor partners continue to wield over the largely small and weak African economies. Indeed, the Bank and IMF staff have argued that a government can present whatever plan it wants, however, both institutions will only support PRSs that concur with their philosophy of what constitutes an appropriate strategy for poverty reduction and growth. Following the drafting of a PRSP the Bank and IMF staff write a "Joint Staff Assessment" (JSA) which highlights areas of disagreement and perceived weaknesses. A positive JSA does not signify agreement with all the analysis, targets, or actions included in the PRSP or that the PRSP represents the best possible strategy for the country. What it does indicate is staffs' judgment as to whether the PRSP is a credible framework within which the World Bank and IMF will provide financial and other support. Without a positive JSA and Board concurrence in this assessment, the government will not get Bank or IMF funding and will be unlikely to get bilateral funding.

Invariably, financially strapped governments are likely to opt for programs that they know will be accepted even if such programs conflict with priorities identified through consultative processes. Thus, it is ultimately questionable whether a program can be truly government or nationally owned. It is more honest to say that the process is government-led. Even a government-led program would not be country-owned without broad participation that translates into objectives. In other words IFIs continue to impose the same conditions, which characterized structural adjustment with scant regard for national ownership.

In addition it seems that little changed in terms of the Fund's and the Bank's "negotiating style." Loan negotiations are still conducted behind closed doors within Ministries of Finance and Central Banks, and lack disclosure, public involvement and oversight. Thus, there has been only a marginal increase in the openness to civil society participation and their proposals and recommendations have had a minimal effect on most PRSPs.[19]

Quality and Quantity of Donor Assistance

Effective ownership of PRSs implies that resource allocations and expenditures reflect the priorities of the PRSP. Specifically true ownership requires alignment of both domestic and donor resources with the priorities of the strategy. In practice however, donors have been slow to harmonize their aid modalities with national priorities or with one another. In Ghana, a Multi-Donor Budget Support initiative was set up to ensure harmonization of aid modalities among donors and to shift a larger share of donor resources into direct budgetary support. However, while the MDBS initiative represents a useful step in the direction of resource alignment several key donors are yet to accede to the initiative. Furthermore, donors have been more willing to align their resources with the social

Table 4.1 Distribution of Donor Funds: 2001-2003 (percent)

	2001	2002	2003
Economic Services	40.2	35.4	20.28
Agriculture	22.3	8.5	10.69
Energy		21.5	4.55
Infrastructure	30.5	38.2	51.55
Social	11.8	15.0	16.72
Education	6.9	6.8	6.70
Health	4.9	8.0	9.88
Public Safety	0.0	1.0	1.55
Contingency	0.0	0.0	0.0

Source: 2001–2003 Budget Statements

sector as opposed to the economic sector priorities of Ghana's PRSP. Alignment with the economic sector priorities, particularly agriculture, has largely been weak. As shown in Table 4.1, the share of donor resource flows to the economic service sector halved between 2001 and 2003 with agriculture and energy experiencing the greatest shifts. Correspondingly, resource flows to social services particularly health, increased appreciably. Skewed resource flows to the social sector in part explain the inability of the country to achieve growth rates in excess of 6 percent since the implementation of PRSP.

Indeed in many countries including Ghana, PRSs have been only partially implemented. For many countries, the PRSP was drawn up on the basis of estimated resource inflows linked to expectations of aid and or debt relief. Furthermore, project-focused approaches continue along with high levels of tied aid, both of which work against aid effectiveness and accountability.[20]

Civil Society Participation

Civil society organizations have not been adequately involved in consultations on the macroeconomic policies in PRSPs. Capacity constraints and limited government interest in engaging civil society have hampered the quality of participatory processes, which, for the most part, have not been institutionalized. Furthermore, civil society organizations do not necessarily represent the poor. Indeed, several NGOs are viewed with suspicion as donor mouthpieces since they are funded by donors. Often consultation with the large and the most vocal NGO's is considered sufficient indication of substantive involvement of civil society even though such organizations may only represent their parochial interests and agendas. Community based organizations (CBOs) tend to receive relatively less attention in the consultation process.

The Macro-Economic Framework

Generally speaking the macro-economic framework has been little subject to debate and has changed little from the framework that underpinned the SAPs. For instance, in Ghana the only components of the macro-framework discussed with civil society were the overall GDP, sectoral growth rate projections, and the broad macro-economic policies designed to ensure stability, including the need to establish a contingency fund to cushion the country against shocks, and the need to ensure competitive real exchange rates and interest rates. However, the details regarding the optimal fiscal deficit required to finance the PRSP, the optimal rate of inflation for poverty reduction and the appropriate sources and level of domestic revenue and options for deficit financing were discussions that were confined to the Ministry of Finance and the IFIs. Most importantly, issues of privatization which were not addressed in Ghana's PRSP mysteriously surfaced as IMF/World Bank PRGF/PRSC benchmarks. In effect, although in theory, the PRSC and PRGF were supposed to be anchored in the PRSP, in reality they were not.

Fiscal and Monetary Policy

There appears to be an inherent contradiction between the SAP inspired macro framework that underpins PRSPs and the objective of poverty reduction. For instance, although in Ghana inflation declined as a result of the implementation of tight fiscal and monetary policies, the gain in price stability has not been associated with any noticeable decline in the real interest cost to businesses (Figure 4.1). On the contrary, the real rate on the interest equivalent of the 91-Day Treasury bill rose even as inflation declined. Furthermore, the spread between the lending and savings rate showed no tendency to decline. This trend can be attributed to weaknesses in the financial institutions, particularly their lack of capacity to assess and minimize exposure to risk; this is not a problem that can be addressed merely through tight fiscal and monetary policy. There is therefore the danger that lower inflation occasioned by tight monetary policy will not be consistent with the overall objective of poverty reduction unless additional measures are instituted to address the credit constraints facing the poor, particularly small and medium scale enterprises.

Export led Growth

Like SAPs, PRSs have not been associated with significant export diversification. Indeed, export growth in Ghana has been driven by the cocoa sector. Attempts are currently being made to expand the range of non-traditional exports beyond pineapples. These measures, however, are still in the early stages of implementation. Progress in the economic sectors of the economy has been slow perhaps because of the heavy emphasis on social sector investments and a decline in relative resource flows to the agriculture sector by both donors and government. The reason for the decline remains unclear. However, it is partly rooted in a deep faith in the private sector to respond to the improved macro-economic climate. In reality the private sector response has been muted. The challenge for government is how to deepen investments in the growth sectors of the economy, in spite of the limited private sector response, without unduly compromising the quality and access to social services.

Figure 4.1 The Year-on-year Change in CPI and the Real Rate on Ninety-one day Treasury bill

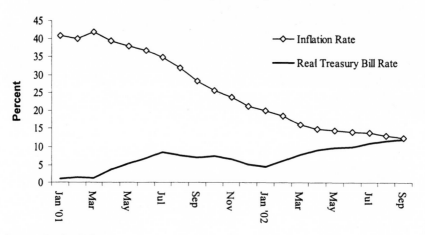

Source: Bank of Ghana

Trade Liberalization

Notwithstanding the paradigm shift from SAPs to PRSs, in Ghana trade liberalization policy has persisted under the PRSP regime even though the PRSP called for a re-examination of the policy in light of its adverse impact on local producers. For instance, in 2003, government reversed its decision to impose a tariff on imported poultry following pressure from the IMF and in contravention of the principle of country ownership. In effect, this development signaled limited policy independence of government and is consistent with the argument that country ownership is a "qualified" concept at best.

Furthermore, the requirement that HIPC eligible countries should have at least three years of successful performance under ESAF explicitly linked the ESAF (and consequently SAP) to the PRS process. It placed great priority on ESAF performance, despite growing unpopularity with the program, and de-emphasized the importance or relevance of country ownership to the PRS.

Table 4.2 Distribution of Discretionary Expenditure: 2001–2003

	percent		
Sector	**2001**	**2002**	**2003**
Economic Services	**15.0**	**18.0**	**9.3**
Agriculture	7.2	4.7	4.0
Infrastructure	11.6	17.2	15.9
Social Services	**30.2**	**34.7**	**39.0**
Education	*22.4*	*24.1*	*26.6*
Health	*6.7*	*9.4*	*11.1*

Source: 2001–2003 Budget Statements

Table 4.3 Trends in the Distribution of GoG Discretionary Funds

	percent		
	2001[a]	**2002**	**2003**
Economic Services	**5.3**	**6.8**	**5.6**
Agriculture	*1.4*	*2.3*	1.8
Infrastructure	**4.4**	**3.7**	**3.9**
Social Services	**37.2**	**47.4**	**46.1**
Education	*28.4*	*35.3*	33.3
Health	*7.4*	*10.3*	11.5

Source: 2001–2003 Budget Statements
[a] *Original 2001 budget figures*

On the positive side, however, the macro-framework did reflect a broad national consensus to apply a portion of savings from the HIPC initiative to amortize the domestic debt. Moreover, it also reflected agreement among broad sections of civil society and government to increase the relative share of social and directly productive spending in total expenditure.

Social Sector Spending

A criticism of SAPs is that because its preferred policy option for reducing fiscal deficits is through reduced government spending, such policies invariably undermine government expenditures on the health and education sectors, to the detriment of the poor. Did this trend change under the PRSP regime? In reality, government spending as a percent of GDP rose (from 14 to 20 percent between 2001 and 2002) in Ghana following the introduction of the PRSP. Furthermore, social expenditures also increased in relative size following the introduction of PRSP even though this occurred at the expense of spending on directly productive services. The relative share of total expenditures (including funding from donor partners) accruing to the social service sector (Table 4.2) increased by

Figure 4.2 Selected sub-Sectoral Allocations of GoG Discretionary

Expenditure

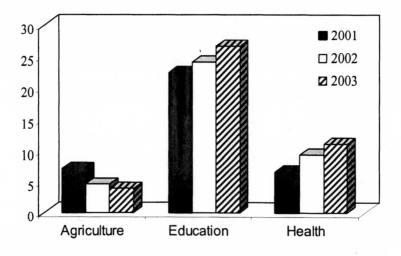

Source: 2001–2003 Budget Statements

9 percentage points while the corresponding share for economic services declined 6 percentage points between the period prior to the implementation of the PRS (2001) and the period following the its implementation (2003). The relative

share of resources devoted to agriculture, presumably a key pillar of the PRSP, also declined markedly. The increase in the relative share of social spending is even more dramatic when one only examines government expenditures excluding donor assistance (Table 4.3). Social spending rises remarkably from 37 to 46 percent of discretionary expenditure with corresponding increases in health and education expenditure (Figure 4.2). In effect, with respect to social spending, the PRS regime was different from the SAP regime at least in Ghana. The PRS has been associated with increased spending on social services, due in part to the poverty focus of first generation PRSP and the increased resources available to countries as a result of their participation in the Enhanced HIPC Initiative.

4. Conclusions and Policy Recommendations

Poverty Reduction Strategies were intended to respond to the growing frustration by civil society and governments with the policy constraints imposed by SAPs. Indeed, the overriding argument against SAPs was that there were externally imposed and not nationally owned. Ownership thus became the mantra of PRSs, heralding hopes of a new policy regime where government would have a greater role in defining their policy directions through their PRSPs. But this was not really the case. Like school term papers PRSs have to be graded by donor partners particularly the Fund and the Bank. Indeed, the threat of a failing grade is sufficient to whip recalcitrant countries in line with the expectations of both institutions. Like SAPs, the macro-economic framework of PRSs remain black boxes partly because of the complexity of the subject matter but largely because it is the "brain box" of PRSPs; control of the macro-framework implies virtual control over the quantum of resource flows required to implement the PRS.

Improving country ownership of the PRSP will require redressing asymmetrical power relations underpinning the formulation of the PRS. National governments must develop the capacity to formulate their own macro-frameworks prior to discussions with the Fund. Currently, such discussions take place around the Funds macro-framework without an alternative framework by government. It is not enough for government and civil society to parrot the old rhetoric about the inflexibility of the existing macro-frameworks; it is time they engaged the Fund and Bank in a frank intellectual debate about the virtues and merits of their alternative framework.

Developing countries must formulate credible alternative macro-economic frameworks that provide the fiscal space for the sustainable implementation of growth oriented development strategies. They must also ensure that their total resource flows are aligned with their priorities and develop effective monitoring systems that inform the dynamic process of program and project implementation.

Notes

1. World Bank, *The Poverty Reduction Strategy Initiative*, An Independent Evaluation of the World Bank Support through 2003, 2004.
2. SAFs were intended to provide loans for medium term programs and to pay greater attention to underlying structural problems than would be possible under normal stabilization arrangements.
3. The Bank has two categories of lending facilities: investment loans and adjustment loans. Unlike investment loans which have a long term focus (five to ten years) adjustment loans have a short term focus (one to three years) and provide quick disbursing external financing for policy and institutional reforms. World Bank, Lending Instruments: Resources for Development Impact, July 2001.
4. The CAS is prepared by the World Bank in collaboration with the borrower, and usually in consultation with donors, civil society, and other public and private stakeholders.
5. Evaluation of Structural Conditionality in IMF-Supported Programs.
6. Double Standards (2005)
7. Double Standards (2005)
8. Double Standards (2005)
9. African Alternative Framework to Structural Adjustment Programs for Socio-Economic Recovery and Transformation
10. African Alternative Framework to Structural Adjustment Programs for Socio-Economic Recovery and Transformation and Double Standards (2005)
11. URL: http://www.eldis.org/static/DOC5511.htm
12. The Bank did not participate in the exercise with El Salvador and Zimbabwe after they halted their participation. However independent SAPRI teams undertook consultations in all ten countries: Ecuador, El Salvador, Mexico, Bangladesh, the Philippines, Ghana, Mali, Uganda, Zimbabwe and Hungary.
13. Jubilee 2000 aimed to get the burden of debt on the world's poorest countries lifted by the Millennium. Therefore, while the Jubilee 2000 organisation had to wind up in 2000, debt campaigning is going on, within a new organisation: *The Jubilee Debt Campaign (UK)*, founded in March 2001.
14. PRSPs were launched in 1999 by the IMF during their annual meetings.
15. The interest and repayment conditions are the same for both facilities.
16. Ruth Driscoll with Karin Christiansen (2004) THE PRSP APPROACH, A basic guide for CARE International
17. As of March 2004, thirty-three countries have full PRSPs and twenty-four more have Interim PRSPs and 4 countries have already produced a second iteration of their PRSP. They are Burkina Faso, Mauritania, Tanzania and Uganda
18. Ruth Driscoll with Karin Christiansen (2004).
19. POLICY BRIEFING (2004) PRSP: Lessons Learnt Recommendations to the World Bank, IMF and donors for the Second Generation of PRSPs.
20. Bretton Woods Project (2003), Poverty Reduction Strategy Papers (PRSPs): A Rough Guide

References

African Alternative Framework Initiative. *Structural Adjustment Programs and Their Impact on the 1980s*, Africa Policy Information Center. <www.africaaction.org/african-initiatives/aaf3.htm> (February 2006).

Avramovic, D. *Structural Adjustment Lending: A Preliminary Analysis*, Policy Based Lending of the World Bank. 1989.

Barry, T. The U.S., the World Bank and SAPs: Implications for Developing Countries. *Foreign Policy in Focus,* 2001. <www.eldis.org/static/DOC5511.htm> (February 2006).

Bretton Woods Project. *Poverty Reduction Strategy Papers (PRSPs): A Rough Guide,* 2003. <www.campaignforeducation.org/resources/Apr2002/prsp_roughguide.pdf> (December, 2005).

Boughton, J. *The Silent Revolution: The International Monetary Fund, 1979-1989*. IMF, 2001.

Double Standards. IMF Structural Adjustment Programs: The Globalization of Poverty , 2005. < www.doublestandards.org/sap1.html> (August, 2005).

Driscoll, R. and Christiansen, K. *The PRSP Approach: A basic guide for CARE International*. Overseas Development Institute, <www.careinternational.org.uk/resource_centre/other/CARE_basic_guide_to_ PRSPs.doc> (June, 2005).

Structural Adjustment and Participatory Review International Network (SAPRIN) The Policy Roots of Economic Crisis and Poverty: A Multi-Country Participatory Assessment of Structural Adjustment, 2002.

IMF. Evaluation of Structural Conditionality in IMF-Supported Programs. Issues Paper for An Evaluation by the Independent Evaluation Office, 2005. <http://www.imf.org/external/np/ieo/2005/sc/051805.pdf> (December, 2005)

Onimode, Bade. "IMF and World Bank Programs in Africa" in Onimode B. ed., The IMF, the World Bank and the African Debt: The Economic Impact. Zed Books Ltd., London and New Jersey, 1989.

TROCAIRE, PRSP: Lessons Learnt Recommendations to the World Bank, IMF and donors for the 2nd Generation of PRSPs. *Policy Briefing, 2004.* <http://www.trocaire.org/policyandadvocacy/debt/prsplessonslearnt.pdf> (December 2005)

World Bank, *Lending Instruments: Resources for Development Impact*, Washington, 2001.

World Bank. *The Poverty Reduction Strategy Initiative, An Independent Evaluation of the World Bank's Support Through 2003, 2004.* http://lnweb18.worldbank.org/oed/oeddoclib.nsf/24cc3bb1f94ae11c85256808006a0 046/6b5669f816a60aaf85256ec1006346ac/$FILE/PRSP_Evaluation.pdf

PART 2

Designing, Implementing, Financing, and Monitoring the GPRS

5

Public Consultations, Bureaucrats and Development Partners in Ghana's Poverty Reduction Strategy

Joe Amoako-Tuffour

1. Introduction[1]

D evelopment planning is not new in Ghana. The scope of public consultations and citizen participation, however, was new under the Ghana Poverty Reduction Strategy (GPRS). As part of the Heavily Indebted Poor Country (HIPC) initiative, the over seventy developing countries which were expected to receive assistance were required to design Poverty Reduction Strategy Papers (PRSPs). The World Bank's Comprehensive Development Framework (CDF) outlined the core guiding principles behind the preparation of the PRSPs. Recognizing the need for country ownership of programs and the importance of democratic decision-making, PRSPs were expected to be country-driven, partnership-oriented, and comprehensive in scope. These strategies were expected to be based on a long-term perspective of poverty reduction and focused on outcomes that benefit the poor. In an apparent response to the lack of transparency in policy-making, each country strategy was expected to be based on a national, consultative process that featured public fora in which civil society, the government and development partners all participate and debate the appropriate pathways to poverty reduction. This last requirement is the subject of this chapter.

Having completed the process, there are questions worth asking. Did the consultative efforts in the GPRS engage citizens in a genuinely participatory exercise? Was the exercise a veil designed to generate evidence in support of pre-established policy preferences? Did the agents see themselves as relatively passive rather than as active participants in the design of the strategy? Was the process merely to satisfy demands for greater citizen involvement without actually requiring the government to respond to the citizens' viewpoint, or explore alternative courses of action? Equally intriguing, what was the role of civil servants and of development partners in the making of the GPRS? Section two of this chapter provides the context of the discussion with a brief look at the policy-making process in the past. In section three, I look at the scope of consultation and the spaces of participation by the different actors in the making of the GPRS. The role of civil society organizations is taken up in section four, focusing on their preparedness and constraints. The fifth section looks at the role of civil servants followed in section six by the role of development partners in their common efforts to develop antipoverty policies. The concluding observations follow in section seven.

2. The Policy-Making Environment in the Past

Throughout much of its post-independence history, the responsibility for policy initiatives and design has been either directly or indirectly conferred upon civil servants and the political elite, who depending on their preferences, could choose to seek policy advice and specialized expertise (Armstrong, 1996; Hutchful, 1997). The first post independence seven-year Development Plan and successive plans followed a similar process without open public engagement. According to Omaboe (1966):

> In Ghana, the politicians are always ahead of the civil servants and the planners in the general consideration and implementation of economic and social objectives. This has meant that almost all important projects have had to be initiated by the politicians who on many occasions have taken decisions and committed the nation to a certain course of action before the technicians were consulted. (p. 461)

Ohemeng (2005) described the policy-making environment in Ghana between 1957–1992 as a "closed circuit network" of politicians and senior bureaucrats with technical assistance drawn from multilateral and bilateral donors. The domestic non-governmental sector played little or no noticeable role in the policy-making process. This lack of local participation is explained by the nature of the political environment which prevailed at that time. The succession of military regimes beginning in 1966 did not allow dissent or public discussions on government decisions (Ohemeng, 2005). To a large extent, public opinion was perceived not as a resource, but rather as a source of potential problems to be avoided, or, on occasions, to be neutralized for political expediency. The short-lived elected governments in 1969–1972 and again in 1979–1981 failed or didn't have the opportunity to open up the political space that welcomed citizens' engagement on national issues.

The transition from successive military regimes to multi-party democracy in 1992 brought limited changes as far as public participation in policy-making was concerned. Having transformed itself from a military government (1982–1992) to an elected parliamentary government, the National Democratic Congress (NDC) government during its (1992–2000) rein continued its authoritarian practices as instruments for policy-making and implementation (Boafo-Arthur, 1999). Indeed, Hutchful (2002) remarked that the difficulties encountered in implementing structural reforms initiated in 1983, were partly because of the failure to solicit the views of the private sector, civil society groups, and the civil service. As unwelcoming as it may have been to the NDC government, the dawn of multi-party democracy in 1992 was a new opportunity for civil society to influence government policies. Private think tanks emerged.[2] The Institute of Economic Affairs (IEA) and Centre for Policy Analysis (CEPA) soon made names for themselves. Through the dissemination of research results and advocacy they sought to influence the government's efforts to develop appropriate policies and institutions as well as to educate the public on policy choices.[3] While some think tanks became major sources of ideas for the government and readily provided input into the policy-making process, consultation remained limited and was certainly not done openly. Potential spaces of consultation provided through various legislative and governance instruments were underutilized or virtually closed by state actors – politicians and bureaucrats.

Most notably, Article 35 (paragraph 6(d)) of the Directive Principles of State Policy of the 1992 Constitution enjoins the state to make democracy a reality by taking appropriate measures to give "possible opportunities to the people to participate in decision-making at every level in national life and in government". This directive finds expression for example in the National Development Planning Commission Act (Act 479) and the National Development Planning System Act (Act 480). Section 15(1) of Act 479 seeks to ensure that national planning is properly integrated and coordinated across sectors. The consultative process envisaged in the legislation is reflected in the required make-up of cross-sectoral planning groups (Act 479, 35(2)). These groups are expected to consist of representatives of various sector ministries, appropriate private and public sector organizations and individuals selected for their knowledge of and relevant experience in each sector.

In furtherance of grassroots participation in a decentralized administrative set-up, Act 480 seeks to provide a bottom-up planning approach rather than the top-down approach that had previously characterized national planning. In theory, district assemblies (DAs) are planning authorities with the power to ensure participation, coordination and integration of different ideas into the preparation of district plans. DAs are expected to conduct public hearings on their development plans and to provide evidence of consultation when submitting their plans to the Regional Coordinating Council for harmonization into regional plans. The latter will in turn feed into national plans (Act 462 (10)). These provisions notwithstanding, consultations in national planning prior to the GPRS were in practice very weak. As observed by Armah in chapter eight in this volume, district plans were frequently put together by consultants without the due consultative process envisaged under Act 479. Moreover, all too often, there was a disconnect between the national plan and the district plans with the result that annual budgetary allocations bore hardly any resemblance to proposals made at the district level (Ayee, 2004). Thus, in practice, planning in Ghana remained at the centre with rather limited open participation and with consultation mainly through the preferred political process. The preparation of the GPRS marked a new era of making, shaping, and implementing antipoverty schemes that involved multi-stakeholder processes. Or did it?

3. Participation and Public Consultation

3.1 Paradigm Shift from Output-oriented to Input-oriented Legitimacy

Using concepts developed by Scharpf (1997), the new paradigm of participation in policy-making that was expected in preparing the PRSPs changed the balance between output-oriented legitimacy and input-oriented legitimacy in favor of the latter. Output-oriented legitimacy is conferred on a policy-making process that enhances the public good, regardless of who participated in it. Economic policy-making in many developing economies arguably fits this mode. Policymakers typically rely on expertise from the International Monetary Fund (IMF), the World Bank (WB) and bilateral Development Partners (DPs) for technical assistance to design and implement economic policies. Legitimacy is justified purely in terms of results. Partly because of the extensive in-house expertise of donors, and partly because of the reliance of recipients on external resources for development, it is not difficult to see why the incentives to encourage or to acquire local analytical capacities have been minimal. It is also not difficult to see why the IMF and the WB have historically monopolized and led the way in policy design and programming without the need for local consultations.

Critics have argued that this approach is unsatisfactory and for good reasons. Driven by their country or institutional ideology, foreign experts are often too removed from the concerns of ordinary citizens on matters of social development and equity. A dominant role of outside experts in sectoral policies often subordinates social concerns and country ownership. No less a concern is that both the experts and the institutions they represent typically are not accountable to the citizens of recipient countries in the event of program failure.

The trends and developments in various countries have seriously challenged output-oriented legitimacy in dealing with development problems. The catalyst has been the persistence and threat of poverty. The World Bank's CDF emerged as a planning tool largely as a result of the slow or lack of progress in developing sectoral policies in many developing countries. With those lessons in mind, consultation between government and civil society was to be the key foundation in sectoral planning for poverty reduction strategies. The emphasis on public consultation acknowledges the need to pay more attention to input-oriented legitimacy. Public consultation, many believe, should better diagnose the incidence and depth of poverty beyond what is revealed in conventional statistics, which are often limited in many developing economies. It may also offer a better grasp of the causes of poverty, and provide for a creative course of action that otherwise may not be possible.

Input-oriented legitimacy depends on the extensiveness of public participation and consultation in the policy-making process (Pierre, 1998; Walters et. al., 2000; Montpetit, 2003). It also depends on the willingness of donors to truly let countries nurture their own paths through learning by doing. Ownership is conferred upon policies when a large segment of society feels it has been consulted and heard. As Montpetit remarked, output-and input-oriented legitimacies are not mutually exclusive. Experts are needed to lead the process. As long as experts do not present their own or official preferences as the ratified public policy, it is reasonable to assume that ordinary citizens would maintain their interest in policy-making. Clearly the stress on consultations in preparing the PRSPs called for a paradigm shift.

3.2 The Consultative Process

In August 2000, five teams were established to match the thematic areas of the PRSP.[69] Each team consisted of a range of change agents and stakeholders representing the appropriate Ministries, Departments and Agencies (MDAs), non-governmental organizations (NGOs), Civil Society and development partners. A consultant was appointed to serve each team. The opening of networks and the calendar of consultation are summarized in Table 5.1.

We see from Table 5.1 that the consultation process was extensive. It drew upon a cross-section of stakeholders identified by various characteristics: gender, political, educational and occupational background, knowledge and area of expertise and religious associations. Community consultations had four major tasks: disseminate information and obtain perspectives on poverty, identify the priorities, identify the obstacles—especially the physical barriers that often find no place in conventional statistics—and find the exit routes out of poverty. By going to the community and district levels, the consultations became a source for supplementary and qualitative information gathering. This was particularly useful since the official survey data which formed the basis of the poverty diagnosis was only available at the national and regional levels and contained no disaggregated district level data.

The Appendix F of the GPRS document identifies the activities undertaken or expected to be undertaken by the different stakeholders in the formulation and implementation of the GPRS. A sample of activities, albeit voluntary, is reported

Table 5.1 Calendar of GPRS Preparation and Consultation

Dates	Activity	Participants/Output
YEAR 2000		
March	Conceptualization forum	Cross section of stakeholders on Poverty Reduction
July	Launching of GPRS process	Cross section of Ghanaian society
August	Initial Diagnostic (Poverty) Studies-Core Teams Orientation fora	Core teams
October–November	Community, district and regional consultations	Community groups, districts and regional representatives.
YEAR 2001		
March	Ghana opt for HIPC Initiative GPRS preparation gains further momentum Harmonization workshops	Workshops with Civil Society Organizations (CSOs), Private Sector, Development Partners (DPs)
May	Special forum as input to National Economic Dialogue (NED) NED	CSOs Cross section of Ghanaian society
July	Presentation on draft GPRS GPRS Instructional Workshop for MDAs	Development Partners MTEF Sectoral groupings
August*	7 Separate GPRS Consultation Workshops and call for comments	Chief Directors of MDAs NGOs and Religious Bodies Labour Unions and Civil Society Policy Advocacy Groups & Think Tanks Women's Groups and Media
September	5 consultation and training workshops Policy review workshops with MTEF/Budget Division (MoF) Monitoring and Evaluation Consultation Meetings with Ministries, Department and Agencies	Budget Officers – Ministry of Finance Ministries, Department and Agencies by functional groups: Administration, Economic and Public Safety groups, Social Sector group, Infrastructure Ministries, Ministers and Deputies Several stakeholders, academics, Civil society, NGOs, DPs

Table 5.1 Continued

Dates	Activity	Participants/Output
October	2-day GPRS Retreat	Parliamentarians
November	Review of 2002 Budget with GPRS priorities	Cabinet and Parliament

Private sector umbrella groups—Private Enterprise Foundation (PEF), Association of Ghanaian Industries (AGI), National Association of Small Scale Industries (NASSI)
* Proceedings of August 20, 2001 meeting are summarized in Box 4.1

Source: Ghana Poverty Reduction Strategy February 2003

Table 5.2. Appendix G of the GPRS and identifies actions which civil society organitions (CSOs) may focus on in the implementation, monitoring and evaluation of the RS. Appendix J provides a sample of the comments and questions on the GPRS drafts the responses by the National Development Planning Commission (NDPC). In all, re were 106 questions and comments. They ranged from the definition of poverty that derlies the strategy, to suggestions of omissions, clarifications and other comments that re judged to be outside the scope of the GPRS.

The consultations enabled the planning team to explore some of the difficult issues underlie poverty in the country, especially the physical constraints and the lack of ergy in past development efforts. It is difficult to infer from Tables 5.1 and 5.2 how ch the consultation process may have shaped the content and the direction of the RS. It is equally difficult to argue that it did not influence the outcome. Not least, critargued that too much public debate may have slowed down the process and polarized ne segments of the population who may have felt that their views were not adequately ected in the final product. That impression was evident from gender groups, even ugh several of the issues they articulated may have been captured as cross-cutting iss under the different thematic areas.

Although in principle poverty reduction has long been the goal of every government, efforts developed few concrete measures because of false starts and disjointed initias. It is not without some justification then that some skepticism greeted the consulta process. These sentiments were evident at the August 20, 2001 workshop summad in Box 5.1. While the summary runs the risk of oversimplifying the positions of ticipants, it nevertheless captures the salient issues that surfaced during these consultas.

Table 5. 2 Selected Stakeholders Category of Activities Towards Poverty Reduction

Stake-holder	Formulation	Implementation	Financing	Monitoring and Evaluation
MDAs	Participate in formulation through core teams; validate proposed strategies; identify priorities for poverty reduction	Act as lead agency, undertake preparation of costed activities; ensure inclusion of activities in budget; refocus on-going projects and develop new projects for poverty reduction.	Make proposals for budgetary allocations	Undertake internal monitoring and evaluation; provide information for evaluation to NDPC
Development Partners	Participate in consultation workshops, provide support for process, contribute to identification of priorities	Assess GPRS and re-align existing programs and expand existing programs for poverty reduction	Common GPRS financial support	Undertake independent M&E of GPRS
Traditional Authorities	Participate in community poverty analysis process	Resolve land acquisition issues; commit land for beneficial social and economic uses, undertake community mobilization for project implementation, assist in the rationalization of gender roles and ownership	Commit royalties to social programs, permit land to be given as equity shares for communities.	Ensure traditional norms are not violated.
NGOs & CSOs	Concerns about environment, vulnerable groups, advocate for inclusion of socially important provisions in strategy	Implementation of some poverty reduction activities relevant.	Source external funding and advocacy for increased spending on areas of interest	Conduct participatory M&E with communities
Trade Unions	Assessment of the role of organized labour and effects of strategy on employment levels	Resource to members	None	Independent M&E of effects on incomes and employment

Source: Extract from GPRS Appendix F " Roles of Stakeholders"

Box 5.1 Summary Proceedings of GPRS Consultation Wrokshop

(Think Tanks, Civil Society and Public Institutions)

Venue: Institute of Economic Affairs, August 20, 2001*

The Institute of Economic Affairs hosted a one-day workshop organized by the National Development Planning Commission. Workshop participants included donors, the press, NGOs, charity groups, and research think tanks. The GPRS technical team (consulters) made presentations on the different thematic areas of the GPRS, followed by comments and questions from other participants.

Internal Economy: Participants drew attention to the fact that management of the internal economy is hampered by macroeconomic instability, supply-side shocks and persistent corruption. As with many programs before, many feared that corruption of the key change agents can pervert the prioritization of programs, the allocation of resources, the implementation of programs, and the monitoring of outcomes. There was a shared belief that bureaucratic practices and the collusion between the public sector managers and private sector contractors in the past have been detrimental to serving citizens in ways that accord with national priorities and preferences. The shoddiness of road construction was a frequently cited example. The need for accountability and transparency, many argued, was not emphasized enough in the strategy.

Governance: The presentation on governance sought to address queries about how government plans to facilitate the implementation of the GPRS. Although the proposed measures were well received, some participants saw some missing links; for example, how to maximize the complementary roles of the public and private sectors in poverty reduction and sustainable growth, and how to strengthen the links between national, regional and district administrative structures. The latter query reflects the fact that weak or improperly defined administrative links and the poor flow of information and feedbacks can make implementation of programs more difficult and virtually impossible to monitor.

Dependency on External Assistance: There was even greater concern about the high dependence on external assistance. Many wondered about (a) the ability of government to carry through the program of work in light of its fiscal constraints; (b) the relationship of the GPRS to the HIPC Initiative; and (c) what might become of the GPRS if the expected external funding did not materialize. It was pointed out that there was not enough emphasis on domestic resource mobilization as part of the poverty alleviation measures.

Outward Orientation Strategy: There were concerns that the export orientation of the growth strategy, many feared, will be at the expense of ensuring domestic food security.

Statistical Data: There were questions about the reliability, accuracy, and timeliness of data, which formed the basis of planning; data which will also be needed for monitoring and evaluation of outcomes. Participants wanted to know more about the targets and indicators, the instruments of data gathering, and what capacity building measures were being put in place to remove deficiencies in data gathering and analysis.

Community Participation and the Role of NGOs: Closely linked to community participation concerns was the role of NGOs. While none disapproved of NGOs' in the GPRS implementation, especially since many were already engaged in different poverty-related projects, the concern was that communities would be best served and the benefits of NGOs' contribution maximized if their activities were better coordinated at the district levels. This concern also put the spotlight on the need for development partners to align their development strategies and program delivery with the GPRS.

Youth Employment: There was general dissatisfaction with the link between poverty reduction and skills development of the youth. Many argued that entrepreneurial training received only brief mention in the document. And that the proposed steps to develop the entrepreneurial capacity of the youth were not concrete enough. Participants suggested that since the thrust of the GPRS is on the agricultural sector and human resource development, important career paths must be introduced in the vocational and technical training of the youth in such areas as agro-business management, food processing and storage, farm management, feeder roads maintenance, livestock and poultry management, and community health management, among others.

Social Welfare/Family Support: The role of the Department of Social Welfare, especially in the protection of the aged and children, many argued, was overlooked or marginalized in the strategy. Groups that work with the aged and children stressed the vulnerability of these groups and called for greater recognition in the fight against poverty. Participants also cautioned against equating disability with vulnerability and stressed that doing so carries the risk of overlooking the potential of the disabled in productive ventures.

Community Health and Sanitation: The proposed actions for the provision of safe and clean water, expeditious removal and disposal of waste products, especially in the urban areas, and the push for better community health management were endorsed as steps in the right direction. There was a call to integrate the needed public education into the primary and secondary schools curriculum.

* Proceedings were prepared by the author for the Institute of Economic Affairs, Accra, Ghana

First, the macroeconomic framework, the inflation and fiscal targets, and the financial programming were not part of the public discussion. While for many CSOs that exclusion may have been a matter of their limited technical capacity in this area, the established think tanks (CEPA and the IEA) saw things differently. It was a matter of "business as usual," they argued. From their perspective, the environment, as defined by the desired fiscal-monetary policy mix and targets of the GPRS, was pre-determined. And this perception had implications for the choice and scope of anti-poverty policy instruments.

Second, and closely related to the preceding concern, the GPRS discussion was not open to the fundamental question of whether or not there was an alternative path to tackling the poverty problem. For example, the use of income support systems and safety nets as instruments for aiding the elderly, those in chronic poverty, and those whose livelihoods were vulnerable to drought or natural calamities were not at all considered for public discussions. These pathways to poverty reduction must have been deemed as outside the scope of the poverty reduction exercise, largely because of their fiscal implications. It was evident that the GPRS explicitly aimed at reducing poverty through broad macroeconomic policies, education and training, manpower development, increased supply of and access to public goods, and improvements in social infrastructure, rather than through any fundamental form of welfare measures. Consultation was to let people share their views on how to move forward using the former instruments and to ensure that the action plan that emerged was consistent with the broad goals of the GPRS.

Third, the workshop highlighted some critical aspects of the participatory process. Among these was the view that it is possible to participate in public consultations without understanding the issues at stake. As the then UNDP Resident Director, Alfred Fawunda, put it, "it is like asking a student to participate in something that he is still learning." This observation applied not only to individuals but, as elaborated below, also to CSOs which sought to be part of the participatory process. For some, participation provided an opportunity to understand the process and the direction of government policies, rather than to provide specific input. They endorsed the strategy if they understood and concurred with the broad policy preferences presented to them. Arguably, this in itself is useful because it engaged the interest of citizens in the policy-making process even if they only marginally altered the course of decision-making.

Fourth, the workshop highlighted key areas of concern, omissions and the process of implementation, monitoring and accountability. In specific areas such as the health sector, substantial changes in the GPRS were influenced by stakeholder inputs and recommendations. These included a focus on human development, staff accommodation, and an expanded fee exemption program. The last of these sought to rectify some of the pitfalls of the user fee scheme introduced under the Economic Recovery Program (ERP).

4. Non-Governmental and Civil Society Organizations

The GPRS process provided opportunities for participation, through district, regional and national workshops, but the capacities of the different stakeholders as effective participants varied widely. Open public consultation was not typical of public policy-making in post-independence Ghana. It was not be until the late 1980s to early 1990s that Civil Society Organizations (CSOs) sought ways to participate in and influence the policy-making process. The trend gathered momentum in the late 1990s. The World Bank and other development agencies sought to involve civil society in the assessment of government; specifically, in the broader public sector performance, in the wider debates about national and sectoral priorities, and in assessing progress in achieving development goals.[5] When the GPRS consultation came along, many of the CSOs had only recently emerged and were in the process of their own training and capacity building. Many were in the process of identifying opportunities for their engagement in policy making, as well as seeking ways to legitimize their activities.

In fact, a reasonable thesis is that the GPRS provided CSOs an opportunity to test the role they had sought to play, without much success, under the previous regime during the ERP era. Poverty alleviation brought a new vibrancy to the public policy debate. The CSOs sought an expanded role: to engage policy-makers to develop and refine policies, to be involved in policy formulation and implementation processes, and to provide information on the status of citizens' conditions, social welfare needs and the opportunities for action by government.

But, with the exception of the established think-tanks (CEPA, IEA, ISSER, PEF and CDD),[6] many of the CSOs which sought to be part of the policy process were less established and had limited research capabilities. Many were severely limited in their experience and in their capacity to carry out a comprehensive, participatory consultation exercise with all its requirements in terms of personnel, expertise and documentation. New at this level of policy engagement, their access to information was limited and, perhaps, so was their knowledge of how to access information and their capacity to analyze the information. The workshop proceedings summarized in Box 5.2 illustrate another space for consultation led by CSOs. It is also one of the instances where development partners used their leverage to create an opportunity for CSOs, technocrats and policymakers to communicate with the view to maximize inclusion and consensus.

In principle, participation determines ownership of processes by citizens. However, this depends on the willingness of state representatives to allow space for civil society voices. It also depends on the amount of information made available to CSOs on a continuous basis (AFRODAD, 2000). Common complaints included inadequate information, late invitations to meetings, and that the NDPC chose organizations it wanted to deal with. The result, critics argued, was that sometimes those invited to workshops were the agreeable ones, not necessarily the most knowledgeable on the subject being discussed.

Box 5.2 Poverty Reduction Network Brown Bag Workshop

Organized by Canadian International Development Agency
Highlights of Presentations by NGOs and CSOs (Accra, October 5, 2001)

Commitment and Ownership—It was acknowledged that the degree of commitment and ownership was considered very high at the highest political level. However, ministries did not seem to be on board because their sector programs were poorly integrated into the process. The ministries were unable to relate their sector programming along the thematic areas of the GPRS. The absence of participation and ownership of the ministries was considered problematic considering their central role in implementation, monitoring and evaluation.

Consultation and Participation—Participants acknowledged the extensive consultation process. The perception, however, remained that NGOs and CSOs were selected in an arbitrary manner. Those consulted were judged to be the highly educated urban based elite, while organized labor was less formally engaged, and rural dwellers had no platform to articulate their concerns. Some NGOs and CSOs argued that their views were "lost" in the process of harmonization and consolidation of ideas. From their standpoint, the process was largely viewed to be "mechanisms of validation and containment" rather than those of "inclusiveness and partnership."

Too Ambitious—Recognizing the link between governance and poverty reduction, the draft GPRS spelt out the need for far reaching reforms to improve governance. However, it failed to outline the operational action plans and the specific assignments for different bodies within government to achieve these goals. In the absence of such operational goals, participants remarked, it is doubtful how much of these reforms can be achieved while also undertaking the more direct poverty reduction programs.

Some Questions and Answers:
Q1: Is one year adequate for preparing a PRSP?
Consulters: It is limited but enough to make a start.
  Q2: Why was donor's participation low and what role do they have now?
Consulters: It was a deliberate attempt to encourage ownership of the process. They can be active in facilitating implementation at the local level.
Q3: Are priorities identified in the GPRS?
Consulters: The GPRS does not list strategies or programs according to priorities. It focuses on sector programs.
Q4: Did the GPRS include consultation with Parliament?
Consulters: No. It would have helped foster greater buy-in had this been the case. But MPs only want to participate in the process through the Parliamentary sub-committees. One disadvantage of involving parliamentarians in the process is that the process would have become too centralized.

Source: Adapted from Canadian International Development Agency PRSP Brown-Bag Series. http://www.acdi.gc.ca/cida_ind.nsf October 23, 2003.

It is, however, fair to say that except by their self identification that I am from this or that civil society group, many of the CSOs (except for the established think tanks mentioned earlier) had no proven record of expertise in any specific policy area——a shortcoming which undermined the role some had hoped to play. Moreover, many had little or no identifiable domestic stakeholders or ownership. Therefore their legitimacy and political neutrality were questionable. It is difficult to make a case for the active role many publicly unaccountable organizations sought in policy-making. Besley and Ghatak (2004) have remarked that in countries with high unemployment and weak job prospects in the private sector, such organizations often become instruments for rent-seeking activity often at the expense of donors. Although there must have been some satisfaction with the actual presence of CSOs at these workshops, only a few CSOs actually dominated the formal and informal contributions. Their future role in policy-making depends on whether the general public and government consider them a planning resource or merely as watchdogs sponsored by external agents and unaccountable to local authorities.

5. Making the GPRS Work—The Role of Civil Servants

Civil servants are sometimes both the producers and the distributors of goods and services that governments desire to make available to improve the lives of citizens. Insofar as civil servants influence the cost of producing public goods, their behavior, as Armah points later in chapter 6, is an important determinant of the terms of delivery and the efficiency of implementation of poverty reducing programs. In this role, they can be a force that moves forward or impedes the ambitions of politicians. The intent here is not to set up the civil service as scapegoats for any imminent failure of the poverty reduction strategy, but simply to identify its role in three key areas: the formulation and design of the GPRS, the costing of the activities, and budgeting for their implementation. First we need to set the scene.

5.1 Background

The New Patriotic Party (NPP) took office after two decades in opposition from 1981 to 2000.[7] Generally, whenever a new party comes into power, the established senior bureaucrats fear for their jobs. When the NPP assumed the role of the governing party there was widespread speculation that the public service, dominated by appointees of the previous National Democratic Congress (NDC) government, would not cooperate with the new government. Furthermore, even if they did, such cooperation would not come easily. Change was inevitable if the new government hoped to carry out any radical process of institutional reform. Believing that continuity is important, and perhaps also wary of the potential backlash that could accompany any radical public service shakeup, the government adopted an inclusive strategy and a gradualist approach to change.

On the whole, most Ghanaian public servants, like most of their counterparts worldwide, prefer to pursue their career paths along lines that are predictable and within their control. Left on their own, bureaucrats would like to maximize the resources allocated to their ministry, department, or agency, attend to the needs of their ministers, managing the latter as much as possible. Communication goes down the civil service hierarchy. Feedback is in a reverse direction. Much gets lost or reinterpreted along the way, often not out of ill intent. In the best of political circumstances, such a system is not amenable to dealing with change. And if change has to occur, senior civil servants prefer that it takes place at a modest pace under their control, or at the very least with their full endorsement of the nature and the direction of change. They are skeptical if change is rapid and, especially so, if change has resource allocation implications, as the GPRS promised to be. Several Ministries, Department and Agencies (MDAs) saw the GPRS as potentially taking away their power to plan their individual activities. Their wariness was not helped by the perception that the Ministry of Economic and Regional Cooperation (MEPRC)—whose minister also happened to be chairman of the National Development Planning Commission (NDPC)—would act as a super ministry in charge of planning and, possibly, of the allocation of resources.

The Minister in charge of NDPC, Paa Kwesi Ndoum, himself a political outsider, a businessman, a member of the Convention People's Party (CPP), who contested unsuccessfully in the 2000 parliamentary election. He was the beneficiary of the NPP government's philosophy of inclusiveness. He would be assigned the daunting task of fashioning a development strategy for the nation. Though not a planner or economist by training, many believed that he could bring a fresh perspective and a different work ethic to the Planning Commission and therefore to the development of the GPRS. But his background and management style and not being an insider to the ruling party became a double-edged sword. He was most interested in the practical dimensions of strategies: what may work and what may not work. He was not wedded to a party manifesto and felt that the latter was not based on broad-based national consultation, a process which the GPRS was to be subjected to. The party manifesto lacked the required consensus across the political spectrum. However, being an outsider of the party undermined his capacity to influence on the key party men capable of selling the GPRS document. The stage was set for the interplay of state actors in the making of the GPRS.

5.2 Preparation of the GPRS

With respect to the preparation of the GPRS, many MDAs delegated their middle or junior level officers to attend the consultative workshops, and frequently they were not the same officers. This manner of delegation adversely affected communications between the NDPC, MEPRC and the individual MDAs. Much information got lost or was misrepresented. The consequent asymmetry of information between the NDPC and the senior civil servants only reinforced mutual mistrust.

The seasoned bureaucrats, many of whom were appointees of the previous government, operated on the quiet, avoiding any frontal attacks, lest they would be seen as opposing the new government. By being subtle in their approach, many may have thought that the GPRS process would perhaps suffer the same fate as other development plans. The senior civil servants, however, should not be viewed as a single conscious cohesive group who gathered together to undermine the process. They are not cohesive or deceptive enough for that. To operate that way would be contrary to their style of always appearing to be "good civil servants" even among themselves. And such a behavior would have backfired anyway, especially in the prevailing political atmosphere. It would have given some party stalwarts ammunition for a radical shake-up of the civil service rather than pursuing the gradualist approach favored by the party elites.

To their credit, Ndoum and the Senior Minister, J. H. Mensah would turn a once sleepy MEPRC and NDPC into institutions with presence in policy planning and design. With the help of the Office of the Presidency and the World Bank Country Director, Peter Harold, the GPRS would be turned into *un projet de société*. For the government, the GPRS would have to be the vehicle to carry forward its development agenda, as expressed in the party manifesto *Agenda for Positive Change*. The World Bank, in particular, was relatively successful in making it difficult for MDAs to hold out. On behalf of all donors, the Bank made it known that the GPRS would form the exclusive basis for donor-government relationship. This highlighted the need for MDAs' programs and activities to be included in the GPRS.

5.3 Costing the GPRS

Despite the obvious urgency that faced the country, the cooperation of civil servants could not be taken for granted. While not openly resistant, there were signs of passive resistance and non-cooperation. This was evident in their less than enthusiastic approach to the release of information. These would include information on the range of ongoing programs and activities that are poverty or non-poverty related, the cost of such programs, and the status of aid-funded programs. While some MDAs may not have had the necessary information from donor counterparts, many did, but were reluctant to fully disclose financial information to the GPRS planning team. While they would usually cooperate if asked directly (to avoid the danger of obvious non-cooperation), all too often information was not provided in the form requested or was provided with limited documentation. This lack of information across MDAs meant that it was difficult to rationalize existing programs to save costs and to enhance inter-ministerial cooperation.

5.4 Translation of the GPRS into the budget

The understanding of the civil servants of the GPRS and the extent of their co-operation became more apparent in the budget preparation stage. As Armah discusses in chapter six, if the GPRS was to become the document guiding the government's development plan, then its priorities must be reflected in the budget. Indeed the budget must take its directions from the GPRS. This is only possible if the programs and activities of the MDAs are already embedded in the GPRS. To a large extent, that was not the case for the 2002 budget. The programs and activities of several MDAs were different from what they were expected to be from the draft GPRS. The result was that the 2002 budget was less effective in moving Ghana towards achieving the specific GPRS targets, which were also necessary to reach the HIPC completion point. For the latter reason alone, implementation failure would have been costly to Ghana. But after considerable work by the NDPC and the Ministry of Finance, implementation failure was averted. The 2003 Budget was very closely aligned to the GPRS. Despite the MDAs earlier apprehensions, the Minister of Finance, Yaw Osafo Maafo's endeavour to improve transparency in the budget-making environment, especially in the expenditure process, was compelling. The earmarking of HIPC funds specifically for poverty-alleviation programs and activities was attractive enough to induce the cooperation of the MDAs.

Looking back, the GPRS process also uncovered some of the manpower limitations of the MDAs. The general deterioration in the remuneration and conditions of service over the years had depleted the public service as a reservoir of expertise for policy making, program design, budgeting, implementation, monitoring and evaluation. There were noticeable deficiencies in their technical capacity to prepare budgets in line with the three-year Medium-Term Expenditure Framework introduced in 1999.

6. Ownership, Partnership and the Role of Outsiders

Government—donor engagement in the GPRS took place at two levels: in the preparation of the document, and in the financing and implementation of the strategy. The latter is the subject of chapter seven in this volume. There I examine how development partners used their financial support through the multi donor budgetary support program to influence critical process and institutional reforms. The role of development partners (DPs for short) in the preparation of the strategy can be seen at two levels: the specific and the general.

On the specific issues, first the DPs, as we saw in Table 5.2 and Box 5.2, followed a range of paths in participating and contributing to the design of the GPRS. At the grassroots level, they used their leverage to create spaces for dialogue among CSOs, the GPRS technical team and policy makers. Second, and perhaps controversial, many DPs used their interactions with sector ministries (through the sector working groups) to point to programs and activities they perceived could have the greatest impact on poverty alleviation. In some sectors, particularly in health, education, agriculture, and local government, critics saw this level of involvement as an opportunity for donors to promote their preferences since these activities would form the basis of devising a country assistance strategy and determining entitlements to donor support. Third, under the leadership of the UNDP, development partners collectively provided comments on different aspects of the strategy.

At the general level, there was a noticeable absence of open criticisms of the process and the content of the GPRS, even when perspectives differed markedly between the government and the DPs. Debate ensued when the government unveiled its medium-term priorities. Improvements in physical infrastructure and the development of social infrastructure were presented as important initiatives that would eventually stimulate economic growth. While this policy direction was seen by the DPs as a departure from the PRSPs guiding principles, it also reflected somewhat the notion that the principles underlying the GPRS were externally imposed, and perhaps were too rigid to construct an effective development strategy. The ensuing debates highlighted the tensions between development partnership and the ownership of the development agenda.

From the DP's perspective, the lack of access to social infrastructure and the opportunities for human development were important causes of deprivation for a large majority of the poor. As a result, improving access to education, health facilities, and safe water, improving sanitation, female child education, child nutrition, improving programs for the vulnerable and excluded, and improving law and order and public safety ought to be the immediate focus of the policy.

The need for improvements in physical infrastructure was not in doubt. What was in doubt, however, was whether investment in roads, highways, ports and telecommunications would take resources away from improvements in social infrastructure, or what the needed capital investment would mean for the fiscal and monetary constraints that underpin the GPRS. Utmost on the minds of many DPs was whether Ghana would be able to carry out its medium-term priorities without compromising the macroeconomic framework agreed to with the

International Monetary Fund, and, potentially jeopardizing the Poverty Reduction Growth Facility available from the Fund.

The government's narrative of the poverty problem emphasized both the physical and social infrastructure as barriers to growth and thus to poverty alleviation. From the government's perspective, the improvements in social infrastructure and public amenities, important as they are, are only intermediate targets. By themselves, these targets did not constitute the complete vision of the transformation envisaged in the party manifesto or in the Vision 2020. In the government's view the development of physical infrastructure, improvements in communication links and energy supply could hardly be a fault. In fact, the inadequate transportation and communication links between rural and urban centers were seen as major impediments to sustaining adequate social services in many parts of the country. Lack of access limits internal trade. It is also a major disincentive for health personnel and teachers to relocate to rural areas where poverty is most prevalent. In short, the mechanisms for the effective delivery of public goods and services are central to any credible anti-poverty scheme. How to sustain these mechanisms and at the same time expand the opportunities for income earning will depend on improvements in the physical infrastructure of the country.

Clearly, the way that poverty is perceived had an important influence on the process of shaping and implementing poverty reduction policies. While the perspectives of the DPs and government were not entirely dissimilar, their frames of reference, the perceived constraints, and the planning sequencing appeared dissimilar. After nearly a decade and a half of economic reforms, the poverty diagnosis from the 1998/99 Ghana Living Standards Survey must have been disappointing. The DPs' perspective, led by the World Bank, was that the poverty fighting impact of economic growth, which averaged 4.5 percent over the period of reform, had been minimal at best. As a result, there was a need to empower the poor, and promote economic and social progress through investments in health, education, water, sanitation and in social protection.

For the government, the economic growth record fell short of the 6 to 8 percent needed to sustain improvements in the standard of living for the growing population. The economy was described as trapped in a "low quality growth equilibrium" path (Economic Commission of Africa, 2003, 155).[8] The proceedings of the workshop on "Macroeconomic Stability, Growth and Poverty Reduction in Ghana" (Aryeetey and Kanbur, 2001) shared the same prognosis of the economy. Moreover, the structure of the economy had remained unchanged, predominantly agricultural. Diversification efforts under the Economic Recovery Program had not been entirely successful. The economy continued to suffer from structural bottlenecks that impeded production. From this diagnosis, it was apparent that HIPC and poverty mitigating strategies may provide only interim relief; but hardly the panacea for the country's development problems in the long run. The surprising fact was that the DPs, including the World Bank, were aware of these structural problems. The obvious explanation for their position in the debate is that they were caught up in the paradigm shift in the global development agenda. The focus of international development efforts under the conditional debt relief of HIPC was on meeting specific measurable targets relating to improvements in the human conditions determined by the Millennium Development Goals (see Annex).

These differences in the basic understanding of the causes and nature of poverty and how best to deal with them in the short, medium and long term only put a sharper spotlight on the issue of ownership of the strategy, which key DPs perhaps were reluctant to usurp openly. In the end, the emphasis on accelerating growth and on reducing poverty was welcome. When the comprehensive volume outlining the strategy was published in February 2003, it carried the subtitle "An Agenda for Growth and Prosperity" in line with the governing party's Manifesto. For the development partners, the nexus of contention will now shift to the actual implementation of the strategy and how to leverage the poverty alleviation component of the strategy.

7. Concluding Observations

At the beginning of this chapter, I posed a number of questions. These included whether the pubic saw themselves as passive or active agents in the consultative process, whether the process was merely a veil to satisfy the demand for participation, and whether the resulting strategy reflected citizens' viewpoints. There are a number of useful lessons.

First, it is difficult to judge the comprehensiveness and inadequacies of the GPRS consultative process. It is also difficult to conclude that the consultations did not influence the content of the strategy. The key issues turn on (a) how much consultations would have been enough to make the process truly participatory and country owned; (b) what format of consultation would have been considered appropriate to maximize public input, (c) the readiness of stakeholders to engage meaningfully in the process, and (d) how sufficiently flexible were the technocrats to accommodate changes in content and direction. Some critics argued that too much public debate may have slowed down the process and polarized some segments of the population, who may have felt that their views were not adequately reflected in the final product. Moreover, it is not easy to define an acceptable output from such consultations because much depends on the reciprocal involvement of the public. The requirements of open consultation in policy-making were new to both the government and the governed. Both groups were on a steep learning curve. Noteworthy, some pointed out that the "poverty reduction" label itself did not galvanize public consensus for progress or imbue public minds with challenging practical goals.

Second, the story of the time constraints appears to be the same everywhere, as in the cases of Mauritania, Tanzania, Mozambique, Uganda and Burkina

Faso. In all these countries, the desire to get the PRSP completed so that debt relief can be applied, inevitably created time constraints that likely compromised both process and content. More worrying for some was the perception that the time constraint was largely externally imposed. Because the GPRS was tied to the HIPC, there was the need to have a document as a trigger for the HIPC Decision Point, which Ghana subsequently achieved in February 2002. Faced with daunting macroeconomic pressures there was great "political" and economic urgency for a new government to access financial resources to implement its program of action. The time constraint, even if well intended, did not take into account the political environment and the resources that countries needed to undertake nationwide, comprehensive consultations. The stakeholders themselves needed time to understand the complexities of developing a poverty reducing strategy in order to make informed contributions.

Third, while there is some validity to the criticisms of time constraints and the lack of opportunity to explore different pathways out of poverty, the GPRS can show, as it did in the appendixes to the document, that it opened up spaces for dialogue and responded to a wide range of comments. Here, I will have to agree with Gyan Baffour, the Executive Director of the NDPC, who managed the entire GPRS process, that the GPRS is not a static but rather a "living" document. The strategy is not crafted once and for all. It may change in the process of implementation based on the feedback from the monitoring and evaluation. The strategy recognized the endogenous nature of the poverty policy process. It opened up new policy spaces to influence the intended outcomes and possibly those intended to benefit from these outcomes. Change may arise not only from the annual progress report, but also from the annual forum of the National Economic Dialogue (NED). As people become more aware of the policy-making process, the greater is their ability to contribute to the debate on subsequent directions of government policy.

Fourth, GPRS provided CSOs the opportunity to seek legitimacy, to deepen and to test the role they sought to play going beyond acting as mere watchdogs of public sector performance. Their contribution could have been strengthened by having more capacity to carry out comprehensive, participatory consultative exercises with greater expertise and documentation. At a different level of engagement, the buy-in by civil servants early in the process would have made for greater coherence of content and helped in the translation of the agenda into the budget, in the execution of the budget, and in the monitoring and evaluation of the outcomes. Equally noteworthy was the limited role of parliament in fashioning out the strategy.

Fifth, the role of the DPs remains mixed and debatable. Most donors admitted that the GPRS is Ghana's main development strategy and were willing to facilitate dialogue and consensus building. Some donors initiated their own consultative processes in developing country assistance plans, and sought greater coordination in donor activities. Controversial, however, was that some sought, through their dealings with MDAs, to influence the content of GRPS programs and projects to suit their preferences. For some, it was business as usual. The GPRS did not make any fundamental difference in their approaches to dealing with country government. They continued to follow their closed door approach to country assistance programs.

How useful was the process for social accountability? The GPRS process highlights two important facets of public engagement. First, as seen in the workshop proceedings, the process compelled a re-packaging and dissemination of information about government policy-making – in this case, about the HIPC initiative, its expected benefits, and about Ghana's relationship with her DPs. Several of the issues raised in the consultation process could have been pre-empted if the government was forthcoming at the start of the whole process: information about the policy goals, what was to be done, how it was to be done, the modes of consultation, and the expected outcomes.

The GPRS process also triggered an unprecedented demand for social and public accountability of public expenditures. There emerged a great deal of interest in tracking the disbursement of HIPC funds and, in particular, in providing concrete evidence of the disbursements in programs and activities at the local level. The think tanks (CEPA, ISSER, CDD, IPA) and other civil society groups (such as the Northern Ghana Network, Budget Advocacy, Action Aid, SEND) all created networks for tracking the HIPC expenditures and assessing their possible impact at the district and grassroots level. While accountability of resource use could be enforced at the constitutional level through parliamentary committees, many stakeholders recognized that social and public accountability under GPRS required no constitutional reforms. It simply required the government to increase access to information on disbursement, and to open up spaces for public participation in the policy-making and implementation process.

Finally, as noted earlier, the need for a democratic approach to policy-making is explicit in Article 35, paragraph 6(d) of the "The Directive of State Policy" of the 1992 Constitution. It enjoins the state and its representatives to provide for and to allow spaces for participation, and to make the policy-making process predictable and transparent.

There are three ways to achieve this goal: through the National Economic Dialogue (NED), through the workings of parliamentary committees, and through pre-budget consultations. While these avenues currently exist and are in use, they are not as effective as they could be. The current structures do not encourage broader participation. While the NED has become a useful forum, it is currently based in the nation's capital with no formal mechanisms to collate inputs from the regional or district levels or for participation on behalf of these levels of government.

Second are bi-partisan parliamentary committees. They are limited in their capacity to organize, to deepen understanding of issues or to provide opportunities to share knowledge and ideas. To open spaces for public input, parliament should consider, as a matter of routine practice, engaging independent bodies outside parliament to provide submissions to inform the deliberations of relevant committees. And finally, pre-budget hearings remain limited to closed-door formal presentation by the ministries, departments, and agencies. These too need restructuring to maximize public input. A greater use of parliamentary committees, district and regional pre-budget consultations, town-hall meetings and invited position papers should form the core of public involvement in the policy-making process.

Notes

1. This chapter benefited immensely from conversations with Dr. J. L. S Abbey, Dr. P. K. Ndoum, Mr Alfred Fawundu (former UNDP Resident Representative in Ghana), Mr. Mpianim (private consultant), Dr. S. Adei (Director of GIMPA), Dr. Ernest Aryeetey of ISSER (Legon), Dr. Asenso Okyere (former vice Chancellor of the University of Ghana), Dr. Baffour Gyan (former Executive Director of NDPC), and comments from Dr. Santo Dodaro, Dr. Aryee, and Ms. Abena Oduro.

2. The Institute of Economic Affairs (IEA) was established in 1989, followed by the Centre for Policy Analysis (CEPA) in 1993, Third World Network (TWN) in 1994, Africa Security Dialogue and Research (ASDR) in 1995, Centre for Democracy and Development (CDD) in 1998 and Institute of Policy Alternatives (IPA) in 2000.

3. See Ohemeng (2005) for more on the history of think tanks in Ghana.

4. The five thematic areas are: Macroeconomic Stability, Production and Gainful Employment, Human Development and the Provision of Basic Services, Special Programs for the Vulnerable and Excluded, and Good Governance.

5. The initiative was boosted by a day-long consultative workshop on October 18, 1999 hosted by the World Bank to deliberate on the actual and potential role of Ghanaian civil society in assessing public sector performance (Mackay and Gariba, 2000). This was preceded by the Structural Adjustment Participatory Review Initiative which begun in Ghana in 1997.

6. Centre for Policy Analysis (CEPA), Institute of Economic Affairs (IEA), Institute of Statistical and Socio-Economic Research (ISSER), Private Enterprise Foundation (PEF), and Centre for Democracy and Development (CDD).

7. The nearly two decades in opposition span first, under the military regime of National Democratic Congress (NDC) the period 1981—1992, officially as the opposition outside of parliament in 1992—1996, then as the official opposition in parliament in 1996-2000.

8. "Ghana—The Danger of Fiscal Exuberance," Economic Report on Africa, Economic Commission of Africa, 2003.

References

Ayee, J. "Ghana: A Top-Down Initiative." Pp. 125—154 in *Local Governance in Africa* edited by Dele Olowu and J.S Wunsch, Lynee Reimer Publishers, Inc. 2004.

Brock, K., Cornwall, A. and Gaventa J. "Power Knowledge and Political Spaces in the framing of Poverty Policy." *Institute of Development Studies,* Working Paper 143, Brighton Sussex, UK. 2001

AFRODAD. "Comparative Analysis of Five African Countries with Completed PRSP." African Forum and Network on Debt and Development, Zimbabwe. 2002.

National Patriotic Party, *Agenda for Positive Change: Manifesto 2000*.

Armstrong, R. P. *Ghana Country Assistance Review: A study in development effectiveness*. Washington. D.C. The World Bank. 1996.

Boafo-Arthur, K. "Structural Adjustment Programs (SAPs) in Ghana: Interrogating PNDC's implementation." *West Africa Review* 1: 1—25. 1999.

Gariba, S. "Participatory Approaches to Social and Public Accountability of Expenditures." Presentation made at the Second World Bank Development Dialogue series, Accra May 23, 2003.

Government of Ghana. *The Constitution of the Republic of Ghana*, 1992.

———. *Ghana Poverty Reduction Strategy: 2003—2005*. February 2003.

———. Government of Ghana, *Local Government Act*, (Act 462), 1993

———. Government of Ghana, *National Development Planning Commission*, Act 479, 1994.

Hall, P. A. "Policy Paradigms, Social Learning, and the State: The Case of Economic Policymaking in Britain." *Comparative Politics* 25 (1993): 275—296.

Hutchful, E. "The Institutional and Political Framework of macro-economic management in Ghana." Geneva: *UNRISD Discussion Paper* 82. 1997.

———. *Ghana's Adjustment Experience: TheParadox of Reform*. Oxford: James Curry. 2002.

Mackay K. and Gariba S. (eds.) "The Role of Civil Society in Assessing Public Sector Performance in Ghana." Proceedings of a Workshop. The World Bank. 2000

Montpetit, E. "Public Consultations in Policy Network Environments: The Case of Assisted Reproductive Technology Policy in Canada." *Canadian Public Policy*, 24(1): Pp. 95—110. 2003.

Ohemeng, F. L. K. "Getting the state right: think tanks and the dissemination of New Public Management ideas in Ghana." *Journal of Modern African Studies*, 43(3) (2005): 443—465.

Omaboe, E. N. "The Process of Planning." *In A Study of Contemporary Ghana: the Eeconomy of Ghana Vol. 1*, edited by W. Birmingham, I. Neustadt and E.N. Omaboe. Northwestern University Press. 1966.

Pierre, J. "Public Consultations and Citizen Participation: Dilemmas of Policy Advice." Pp. 137-163 in *Taking Stock: Assessing Public Sector Reform* edited by B. Guy Peters and Donald Savoie, McGill-Queen's University Press, 1998.

Scharpf, F. W. *Games Real Actors Play: Actor-Centered Institutionalism in Policy Research*. Boulder: Westview Press. 1997.

Walters, L. C., J. Aydelottee and J. Miller. "Putting More Public in Policy Analysis." *Public Administration Review* 60, 4 (2000): 349—359.

World Bank. World Development Report 2000/2001: *Attacking Poverty*, Washington, D.C. The World Bank, 2000.

6

Linking Poverty Reduction Strategies to the Budget

Bartholomew Armah

1. Introduction

Effective implementation of PRSs (Poverty Reduction Strategies) requires that the projects and programs identified in each strategy be linked, in a non-superficial way, to the annual budget and expenditure framework. This requires that: sector strategic priorities are consistent with national strategic priorities; sector priorities are appropriately costed and reflected in national budgets and existing expenditure frameworks; the revenue side of the budget reflects the total (domestic and external) resource envelope; budget allocations are aligned with PRS priorities; disbursements are predictable and timely; and monitoring and evaluation systems are effective and appropriately inform budgetary allocations in line with changing national priorities.

Experience has shown that invariably several PRSP projects and programs are either not funded or are financed outside the budget. Off-budget expenditures tend to be sub-optimal especially when they are made in a non-transparent way. Often, they risk duplication of effort and undermine expenditure tracking and performance monitoring. Obviously, in the extreme case where PRSs are not funded, implementation of national priorities is bound to fail; PRSs default into mere academic exercises aimed at satisfying donor benchmarks or conditionalities.

Using Ghana as a case study, this chapter examines the challenges associated with embedding the Ghana Poverty Reduction Strategy (hereafter referred to as GPRS) in the national budget and the Medium Term Expenditure Framework (MTEF).[1]

The chapter is organized as follows. The first section provides a brief background to the introduction of the MTEF process in Ghana. The second section describes the MTEF process in Ghana and highlights the practical challenges associated with embedding the GPRS in the MTEF. The third section identifies the lessons from Ghana's experience and makes policy recommendations. The fourth section concludes the chapter.

2. Background

The Medium Term Expenditure Framework (MTEF) was introduced in Ghana to address weaknesses in the budget preparation and management practices. MTEF is one component of the Public Financial Management Reform Program[2] (PUFMARP), a comprehensive public sector reform initiative, addressing deficiencies in the budget system. The MTEF is an integrated, broad-based performance budget that sets out government's expenditure for a three year period.

PUFMARP on the other hand, is a comprehensive medium term strategic program aimed at addressing public financial management issues in general. These issues include weak budgetary frameworks; lack of proper accounting; ineffective audit systems; lack of reliable, accurate and timely information for management decision making; ineffective public expenditure monitoring and control; and lack of budget ownership.

One of the two main objectives of the MTEF was to provide a tool for improved deficit management through realistic revenue projections that take into account various factors that may contribute to revenue instability, including seasonalities. The second was to identify and appropriately fund expenditure priorities. Prior to the introduction of the MTEF in 1998, Ghana had undertaken Public Expenditure Reviews in 1993, 1994 and 1995, to evaluate the impact of government expenditure on productivity, growth and development. The reviews identified the following weaknesses in the budgetary system:

a) Failure to link the development plans, (such as Ghana Vision 2020 document and the Medium Term Development Plan, MTDP) policies and priorities with the annual budget through a macroeconomic framework. As a result, annual budgetary targets and policies were often inconsistent with those stipulated in the Vision 2020 and the MTDP. In addition, the resource envelope was often insufficient to realize the desired objectives.

b) A disconnect between the recurrent and development budgets because they were prepared independently of each other. As a result, the recurrent costs arising from new investments were not planned for. For instance, bridges would be built without providing sufficient funds for maintenance; hospitals would be constructed without taking into account the resources required to employ new nurses and doctors.

c) Failure to link the budgetary allocations to the performance of Ministries, Departments and Agencies (MDAs).

d) The tendency to prepare the recurrent budget on an incremental basis without reviewing the relevance of the activities being funded.
e) The tendency for budget classification to reflect types of expenditure (e.g., traveling) without indicating the purpose of expenditures (e.g., provision of extension services).
f) The failure of the development budget to link project activities to the government's priorities.
g) The failure to re-prioritize activities as resources declined. There was a tendency to continue funding most activities from year to year while resources were declining in real terms, resulting in the under–funding of priority activities.

The introduction of the MTEF was preceded by attempts to address several of the above problems through the preparation of Sector Investment Programs (SIPs) in the roads, health and education sectors. A SIP is a program of priority activities (comprising both recurrent and capital expenditure) designed by a line ministry and funded by the government and donors. In fact, the Roads, Health and Education line ministries were initially reluctant to participate in the MTEF program since the staff believed it was a duplication of the SIP initiative. While the SIP approach shares many of the same characteristics of the MTEF, particularly the emphasis on funding priority activities, as defined by government, it falls short on the following grounds. First, it is not always linked to a reliable macroeconomic framework; the projections of resource availability for the sector are not based on estimates of national resource availability. Second, the SIP approach does not take into account inter-sectoral linkages; SIPs are sector specific with little regard for inter-sectoral interactions. Third, in some cases, not all the activities within a sector are included hence choices within a sector are not comprehensive. The MTEF approach took the SIP process a few steps further by taking into account inter and intra-sectoral trade-offs and linking sectoral choices to an albeit rudimentary macroeconomic framework that provides an indication of the overall resource envelope.

3. The MTEF Budget Process

In one sense, the MTEF process in Ghana is a *top down* process, determining resource availability and allocating these resources between sectors. In this context, the Ministry of Finance and Economic Planning (MoFEP) estimates the total resources available and cabinet decides how these resources should be allocated between the broad sectors[3] of the economy based on government priorities.

At the same time, the MTEF process is a *bottom up* process, estimating the actual requirements or inputs needed to implement policies in each sector. This component of the MTEF involves the preparation of a *strategic plan* and an *activity based budget* by all line ministries. In effect, the top down process of allocating resources to MDAs is informed by a bottom up *policy review* process, where MDAs assess and appropriately revise their strategic plans and policies in the context of evolving national priorities. Following MDA sectoral reviews, sectoral expenditure ceilings are developed and communicated to all MDAs in a *budget guideline.* This indicates the total resources to be available for the forthcoming three years, including donor resources.

Box 6.1 Steps in Ghana's MTEF Process

The MTEF is a means to integrate both top down and bottom up approaches. The steps in Ghana's MTEF process can be summarized as follows:

Step 1: Develop a macro-framework as the basis for projecting resource availability based on the macro-environment (i.e., economic growth, domestic revenues and availability of donor funds)

Step 2: Develop preliminary sectoral expenditure ceilings by allocating resources between sectors on the basis of government priorities. The objective is to provide line ministries with an indication of their likely resource envelope before they commence their detailed costing.

Step 3: Require each ministry to estimate its input requirements for the medium-term based on national government policies and priorities. Sectoral priorities are in turn based on policy reviews (MDA specific) and cross-sectoral discussions (sector-specific; MDAs within a specific sector). During this phase sector ministries (i.e., Ministries classified in the same sector):

- Review sectoral objectives, policies and strategies pursued in previous years.
- Review activities needed to achieve the agreed upon outputs and objectives. (This involves a review of existing activities for whether they are in line with sectoral policies and priorities and whether new activities are required).
- Estimate the actual costs of activities (recurrent and development, government and donor).
- Prioritize activities within the constraints of the sectoral resource ceiling and identify those activities which should continue, those that need to be scaled back and those that have to
- be terminated.

Box 6.1 Continued

Step 4: Revise sectoral ceilings on the basis of additional information gathered in the sector reviews by MDAs;

Step 5: Finalize three year estimates: sector ministries make final adjustments to the three year estimates at an aggregate level (i.e., at the program and sub-program level), with the first year's estimate shown in detail.

Step 6: Review and Finalize the Estimates: Once ministries have completed their plans and estimates, they are reviewed by the Ministry of Finance to assess whether the estimates are consistent with national policies, plans and priorities and within the ceilings. The estimates are subsequently, discussed at *Budget Hearings* and presented to Cabinet and Parliament for discussion and approval. The first year's estimates are approved while the second and third year's estimates are indicative.

3.1 Key Elements of the Top-Down Process

Estimating the Total Resource Envelope
The budget allocation process begins with the Ministry of Finance and Economic Planning (MoFEP)[4] estimating the total (domestic and external) resource envelope as a basis for expenditure allocations. This is achieved through the use of a macro-model to estimate targets for key macro-indicators including the GDP growth rate, the rate of inflation, the balance of payments, and the rate of monetary expansion.[5] The targeted values of these variables then determine the total resource envelope which serves as the basis for establishing sectoral/MDA expenditure ceilings. For this purpose, a *Macro Group* was established comprised of representatives from the Ministry of Finance and Economic Planning's Research and Budget Divisions, the revenue agencies, the Bank of Ghana, the Statistical Services, and the National Development Planning Commission (NDPC). Consultants helped the Group develop a simple spreadsheet model, to estimate the resource envelope and establish sector expenditure ceilings.

In reality, the institution responsible for developing the national plan (the NDPC) has not played a significant role in either the development of the macro-model or the design of the PRS macro-economic framework. The operational reality is that the total resource envelope is based on incremental projections by MoFEP of the existing revenue base. This narrow interpretation of the macro-framework has resulted in systemic weaknesses in the estimation of the total resource envelope resulting in unrealistic estimates. The credibility of the estimates is further undermined by the fact that, the MoFEP's aggregate number evolves largely out of an agreement with the IMF with relatively little input from academics, the private sector and leading think-tanks in the country.

Indeed, for several key macro-economic indicators, the substantial disparity between actual outturns and budgetary targets suggests the need to pay greater attention to the revenue side of the MTEF process. This focus would ensure more reliable estimates of the total resource envelope. This calls for a more expeditious adoption and implementation of a macroeconomic model to arrive at credible estimates of the resource envelope. It also calls for improved coordination of skills and resources among the key stakeholders, particularly the NDPC and the MoFEP.

Contributing to the poor estimation of the resource envelope is the lack of transparency in estimating internally generated funds (IGFs) and donor funding. A substantial amount of "earmarked" donor assistance and funds generated by line ministries are not captured in the MTEF. A major reason for this trend is the concern by MDAs that full disclosure would lead to a corresponding reduction in government allocations. However, failure to include all elements of funding within the MTEF obviously compromises the government's ability to estimate its total resource envelope and to frame a comprehensive and consistent planning and budget process.

Table 6.1 Macro Targets Versus Actual Performance
(in percent unless otherwise stated)

	1999		2000		2001
	Target	**Actual**	**Target**	**Actual**	**Target**
GDP	5.5	**4.4**	5.0	**3.7**	4.0
Monetary					
Inflation (end of period)	9.5	**13.8**	12.5	**40.5**	25
Inflation (average)		**12.4**		**25.2**	35.0
Money Supply Growth	15.0	**16.1**	16.0	**39.8**	32
Fiscal Indicators					
Tax Revenue (¢ billion)	3294	**3084**	3,957	**3,731.7**	5,802.9
Non-Tax (¢ billion)	310.4	**475**	344	**396.1**	300
Expenditure (¢ billion)	6,063.7	**5,845.5**	7660	**7,524.9**	13,539.2
Broad Deficit/GDP	5.2	**6.5**	6.1	**8.5**	5.2
Primary Balance/GDP	3.8	**2.3**		**2.4**	3.4
International Trade					
Balance of Payments ($ millions)	60.0	**-93.4**	0	**-194.8**	165.7

Source: 1999–2001 Budget Statements

Forecasting inaccuracies are often exacerbated by external shocks. In particular, Ghana's macro-economic indicators took a dramatic turn for the worse in mid-1999 as the economy suffered from the combined effect of rising crude oil prices and declining prices of her major commodity exports. The situation was further compounded by delays in donor disbursements, deterioration in the government's fiscal position and a substantial increase in the budget deficit from 6.5 percent of the budget in 1999 to 8.5 percent of the budget in year 2000 (Table 6.1). These trends resulted in slower than projected increases in both expenditure and revenue.

In sum, difficulties in estimating the total resource envelope invariably undermine the credibility of the sector ceilings and consequently, the ability of MDAs to fund the activities necessary to achieve their objectives. This can create frustration on the part of MDAs and also undermine the successful implementation of the MDAs program of activities.

The lesson is that the revenue side of the MTEF process needs more attention to ensure realistic estimates of the resource envelope. This will involve: the cooperation of donors with respect to the timeliness of their disbursements; greater transparency in the disclosure of both donor and internally generated funds; and greater accuracy in macro-economic modeling and revenue forecasting. To reduce the budgetary impact of external shocks, the government could set up a contingency fund exclusively for the purpose of addressing any overestimation of the resource envelope. Furthermore, to avoid the possibility of the contingency fund degenerating into a "slush" fund, there must be explicit monitoring of the rules for its allocation.

Allocating Resources
The MTEF process stipulates ceilings for MDAs in the broad expenditure categories. As of 2003 these categories were: Administration, Economic Services, Infrastructure Services, Social Services and Public Safety. The indicative MDA ceiling for the three-year period is based on total expenditures (both recurrent and development expenditures, and both donor and government resources) and is apportioned between the various cost centers where the budget is prepared and managed: Departments, Divisions, Regions, and Agencies.

For instance, the allocations for 2000 and 2001 (Table 6.2) reflected the importance of administration and social services in the overall policy framework. The relatively large share of resources devoted to social services was consistent with government's policy objective of poverty reduction. Furthermore, the allocations pointed to the importance of donor funding to develop key infrastructure and economic services. For both categories of expenditure, donor funding was concentrated in investment and service activities.

In 2000 while actual statutory expenditure exceeded programmed expenditures, discretionary expenditures were generally restrained as a result of slow disbursements of funds to the various line ministries. Unfavorable trends in discretionary expenditure are noteworthy since all MDA allocations are drawn from this category of expenditures. With the exception of salaries, disbursements to MDAs were below their sectoral ceilings in both 2000 and 1999. In

1999, MDAs only received their allocations for the first two quarters of the year. The situation worsened in 2000 when they only received allocations for just one quarter. In some cases, the timing of the release was so late as to be counter-productive. For instance, in the case of the agricultural sector, where the timing of releases is crucial due to the agricultural cycle, erratic release of funds could undermine the realization of sectoral and PRS objectives. Furthermore, the monitoring and evaluation of the PRS process has been constrained by a lack of funds since MDAs charged with monitoring responsibilities have also been under-funded.

The lesson here is that reflecting the PRS in the national budget goes beyond resource allocation for priority projects. It encompasses the issue of timeliness of disbursements, and the relative share of the funds allocated to salaries as opposed to complementary investments in goods and services necessary for program and project implementation. There is the tendency for wages and salaries to account for the bulk of the resource allocations. While this may be warranted in some cases, such as in the delivery of education services, in others, such as infrastructure development, it is clearly wasteful.

3.2 Key Elements of the Bottom-Up Process

Strategic Planning by Sectors
The bottom up process of determining the actual costs of implementing policies in each sector is informed by the strategic plans of MDAs. Prior to the introduction of the MTEF, program proposals from the sector ministries tended to be mere extensions of past programs, which had nothing to do with new approved policy issues under the existing national development framework (i.e., Ghana-Vision 2020).

The strategic planning process was adopted to ensure that the mission, objectives and outputs of line ministries are consistent with national and sectoral goals. It was also to encourage MDAs to define the activities needed to produce outputs and fulfill their objectives. Since it was intended that activities would be costed rather than have automatic increments over and above previous year estimates. The strategic planning approach represented, in theory, an improvement on the incremental approach to budgeting. By costing both the recurrent and development budgets as an integrated whole, the strategic approach avoided the practice of ignoring the recurrent costs arising from development expenditure. Moreover, through improvements in budget classification and presentation, Ghana's strategic planning also ensured that expenditures were linked, in a more transparent way, to the activities, outputs and objectives of MDAs.

Table 6.2 Sectoral Allocations by Item and Sources of Funds: 2001

Item	Administration		Economic Services		Infrastructure		Social Services		Public Safety	
	Cedis (¢, bn)	Percent of Total	Cedis ¢, bn	Percent of Total	Cedis ¢, bn	Percent of Total	Cedis ¢, bn	Per-cent of Total	Cedis ¢, bn	Per-cent of Total
Personnel	1,043.6	16.5	161.2	2.6	64.0	1.0	1320.6	20.9	298.7	4.7
Administration										
GoG	176.5	2.8	31.9	0.5	15.7	0.3	128.4	2.0	86.1	1.4
Donor	5.5	0.1	3.2	0.05	0.0	0.0	5.8	0.1	0.0	0.0
Services										
GoG	124.15	2.0	34.6	0.5	19.7	0.3	139.5	2.2	43.3	0.7
Donor	103.14	1.6	308.5	4.9	8.0	0.1	124.9	1.97	0.0	0.0
Investment										
GoG	555.7	8.8	41.9	0.7	101.9	1.6	115.6	1.8	75.1	1.2
Donor	197.5	3.1	367.5	5.8	527.2	8.3	75.3	1.2	0.0	0.0
Total	**2206.2**	**34.9**	**948.9**	**15.0**	**736.5**	**11.6**	**1910.2**	**30.2**	**502.6**	**7.9**

Source: 2001 Budget Statement

The overall mission, goals and objectives of an MDA must however, be consistent with the national goals and objectives of the poverty reduction strategy. As part of the strategic planning process, line ministries are required to examine their current situation through an environmental scan and SWOT (Strengths, Weaknesses, Opportunities and Threats) analysis. They also define their mission statement, objectives, outputs and activities and identify inputs required to implement the agreed upon activities. For instance, in 2001, the

Box 6.2 Elements of the Strategic Plan

Elements of Sector Strategic Plans

- *Internalization of National and Sectoral Goals*: The strategic plans of MDAs must be placed in the context of achieving the broad goals of the country as articulated in key development programs such as the Ghana Poverty Reduction Strategy (currently the Growth and Poverty Reduction Strategy 2005) and the Medium Term Development Plan.

- *Identification of Outcomes*: These are the direct or indirect impacts of the outputs of MDAs. They provide concrete evidence of success or failure of respective MDAs in the achievement of national goals.

- *Articulation of Mission Statements of MDAs:* spell out each MDA's reason for being, their core business areas, their stakeholders and the values guiding their operations.

- *Specification of MDA Objectives:* these constitute short term goals, which the MDA aims to achieve in order to fulfill its mission. For example, one of the objectives of the Ministry of Communications in 2000 was to provide guidance for the national effort in solving the Y2K problem.

- *Identification of MDA Outputs:* these comprise services and facilities to be provided by the MDA over the three years in order to achieve the agreed objectives. For instance, to solve the Y2K problem, the Ministry established a Local Area Network. Furthermore, to achieve its objective of monitoring, evaluating and providing feedback to Government on its policies and programs, the same Ministry organized public awareness campaigns and actively promoted the programs and activities of the Ghana film industry.

- *Clear Specification of MDA Activities*: The concrete actions or measures that need to be undertaken to generate the agreed outputs required to achieve the MDAs objectives must be clearly spelled out in an MDA's strategic plan. Activities fall into two categories: services and investment.

stated mission of the Ministry for Communications was to develop and coordinate the implementation of policies that help integrate communications technologies and public information systems and also harness the full potential of resources within our society for accelerated and sustainable national development by (a) Providing public relations and communications services supporting national development programs; (b) Assembling, processing and disseminating information to relevant bodies and institutions; (c) Engaging in research and submitting reports to the government for the refinement and reformulation of policies.

Policy Review
Following a full year of MTEF implementation, line ministries undertake a review of their activities to determine whether the objectives, policies, outputs and activities identified in their Strategic Plan are the best means of achieving the PRS. Furthermore, the additional information from the review is used by MoFEP to revise the three year ceilings. In addition to annual reviews, the MTEF, at least in theory, provides MDAs an opportunity to reprioritize their objectives, outputs and activities both within and between years, in response to changing circumstances.

3.3 Implementation Challenges

Weak Institutional Coordination
Institutional coordination between the key sectors responsible for facilitating the links between sector strategies and the budget has been weak. The NDPC, at the apex of the planning machinery, is responsible for coordinating and harmonizing sector strategic plans from MDAs and District plans from District Assemblies into a comprehensive, integrated and broad national plan. The Ministry of Finance and Economic Planning (MoFEP) on the other hand, directly controls the budgetary allocation process. The operational reality, however, is that there has been little coordination of effort between the NDPC and MoFEP. The MTEF process appears to be controlled by the MoFEP effectively leaving the NDPC sidelined. One possible reason for this is that the strategic plans of the MDAs were supposed to be formulated in the context of sector plans developed by the NDPC. However, these plans were not available at the time that the MTEF initiative was being implemented. As a result, initially, the strategic plans of MDAs were not linked to the PRS through the sector plans. With the sector plans no longer relevant to the MDA's budgeting process, MoFEP assumed greater control of the MTEF process. Hence, the strategic plans of MDAs were crafted in the context of MoFEP as the key player in the MTEF process. As a result, the sector plans from the MDAs were inconsistent and only superficially linked with the PRS.

Most importantly, the implementation of the PRSP was plagued by an institutional turf war that raged between the Ministry of Finance (now the Ministry
of Finance and Economic Planning), the Ministry for Economic Planning and
Regional Cooperation (MEPRC),[6] and the National Development Planning
Commission (NDPC). The issue centered on control over the PRSP process and
was exacerbated by personality conflicts between the Ministers of the respective
ministries. The Ministry of Finance argued for greater control of the PRSP especially when the fiscal implications of the document became apparent. However,
MEPRC and NDPC had led the process of formulating the document and under-
standably, were reticent about ceding control to the Ministry of Finance. Besides, they argued that the PRS was largely a strategic planning document and
therefore appropriately lay within their mandate.

In this context, it did not help that the then Minister for MEPRC, Paa Kwesi
Nduom, was not a member of the ruling party. This placing of a party-outsider
in control of a process that had significant fiscal and political implications added
another dimension to the coordination problem.

In April, 2002, the MoFEP, NDPC and several MDAs convened a meeting
to address the issue of institutional coordination. The meeting identified several
gaps in the national planning and budgeting process. These gaps included weak
linkage between the national strategic plans developed by the NDPC and the
sector strategic plans of MDAs; the lack of well-defined responsibilities for
NDPC and MoFEP with respect to the development of a macro-economic
framework and the formulation of policy guidelines for the MDAs; and the limited consultation with the NDPC by the MoFEP in the policy review and allocation of ceilings to the MDAs.

As a result of these meetings the NDPC began to assume a more active role
in training line ministries on the content of the PRSP and on improving the consistency between their strategic plans and the PRSP. However, the NDPC continues to play second fiddle in the budget preparation process. It is hardly involved in consultations leading up to the formulation of the macro-framework.
For instance, the macro framework of Ghana's second PRS was developed parallel to the formulation of the other components of the strategy. The NDPC's
input was largely restricted to setting broad national and sectoral growth targets.
Elements of the framework relating to the fiscal envelope were seemingly off-
limits to the NDPC.

This development raises the issue of whether the macro-framework can be
consistent with the targets and policy objectives stipulated in the PRS. Can the
resources projected in the macro-economic framework be consistent with the
PRS objectives? The obvious lesson from this experience is that institutions responsible for setting national priorities and those engaged in the budgeting process must coordinate their activities for the MTEF to be successful in realizing
the PRS targets. Ideally, the budgetary institution must coordinate its processes
with the planning institution if the system is to work smoothly.

In an apparent effort to address the institutional issues identified above, in 2003, the Ministry of Economic Planning was merged with the Ministry of Finance.[7] In reality this reconfiguration did not solve the underlying problem since the NDPC still leads the PRS process given its constitutional mandate. In effect, the need to improve harmonization and institutional synergies between the NDPC and the new Ministry of Finance and Economic Planning remains. Furthermore, the planning functions currently undertaken by the MoFEP need to be clearly defined and distinguished from the NDPC to mitigate the tendency towards turf wars over the planning process.

Issues of Prioritization

There are also indications that line ministries lack flexibility, within any given year, in re-allocating resources because of changing priorities arising out of funding and other shocks. The rigidities apply largely to allocations for services and investments.[8] This lack of flexibility somewhat undermines the MTEF process and compromises its effectiveness in achieving the PRS.

Slow Internalization of the MTEF

In reality, the process of ensuring that the PRS found expression in the budget was plagued by several weaknesses. Key among these was that the MTEF had not been adequately internalized by the line ministries. This was in part due to the complex nature of the framework and partly because the line Ministries rarely received the full promised allocations because the government consistently overstated the total resource envelope. As a result of government's consistent failure to deliver on its resource commitments, the MTEF process lost much credibility. This development invariably compromised the effectiveness of the budget as a vehicle for financing the programs and projects of the PRSP.

The Primacy of Sectoral Interests

Another dimension to the problem was largely political. The pre-eminence of the PRSP as the primary framework for both donor and domestic financing priorities, implied that line ministries with programs and projects which did not list high on PRS priorities would invariably receive low funding. As a result, several line ministries reflected PRS priorities in their strategic plans in a very superficial way. While some failed to reprioritize their strategic plans to reflect the emerging priorities of the PRS.

The constitutionally mandated planning institution——the National Development Planning Commission (NDPC)——was charged with the task of ensuring that the strategic plans of line Ministries did indeed conform to the dictates and spirit of Ghana's PRSP. However, it was constrained by the failure of several Ministries to submit copies of their revised strategic plans to the NDPC for review, and also by the NDPC's limited capacity to thoroughly examine such reports for consistency with the PRS.

Issues of Costing

In line with MTEF, the Government of Ghana moved the budget process from annual increments in funding to an explicit focus on costing of activities and policies. Prior to the MTEF, program funding proposals from the sector ministries tended to be merely incremental, with little connection to the actual costs of production and the changing input requirements of the MDAs. Furthermore, the estimates were usually inflated in the knowledge that MoFEP would always find an excuse to "cut the estimates" of any Ministry.[9]

Budget Classification and Integration

Budget expenditures in Ghana fall into two broad categories: overhead costs and variable costs. Overhead costs are made up of salaries and administrative costs associated with running an MDA. Variable costs include investment expenditures and expenditures for the provision of services.

Table 6.3 Expenditure by item: Ministry of Communications, 2000
(Millions of Cedis)

Item	GoG	Donor	Total
Overheads	**23,482.7**	**0**	**23,482.7**
Admin	19,439.0	0	19,439.0
Personnel	4,043.6	0	4,043.6
Objective	*To monitor, evaluate and provide feedback to Government on its Policies and Programs*		
Service	143.2	0	143.2
Investment	210.0	0	210.0
Sub-Total	**353.2**	**0**	**353.2**
Objective	*To provide staff development to facilitate increased efficiency in the Comm. Sector*		
Service	915.7	0	915.7
Investment	904.0	0	904.0
Sub-Total	**1819.7**	**0**	**1819.7**

Source: Ghana Statistical Service

In the strategic plans of line ministries an attempt is made to relate expenditures within these broad categories to the overall objectives of an MDA. However, currently this is only done for variable costs and not overhead costs. Thus, Ghana's MTEF does not reveal an explicit relationship between expenditures on overhead costs and the overall objectives of an MDA. This is due to methodological difficulties in attributing some components of these costs to specific objectives. For instance, it would be quite challenging, perhaps even unproductive, for a line Ministry to estimate the proportion of its electricity bill that is attributable to the realization of a specific activity or output. The situation is even more complex where outputs are generated from interrelated activities. However, it is relatively easier to attribute manpower wages to specific outputs simply by recording time spent by staff on different projects and programs. Yet, MDA strategic plans only relate variable costs (i.e., service and investment) directly to their objectives. It is expected that, eventually, salary overhead costs will be linked to the objectives of line Ministries. This would be an important step in assessing the manpower needs of MDAs. This information would be useful for institutions charged with the responsibility of reforming the public sector.

The expenditure breakdown by the Ministry of Communications is illustrative. Table 6.3 reveals that approximately ¢23.5bn was spent on overheads by the Ministry of Communications. Unlike service and investment activities, overhead costs are not disaggregated by objective. For instance, ¢353.2 million was spent on services and investment to monitor, evaluate and provide feedback to government on its policies and programs, while ¢1.82 billion was allocated for staff development. However, it is not obvious what proportion of the total overhead expenditure of ¢23.48 billion was used to evaluate and provide feedback to government on its policies and programs. Each of the four broad categories of expenditure has sub-categories reflecting the specific needs and objectives of an MDA. Thus, under each of the broad categories, MDAs are free to include additional sub-items in situations where they require inputs specific to their organization.

Table 6.3 also reveals that currently, MDAs only relate their activities to their overall objectives not to their outputs. As a result, it is not easy to assess the link between their activities and outputs, and in turn, how their outputs relate to their overall objectives. In the current MTEF framework, MDAs do not account at the output level – the level of accounting is at the objective level only. The implication is that line Ministries need not indicate how their outputs are linked to their objectives and in turn the larger objectives of the PRS. It would be necessary to engage in accounting at the output level in order to ensure that the activities of line ministries are linked to the PRS, and to appropriately monitor and account for activities and expenditures under the MTEF. However, there is a concern that accounting for detailed activities in a budget may be counterproductive. Thus, there is the need to strike a balance between providing adequate information and superfluous information. In order to monitor and account for poverty related activities and expenditures, line ministries must at the very minimum map their outputs to their objectives.

Linking the PRS to the budget in a meaningful way requires that priorities are appropriately reflected in the budget. Where there is the possibility of misrepresenting activities or outputs there is a tendency to pay lip service to the

notion of budgetary alignment. For instance, the "investment expenditure" category in Ghana does not distinguish productive investments from expenditures on
durable consumer items. For instance, the development implications of investments in televisions and refrigerators are quite different from investments in
irrigation, school buildings and bridges. While the nation could align its resources to the high priority area of agriculture by devoting resources to agricultural investment, the bulk of these funds may be used for the purchase of consumer durables such as air conditioners and refrigerators.

4. Conclusions and Lessons from Ghana's Experience

Poverty Reduction Strategies (PRSs) must find expression in the national budget
if they are to be implemented. Embedding PRSs in the national budget requires
that the costed activities, inputs and outputs are consistent with both the spirit
and letter of a nation's PRS. Where there is tension or a disconnect between the
priorities of line Ministries and the strategic objectives of PRSs, the line ministries costed items may not be "PRS compliant"; PRSs will in such cases remain
at the level of ideas, not actions and outputs with expected outcomes and impacts. Ghana's MTEF is experiencing severe operationalization problems which
have undermined confidence in the budgeting process. These problems are reflected in the challenges to the embedding of the poverty reduction strategy in
the budget. In several cases, the activities and programs of the strategy were
reflected in the MTEF in only a superficial way and overall the process has been
slow. The implication is that implementation of PRSs must take into account the
institutional and practical constraints associated with restructuring budgets to
reflect the new priorities of PRSs.

Notwithstanding the lapses, the MTEF process has yielded some notable
achievements including an increase in the coverage of donor funds in the
budget. Prior to the MTEF a substantial portion of donor funds were not captured in the budget. The initiative has also transformed MoFEP's role from specific control of line items to one of ensuring that MDAs allocate and use their
resources in line with their stated objective and priorities. To the extent that
these objectives are linked to the PRS, resource allocations will also be consistent with the PRS.

Furthermore, the MTEF has resulted in a greater integration of the development and recurrent budgets. Operationally, this was accomplished through the
merger of the Budget Division (responsible for the recurrent budget) and the
Investment Policy Analysis Division (responsible for the development budget).
The process has resulted in an increased emphasis on performance by MDAs
through the achievement of objectives and production of outputs. Concurrently,
the new initiative has facilitated the devolution of responsibility for budget
preparation and management to the cost center level. This has nurtured a partici-

patory approach to budgeting although much more needs to be done in this area to reflect the views of civil society. Overall, Ghana's experience with MTEF has generated the following useful lessons.

Budgeting and Planning Ministries must Collaborate

Ghana's experience reveals the importance of harmonizing national goals and objectives such as those embodied in the PRS with the objectives and policies of MDAs. To this end, institutions responsible for the formulation and articulation of national plans must work closely with the institution charged with budgetary allocations. Since MDAs view Finance ministries as their source of funds, they are more likely to align themselves to the Finance ministry than to the planning institutions in the event of deterioration in relations between the two key institutions.

Resource Envelope must be Credible

Furthermore, Ghana's experience shows that the failure of the macro-framework to provide realistic estimates of the resource envelope breeds frustration and undermines the credibility of the MTEF process. Since the MTEF essentially embodies the funded elements of PRSs, a failure of the MTEF is tantamount to a failure in the execution of the PRS. Hence, there is the need to maintain the MTEF's credibility, by ensuring that budgetary ceilings are realistic and that resource flows are predictable. Predictability encourages performance by MDAs and, with an effective performance management system, militates against complacency in budget execution.

Rushing Reforms may be Counterproductive

Sweeping reforms must be implemented gradually if they are to be effective. The rapid introduction of the MTEF process has compromised the quality of implementation, as reflected in the formulation of strategic plans. The key reason is that the technical complexity of the process requires that more time is needed for it to be internalized. In this regard, it was not unusual for MDAs to "appropriate" mission statements and objectives directly from training manuals even when they were irrelevant to their mandate. This places a greater burden on the Policy Review aspect of the MTEF process with respect to line ministries, where there may be difficulties internalizing the new thinking.

MTEF Needs Planners as well as Accountants

These developments highlight the importance of nurturing a cadre of planners in line ministries, to lead the strategic planning process. Accountants, normally in charge of the old budgeting process are not well suited to assume the role of planners required by the MTEF process.

Effective Monitoring is Imperative

Ghana's MTEF experience also highlights the importance of monitoring budgetary outcomes to ensure consistency in at least two levels: internal consistency
between MDA goals and objectives, activities, and outputs; and consistency
between MDA goals and the national goals in the PRS.

Weaknesses in the implementation of Ghana's MTEF must be addressed if
the country is to successfully implement its second growth and poverty reduction strategy. Will the goals and objectives of the Growth and Poverty Reduction
Strategy (GPRS II) be effectively captured in the MDA strategic plans and will
the activities and outputs of the MDAs have substantive or merely superficial
links with GPRS II?

Notes

1. Adopted in 1998, the MTEF is a three year rolling budget that attempts to link budgetary expenditures with national development goals and objectives.
2. PUFMARP was launched in July 1995 and officially initiated in May 1996.
3. In the case of Ghana they are: Administration, Infrastructure, Economic Services,
Social Services and Public Safety.
4. This exercise is done in close collaboration with the International Monetary Fund.
5. In reality the International Monetary Fund is heavily involved in the process.
6. Following the merger of the Ministry of Finance with the Ministry for Economic
Planning, the Ministry for Economic Planning and Regional Cooperation was renamed
the Ministry for NEPAD and Regional Cooperation.
7. As of 2005 he was the Minister for public sector reform.
8. Service refers to services such as extension, and other support activities provided by
the line ministry to generate its outputs. Investment comprises projects undertaken by line
ministries such as construction of schools and clinics. It also refers to the purchase of
consumer durables such as refrigerators and vehicles.
9. Originally, the intention was to restrict the introduction of the costing part of the
MTEF process to three pilot Ministries: Health, Education and Roads and Transport.
However, the response of the MDA's was presumably so enthusiastic that this component
was extended to all Ministries. Consequently, all ministries were trained to produce three
year estimates and all Ministries prepared their 1999 expenditure estimates in the MTEF
format.

References

Armah, Bartholomew. "Links Between the Budget and the GPRS." in *Implementation of
the Ghana Poverty Reduction Strategy: Annual Progress Report 2002,* May 2003.
———. The Medium Term Expenditure Framework: A Case Study of Ghana. *Legislative
Alert:* October 2001. *A Publication of The Institute of Economic Affairs (IEA).* 2001.
www.worldbank.org/wbi/attackingpoverty/activities/dakar-armah.pdf
———. "Ghana's 1999 Budget and the Vision 2020 Statement: Where's the Vision?"(IEA-Ghana; Legislative Alert, 1999.

Consulting Africa Ltd. Medium Term Expenditure Framework: Draft Handbook. Government of Ghana, Ministry of Finance PUFMARP. 1999.

Government of Ghana. Ghana Poverty Reduction Strategy Volume I. February 2003.

———. (2001). Budget Statement. 2001.

———. (2000) Budget Statement. 2000.

———. (1999) Budget Statement. 1999.

7

Towards an Architecture for the Delivery of International Development Assistance: The case of the GPRS

Joe Amoako-Tuffour

1. Introduction

What financing strategy should underpin a nation's poverty reduction strategy? There are three options: build on the strength of domestic revenue capacity; build on the basis of expenditures that will be needed to reach minimum social development targets but relying mostly on domestic financing; or build on the basis of expenditures that will be needed to reach some international development targets. The first option is a minimalist approach, but it's not likely to move poor economies forward appreciably especially when domestic revenue capacity is low. The second option expands the scope of poverty reduction, but runs the risk of debt expansion and inflationary financing if expenditure needs are to be met fully. Ghana's Poverty Reduction Strategy (GPRS) was built on the basis of the third option. The strategy set a subset of its development targets in line with the Millennium Development Goals (MDGs) which was set up to reduce global poverty by half by the year 2015.

It soon became apparent that the scope of spending that needed to achieve the desired targets far exceeded domestic non-inflationary finance. Even with the savings from debt relief, additional external financing will be vital if Ghana was to make progress towards achieving the benchmarks set by the MDGs. The Multi-Donor Budgetary Support (MDBS) was the financing arrangement between Ghana and its development partners (largely the World Bank and bilateral donors) to mobilize additional funding to support the implementation of the activities and programs outlined in the GPRS. The objectives and the rationale for direct pooled budget support, the background and the drivers of the shifting aid delivery, its potential benefits and risks, and the challenges form the content of this chapter.

A brief background to aid flows in Ghana and the major challenges are presented in section two. Section three traces the genesis of the development of the direct budget support as an aid delivery instrument, focusing on the institutional arrangements, the guiding principles, and the key elements that were used as levers of reform to accelerate the implementation of the GPRS. This is followed in section four by the results of a field survey of donors and government stakeholders as an assessment of the experience in Ghana. The lessons learned are summarized in section five.

2. Aid Flows to Ghana

Ghana has for long remained one of the aid community's favorite countries in the West African sub-region. Aid flows of any kind were relatively small until the mid 1960s.[1] The regime change following the overthrow of the first post colonial government in 1966 would change all that. Overseas development assistance (ODA) as percent of GDP increased from a miniscule 0.002 percent in 1960 to 0.036 percent in 1969. Aid flows declined in the early 1970s but rebounded in the second half of the 1970s as the geographical interest in Africa increased.

Beyond the historic and geopolitical considerations, Ghana in the late 1980s and early 1990s also benefited from its willingness to undertake needed reforms and structural adjustments. The pursuit of democratic governance in the nineties endeared Ghana to the aid community. Subsequently, a number of factors reinforced donors' enthusiasm. These include the successful transfer of power from one elected government to the other in 2000, the new government's commitment to the rule of law and democratic governance, the commitment to poverty reduction as well as the enthusiasm for improvements in corporate governance and private sector led-growth. These were reinforced by the search for peace and stability in West Africa and perhaps by the need to strengthen Ghana to provide the core of sub-regional stability.

Tables 7.1, 7.2 and Figure 7.1 capture Ghana's dependence on development assistance for both fiscal and balance of payment support. At the close of the 1990s, tax revenue hardly exceeded 60 percent of total budgetary expenditures. With a negative domestic savings-investment gap, Ghana historically has had to rely on other sources to support budget implementation. The persistent need for balance of payment support is apparent from Figure 7.1. After the economic slump of the late 1970s to the early 1980s, much of the current account deficit became necessary to restructure industry and to build new capacity. The year-to-year changes in external debt closely matched the trends in the current account deficit, especially beginning in the early 1980s. The cumulative current account deficit of $6.2 billion from 1984 to 2000 is matched by the increase in external

Table 7.1 Tax Indicators and Domestic Resource Gap

Tax Revenue as percent of	1981-1985	1986-1990	1991-1995	1996-2000
Total revenue	81.9	75.7	67.6	82.1
Domestic-Financed Expenditures	54.5	87.2	78.6	68.3
Total Expenditures	52.2	66.2	60.0	54.2
	1986-1995	1991-1995	1996-1998	
Percent of GDP				
Domestic savings	7.2	6.3	13.1	
Domestic Investment	13.1	14.6	20.3	
Savings-Investment gap	-5.9	-8.3	-7.2	

Data on domestic savings and domestic investment are taken from CEPA: Macroeconomic Review and Outlook, various issues

Table 7.2 Comparative Aid Dependency Ratios

	Ghana	Sub-Saharan Africa
Net aid as percent of gross national income	13	4
Net aid as percent of gross capital formation	52	23
Net aid as percent of imports	18	11
Net aid per capita ($)	32	20

Source: Evaluation of the Comprehensive Development Framework (CDF), World Bank, Ghana Case Study, Working Paper series, undated.

loans of $5.6 billion and the rise in other non-debt resource inflow of about $672 million (Amoako-Tuffour, 2001).

Ghana's foreign aid per capita (loans and grants) rose sharply from $18 in 1980 to a peak of $38 in 1998 before falling to $32 in 1999-2000 (Table 7.2). The sharp rise in the 1980s reflects the massive inflow of donor assistance in support of the economic and structural reforms which begun in 1983. Ghana's net aid as a ratio of gross national income of 13 percent is nine full points above the sub-Saharan average of 4 percent. The high dependency of public investment and imports on foreign aid reflects in the net aid to gross capital formation ratio of 52 percent and the net aid to imports ratio of 18 percent in FY 2000; both ratios are higher (the former considerably higher) than the sub-Saharan averages.

Traditionally, both multilateral and bilateral agencies have supported Ghana's development efforts through aid pledges, which historically has been volatile. For the period 1989 to 1998 pledges ranged between US$518 million to

US$1,095. Disbursements as percent of total pledges ranged between 29 percent and 81 percent, making dependence on development aid precarious. The impact of the shortfalls on the budget reflected mainly in the rise in domestic borrowing and in the decline in international reserves.

Figure 7.1   Growth of Real GDP, Current Account Balance, and Flow of External Resources

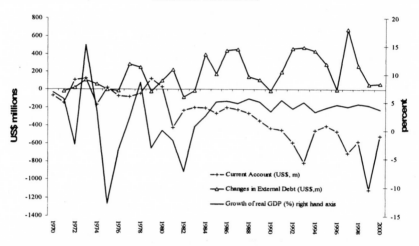

Source: *Ministry of Finance and Economic Planning, Ghana*

Historically aid flows have taken many forms, most commonly commodity aid, technical assistance, project, and program aid, and often as part of a broader package. Early aid flows to Ghana came largely in the form of loans and commodity aid; the latter mainly from the Eastern bloc countries because of the government's ideological leanings. Following the overthrow of the regime in 1966, aid flows in the late 1960s were allocated to clearing commercial credits, external debt arrears and for supporting balance of payments. Aid flows declined in the early 1970s and when aid rebounded in the second half of the 1970s, the development community had lost confidence in economic growth as the means to improving living conditions (Harrigan and Younger, 2000). As real GDP growth plummeted (Figure 7.1), the donor community began to shift emphasis towards more direct interventions by way of project aid in the hope to provide basic human needs. Aid also came more as loans than grants. Coming as it did at a time of economic decline in the late 1970s and early 1980s, Ghana's debt service arrears mounted and by 1983 Ghana's source of external assistance had dwindled to a small number of donors who concentrated largely on project aid and technical assistance.

In Figure 7.2 the decline in grants and program aid as percent of total aid in-flows coincided with the rise in project aid. The trend signaled the growth of uncoordinated donor activities and there was little attempt on the side of gov-ernment, line ministries, and development partners to relate donor activities with national development agenda. The 1999 study "Study of Aid Flows" by the then Ministry of Finance made the following observations. First, there was a shift beginning in 1990 in official multilateral and bilateral aid inflows from quickly disbursing program aid to project aid. Second, program aid fell sharply as a share of total aid—from 41 percent in 1989–1990 to 15 percent in 1996–1998. Third, the ratio of program aid to budget revenue declined dramatically from 37.5 percent in 1989–1990 to 10 percent in 1996–1998. And fourth, in most years since 1990, actual program aid disbursements fell below projections.

Figure 7.2 Program and Project Aid Disbursements

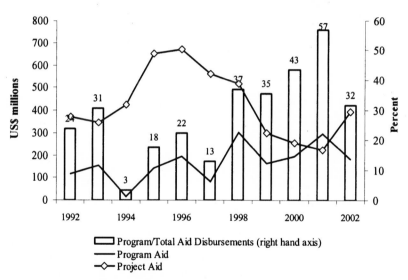

Source: *Ministry of Finance and Economic Planning*

The data in Figure 7.2 may understate the total project and program aid flows and therefore may not reflect total aid flows into government systems. This is likely to be the case if some aid flows escape budget capture. In fact, in both the monthly and annual reports of the Accountant General, the execution of foreign-financed projects is not captured whenever transactions are made out-side of the public accounts. When aid benefactors administer projects as "off-budget" items, when donors insist on transferring funds directly to non-central government agencies (and often through commercial banks), they inadvertently reinforce a vicious circle of weak government systems. They undermine public financial management and weaken the accountability of public institutions in the recipient country. Commenting on the 2002 Ghana Public Accounts, the Controller and Accountant-General remarked that it could not produce broad-based financial statements largely because the Ministries, Departments and Agencies (MDAs) that benefited from direct donor resources failed to provide adequate information of their accounts in breach of Article 187(3) of the 1992 Constitution of the Republic of Ghana.[2]

According to the 1999 study "Study of Aid Flows,"[3] the problem Ghana faced in the late 1980s and throughout the 1990s was the large number of uncoordinated donor projects and programs sitting in different boxes. In a survey conducted in May 2002 as part of the evaluation of Ghana's Comprehensive Development Framework (CDF), seven donors had a total of 131 projects (including non-project and programmatic assistance). Three major donors Japan, UK and USA- did not respond to the survey. The rate of expansion of project aid, the diversity of aid agencies, the increased complexity of donor operational policies and procedural requirements all made it difficult for government to keep pace with the demands for managing and coordinating the aid environment. The transaction costs associated with the preparation, negotiation, implementation and monitoring of agreements made it difficult for the government, with its thin management capacity, to keep pace with the requirements for effective coordination.

The 1999 study further echoed the 1993 Public Expenditure Review's observations about the preponderance of matching fund projects.[4] The latter accounted for about a third of Ghana's development budget in 1999. As of March 2003, there were 131 known project loans and conditional grants outstanding (supported by 27 development partners and agencies) of which 77 percent were identified as matching funds projects.[5] The major drawbacks include (a) the precondition of blocking matching funds for specific project without regard to the timing of domestic revenue inflows, (b) the excessive levels of matching funds requirements as a percent of project cost, and (c) the limited information sharing between government and donors on grant-aided projects. In most instances, bilateral donors often operate as if government officials have little "right" to full disclosure of project information because of their grant-aided nature. Typically, these projects are negotiated at the sector level. They are often inadequately budgeted for because the implementing ministries may not always assess the availability of funds and the implications of the project for overall budgetary outcomes.[6]

3. The Evolution of Multi Donor Budgetary Support

As part of the search for common efforts to accelerate the implementation of the Ghana Poverty Reduction Strategy (GPRS), the Government of Ghana (GoG) and its development partners (DPs) convened a consultative group meeting in April 2002 in Accra. There was concurrence that the resources Ghana needed to implement its poverty reduction strategy and to reach the Millennium Development Goals was extraordinarily high.[7]

Despite the structural transformation of the economy which begun in the mid-1980s, domestic revenue had leveled off somewhat in the late 1990s. Moreover, the new government that came into office in 2001 inherited a destabilized economy and at the heart of it were fiscal slippages.[8] There was an urgent need to boost domestic revenues if there should be any chance of deepening public expenditures in poverty related areas without igniting inflationary pressures. Also needed were general improvements in public financial management. Interestingly enough, both the needed revenue boost and the expenditure measures, especially the institutional re-building, were themselves part of the GPRS process and needed to be funded. Additional development assistance over debt relief savings therefore became essential to the immediate implementation of the GPRS.

To a large extent the major DPs, who had worked with the previous government, had a better sense of the challenges ahead on both the revenue mobilization and expenditure management fronts. They were all too aware that the lack of improvements in public financial management could derail the effective implementation of the GPRS no matter how much debt relief may be forthcoming. The lessons of reforms in the 1980s had been learnt. Most notably, that it is not sufficient to have a democratically elected government, necessary as it is. It is also important to ensure that the policy environment is sound, that the broad processes of policymaking works, and that government's systems are transparent and accountable.

3.1 Risks and Benefits of Direct Budget Support

Direct Budget Support (DBS) is a form of program aid in which funds are provided by donors to recipients in support of government expenditure plans. Once transferred these funds become part of the consolidated funds and subject to the same financial management and accountability systems of the recipient government.

Like any other activity in which different agents must apply imperfect judgments and limited knowledge to a changeable and unpredictable environment, development partnership dialogue is an uncertain art. Principles of good practices and management must co-exist uneasily with trust, balancing potential gains and risks. Donors perhaps were more aware of the risks than the government did. From donors' perspective the risks include the commitment of government to budget implementation, the fungibility of the funds made available to government, and the extent to which donors can achieve consensus on the key elements of budget support.

The April 2002 meeting was preceded by the Government of Ghana's request to Denmark to provide budget support to Ghana in order to deal with the inherited financial pressures on the economy. A Danish mission in May 2001 was charged with (a) developing important criteria that will guide possible future budget support; (b) identifying the conditions that should be in place before determining the appropriateness of budget support; (c) making preliminary recommendation as to the scope, size, disbursement mechanism, timing of a potential budget support, and whether the support should be general or sector specific; and (d) identifying the performance indicators that should be monitored as trigger devices for budget support disbursement.

In addition to making recommendations to these specific terms of the mission, the mission pointed out the potential uses of budget support, how to maximize the potential impact, and how to mitigate the risks. Perhaps most telling was the conclusion that "the potential impact would be higher if like-minded donors teamed up using the same type of budget support and the same sort of indicators and conditionalities."[9]

The Danish report identified several key issues to be taken into account and hinted at others that were likely to emerge in putting together a multi-player budget support. Pertinent concerns included the appropriateness of the policy environment, the potential disincentive effects, the moral hazard behavior of the government, the risks of fungibility, the use of essential and potential indicators that might serve as disbursement triggers, how to balance general budget support and sectoral support without undermining government systems, and the potential coordination problems among donors. The report recognized in particular the need for harmonization of disbursement triggers if bilateral donors are not to be seen as operating at cross purposes and, perhaps, more crucial, if bilateral donors' trigger values are not to be seen as "softer" or "harder" than those of the IMF under the Poverty Reduction Growth Facility (PRGF).[10]

With respect to both multilateral and bilateral donors, there were precedents to active budget support in Ghana: on grants basis, the Netherlands, the United Kingdom, the European Union and Denmark, and on loan basis the World Bank, African Development Bank and the IMF. These have had mixed outcomes and the lessons learnt would inform future initiatives. These included general policy shortfalls that required waivers, reporting and accountability shortfalls by sectors, shortfalls in release of matching funds, high administrative and transactions costs, delays in donor disbursement, and the risks of donor competition and rivalries.

The Danish report also identified three conditions that needed to be "in place" before general budget support can be initiated. These are (a) the macroeconomic framework, the overall policy-making environment and the capacity to conduct macroeconomic policy; (b) the public budget, including its breakdown into sectors and sub-sectors and the capacity to use resources efficiently; and (c) the capacity within financial management to account for the use of resources. The first condition was within the scope of the PRGF, and therefore bilateral funding was technically linked to a satisfactory assessment by the IMF. The MDBS focused on the latter two conditions. While there had been notable shortfalls in all these areas, especially in public financial management, direct budget support was seen as providing an avenue for high level policy dialogue that can focus attention on and, in discrete steps, accelerate desired improvements in government systems in a consistent fashion. By having the opportunity to engage in close and frank dialogue with government, donors could learn more about the institutions and the political economy of the policy-making environment of the new partner government.

The opportunity that DBS provides in policy dialogue is an important avenue in encouraging gradual improvements in government systems, building institutional capacity and strengthening the efforts and commitment of people and government to their own progress. Gradualism and open dialogue also provide the opportunity to encourage buy-in by line ministries and departments. Their managers and front-line civil servants must be brought closer to any reform process if only because they must adopt, implement and sustain desired innovations in government systems.

With direct budget support, general or sector specific, donors may also see themselves on a personal level with citizens of the receiving country who also contribute resources through taxes into a common pool to finance development. Donors in a sense become "voluntary taxpayers" into the recipient country's consolidated funds, yet cohesive enough to use their 'tax' contribution to leverage for policy changes. There are other advantages even if of less strategic importance. Ideally, DBS should enable substantial savings in administrative and transactions costs of aid delivery if donors are willing to collapse their parallel and separate systems of project management and project implementation units into government systems.

What about the recipient country government? In principle, with the commitment to donor harmonization, direct budget support should reduce the proliferation of donor conditionalities, the multiplicity of appraisals and reviews, the unpredictability of donor funding, and the time inconsistency between donor and government budget cycles. With multi-year pledges, government gains the assurance to carry out multi-year budgeting as envisaged under a medium-term expenditure framework.

Equally noteworthy, once the donors had accepted the GPRS as the plan to work towards and the commitment to direct budget support as the specific form of disbursement, it should make it easier for government's own internal coordination of line ministries, departments and agencies (MDAs) in the management of donor funds. If it works, sector wide approaches and basket funding should gradually be folded into direct budget support. MDAs should have no separate dealings with individual or group of donors. All of them should interact through the joint process and obtain their funding through normal government system of budgeting. It is interesting to note that on the government side there was concurrence that the potential benefits, (including simplicity, predictability, higher flexibility in the use of funds, better coordination, the potential for higher quality cooperation between donors and government, and the certainty of support) far outweighed the potential risks of coercive, collusive behavior of donors that can lead to an "all or nothing" outcome.

3.2 The Framework Memorandum

For direct budget support to work the recipient government must develop a common policy framework that will serve as a reference point for the development dialogue. In this instance, the Ghana Poverty Reduction Strategy would become an important driver of policy direction. Here there were four key assumptions.[11] First, that the GPRS articulate a coherent set of policy objectives, programs and activities that would guide economic policy-making to accelerate growth and poverty alleviation in the medium-term. Second, that the GPRS identify the key areas of policy focus and the priority setting process. Third, that the central government budget would be the main tool to reach the GPRS objectives, to tackle the priority sectors, and to implement all programs and activities as defined in the GPRS. And finally that the priority sectors –education, health and agriculture- towards poverty alleviation would be protected in the budget in the event of adverse fiscal shocks. Although donors did not accept the GPRS in its entirety, they individually and collectively accepted to support implementation, especially of the poverty-reducing and governance components.

The second condition is the willingness of donors to harmonize aid delivery policies and procedures, appraisals and reviews and accountability rules. On this there were two important considerations. First, there are donor country specific legal restrictions on whether development assistance can be directed into budgetary support. These restrictions often cover procedures for disbursing funds, country-specific conditions for development cooperation, and accountability rules to governments, parliament and audit agencies. It is for this reason that the U.S. withdrew and Japan did not participate because both preferred their own frameworks for donor assistance, largely in the form of technical assistance and project aid. Second, for donors who can deliver aid through DBS, the issues turn on the country-specific administrative and statutory provisions as defined in their bilateral agreements. More often, the nature of cooperation among DPs in the field depends on the operational procedures and regulations of each donor. These considerations determine the scope of harmonization.

The next challenges turn on how much can be harmonized and harmonized around what? Harmonization in this instance was sought in the following key areas: common funding commitment procedures, common disbursements mechanism, common missions and policy dialogue, common reporting requirements and the set of policy reform measures or triggers that would be used to assess progress of GPRS implementation. And to be effective, all these would be harmonized around the government's budget cycle.

While the FM was to be supplemented by bilateral agreements, it was understood in principle that individual DPs would not set up parallel processes and procedures that would impose additional reporting burden on the government. It was agreed that should the quality of regular information flow prove unsatisfactory, both parties would establish by discussion a timeframe and the possible support that DPs could offer to build the capacity needed to provide this information. To the extent that DPs agreed to work towards the goal of harmonization of procedures, assessment missions, disbursements and review missions, it would be done to "the extent possible and consistent with their internal laws, policies, procedures and individual bilateral agreements with the Government." It was understood that the key processes of the FM would be included in individual bilateral funding arrangements to the maximum extent possible and any general conditions differing from the FM processes should be kept to the minimum.

The FM also delineated three over-arching requirements for the government; namely, (a) maintaining an appropriate macro-economic framework usually within the context of a Poverty Reduction and Growth Facility (PRGF) arrangement with the International Monetary Fund; (b) developing an appropriate monitoring and evaluation system which will be used to assess progress and to provide feedback for the further strengthening of the strategy; and (c) ensuring that progress is made in reforms represented in the progress assessment framework as mutually established from year to year. Noteworthy, the FM also provided for (1) clauses against corruption in order to ensure transparency, accountability and probity in the use of public resources; (2) for conflict resolution mechanisms;[12] (3) for modalities of dialogue and reporting mechanisms from both government and DPs. To some observers, the FM was a detailed and perhaps ambitious principle of partnership.

Performance Indicators

On the premise that DBS will be based on ex post performance measures, a key principle is that government and DPs agree on performance indicators that form the basis of disbursements. They must agree on the formula for disbursement and the mechanisms for disbursement. In Ghana, the latter were spelt out in the Framework Agreement. Disbursement was to be made in two equal transfers. The base disbursement in the first quarter is determined by a positive outcome of the annual IMF/PRGF review in the previous year. The performance disbursement is based on satisfactory assessment of achievement of prior indicators jointly chosen by government and donors and, on the government side, jointly agreed to by the implementing Ministries, Department and Agencies (MDAs).

Table 7.3   Budget Support Performance Indicators: 2003

Objective	Trigger

1. Overall Objective: Improve Financial Management

BPEMS implemented in all ministries	1 A computer based financial management information system operational on a pilot basis.
Improved quality and usefulness of financial reports produced by CAGD	2. Monthly financial reports (commitments and expenditures) produced, reconciled with the BoG within 8 weeks.
Transparency and value for money in public expenditure	3. Procurement Bill laid before Parliament

2. Translation of the GPRS into the Budget

Total budget is consistent with the expenditure priorities outlined in the GPRS.	4. Shift from 2002 to 2003 discretionary budget broad sector allocations is consistent with the GPRS
	5. Budgeted Poverty Reduction Expenditure of GoG (including HIPC) increases over the 21.7 percent of the total Government Expenditure in 2002.
Regular M&E of GPRS implementation	6. Annual Review of the GPRS implementation conducted by MEPRC.

3. Public Sector Reform

Efficiency and service delivery of civil service improved.	7. Census of public sector employees completed.
	8. Independent Review of Public Sector Reform considered by the steering committee
	9. Develop policy to encourage deployment of teachers and health workers to remote and rural areas.

4. Decentralization

Establishment of a decentralization policy framework to improve service delivery.	10. Local Government Service Bill laid before Parliament

5. Governance

Improved transparency and accountability	11. Freedom of information Bill submitted to Cabinet by Attorney General
Improved operational efficiency of key institutions dealing with governance and corruption	12. Real increase in the GoG budget allocation to good governance statutory bodies (for example, CHRAJ, Audit Service, Electoral Commission, Office of Parliament and the Media Commission

Notes: (1) Table is derived from the maiden policy matrix of the 2002/2003 Framework Memorandum. (2) MoFEP = Ministry of Finance and Economic Planning, CAGD = Controller and Accountant General Department, GoG = Government of Ghana, BoG = Bank of Ghana

The performance indicators are of three types: input, output, or process indicators. In other words the indicators may represent a set of actions, activities or measures that are spelt out as inputs to a policy implementation, as steps to have been taken, as measures of progress, or as expected outcomes. Performance indicators thus may be a set of qualitative verifiable stages in the process of reform or quantitative measures of input or outcome. Where donors want to support the autonomous efforts of partner governments, the performance indicators may consist of very limited set of measures which have very high likelihood of being met or are achievable.

Table 7.3 summarizes the maiden performance indicators. The indicators were the outcome of joint consultations and emanated directly from the five key elements of the GPRS; namely, public finance management, linking the GPRS to the budget, public sector reform, decentralization and governance. In this instance, the performance matrix focused on the "baby steps" necessary for the successful implementation of the GPRS.

Rearranged, the specific twelve indicators (Table 7.3) fall into three *input triggers* (4, 5 and 12), seven *process triggers* (1 - 3, 8 - 11) and two *outcome triggers* (6, 7). They were about taking steps to lay the legislative framework, shifting aggregate spending, and developing strategies in each of the areas of crucial central reforms. They focused on processes of institutional development, budget execution, accuracy and timely financial reporting, improved transparency and accountability in government system. The poverty leverage was sought through a number of channels by focusing on the translation of the GPRS into the budget, on budget design, on the allocation of discretionary budget, on monitoring poverty outcomes, and to ensure that the steps to improve the delivery of public services at the decentralized local level are being taken.

4. Survey Findings

A way to measure success is whether the direct budget support is achieving the positives which are the basis for its dominance over other forms of aid delivery. The following survey of perception is only half the story. The survey was conducted by the author in June-July 2004, the second year of implementation of direct budget support. On the government side, the respondents were the line ministries, departments and agencies (MDAs). The response rate was higher among the more active participating institutions. On the donor side the survey covered all development partners with about a third responding.

Preferences for aid delivery mechanisms differed between donors and government sector respondents (Figure 7.3). On the government's side, DBS was most preferred and commodity aid, specifically food aid, the least preferred.

Figure 7.3   Preferences for Aid Delivery

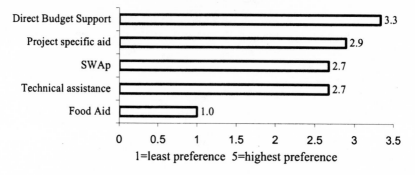

Preference for form of Aid Delivery (Ministries, Department and Agencies)

1=least preference 5=highest preference

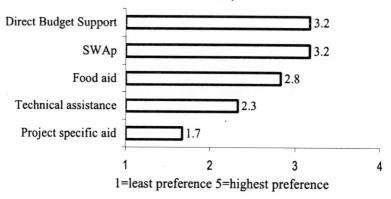

Preference for form of Aid Delivery (Development Parteners)

1=least preference 5=highest preference

Source: Survey Data.

Project specific aid ranked second while sector wide approach (SWAp) and technical assistance ranked above food aid. The DPs ranked DBS, SWAp, food aid, technical assistance, and stand-alone project aid in descending order of preferences. That DPs least preferred stand-alone project aid is not surprising since the survey response was highest among the donors already participating in the DBS arrangement.

Noteworthy, the MDAs preferred stand-alone project aid to SWAp and technical assistance. Although stand-alone project aid is administratively cumbersome with high transaction costs, it does offer greater overhead benefits directly to the implementing ministry or agency than SWAps. The benefits from the latter tend to spread across different sector institutions, and therefore there is less control by any single one of them. Hence, there is a hidden yet powerful resistance to integrating projects into ministries' overall program of action to be funded through normal government system. In a weak aid coordination environment, civil servants, acting alone or in conjunction with sector ministers, believe that they can maximize their budget by seeking out projects on bilateral basis with donors. The potential benefits from such project arrangements include overhead and administrative expenses and the top-up allowances to the project implementing and monitoring units. MDAs are prone to accepting offers of project aid even when such are driven by donors' priorities rather than those of country government's.

Overall level of satisfaction of the direct budget support arrangement was ranked as good to excellent by 63 percent of respondents. The top panel of Figure 7.4 suggests that the overall conditions for harmonization, the readiness of donors to coordinate their development activities, the transparency of rules and the quality of policy formulation were ranked as above average to satisfactory by donors. From the middle panel, DPs' efforts at harmonization were judged as good to very good. The concerns about donors' intrusiveness in policy making are apparent in the bottom panel. At the same time, nearly 75 percent of respondents rated government negotiating stance as reasonably good, strong or very strong, reflecting in part the improvements in internal coordination among the MDAs in the development dialogue. For the responding MDAs, 71 percent were concerned that DBS has the potential to make the recipient country more aid dependent. About 14 percent thought that direct budget support made Ghana no more or less dependent than it has always been.

Also noteworthy, nearly half of the responding MDAs were not satisfied with how the performance indicators were developed. Some suggested that the indicators were selected to impress donors. Truth, however, is that the first policy matrix was developed with high achievability in mind and also to facilitate learning in the making of the new aid delivery mechanism. With the symmetry of interest between DPs and government, DPs must have felt that as long as the indicators were in line with the implementation of the poverty reduction strategy, and with proper monitoring and evaluation, the "baby steps" should provide useful feedback for the next steps. The selection of the performance indicators also recognized that it is better to pursue incremental policy leveraging, hoping to make modest adjustments to the indicators, on year-by-year basis, as donors' comfort level with, and understanding of, government systems increase. Certainly, the performance indicators must move gradually away from input and processes triggers to more activity-based processes and outputs, which reflect medium-term strategic policy outcomes with well-defined trends against which progress could be measured.

Figure 7.4 Rating of the Policy Environment and Harmonization Efforts

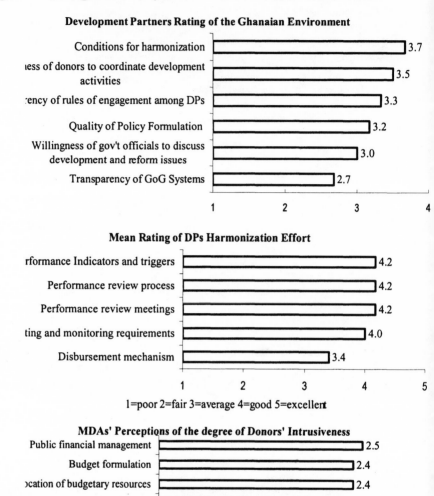

Development Partners Rating of the Ghanaian Environment

Source: Survey data

Nearly three in four of the MDAs noted that donor-led aid coordination may become stronger partly because of the high level engagement in policy-making. DPs had become more active in discussions in public financial management, budget formulation, and in the allocation of budgetary resources. They acknowledged progress in harmonization, especially in the areas of setting performance indicators, common review missions, and in reporting and monitoring mechanisms. The result was a decrease in the amount of paperwork prepared for, and the time spent in meetings with, DPs. However, other activities such as procedural requirements and the number of sector projects remained nearly the same. Perhaps, this should be expected in the transition stage of the aid delivery arrangements.

Nearly all respondents acknowledged the increased participation of DPs and MDAs in development dialogue and the general improvement in the quality of the dialogue. There was a noticeable shift away from the more political and diplomatic level of dialogue that takes place in the Mini-Consultative Group setting to the more technical and development oriented dialogue which provides greater room for policy path experimentation. Since DBS provides for open dialogue, all donors benefited equally from the information flow, including those who made no clear commitment to budget support because they preferred bilateral project aid approaches.

Table 7.4 Expenditures, Taxation and Budget Support

	2000	2001	2002	2003*	2004	2005
Expenditures (¢, bn)	9,916	13,570	15,447	21,997	28,739	34,227
Grants/Expenditures (%)	15.85	19.35	9.86	14.17	17.19	15.64
Grants/ GDP (%)	5.78	6.9	3.19	4.77	6.19	5.51
Tax/ GDP (%)	16.3	17.2	17.9	20.2	21.7	22.1
Tax/Expenditures (%)	51.7	52.7	55.3	60.8	62.2	67.7
Poverty Related Exp/GDP (%)		4.5	4.8	6.8	8	8

Source: Government of Ghana Budget Statements.

* *Direct budget support commenced in 2003. Grants are defined as budget support plus debt relief assistance (or HIPC Assistance). Poverty related expenditures include spending on education, health, sanitation and expenditures to improve water and electricity access.*

Has direct budget support delivered where it counts? While many respondents did not believe that there will be a substantial increase in aid as a result of direct budget support arrangement, they shared the view that it may enhance aid effectiveness. In 2002, a year before DBS was formally introduced, less than half of planned budget support was disbursed. Disbursements rose to 90 percent of the planned amount in 2003, and about 100 percent in 2004. It is debatable whether the drop in aid disbursement in 2002 was in anticipation of the onset of the direct budget support arrangement in 2003. When we see in Table 7.4 an average grants/GDP ratio of 5.5 between 2003 and 2005, (with GDP growth also averaging about 5.5 percent between 2002 and 2005) it must be the case that budget support and debt relief assistance must be growing by as much as GDP.

Will direct budget support encourage governments to postpone reforms needed to mobilize domestic resources for development? Evidence from Table 7.4 suggests that this was not the case. Increased external resource mobilization through program support did not diminish the domestic tax effort. Legislative improvements, increased capacity of revenue agencies, increased efficiency of revenue administration and diminished political interference in tax administration were key contributory factors.

Figure 7. 5 Assessment of Direct Budget Support in Specific Policy Areas

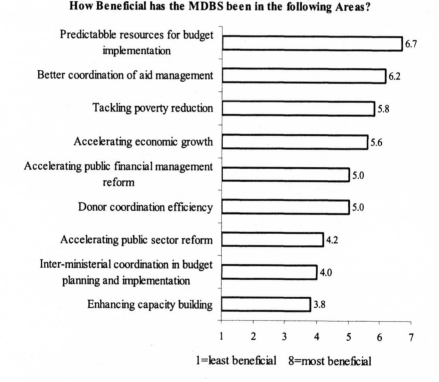

How Beneficial has the MDBS been in the following Areas?

1=least beneficial   8=most beneficial

Figure 7.5 summarizes the mean ratings of the impact the new aid delivery arrangement may have had on key activities and policy areas from the point of view of government respondents. In their assessment, the process has contributed to greater predictability of resource inflow for budget implementation, enhanced growth prospects, accelerated public financial management reform and improved efficiency in donor coordination. The effect on public sector reform, inter-ministerial coordination, budget planning and capacity building, however, were ranked to have been minimally beneficial.

While acknowledging progress in public financial management and budget implementation, DPs noted a number of challenges. These include the slow progress in overall public sector reform and to a lesser extent public financial management. Second is the reluctance of MDAs in rejecting project assistance and their slow response to embracing the DBS approach. Key MDAs were noted not to have incorporated all the relevant triggers and targets in policy making and implementation into their program of action. Sectors such as roads, water, energy, agriculture and natural resources may have found it challenging to engage in the DBS process. According to Walters (2005) this partly reflects the reliance of these ministries on donor financing systems, procurement systems, and project management units that historically divert the ministries' attention away from any meaningful engagement with the national budget process.

On the donors' side, there are new challenges. Can DBS capture the divergent interest of donors? And how far are donors willing and able to harmonize. By 2005, fault lines had begun to emerge. First, there were problems with alignment of priorities, with procedures and with the setting of disbursement triggers. The fact that individual donors had recourse to bilateral agreements meant that harmonization was constrained by individual donor policies and procedures some of which could not be brought to the table. DBS may reduce the number of appraisals and review missions, but it may not necessarily reduce the number of individual projects and accountability rules. Different donors were constrained by their responsibilities to account for public expenditures to their government, parliament and audit agencies differently.

Second, in the design of the policy matrix, it was evident that different donors put different emphasis on what should be included as triggers and in what form the trigger should be. The degree of donor flexibility varied, being more flexible for bilateral donors than for the dominant donor, the World Bank. As the dominant partner, the Bank's Poverty Reduction Support Credit (PRSC) invariably will dominate the set of disbursement triggers. In that sense little may have changed as far as the Bank's program is concerned. The Bank's limited flexibility in partnership dialogue reflects in part the limited degree of local decision-making autonomy. Third, the consensus building approach of DBS often means more negotiations. This has its downside. It has meant making fewer decisions on which there is a consensus. One respondent acknowledged that "the time spent in discussions amongst donors has sharpened the focus of donors' contributions to policy dialogue and has raised the game of individual participants". It has also served to reduce the data requests and clarifications that used to be directed towards government often at the inappropriate level.

Fourth, there is also the problem of the assignment of responsibility among donors with respect to who takes the lead role in the different aspects of the

DBS process. Differences in the technical capacity of the resident staff of the different DPs partly account for this. Donor countries with low level decision-making authority on he ground are more likely to become the silent partners in the dialogue. They are also less flexible in their perspectives on how things ought to be done. It is reasonable to assume that these are all part of the teething problems in a new paradigm of aid delivery.

Finally, the first review mission on budget support brought out some important lessons. First, ex ante, performance indicators must be clearly defined, easily verifiable and or measurable. Improperly defined indicators may prove consequential in the review stage. For example, exactly what was meant by "operational on pilot basis" (Table 7.3, trigger #1) was given different interpretations between government and donors and among donors in the performance review stage. Loosely specified disbursement triggers have the merits of simplicity and flexibility, but are hardly risk free. Controversy is more likely to be the case if there is a high turnover of donor staff between the period when the performance matrix is developed and agreed to and when the review or assessment mission occurs. Second, where there is a process indicator, the administrative steps to carrying out a particular course of action must be clearly spelt out ex ante and well understood by both parties. This clarity hinges on an understanding of government systems. Sometimes, it may be worthwhile making intermediary steps as achievable benchmarks. Third, develop clear, simple and mutually acceptable disbursement rules in advance of performance review missions.

5. Conclusions

Against the background of a fiscally weak economy, increasing incidence of poverty, and the problems of aid coordination in the past, direct budget support is meant to improve the domestic ownership of donor support funds and higher flexibility in the use of funds. Ghana's limited experience in developing direct budget support program is instructive. A country's own development strategy must be in place to form the common basis of dialogue. That strategy must be the key driver of policy direction, sectoral reform, poverty reduction and spatial allocation of resources.

Donors' willingness to harmonize their common procedures for disbursements, monitoring and reporting, review missions and willingness to rely on government systems are essential catalyst to the direct budget support program. On the donors' side, the challenges are how to reconcile the divergent interest of donors, and how far are donors willing and able to harmonize preferences, reporting and disbursement procedures in a single framework? There is also the challenge as to how best to design the disbursement package in ways that encourage the process of development, and increase the incentives for government's domestic revenue mobilization effort and effective institutional building.

For the recipient country the challenges are in how to improve inter-ministerial coordination.

Finally, will budget support create perverse incentives for recipients to mobilize domestic resources or to make public sector more efficient? Although by all indications tax effort has not waned in Ghana since 2001, there is no reason to believe that governments may not relent in their efforts to marshal resources for development outside of aid. Obviously a key tool to minimizing these moral hazards is to impose conditionalities and triggers, too many of which can readily compromise ownership and the flexibility in the use budgetary funds.

Direct budget support must be terminal. It must be scaled down in phases while still encouraging recipient government to marshal domestic resources for development. We must recognize, however, that not all aid recipients (example, Mali, Burkina Faso) have the capacity to generate internal resources because of the general lack of revenue capacity. For these countries, direct budget support may concentrate on encouraging institutional building to increase the efficiency of the resources made available to them. Increased efficiency in budgeting, in the allocation of, and accountability for, financial resources may progressively translate into more cost effective measures to improve living standards.

Notes

1. The early history of aid flows draws from Harrigan and Younger (2000).
2. Report of the Auditor-General on the Public Accounts of Ghana, 2002
3. Prepared by the Ministry of Finance and Bank of Ghana.
4. Matching funds represent the contribution that central government (or other local agencies) makes to the financing of donor-assisted projects or programs.
5. J. Amoako-Tuffour and D. Twerefou, "Matching Fund Conditionality and the Implication for Budgeting and Budgeting Outcomes." A Study conducted at the Ministry of Finance and Economic Planning, May 2003.
6. Where MDAs were unable to fulfill the terms of the contract and the grants are withdrawn, the transaction cost in terms of time, money and effort spent by the representatives of the MDAs and donor countries in discussing, negotiating and finalizing the terms and conditions of the project assistance are wasted. Also, pulling out of a donor counterpart project sends wrong signals to other DPs that may want to extend similar assistance.
7. Initial estimates put the total resource requirements at about U.S.$8 billion (or an average of U.S. $2.7 billion for each of the 3 years, 2002—2005). This provoked debate and prompted a re-working, a re-prioritizing and re-costing of the GPRS down to U.S. $5.2 billion. Even after re-costing the poverty reduction strategy, it was acknowledged that the revenue needs will be substantial if Ghana is to successfully implement its poverty alleviation program..
8. "Overview: State of the Ghanaian Economy 2002-2003," *Ghana: Selected Economic Issues*, No.6, Centre for Policy Analysis, 2003.
9. DANIDA Report on Budget Support, May 2001 p. 37.

10. DANIDA, May 2001 pp. 35-36.

11. The framework memorandum was accepted by the Government of Ghana and Development Partners and became operational in June 2003.

12. Conflicts are to be settled by means of dialogue and consultation. The government and partners will promptly consult with the other participants whenever a partner proposes to suspend or terminate, in whole or in part, support to the GPRS. If a partner invokes remedial measures or if support is no longer available, the government will promptly review and make necessary revisions to the program, in consultation with the other partners, to ensure that the expenditure framework corresponds with the available resource envelope.

References

Adam C. S. and Gunning J. W. "Redesigning the Aid Contract: Donors' use of Performance Indicators in Uganda." *World Development*. 30(12) (2002): 2045—2056.

Akatwijuka M. H. "Coordination Failures in Foreign Aid." *The World Economy*, 1-49. and background Paper for World Development Report 2004.

Amoako. K. Y. "Making Aid Work Better for Africa." Statement made to Houses of Parliament, London, United Kingdom, 13 February 2005.

Amoako-Tuffour, J. "The Growth of Public Debt in a Reforming Economy," Pp. 41—76 in Kwadwo Konadu-Agyeman (ed.) *IMF and World Bank Sponsored Structural Adjustment Programs in Africa*, Ashgate, 2001.

———— and D. Twerefour. "Matching Fund Conditionality and the Implications for Budgeting and Budgeting Outcomes." *CG/MDBS Secretariat and Ministry of Finance and Economic Planning*, Accra. 2003.

Aryeetey, E. J. Harrigan and M. Nissanke. *Economic Reforms in Ghana: The Miracle and the Mirage*. Accra: Woeli. 2002.

Burnside, C. and Dollar D. "Aid, Policies and Growth." *American Economic Review*, 90(4) (2000): 847—68.

Cordella, T. and Ulk, H. "Grants Versus Loans" International Monetary Fund Paper. WP/04/61.

Devarajan, S. and V. Swaroop, "The Implications of Foreign Aid Fungibility for Development Assistance." Pp. 196—209 in *World Bank: Structure and Policies* Cambridge University Press 2000.

Easterly, W., Levine R., and Roodman, D. "New Data, New Doubts: A Comment on Burnside and Dollar's Aid, Policies and Growth." (2000).

Elbadawi, I. and A. Gelb "Towards Africa's Development: Towards a Business Plan?" Paper for Africa Economic Policy seminar, Dar Es Salaam, February 2003.

Government of the Republic of Ghana. *Ghana Poverty Reduction Strategy: 2003—2005. An Agenda for Growth and Prosperity*, Volume 1. February 2003.

Harrigan, J. and S. Younger. "Aid, Debt and Growth" Pp. 185-208 in Aryeetey, Harrigan and Nissanke (eds.). 2000.

Kosack, S. "Effective Aid: How Democracy Allows Development Aid to Improve the Quality of Life." *World Development* ,31(1) (2004): 1—22.

Morrissey, O. 2004. "Conditionality and Aid Effectiveness Re-evaluated." *The World Economy*, 27(2): 153—171.

Mosley, P., Harrigan, J. and Taye J. *Aid, Power: the World Bank and Policy-based Lending*. London, Routledge, 1991.

Odedokun, M. "Multilateral and Bilateral Loans versus Grants: Issues and Evidence." *The World Economy*. Feb. 27(2) (2004):239–263.

Walters, P. "Multi-Donor Budget support and Capacity Development: Emerging lessons from Ghana", The LENPA forum Case Study, April 2005.

World Bank. *Evaluation of the Comprehensive Development Framework: Ghana Case Study*. April–May 2002.

———. *Implementation Completion Report: Republic of Ghana for a Public Sector Management*. 2004

UNECA. Our Common Interest, Report of the Commission for Africa, Commission for Africa, 2005.

8

Monitoring Poverty Reduction Strategies

Bartholomew Armah

1. Introduction

A major drawback to project and program implementation in developing countries is the low priority placed on monitoring. Notable exceptions are projects conceived and administered by donor partners. Although the last half decade has seen improvements in expenditure monitoring due to concerted efforts by governments to maintain fiscal discipline, most of these initiatives have been driven by the imperatives of donor "benchmarks" or "triggers."

These improvements notwithstanding, fiscal reforms, such as Ghana's Public and Financial Management Reform Program, which aim at improving expenditure tracking, have been slowly implemented. In particular, as of 2004, Ghana's Budget and Public Expenditure Management System (BPEMS) which was specifically intended to track government expenditures, was still in the pilot stage almost eight years after it was conceptualized.

However, monitoring is more than an exercise in expenditure tracking. It is not enough to know that resources allocated for constructing a school have indeed been utilized for that purpose. Merely tracking expenditures does not tell you whether the school achieved the objective for which it was built. It fails to answer questions such as: Did enrollments rise following the construction of the school? Did the school attract teachers and pupils after construction? Has the literacy rate improved since the school was constructed? Have gender disparities in enrollment declined following the construction?

Answering such questions requires a well conceived monitoring strategy involving the design of indicators that track performance at the input, output, outcome and impact levels. Such strategies must be anchored in effective and competent monitoring systems. In reality, such systems are few and far between in most developing countries including Ghana.

This chapter assesses the performance and practical realities of monitoring and evaluation systems in developing countries using Ghana as a case study. It highlights concrete issues and problems associated with implementing Monitoring and Evaluation (M&E) systems in developing countries. The next section discusses the importance of monitoring. Section three addresses the scope of monitoring. In the context of poverty reduction, should monitoring systems focus exclusively on poverty-focused development programs such as the PRSP or on poverty in general? The fourth section analyzes the practical challenges associated with identifying appropriate indicators to monitor towards the achievement of national goals. The fifth section discusses institutional roles and responsibilities associated with monitoring. Specifically, this section describes the institutional framework governing Ghana's M&E plan and chronicles the challenges of operationalizing effective monitoring systems. The sixth section focuses on the particular M&E challenges confronting sub-national or regional and district level administrative units. The concluding section provides some policy perspectives on the M&E process.

The key message of this chapter is that monitoring systems in Ghana are generally weak and rudimentary because of weak demand for M&E outputs by policymakers and other domestic stakeholders. While weak demand is partly attributable to a lack of resources and capacity, an overriding factor is a lack of an M&E culture. Indeed, until the advent of Poverty Reduction Strategy Papers (PRSPs) which required the development of active monitoring systems by participating governments, M&E received low budget priority. Furthermore, the meager resources allocated for M&E were often reallocated to other activities. Undoubtedly, the weakness in M&E systems has encouraged misuse of public resources.

This chapter highlights the importance of designing demand-driven M&E systems. Furthermore, it emphasizes that monitoring outputs must inform the policy formulation process if this process is to be relevant. The extent to which policymakers respond to the findings of M&E outputs, can influence the behavior of economic agents, through a system of rewards and penalties represented by resource reallocations and policy changes.

2. Why Monitor? The Case for Monitoring

The PRSP process has given prominence to monitoring and evaluation in Ghana. Since their inception in late 1999, PRSPs have been guided by the principles of country ownership, results orientation, comprehensiveness, partnership and a long term perspective. In addition, PRSPs rest on three pillars which provide a coherent link between policy formulation, implementation and monitoring. The pillars are: poverty analysis, which entails generating a comprehensive understanding of poverty and its determinants; the formulation of a poverty strategy through the choice of interventions with the maximum anti-poverty impact; and a monitoring system that sets targets and monitors success based on indicators, largely at the level of outcomes.

Box 8.1 Underlying Principles of PRSPs

Country Ownership means that the PRSP formulation will be led by government but anchored in broad-based participation of civil society in the adoption and monitoring of the process.

Results-orientation suggests that the strategy must set medium and long term goals for poverty reduction including key outcomes and intermediate indicators to ensure that policies are well designed, effectively implemented and carefully monitored.

Comprehensiveness implies that PRSP must adopt a multifaceted approach to poverty, given the multidimensional nature of poverty. Hence, PRSPs must cover a number of areas including macro-stabilization, structural reforms, economic growth and social development.

Partnership Oriented involves the coordination, harmonization, and collaboration with donors to achieve the objectives of the PRS.

A long term horizon is necessary to consolidate and sustain progress towards poverty reduction.

Monitoring is essential for several reasons. First, it provides an opportunity for policymakers to take stock of the effectiveness of their interventions using established benchmarks as yardsticks of performance. Secondly, when monitoring is done in a transparent and inclusive manner, it tends to promote and reinforce buy-in on the part of stakeholders by involving them in the process. Third, it is an opportunity for policy makers to identify policy and implementation gaps. In this context, it is important to distinguish flawed policies from policy implementation failures. Effective monitoring and evaluation systems underpinned by an appropriate balance of process and outcome indicators should be able to make that distinction. Thus, M&E can ensure that policymakers do not "throw the baby out with the bathwater." Fourth, effective monitoring demonstrates greater accountability in the use of resources to all stakeholders, including the general public and the government's internal and external development partners. Fifth, M&E requires data and can indirectly improve data gathering, processing and storage systems. Inclusiveness and the choice of mechanisms for verifying M&E outcomes can discourage data distortions aimed at generating "politically correct" outcomes.

The benefits of monitoring are enhanced by the level of inclusiveness of the process since this tends to maximize its credibility. Nonetheless, merely increasing the number of stakeholders is not sufficient; the quality of engagement shown partly by the capacity of stakeholders to interpret and analyze indicators of progress is paramount. This is particularly relevant where the issues being monitored are technical and complex, requiring specialized knowledge. In such scenarios, the resources and experience of independent think-tanks and academic institutions should be fully exploited.

3. What to Monitor: The Scope of Monitoring

Given the apparent benefits of monitoring, the obvious question is what to monitor? In most African countries including Ghana, monitoring has assumed a prominent role since the introduction of PRSPs. This is not to imply that such countries had no monitoring systems prior to that period. It merely suggests that M&E was of low priority until that point. This is understandable particularly in the context of the resource constraints facing most developing countries. In Ghana for instance, the estimated resource envelope was consistently overstated and as a result actual budgetary allocations under the Medium Term Expenditure Framework (MTEF) were woefully below budget ceilings. Worse still, the budget ceilings were often well below the level of resources requested by Ministries Departments and Agencies (MDAs).

Furthermore, resources were disbursed on the basis of availability rather than the timing of MDA activities. For instance, to be effective, agricultural extension interventions must be provided during specific months of the agricultural cycle. Limited resources availability, erratic and often back-loaded disbursements often result MDAs being more preoccupied with ensuring they had enough resources to produce outputs than they were about allocating resources for M&E. What good was M&E if the outputs could not be produced? In effect, in the scheme of prioritization, M&E was at the bottom.

But should this necessarily have been the case? After all is M&E not the mechanism to expose policy and implementation gaps? The obvious answer to these questions is a resounding yes . . . but it depends. It depends on the importance that policymakers attach to M&E. Would the M&E reports have been read let alone influenced policy and if so in what direction? In the case of Ghana, the objective reality is that interest in M&E was largely externally driven by the requirements of the PRSP; prior to the implementation of PRSPs, M&E systems remained largely dysfunctional, being under-funded and under-utilized. The notable exceptions with respect to M&E funding were the Health and Education sectors where significant M&E investments had been made. But coincidentally these were also sectors where donors were very active in terms of financial and technical assistance. Ironically, the National Development Planning Commission (NDPC) which is charged with coordinating the M&E of government plans and policies, was grossly under-resourced for M&E.[1]

Following the formulation of the GPRS and the drafting of an M&E plan, monitoring began to assume greater importance in the development debate. But challenges still remained particularly in terms of how to revitalize the nation's fledgling M&E systems. Even more important, because interest in M&E was stimulated in the context of the PRSP, the initial focus of the M&E debate was the PRSP. Not surprisingly, policymakers and other stakeholders began to question whether monitoring the PRSP could be equated with monitoring poverty. This question was particularly poignant in light of events that had occurred at Ghana's Consultative Group meeting with donors in 2002. During this meeting, donors questioned the feasibility of Ghana's PRSP, given the apparently high cost of implementation (approximately $10 billion). As a result, the original PRSP was scaled down and replaced by the "Medium Term Priorities" (MTP), a development program which was largely criticized as a departure from the PRSP. Indeed, the sudden birth of the MTP further confused the monitoring process because what to monitor became even more unclear, the PRSP, the MTP or both?

Further complicating the process was the fact that the government had meanwhile required MDAs to compile a list of activities and objectives which they considered to be a priority in the context of poverty reduction. The idea was for government to prioritize expenditures on the basis of these priorities. This collection of activities and outputs became part of the Government Book of Business. A close analysis of the MDA priority activities however revealed an apparent disconnect with the PRSP and the MTP. Apparently, given the priority accorded to poverty in the development agenda and the expected allocation of resources on the basis of poverty focused initiatives, several MDA's reinvented their activities and outputs within the framework of the new agenda.

The M&E waters in Ghana became even more muddied, when it was suggested that the process be expanded to include monitoring the government's manifesto. After all, the government was elected presumably on the strength of its campaign promises articulated in its manifesto. These promises included moving the nation out of poverty through private sector initiatives carried out in an environment of good political and economic governance. In this context it was reasonable to argue for the scope of M&E to include the manifesto.[2]

These broad and sometimes conflicting monitoring objectives had to be resolved by a team of technical experts charged with the task of designing an M&E plan. The resolution was to develop a core set of indicators designed to monitor key poverty indicators that were not necessarily limited to or inclusive of the PRSP, MTP or Government Book of Business activities. In effect, the thinking was that these initiatives were a means to achieve the overall objective of poverty reduction. Hence, the focus of the M&E plan should be to monitor progress towards the achievement of this broad objective using a comprehensive set of indicators.

The government had a technical obligation to monitor the implementation of its PRSP in the context of the Annual Progress Report (APR). Thus, the APR had to have an element of PRSP specific monitoring. Furthermore, the IMF and World Bank had, in partnership with government, agreed on performance benchmarks as conditions for resource disbursements in the context of the IMF's Poverty Reduction and Growth Facility (PRGF) and the World Bank's Poverty Reduction Support Credit (PRSC) programs. Embedded in these benchmarks were the so called HIPC triggers which were essentially the conditions for reaching the HIPC completion point. Although several of the benchmarks were extracted from the GPRS (not necessarily the MTP), they also included elements such as privatization of the Ghana Commercial Bank and Ghana Airways, and the adoption of a lifeline pricing mechanism for electricity, which were not explicitly addressed in either the GPRS or MTP. Progress towards achieving these benchmarks had to be monitored.

Finally, the Millennium Development Goals (MDGs) had also assumed great visibility in this period and would have been conspicuous by their absence from the monitoring indicators. Coincidentally, several of the MDGs goals, objectives and indicators had been included in the GPRS; therefore including them in the M&E plan did not pose much difficulty. Nonetheless, only thirteen out of thirty-nine[3] applicable MDG indicators were captured in the initial list of fifty-two[4] indicators. Thus, to respond to the sometimes competing monitoring demands of donors and government, the scope of monitoring widened. This widening blurred its focus. Furthermore, in the context of the nation's dire M&E capacity constraints, widening the scope of the M&E mandate placed considerable strain on the national monitoring system and may have compromised the quality of monitoring outputs.

4. Designing Coherent Indicators: A Reality Check

A poverty monitoring system must monitor processes, outcomes and impacts to provide a comprehensive view of policy performance. In this context, processes are defined as the intermediate steps to achieve desired outcomes and impacts; they include inputs and outputs. The reason for process monitoring is quite obvious. There is generally a lag between the initiation of a policy intervention and the realization of the outcome or even the specific output of that intervention. For instance, improving functional literacy (outcome) requires intermediate activities such as resources (inputs) to build schools (outputs) and train teachers (outputs). Assuming it takes a minimum of ten years to realize the desired outcome of improved functional literacy, in the absence of intermediate indicators it would be difficult to assess progress towards the realization of the outcome prior to the ten year period. This implies that monitoring indicators must consist of a rich balance between intermediate (input and output) and final (outcome and impact) indicators.

At the same time, the number of selected indicators must not be so large as to overwhelm the monitoring systems especially where there are capacity constraints as in Ghana. Satisfying both conditions, however, poses a practical challenge. The first condition requires that each target must be linked to at least three types of indicators (input, output and outcome, not to mention impact). Based on this logic, monitoring thirty targets requires a minimum of ninety indicators. Given the imperative to broaden the scope of monitoring in Ghana, it was practically impossible to satisfy the apparently competing conditions of parsimony and balance in the selection of indicators. As a result, 65 percent (thirty-four out of fifty-two) of the core indicators adopted in Ghana were outcome (eighteen) and output indicators (sixteen). This violates one of the theoretical tenets underpinning effective M&Es relating to balance. Furthermore, these indicators did not represent a coherent chain of intermediate and final indicators since each policy goal or objective was only associated with one indicator.

Even where there is a balance between intermediate and final indicators, establishing the relationship among indicators on the one hand, and between indicators and targets on the other hand is practically a subjective exercise. Ghana's experience is a case in point. For instance, assuming that the target is to reduce infant mortality by 67 percent by 2006, and assuming the output indicator is twenty health clinics built by 2004, then the presumption is that there is a relationship between the number of health clinics constructed and the realization of the target. In reality, a number of outputs collectively contribute to achieving the target. However, it is a daunting and intensive task to map indicators to targets in a precise way. In Ghana, with the possible exception of the education sector, little was done in this area prior to choosing the indicators. As a result, it is not obvious whether achieving progress with respect to output indicators (for example, thirty schools constructed), necessarily implies progress towards the realization of broad impacts or goals (for example, poverty reduced by 50 percent). MDG "needs assessments" attempt to answer these questions by identifying and costing the inputs required to generate desired outputs. But even mapping inputs to outputs requires knowledge of input-output coefficients which may be lacking at the level of monitoring institutions. Furthermore, the relationship between costed outputs and outcomes and impacts, is even more diffused requiring "time series data analysis." This is generally lacking in M&E institutions in developing countries including Ghana. In addition, costing in a changing world is a dynamic process that must take into account, population growth and a dynamic macro-economic environment.

Ghana attempted to address attribution through poverty and social impact assessment studies that examined the impact of selected government policies on vulnerable groups. However, this is not the same as validating the causal links between a chain of input, output and outcome indicators, leaving aside for a moment, impact indicators.

The problem is further compounded when national targets have to be reconciled with international targets such as the MDGs. In this case, intermediate inputs must not only achieve national targets but must also be reconciled with international targets. For instance, in the case of Ghana where the MDGs were not explicitly factored into the GPRS, ensuring consistency between the GPRS and MDG targets essentially required a recalibration of the GPRS targets. However, this was not done. At the broad macro level, it may be relatively easy to quantify a growth rate consistent with halving poverty by 2015. However, estimating the level of inputs and outputs that are consistent with achieving the required national growth rate is a challenge to most planning and M&E systems in developing countries. A "needs assessment" exercise, either in the context of PRSs or MDGs, which is not based on a credible chain of input, output and outcome indicators, is bound to estimate costs that have little bearing on expected objectives and goals.

In Ghana, linking targets with indicators was problematic for additional reasons, including the disconnect between the GPRS, the MTP and the core poverty indicators developed by the M&E system. A decision had been taken to monitor poverty and not necessarily the GPRS/MTP. On the face of it, this made sense since the overall objective was to reduce poverty. However, this implied that the core indicators were not directly linked to the MTP and the GPRS. Hence in the absence of MTP or GPRS-specific indicators, the core indicators could not be used as the basis for monitoring either the GPRS or the MTP. In particular several of the core indicators were not linked to the MTP. Because the MTP was weak on verifiable indicators it contributed little to the pool of core indicators. Furthermore, only eleven of the fifty-two core indicators were derived from the GPRS. To the extent that the MTP programs were not underpinned by a coherent set of intermediate and final indicators the framework for monitoring the MTP was weak. In addition, only thirty-one of the final sixty core indicators had corresponding targets. In recognition of this constraint, the 2002 APR for Ghana observed that:

> targets for agricultural modernization are largely unavailable, which undermines efforts to assess the extent of progress. Furthermore, the lack of baseline data on several of the indicators (e.g., farmer tractor ratio) will make it difficult to assess the future performance of the indicators. . . . (2002 Annual Progress Report: 36.)

In addition to these issues, the choice of indicators in Ghana was made more challenging because of the limitations of data. In some cases the data existed but was not routinely published. In other cases it existed in fragments dispersed within and across institutions and required a systematic methodology for assembling and processing the information on a routine basis. Other data challenges relate to accuracy and timeliness of data, infrequent national surveys due to inadequate resources, and lack of motivation of staff in the line ministries and districts to institutionalize the collection and dissemination of data.

The obvious implication for the monitoring process was that it could not routinely track progress in several areas of interest because the choice of indicators was constrained by access to data. For instance, assessing the welfare of food crop farmers requires information about farm gate prices since their outputs are sold at producer prices not retail prices. Such information is not readily available. Hence, per-capita food crop production is used as a proxy indicator of welfare of food crop producers, even though per-capita production is a weak indicator of the welfare of food crop producers. Higher food crop output may actually be associated with lower prices and earnings for farmers. Secondly where large disparities exist between farm gate and retail prices, food crop production valued at retail prices may overstate the benefits accruing to rural farmers who constitute the bulk of the poor in Ghana. Based on these observations, Ghana's 2002 Annual Progress Report (APR) recommended that the government routinely publish data on agricultural producer prices to ensure a more accurate assessment of the impact of changes in agricultural output on producers.

5. Who Monitors? Systems, Institutional Roles and Relationships

Effective monitoring systems must clearly identify and define monitoring roles to avoid duplication of effort and eliminate turf wars among institutions. The experience of Ghana is instructive in this respect; it demonstrates that even clearly assigned roles may not be a sufficient condition for ensuring a harmonious relationship among institutional actors.

In August 2002 the government of Ghana, in collaboration with the Department for International Development (DfID), initiated the process of developing an M&E plan to monitor Ghana's PRSP. The key institutional actors in this plan included the:

- Ministry of Finance and Economic Planning (MoFEP),[5]
- M&E Division of the National Development Planning Commission [NDPC]
- Ministries Departments and Agencies (MDAs)
- National Inter-Agency Poverty Monitoring Groups (NIPMGs)
- M&E Technical Committee
- Office of the President,
- Parliament
- Ghana Statistical Service.

Of this group, the office of the President and the parliamentary sub-committee are mainly users of the M&E outputs produced by the NDPC M&E Division in collaboration with the Technical Committee and the National Inter-Agency Monitoring Groups. The Ministry of Finance is both a producer and a user of the NDPC monitoring outputs. It uses the monitoring information produced by the NDPC to inform its budgetary allocations and at the same time track budgetary expenditures. The latter role is essentially a narrowly focused type of monitoring.

Monitoring Role of the Ministry of Finance

There is some confusion among development practitioners and policymakers about the monitoring roles of the Ministry of Finance and the Ministry of Planning. In Ghana, lack of clarity on this issue fuelled antagonism between the two institutions. The Finance Ministry's role in the monitoring process is to track public expenditures and use the M&E information gathered by the NDPC to inform the Medium Term Expenditure Framework (MTEF) and the budget preparation process. The MoFEP monitors all aspects of government expenditure. The prime objective of expenditure tracking is to determine whether funds are properly accounted for and used for their intended purpose. The Heavily Indebted Poor Country (HIPC) expenditure tracking system focused on expenditures on anti-poverty programs or projects. Unlike the NDPC, MoFEP's monitoring role does not include ensuring that the projects and programs for which monies have been allocated are achieving their intended objectives. For instance, with respect to road construction, MoFEP grants certificates authorizing payment for the delivery of outputs (i.e., constructed roads), however, it does not assess the outcomes or impact of the outputs. In addition to tracking expenditures on poverty-focused activities the Finance Ministry also tracks expenditures on public sector wages and salaries, overheads, services and investments.

Thus, the monitoring focus of MoFEP addresses questions such as: Is the nation spending on the items for which the monies were originally contracted and spending within its budget constraint? On the other hand, the primary monitoring focus of the NDPC is not on expenditures but on performance indicators at the multi-sectoral level. For example, it is not enough that the Ministry of Education spends its budget on employing more teachers. It needs to know whether this expenditure realized the impacts projected. The extent to which public expenditure facilitates the realization of broader objectives relates to all relevant ministries and to the progress of the nation as a whole?

Role of the NDPC M&E Division

The M&E division of the NDPC is at the heart of the monitoring framework. It is the focal point responsible for coordinating the monitoring activities of line ministries and districts, preparing the PRSP Annual Progress Report (APR), and identifying baseline values for the core M&E indicators. However, because the NDPC lacked the capacity to assume this monitoring role, a consulting firm was engaged to carry out the NDPC's role in the interim. This raised the issue of an appropriate mechanism for the transfer of knowledge from consultants to the regular staff of the NDPC. Resentment arising from disparities in salaries between the consultants and regular NDPC staff was real and had to be carefully managed to ensure cooperation between the two groups. This was not very successful and further added to the monitoring challenges for the consultants. In a larger context, what was happening was the creation of parallel processes. New capacity was being grafted on to an under-capacity civil service. Ultimately the new layer has assumed a quasi-permanent role in the overall institutional set-up of the NDPC.

The monitoring role of the NDPC is to ensure that the GPRS is aligned to the budget in a non-superficial way. Unlike MoFEP, The NDPC's role extends beyond expenditure tracking. It involves evaluation and impact assessment to ensure that national programs and projects move the economy closer to achieving agreed poverty targets. The NDPC had to ensure that the proposed projects and programs of MDAs requesting HIPC funds were benefiting the poor. The MoFEP was to ensure that MDAs eligible for HIPC funding had the capability to track such expenditures. The MoFEP trained a pilot group of ministries to track HIPC expenditures. Training was subsequently extended to all ministries that qualified for HIPC allocations.

Role of Line Ministries Departments and Agencies
The role of both the MoFEP and NDPC can be distinguished from monitoring at the level of Ministries Departments and Agencies. Unlike the NDPC and MoFEP, whose monitoring role is multi-sectoral, an MDA's monitoring and evaluation role is largely limited to an analysis of performance indicators within its sector.

In addition to monitoring their programs and projects, MDAs inform the national monitoring process through their representation on the National Inter-Agency Poverty Monitoring Groups. The latter are organized around the thematic areas of Ghana's PRSP. Each MDA's activities fall within one or more of the thematic areas of the NIPMGs. MDAs provide technical advice in the selection of core monitoring indicators based on their thematic alignment. They are an indispensable source of information on indicators that fall within their thematic purview. In addition to its representation on the NIPMG each MDA is also charged with monitoring the performance of its specific programs and projects.

Ideally, the MDA monitoring should be based on performance relating to verifiable indicators. However, personal interviews with MDA representatives revealed that monitoring and evaluation assumed low priority in their budgets and in reality, very little is done in the area of monitoring. None of the MDAs interviewed was able to produce an M&E report. In practice, MDAs find it difficult to conceptualize and formulate input indicators. Input indicators are largely couched in terms of financial resources not specific activities designed to achieve verifiable outputs. Emphasis on financial resources, however, obscures the link between inputs and outputs; merely stating that an MDA requires a certain amount of dollars to produce a stated output does not explain how those resources will contribute to the achievement of the required outputs. Furthermore, using financial resources as an input indicator requires good estimates of the cost of the expected outputs. The problem however, is that MDA resource requirements are constrained by budget ceilings (and actual allocations) and hence, tend to significantly understate the resources required to generate their expected outputs.

Role of National Inter-Agency Poverty Monitoring Groups (NIPMGs)

NIPMGs were created to provide technical advisory services to the NDPC M&E division. They are five groups each being responsible for assessing the monitoring performance in one of the five thematic areas of the GPRS. In particular, they evaluate the choice of monitoring indicators in their respective thematic areas and review the M&E reports of the NDPC. They are expected to report to the Technical Committee through the NDPC M&E division once it is established.

Monitoring Role of the M&E Technical Committee

The M&E Technical Committee is intended to provide broad strategic direction to the M&E division on all aspects of the M&E process. It is intended to serve as an advisory board to the NDPC and the Office of the President and Cabinet. Its roles include reviewing the goals, indicators and targets of the GPRS to ensure relevancy and reviewing and approving the quarterly and annual reports from the M&E Division to ensure they are user friendly. However, as of October 2005, this committee had not been established. When established it is expected that membership of the committee will be drawn from a wide range of stakeholders with a strong M&E interest and or expertise including the Director of Policy Co-ordination, Monitoring and Evaluation in the Office of the President, the Budget Director of the Ministry of Finance, the Director of the Ghana Statistical Service, the Director of the M&E Division of the NDC and a representative of the private sector.

The Office of the President (OoP)

The Office of the President's Policy Co-ordination, Monitoring and Evaluation Unit uses the M&E information to inform policymaking. Such information enables government to distinguish bad policies from policy implementation failures. This is important since corrective measures will depend on the nature and source of the problem. Inappropriate policies can be addressed by policy reforms while weaknesses in policy implementation will require corrective implementation strategies that explicitly take into account the political aspects of the policy implementation environment. The OoP is also supposed to ensure that the NDPC is adequately resourced and has the requisite manpower skills to carry out its monitoring role.

Regional/District Poverty Monitoring Groups (RPMGs)

It was intended that the input of regions and districts into the national M&E process was would be captured through the Regional and District Poverty Monitoring Groups (RPMGs). The original idea was for the RPMGs to inform the national monitoring system with regional and district M&E information. Also, the RPMGs were expected to disseminate national level M&E data to the regions and districts to inform their local development programs. However, given the generally weak regional and district level capacity, it was unrealistic to expect substantive information flows from the district M&E systems to the national systems. Thus, the consensus was that, in the interim, the RPGMs would only serve as a source of information for the regions and districts and not for the national monitoring institution. Meanwhile, several initiatives would be put in place to address district and regional level capacity constraints.

6. Challenges of Sub-National Level Monitoring

The role of sub-national governments or district assemblies (as they are referred to in Ghana) in the poverty monitoring process is to monitor the implementation of anti-poverty projects and programs in their districts. Presumably, these programs and projects are derived from district medium term (five year) development plans which are expected to be consistent with national priorities as reflected in the GPRS. Ideally, the outcomes of district level monitoring activities inform national monitoring systems by providing data on district level performance indicators. Furthermore, sub-national level monitoring can reveal spatial and income inequalities at the regional and district levels and thereby provide detailed information for targeted policy interventions.

As Ghana moved in the direction of fiscal decentralization, district level monitoring evolved to encompass monitoring the performance of decentralized MDAs in addition to projects and programs undertaken at the district level by development partners. District level monitoring is thus cross-sectoral.

M&E at the district level is funded largely by the central government and donor partners. Resources from the central government flow indirectly to districts through sector ministries (e.g., education, health, water and sanitation) and are also channeled directly to the districts through the district assembly common fund.

District monitoring occurs at two levels: the district assembly level and at the level of the decentralized line ministries. The district assemblies monitor the implementation of their development programs, while the decentralized MDAs monitor their sectoral[6] programs implemented at the level of the district. To ensure harmonization of the district level monitoring process District Planning Coordinating Units (DPCUs)[7] were established to coordinate both levels of monitoring. Although the monitoring role of district assemblies is clearly defined, they lack the capacity to effectively monitor district level programs and projects. Indeed the GPRS Monitoring and Evaluation Plan noted that:

> the level of activity within DPCUs depends on the personalities involved and the level of external support. Monitoring is narrowly limited to expenditure tracking. Staffing is often very limited and inadequately prepared. Data management hardware and software, and expertise are generally lacking. Little or no budgetary disbursements are made specifically for M&E. Very few reports are routinely prepared by DPCUs and evaluation is virtually nonexistent. District level resources intended for M&E are usually reallocated for other activities. [p. 25].

The quality of monitoring at the district and municipal levels varies by sector, and by the intensity of project activity. Generally, the Health, Education and Agriculture ministries tend to have relatively stronger capacity, better developed administrative systems and more vibrant monitoring systems even though these also tend to engage in rudimentary monitoring activities. They tend to generate reports on project performance based on subjective evaluations and not on verifiable indicators of performance. Furthermore, district-level monitoring tends to be donor driven and characterized by poor coordination and limited interaction between the district assemblies and the decentralized line ministries; and there is limited grassroots involvement in the formulation of district development plans. There also appears to be a disconnect between district plans and projects implemented at the district level. This is largely the result of the low level of interaction between the district assemblies and the sectoral ministries.

Weak Institutional Coordination at the Sub-National Level

Development Planning
In theory, each district is tasked with the responsibility of drafting a district wide development plan based on the PRSP and consultations with community stakeholders. But it was evident in the discussions with the district assemblies and decentralized ministries that there is very little coordination between the two institutions. For instance, line ministries tend to have limited input into district development plans. Moreover, the annual budgets of district assemblies, which are supposed to reflect the priorities of district development programs, exclude the activities of several of the decentralized sectors, notably the education sector. As a result, district level plans are not as comprehensive and coherent as they could have been with the collaboration of key sector ministries.

Monitoring

Although in theory, District and Municipal Planning Coordinating Units (DPCUs, MPCUs) are supposed to coordinate all district level monitoring activities, in practice the monitoring activities of the line ministries occur outside the realm of the DPCUs and MPCUs. For instance, the line ministries of agriculture and health have a vertical reporting structure with limited contact with the district or municipal assembly. The monitoring team of the Ministry of Health sends most of its reports directly to the regional office; reports are only sent to the district or municipality when they make a financial contribution to the project. In contrast, the Education Ministry's monitoring reports are sent to both the national headquarters in the capital (Accra) and to the districts.

The health sector appears to have a comprehensive, well organized and well resourced, computerized data collection and storage system which stores information on relevant indicators including, immunization rates, dropout rates, guinea worm infection rates, among others. The sector presumably has the capacity to conduct data analysis at the district, regional and national levels. The health sector's data is however, not routinely shared with the municipalities. Once again, this reflects the lack of horizontal integration at the district level and the failure to optimize synergies. This is particularly important because the dearth of district level monitoring capacity makes it imperative that district level institutions share capacity and information to optimize the use of their limited resources.

Lack of Ownership in District Level M&E Processes
District Development Plans lack strong stakeholder input
In practice the consultative process that underpins development planning at the district level has been weak. District representatives admitted that in the past, district plans were hurriedly put together, in most cases by consultants, and not truly owned by the districts. As a result, the district governing body or assemblymen tend to be disconnected from district development plans. To address this issue they suggested the establishment of a planning task force comprising all stakeholders including heads of decentralized departments, NGOs and traditional authorities to formulate the district plan.

Monitoring at the district level tends to be driven by donor funded projects. In the absence of such projects, monitoring is not given much priority. Indeed programs and projects funded under the District Assembly Common Fund and other government programs tend to receive lower monitoring priority. What is evident is that donor projects compel monitoring because of their stringent monitoring requirements. Since other programs do not have similar compelling requirements, monitoring activities tend to be virtually nonexistent or superficial at best. This suggests that the problem of M&E is not solely due to lack of capacity and resources but is fundamentally one of limited requirements fuelled by a weak M&E culture in Ghana. In effect, if M&E were considered a priority, greater resources would be devoted to developing M&E capacity.

Poor alignment of NGO activities with sub-national priorities
Besides government funded programs and projects, most of the activities under-taken at the district assemblies are in collaboration with NGOs While collabora-tion between districts and NGO's is a welcome development, it appears that NGO's tend to set the terms and priorities of the collaboration even though in theory they are required to operate within the framework of the district level development plans. Indeed, all NGOs are required to register their activities with the District Assembly. In practice however, NGOs do not register with the Dis-trict Assembly unless mandated by their donors. Smaller NGOs tend to be less visible and are less likely to register with the districts.

This trend has implications for the implementation of district level pro-grams. In the absence of effective monitoring systems to flag and correct mis-alignment of donor activities, there is the danger of duplication of effort and project proliferation. .

Poor data collection and storage systems
The key constraints to M&E at the district level are a lack of human capacity and logistical resources underpinned by a low priority for monitoring budgets by policymakers. Logistical capacity constraints include limited access to com-puters for data storage and analysis and lack of vehicles to conduct on-site moni-toring in remote areas. Indeed, the 2004 Annual Progress Report (APR) of Ghana noted a lack of incentives to motivate staff to institutionalize M&E ac-tivities at the level of regional, district and line ministry levels. In addition to resource constraints and perhaps partly due to human capacity constraints, the APR also observed the tendency for regional data to be inconsistent with data gathered at the district level. Resources budgeted for M&E are limited and tend to be used for activities that are not strictly M&E in nature (2003 and 2004 An-nual Progress Reports of Ghana).

Improved monitoring at the district level could generate more effective and reliable statistical information for assessing policy performance. Currently, very few personnel have been trained in monitoring. In several cases data is frag-mented, stored in files and notebooks, and not on computers. In the absence of effective data storage mechanisms most of the data tends to be inaccessible to researchers and policymakers.

Multiple reporting requirements by Donors
Multiple reporting requirements of donors further complicate the M&E process at all levels. Donor partners must harmonize their reporting requirements to ease the pressure on already weak M&E systems. To this end, current efforts to in-crease donor participation in the Multi-Donor Budgetary Support (MDBS) pro-gram are a step in the right direction since the MDBS seeks to streamline and harmonize donor performance benchmarks and reporting requirements (see dis-cussion in chapter 7).

7. Conclusions and Policy Directions

The key message of this chapter is that the current status of M&E systems in Ghana represents an improvement over the pre-PRS era when systems were largely focused on monitoring Structural Adjustment Program (SAP) benchmarks or conditionalities. M&E systems are still generally weak and rudimentary particularly at the sub-national level of governance. Although the reasons for this development include a lack of resources and capacity, an overriding factor is a lack of demand for M&E outputs reflecting a nascent M&E culture in Ghana.

Improving the effectiveness of M&E in Ghana will therefore require more than financial and human resources; it must be underpinned by a commitment to nurture a culture of M&E that reinforces and sustains the demand for M&E. Cultural change can be engendered either domestically (i.e., from within a system) or triggered through external pressure. However, cultural change must be internalized at the domestic level if it is to be sustainable; it must be acceptable to key stakeholders. So far, the process of M&E revitalization in Ghana has largely been externally driven. Indeed, until the advent of Poverty Reduction Strategy Papers which required the formulation and design of vibrant monitoring systems, there had been little incentive or desire to pursue an active M&E program in Ghana. That the demand for M&E in Ghana has been triggered by external imperatives is not necessarily a negative development. The challenge is whether this process will be internalized by constituents and stakeholders that have the clout to sustain evolving progress in this area.

Overall the analysis of Ghana's M&E experience highlights the importance of ensuring that M&E systems are demand driven. At the sub national level there is the need for greater ownership of M&E processes better institutional coordination and improved alignment of development partner activities with district priorities. Furthermore, improving the capacity of sub national units to collect, organize, store and analyze data is critical to improving national statistics and M&E systems. But ultimately, monitoring reports must inform or feed into the policy formulation process if they are to be relevant. When policymakers respond to the findings of monitoring reports, they can influence the behavior of economic agents through a system of rewards, penalties and policy changes.

Notes

1. See *An Agenda For Growth and Prosperity: Ghana's Poverty Reduction Strategy 2003-2005 Monitoring and Evaluation Plan.*
2. This suggestion was however dropped. It was argued that several aspects of the manifesto were reflected in the PRSP.

3. There are forty-eight indicators in all, however nine indicators only apply at international level.

4. The number of core indicators was expanded to sixty following the inclusion of indicators from the Ministry of Agriculture.

5. It was then the Ministry of Finance.

6. The key sector ministries in the district are Agriculture, Health, Education, Water and Sanitation and Social Welfare.

7. DPCUs consist of the Panning Officer, the Budget Officer, the District Engineer and the Chairman of the Works Sub-Committee. The expanded DPCU includes technical personnel from the decentralized line ministries, particularly Agriculture, Education and Health.

References

Booth, D. "PRSP Institutionalization Study." *Final Report, Chapter 1: Overview of PRSP Process and Monitoring* ODI, London. 2001.

Government of Ghana. *An Agenda for Growth and Prosperity: Ghana's Poverty Reduction Strategy 2003-2005, Monitoring and Evaluation Plan.* February 2003.

Marta Foresti et. al. *What Role for Civil Society in Monitoring Poverty Reduction Policies.* Discussion Paper presented at the *Roundtable Role of Civil Society in Monitoring Poverty Reduction Policies.* European Evaluation Society Conference, Seville 9-11 October 2002.

National Development Planning Commission, (Government of Ghana) *Implementation of the Ghana Poverty Reduction Strategy, 2004 Annual Progress Report.* March 31 2005.

————. *Implementation of the Ghana Poverty Reduction Strategy, 2003 Annual Progress Report.* March 31, 2004.

PRSP Monitoring and Synthesis Project, PRS Monitoring in Africa, PRSP Synthesis Note 7, June 2003.

PART 3

Special Topics in Poverty Reduction

9

Decentralization, Poverty Reduction, and the Ghana Poverty Reduction Strategy

Felix A. Asante and Joseph R. A. Ayee

1. Introduction

P overty reduction has not only occupied the development strategies of sub-Saharan African governments since independence, but has also featured prominently on the agenda of donors. Governments and donors alike have sought to design and to implement programs to ensure that scarce resources are allocated to activities that are likely to have the greatest impact on the poor and to decrease their levels of deprivation and vulnerability (World Bank, 2001; Sen, 1999).

One of the strategies that has been used to promote poverty reduction in sub-Saharan Africa and which has won the acceptance and commitment of donors is decentralization. This paper discusses the extent to which decentralization has facilitated or hindered the implementation of the GPRS and the lessons learned. First, the paper identifies the objectives of decentralization in Ghana. Second, it draws the link between decentralization and poverty reduction. Third, it assesses the impact of decentralization on poverty reduction in Ghana using the following indicators: (i) responsiveness to the needs of the poor; (ii) levels and quality of representation and participation of the poor; (iii) social and economic outcomes such as the promotion of human development, social equity, increase in incomes and spatial or inter-regional equality; and (iv) accountability. Fourth, it highlights some of the lessons learnt and their implications for decentralization and poverty reduction.

2. The Objectives of Decentralization in Ghana

Decentralization in Ghana as articulated in 1988 by Rawlings' Provisional National Defence Council (PNDC) is a specific policy construction, with important conceptual and legal underpinnings. At the conceptual level, the policy (at its genesis) was a political construction to translate the "populist" notions of participatory democracy of the erstwhile PNDC into the "democratic fabric". Under this construction, a dual part-elected, part-appointed District Assembly was established, to both ensure some governmental influence alongside with quasi-local engagement and participation. At the level of local government reform, the decentralization policy seeks to establish decentralized administration through the transfer of authority, functions, means and competence from the Central Government Ministries, Department and Agencies (MDAs) to the sub-national institutions such as the Regional Coordinating Councils and the District Assemblies. This is to enhance the capacity of the public sector to plan, manage, and monitor social, spatial and economic development. The policy specifically seeks to:

- Promote popular participation in the decision-making process;
- Promote responsive governance at the local level; and
- Enhance efficiency and effectiveness of the entire government machinery, through a process of restructuring of the institutions responsible for service delivery making them closer to and accountable to the people (Government of Ghana, 1992; 1993; Decentralization Secretariat, 2003).

The policy reassigns functions entrusting policy planning, monitoring, evaluation and promotion to the headquarters of MDAs and program coordination and monitoring to Regional Coordinating Councils, while the District Assemblies (DAs) become responsible for implementing development programs. DAs have thus become the focal points for all development activities at the local level.

Under the decentralization policy, development becomes a shared responsibility of the Government, District Assemblies, Civil Society Organization, the private sector and local communities. The policy is designed to make the DAs more autonomous, more responsive to local needs and technically and financially more capable of expanding and improving service delivery. The thrust of Ghana's decentralization policy, therefore, is devolution (and not de-concentration or delegation). Devolution relates to constitutional or legislative assigned roles, responsibilities and accountabilities at all levels of government, while de-concentration refers to a mere relocation of personnel and their responsibilities to regions and districts (often within the same agencies) without transfer of authority (MLGRD, 2002).

Various provisions in the 1992 Constitution provide ample testimony of this broad-based conceptual and legal basis for decentralization in Ghana.[1] In chapter six of the Constitution (Directive Principles of State Policy), the government is enjoined to make "democracy a reality by decentralizing the administrative and financial machinery of government to the regions and districts and by affording all possible opportunities to the people" (Republic of Ghana, 1992). In addition to these objectives, the individual Establishing Acts (Legislative Instruments) for each of the District Assemblies, which supplement the Local Government Act (Act 462), include a list of 86 specific responsibilities[2] ranging from the provision of basic services in education, health, water supply, sanitation, to public safety and revenue collection.

Developments in Decentralization

The most significant recent developments in Ghana's decentralization policy have occurred since the elections in 2000, which resulted in a change of government. These include a resolution of a political transition problem in 2001; the District Assembly elections of 2002; the completion of the GPRS (also in 2002), which made decentralization reform one of the major governance challenges; and the development of the National Decentralization Action Plan (NDAP) in 2003, as the main strategic document to guide implementation of decentralization.

- *Transition in Local Governance and Extension of Central Government Transition*: At the point of swearing in a new Government in 2001, a dilemma lingered over the status of the District Chief Executives (DCEs), appointed by the previous Government, and the fate of the 30 percent government appointees in the District Assemblies and the Unit Committees (the unelected members). For several months, the DCEs continued to perform their functions, while the government pondered their status. Eventually, their appointments were terminated and new DCEs were appointed by the President. The District Assemblies themselves remained in limbo for several months until new appointments were made by the President to replace the 30 percent of members whose appointments by the previous government were also terminated.

- *The Local Government Elections of 2002*: Almost immediately after the resolution of the transition challenges, there was massive effort by the Government to conduct the District Assembly elections in July-August of 2002. The election was characterized by a high incidence of women's participation, encouraged by the active engagement of civil society groups which supported female candidates through training, capacity building and the promotion of affirmative action measures (Ayee, 2004a).

- *Decentralization Incorporated in GPRS*: The GPRS process gave priority to decentralization reform. It was envisaged that sub-national units would spearhead the implementation of the nation's development programs and projects. The vision of decentralization as contained in the GPRS is to promote responsive and accountable governance at the local levels that allows for effective participation, equity in resource allocation, and effective delivery of services, especially for the poor.

- *National Decentralization Action Plan (NDAP):* At the close of 2003, a NDAP was formulated after broad consultations with various sector agencies and specialized institutions of government and civil society, led by the Ministry of Local Government and Rural Development (MLGRD). Endorsed by Cabinet in February 2004, the NDAP identified the following eight key strategic objectives during the plan period, 2003–2005:

  o Strengthen political leadership and inter-sectoral collaboration for decentralization.
  o Enhance decentralization policy management, implementation and monitoring.
  o Increase discretionary funding to District Assemblies and consolidate the overall District Resource envelope.
  o Strengthen overall district level financial and human resource management and accountability.
  o Strengthen District Assemblies' functional and governance performance.
  o Strengthen decentralized coordination and M&E at the regional level.
  o Enhance and strengthen the sub-district level.
  o Promote popular participation and deepen associations and partnerships between District Assemblies, civil society, the private sector and Tradition Authorities (Decentralization Secretariat, 2003).

A Decentralization Secretariat, established within the MLGRD coordinates the NDAP. A Presidential Advisory Committee on Decentralization inaugurated in late 2003 provides policy direction and oversight. NDAP's overall legitimacy has been enhanced with the establishment of an Inter-Sectoral Committee, comprises of key representatives from various sectors, acting as a functional link to the Public Sector Reform Secretariat in the Office of the Senior Minister.

In response to political pressure, twenty eight new districts have been created, increasing the number of districts from one hundred and ten to one hundred and thirty-eight. However, this development has raised important questions about both the capacity of government to finance these new districts and the ability of the districts to generate revenue from internal sources.

3. Decentralization and Poverty Reduction in Ghana

Decentralization is seen by donors, governments and scholars as one of the most important and appropriate strategies to reduce the levels of deprivation and vulnerability of the poor. There are three ways in which decentralization is linked to poverty reduction (Bird, *et. al.*, 1995).

First, as with many other public services, effective implementation of poverty reduction strategies often requires detailed and specific local knowledge which may be most readily obtainable through a decentralized and locally accountable system of governance. Appropriately designed, decentralized systems enable local government units to implement, in a relatively more informed and participatory manner, their district development plans.

Second, the transfer of fiscal responsibilities to decentralized units can positively influence local spending decisions if it is accompanied by improved fiscal management and monitoring systems that reduce fiduciary risk on the part of the central government. Efficient assignment of revenue and expenditure responsibility to different levels of government invariably means that local government units as a group will depend to a significant extent upon transfers from the central government. While this can deepen dependence on the central government, the current revenue sharing formula rewards districts that increase their share of locally generated revenues. Related to this is the issue of equity in fiscal resource transfers. Given the heterogeneity of district resources, capacities, costs, needs and preferences, some local government units will need much more financial and technical support than others. Fiscal decentralization thus inevitably requires some degree of "equalization" – in the sense of larger fiscal transfers from the central government to poorer regions, and not to poorer people as such (Bird & Rodriguez, 1999; Shah, 1994; Crook & Sverrisson, 2001). This issue is addressed in Ghana by increasing allocations to poorer districts. However, it's important to note that in Ghana, there has been the tendency for the compensating factors in the revenue sharing formula to offset each other ultimately resulting in zero net differences in district level allocations. Thus, the relative weight accorded to under-resourced or poor districts must be sufficiently high to avoid "netting out" the equalization factor.

Third, the relationship between decentralization and poverty reduction depends on the strategies adopted to reduce poverty. Strategies that focus largely on income transfers to the poor tend to be less sustainable than those that focus on facilitating access to productive economic activities by the poor through investments in human capital, infrastructure and income generating activities. The appropriate mix of income transfers and productive economic and social investments will depend on the capacity of sub-national units to design and implement development strategies that promote shared growth. Figure 9.1 shows the conceptual link between decentralization and poverty reduction. According to Jong

Asante and Ayee

Figure 9.1 Linkage between Decentralization and Poverty Reduction

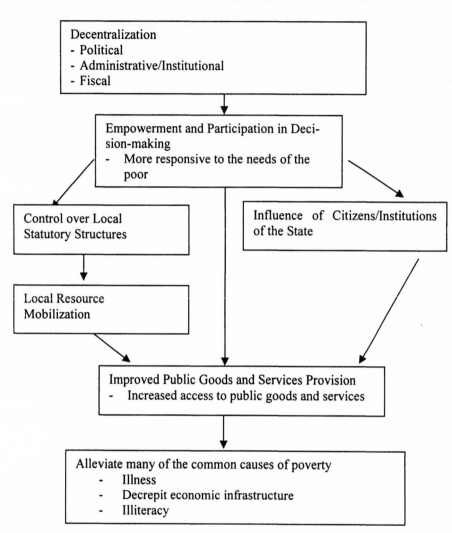

Source: Asante, 2003

et. al, (1999), decentralization is assumed to promote poverty reduction through the following channels:

(i)   Political devolution can aim at reducing poverty by creating "space" for people to effectively participate in the decision making process;

(ii)   Poverty reduction and decentralization might also be linked through a resource mobilization strategy. When people are given greater control over local statutory structures, they may be motivated to commit more assets to the common good; and

(iii)   Decentralized government may also be seen as a more effective means of delivering basic social services, thus reducing many of the common causes of poverty such as illness, decrepit economic infrastructure and illiteracy.

The link between decentralization and poverty reduction in Ghana is explicitly provided by the Ghana Poverty Reduction Strategy (GPRS). The GPRS aims to "create wealth by transforming the nature of the economy to achieve growth, accelerated poverty reduction and the protection of the vulnerable and excluded within a decentralized, democratic environment" [3] (Government of Ghana, 2003: i).

This will be achieved by:

- Ensuring economic stability for accelerated growth;
- Increasing production and promoting sustainable livelihoods;
- Facilitating direct support for equitable human resource development;
- Providing special programs in support of the vulnerable and excluded;
- Ensuring gender equity;
- Ensuring good governance and the increased capacity of the public sector; and
- The active involvement of the private sector as the main engine of growth and main partner in nation-building (Republic of Ghana, 2003: 30).

In addition, the GPRS recognizes that sustainable growth in support of poverty reduction requires decentralization. Consequently, there is the:

> need for a vigorous and progressive deepening of decentralization and the devolution of power. A combination of the latter with permanent mechanisms for a symbiotic relationship between communities, NGOs, civil society organizations, private business and the public sector and between levels of government will strengthen the national government and nation building through dialogue and consensus. The

aim is to decompose power to the District to the extent that the District Assemblies are in effective and total control of their departments and staff within the context of relevant legislation. Ultimately, District departments must have the capacity to carry out all District level programs and projects funded from their own resources and by central government. In the latter case, decisions on resource utilization including priorities and intra-District location must lie with the local authority. Central government must progressively use District Assemblies as agents for the local provision of physical infrastructure and services wholly or part funded by the former. The goal is to provide for a situation where national development plans are an aggregation of local development plans and the latter are a dis-aggregation of national plans. Dialogue between national and local level must achieve a synthesis of mutually supportive measures, which bind together national policies and local aspirations (Government of Ghana, 2003: 41).

In short, the GPRS recognizes that decentralization and the strengthening of District Assemblies goes beyond decongestion of public sector activities and the decomposition of power. It sees decentralization as an "opportunity to involve more people and more institutions in the formulation and delivery of development policy for poverty reduction and growth. Decentralization maximizes the use of human resources, optimizes equity and provides a basis for accountability and transparency" (Government of Ghana, 2003: 135).

As noted earlier, in principle, there are many advantages to making local governments responsible for designing their local poverty alleviation programs. In the bottom-up approach envisaged in decentralization, local governments will design their programs, which are then collated at the regional level and subsequently fed into the broader national plan. Districts may have different levels of need for public services because of differences in geography and differences in income and demographic composition. Arguably, although the GPRS was greatly informed by public consultation, it has not followed the bottom-up approach as envisaged. Poverty alleviation programs were designed at the centre with strong decentralizing provisions to encourage and ensure effective implementation at the local levels. The role of local governments became more central in the implementation and monitoring than in the design of the strategy. There are good reasons for this. For one thing, the national surveys and poverty diagnosis that formed the background to the GPRS had weak district specific dimensions. The original survey data was based on national household sampling and therefore not all districts would have been included in the sample. Consequently, it would have been erroneous to design district specific policies towards poverty alleviation which uniquely reflect the local needs. In this circumstance, one could not have assumed that local governments were better informed about local needs than the central government. Moreover, the administrative capacity of local governments at the time of the design of the GPRS was manifestly weak.

Making them responsible for the design would most surely have been a catastrophe. The picture of poverty that emerged from the national poverty diagnosis called for a comprehensive national plan and relatively large expenditures in most parts of the country and revealed that the short term goals of poverty alleviation would have been difficult to pursue in a fragmented system. The existence of a great number of small, large and varied districts would surely have made it difficult to achieve the required degree of uniformity in program design and equitable distribution of resources as envisaged under the GPRS. Thus, while the design of the strategy may have involved a mixture of bottom-up and top-down approaches, the DAs did have an important role to play in actually delivering the poverty alleviation programs.

The NPP government's Poverty Reduction Strategy seems to differ from that of its predecessor National Democratic Congress (NDC) government which ruled from 1993–2000. Even though the NDC government implemented a radical decentralization program, its main objective of decentralization was not for poverty reduction or the delivery of programs per se but for popular participation. This notwithstanding, it was under the NDC government that the Productivity and Income Generation Fund (or the "District Assembly Poverty Alleviation Fund")[4] was introduced in 1996. The Fund, generated through the allocation of 20 percent of the districts' yearly shares of the District Assemblies Common Fund, created a line of credit in each district (Ayee, 2004a). The GPRS, on the other hand, focused on providing the enabling environment to empower the people to participate in wealth creation and to partake in its benefits. It sought to ensure that the people have access to basic social services and participate in decisions that affect their lives. In translating these commitments towards pro-poor governance, the GPRS calls for a comprehensive program to strengthen the capacities and institutions of local governments to enhance planning, implementation, and monitoring of programs at the national, regional, district and sub-districts levels to support the implementation of GPRS and other development programs (Government of Ghana, 2003).

4. Targeted Interventions and the Impact of Decentralization on Poverty Reduction

4.1 Targeted Interventions and Institutional Structures

The government of Ghana with the support of development partners is implementing several targeted interventions to reduce poverty. Many of these interventions are community-based, and are designed to optimize the involvement of beneficiaries in their implementation. Table 9.1 provides a summary of some of the notable poverty reduction targeted interventions (Ayee, 2004a).

A number of institutional structures and mechanisms have been established to oversee and coordinate poverty reduction initiatives. These include the Government of Ghana/Donor Consultative Group on Poverty, the Inter-Ministerial Committee on Poverty Reduction, and the Technical Committee on Poverty (TCOP). Other permanent arrangements are the decentralized participatory development planning system and the poverty monitoring system. At the national level, the National Development Planning Commission (NDPC) is mandated to monitor and evaluate the performance of poverty-related programs and activities. However, the Ghana Statistical Services (GSS) is the primary Government of Ghana agency responsible for the collection and analysis of data on poverty at the national and regional levels. The key institution responsible for poverty programming and monitoring at the district level is the District Assembly. The technical planning wing of the District Assembly, the District Planning Coordinating Unit (DPCU) is required to update and maintain district poverty profiles. To facilitate the formulation of comprehensive poverty reduction programs for funding under the national budget, ministries, departments and agencies have Poverty Desk Officers (PDOs). They are the direct link between their institutions and the TCOP as well as the focal point and liaison for issues relating to poverty reduction (Ayee, 2004a).

4.2 The Impact of Decentralization on Poverty Reduction

The impact of decentralization on poverty reduction is measured by the following four indicators: (i) responsiveness to needs of the poor; (ii) levels and quality of representation and participation of the poor; (iii) social and economic outcomes such as the promotion of human development, social equity, increase in incomes and spatial or inter-regional equality; and (iv) accountability of officials to the poor. Although these indicators may seem arbitrary, they adequately capture the essence of promoting decentralization in Ghana.

Responsiveness to needs of the poor
One of the objectives of the decentralization program is to ensure that people living in the rural areas have access to basic services and infrastructure. Indeed, the District Assemblies (DAs) have undertaken development projects such as the construction and maintenance of classroom blocks, feeder roads, clinics, public toilets, markets and provision of street-lights in rural areas previously without access to these services. In the Aowin/Suaman, Juabeso and Asante Akim North districts, for instance, recycled engine oil was used to harden road surfaces. Some of these projects were undertaken in collaboration with local and international non-governmental organizations. In addition to projects undertaken by either the District Assemblies or NGOs, other poverty reduction targeted

Table 9.1 Selected Poverty Reduction Programs

Program	Objectives	Duration	Target Geographical Area	Investment (U.S.$)	Leading Government Agency	Partner/Donor Organization
Social Investment Fund	Improve access of poor to basic social and economic infrastructure services; enhance access of the poor to financial services	1999-2004	Target of 80 districts in four years	18.6 million	Semi-autonomous Board of Directors chaired by National Development Planning Commission (NDPC)	African Development Bank and the UNDP
Village Infrastructure Program	Empower local communities and beneficiary groups to identify, plan, implement and maintain small, village-level infrastructure investments	1998-2005	All 110 districts	60 million	Ministry of Food and Agriculture	World Bank, International Fund for Agriculture Development
Rural and Urban Community-based Development Program	Rural: Improve the nutritional status of children and women. Urban: Improve social and economic conditions of the urban poor; assist street children	1994-	Rural: 3 districts in Northern Ghana, Yendi, Builsa and Tolon-Kumbungu 1. Urban: 2 districts in the nation's capital, Accra	Not fixed, depends on community requests. About $1 million in 1998	Ministry of Local Government and Rural Development	UNICEF
Community Water and Sanitation	Provision of reliable and easily accessible sources of safe drinking water	1993-	All the 10 administrative regions	6 million	Community Water and Sanitation Department	World Bank, DANIDA, European Union, CIDA, JICA, GTZ, KfW

Source: Compiled from various donor funded projects of the World Bank, DANIDA, European Union, CIDA, JICA, UNICEF, USAID, ADB and GTZ.

interventions are noted in Table 9.1. For instance, the District Capitals Project, started in 1990 achieved the following:

- Construction of piped water supply schemes completed in Ejura, Nkoranza and Kintampo districts and the communities have been organized to manage them on their own; and
- Constructed markets and lorry parks in twenty-two towns in ten districts in the Brong Ahafo and Ashanti Regions (MLGRD, 2002).

The projects have in turn opened up development opportunities in the districts. Improvements in health and sanitation infrastructure have removed some of the barriers to social and economic development. Even though a look at the budgets of all the original 110 districts in Ghana showed that less than 10 percent of their budget was devoted to financing projects in the health, education, local government and rural development programs, the evidence shows that there has been considerable infrastructure development in the districts compared to the period before the creation of the 110 DAs in 1988/89. This notwithstanding, complaints have come from some rural people that most of these services and infrastructure have been concentrated mainly in the district capitals to the detriment of the rural areas (Ayee, 2003a).

The District Assembly system has greatly enhanced popular participation in local government, and included greater numbers of previously excluded groups. Yet the responsiveness of the DAs to popular development needs and to those of the poor in particular has fallen short of expectations (Crook and Sverrisson, 2001).

Levels and quality of representation and participation of the poor
Another main objective of the decentralization program is to allow for participation of the people in their own affairs and therefore empower them. The activities of DAs have enabled the local people to show some interest in their affairs, creating a spirit of voluntarism and awareness of the need to develop one's community, especially at the beginning of the program. However, people's interest declined when they realized that their expectations cannot be fulfilled because of the weak capacity of the DAs. The DAs lacked the human and financial resources to implement their set development objectives. In addition, as much as possible, district plans are subjected to a public hearing at the sub-district level but the hearing is not patronized by most people. This is mainly because of apathy and the inability of some sub-district structures to be in place due to composition problems. In spite of these difficulties, the DAs created a high level of political awareness, facilitating some political dynamism, with some functionaries of the DAs and members of the electorate demanding greater accountability from the District Chief Executive, Presiding Members and DA members (Ayee, 2004a; 2004b).

The representative nature of the DAs has been criticized on a number of grounds. First, the DAs have provided limited opportunities for formal participation. There are formal and informal procedures and opportunities for popular participation in the local policy-making process through DA meetings and DA members meeting the electorate. These, however, have been grossly inadequate and often irregular. Second, the composition of the DAs is rarely, if ever, representative of the populations they are governing. Elected representatives are usually drawn from mainly professional classes. For example, males in the highly educated and elite occupations are over-represented on the DAs – accounting for over 89 percent. The poor have usually been under-represented, as are women. In spite of the government's directive that 30 percent of government appointments will be reserved for women, men dominate the work of the DAs. For instance, in the 1998 district level elections, only 3.6 percent out of the 15,220 contestants were females. In 2002, however, the ratio increased to 6.9 percent out of the total number of 13,950 candidates. This notwithstanding, the 2002 DA elections witnessed a 74 percent increase in the number of women elected (from 196 in 1998 to 341 in 2002). Third, there is the perception that the 30 percent government appointees are selected without adequate consultation with traditional authorities and other interest groups in the district. This perception undermines the representative nature of the DAs, especially in cases where the Presiding Member (PM) is a government appointee and government appointees dominate the key committees such as the Executive Committee (EXECO). The pro-government stance of most of the government appointees often brings them into conflict with the elected members. This notwithstanding, some government appointees because of their status and education have constructively criticized government policies and programs (Ayee, 2003b).

Social and economic outcomes
The issue of poverty reduction is central to the decentralization program, even though there is the perception[5] that poverty reduction was not part of the original objectives of decentralization in Ghana but rather an objective later forced by donors on the government. Given the central role of poverty reduction to the decentralization program, a number of poverty reduction strategies have been formulated with district implementation in mind. They include the Program of Actions to Mitigate the Social Costs of Adjustment (PAMSCAD)[6] in 1987, the Productivity and Income Generation Fund popularly called the "District Assembly Poverty Alleviation Fund" in 1996 and the Highly Indebted Poor Countries (HIPC) Funds in 2002.[7]

The Poverty Alleviation Fund was to give the poor access to credit to use in investment in job creation. Even though this was a laudable scheme and had assisted hitherto vulnerable groups like women in small-scale industries, it was not well implemented for a number of reasons. First, the means for selection of beneficiaries were unclear. There is the perception, rightly or wrongly, that most of the beneficiaries were selected based on their political affiliations and not on their levels of deprivation and vulnerability. Second, there has been a high default rate in the re-payment of the loans given out because the beneficiaries have not invested these funds to create the expected job but rather treated them as a booty to meet personal commitments. In addition, apart from the smallness of the loan (¢500,000) because this ensured that a large number of the population benefited from it, the credit facility was not disbursed on schedule when people most needed it.

Under the GPRS, the HIPC funds are meant to reduce the plight of the poor and vulnerable groups by directly providing them with basic social and economic services as well as productive assets. Since 2002, a total of ¢4.59 trillion has been transferred into the HIPC account and ¢4.52 trillion disbursed from the HIPC account to support poverty-related spending by Ministries, Departments and Agencies. HIPC funds were also directly allocated to the District Assemblies to be used in providing school infrastructure, health facilities, sanitation services, safe drinking water for their communities and in developing the capacity for disaster preparedness. Thus through the HIPC funds, the government deepens its decentralization policy by providing additional funds for increased access to quality education, health services and sanitation in the rural areas.

Accountability of officials to the poor [8]
The 1992 Ghanaian Constitution requires that District Chief Executives (DCEs), the political and administrative heads of districts, and up to 30 percent of Assembly members are appointed by the President. In practice, this stipulation undermines accountability of the DCEs and government appointees to the people.

A local political process is important to ensure the accountability and responsiveness of decentralized government to the poor (Olowu & Wunsch, 2004; Olowu, 2003). The key institution in this is the DA. It mediates between the public and the District Chief Executive. To be accountable, it must be able then, to assert some control over the executive as well as be accountable to and represent local opinion. Both of these dimensions are now considered.

Effective accountability of the District Chief Executive (DCE) to the DA has yet to be achieved. The problem is that the DCE is centrally appointed, is far more powerful than the Presiding Member (PM) of the DA, and plays the dual role as the local chief executive and the representative of the central government. In these capacities, the DCE exerts great influence over the DAs. In addition, the DCE is the most influential member of the DA, as reflected by his chairmanship of the Executive Committee (EXECO), which serves as the nerve centre of the DA and exercises executive and coordinating responsibilities. Neither in law nor practice does the Presiding Member (PM), the chairman of the DA, ever present a real threat to the dominance and pre-eminence of the DCE. In short, the extremely active role of the DCE has undermined the democratic orientation of the decentralization program.

4.4 Fiscal Decentralization and Poverty Reduction

Fiscal decentralization, that is, the decentralization of governance, expenditure delivery and revenue mobilization, has become the "midwife" between the financing of local government services and the degree of autonomy of subnational governments in making budget decisions. In other words, fiscal decentralization entails the transfer of financial resources from the central government to local government units taking account of the responsibilities allocated to these institutions. The ceding of revenue to local government units by the central government, the mobilization and management of resources by local government units and revenue sharing formula are indicative of fiscal decentralization (Smoke, 2003; Rondinelli et. al., 1989; Olowu, 2003).

Fiscal decentralization addresses the division of fiscal responsibilities between central and local governments and the transfer of such responsibilities and resources from the former to the latter. In specific terms, fiscal decentralization involves expenditure allocation, revenue allocation, intergovernmental transfers, borrowing, financial management arrangements, information technology and legal structures. Indeed, at the heart of fiscal decentralization is the impact of local revenue sources on patterns of expenditure.

As earlier indicated, Ghana's decentralization program is intended to achieve two things. First, it is to stimulate greater popular participation and interest in local government through enhanced representation and influence on local development projects. Second, it is to encourage greater readiness on the part of local populations to contribute to local development efforts (via, among other things, setting the rates and other forms of local taxation). There was, however, a conflict between these aims and the continuous reluctance of the central government (there is a long history of this) to give very much real autonomy to the District Assemblies.

The result has been a vicious cycle. DAs have had little revenue for development projects hence local populations lost interest and were reluctant to contribute more through local taxes to the DAs which seemed to be doing little for them (Ayee, 2003a; Crook, 1994). These problems are compounded first by the variability of the internally generated revenue sources which makes budgeting and cash flow forecasting difficult, and second, by the simple fact that local revenue increases do not match increases in income or population (Ayee, 1995). The establishment of the District Assemblies Common Fund (DACF) under Section 252 of the 1992 Constitution stipulated that not less than 5 percent of total central government revenues are to be allocated to the DAs for development. This was intended to provide some predictability of revenues to the DAs to finance their large and growing needs.

The formula for allocating the DACF among the DAs reflects a combination of the desire to equalize fiscal capacity (or reduce disparities in levels of public service) and to encourage the DAs to mobilize resources. The five underlying principles in designing the DACF formula are: (a) to redress fiscal imbalances; (b) to motivate and encourage the DAs to mobilize resources locally; (c) to provide some minimum level of funding to the DAs; (d) to make provision for addressing environmental degradation caused by pressures on existing services as a result of increased population; and (e) to cater for unforeseen developments.

At its inception in 1993, the five factors that form the basis for the formula are:

- Need is meant to redress current imbalances or disparities in the development of districts;

- Equalization is to ensure that each district has a minimum amount for a significant development program to be initiated;

- Responsiveness is meant to stimulate local mobilization of funds for development;

- Service Pressure is to address environmental, sanitation and health problems facing the big cities such as Accra and Kumasi as a result of urbanization;

- Contingency provides for unforeseen developments in any of the districts or for any problem which might occur in the course of applying the formula.

The formula for the disbursement of the DACF is normally submitted annually to Parliament by the Common Fund Administrator. Transfers from the DACF appear to be consistent with the three basic principles that underpin an effective intergovernmental transfer system, which are: (a) transfers are determined as objectively and openly as possible, ideally by some well-established formula; (b) transfers are relatively stable from year to year to permit rational subnational budgeting; (c) the transfer formula is transparent, based on credible factors and is as simple as possible (Ayee, 2004a).

Extent of fiscal decentralization

Local government fiscal operations can play an important role in macromanagement of the economy (Ekpo and Ndebbio, 1998). At the local level, certain goods and services are best provided through public means, hence issues of efficiency, resource allocation and distribution become relevant. Also certain taxes, levies and rates are better collected by the local government.

The financial provisions of the local government system are contained in Articles 245 and 252 of the 1992 constitution, the Local Government Act, 1993 (Act 462) and the PNDC law 207. The Local Government Act 1993 (Act 462) empowers District Assemblies (DA) to draw revenue from tax and non-tax sources. In addition, the DA as corporate bodies can obtain loans and other credit or earn interest on their investments. Revenue sources in the district depend on the level of socio-economic activities. The DACF as a proportion of the Gross Domestic Product (GDP) has generally been increasing since 2001. The proportion of the DACF in total government spending increased from a low 0.61 percent in 2001 to a high 3.17 percent in 2003 and fell to 2.88 percent in 2004.

5. Lessons

Viewed against the criteria of responsiveness, representation and participation, promotion of human development, social equity, increase in income and accountability, decentralized governance in Ghana has fallen far short of reducing poverty. There is some evidence that the District Assemblies have tended to allocate most of their financial resources toward education, health and local government and rural development programs. In addition, it was realized that though health and education spending are more important aspects of a poverty reduction strategy, the DAs have not been able to introduce programs to improve upon productivity, create employment and generate income. In particular, in spite of the HIPC funds and the poverty alleviation fund, there is still difficulty accessing credit which is a big constraint facing many micro, small and medium enterprises. Despite the slow progress in decentralized governance, about 52 percent of people in 12 districts[9] in Ghana still have faith in the DAs not only as the appropriate institution for solving community problems but also feel they are the key to effective delivery of services and the solution to the grassroots problems (Ayee and Amponsah, 2003).

A number of lessons can be distilled from the paper. First, community or beneficiary participation must be the cornerstone in the design and implementation of poverty reduction projects. Second, projects should be highly flexible, implementing activities according to community readiness. Third, significant investment must be made in training and building capacity among community members, and staff and officials of the Government of Ghana, District Assemblies as well as non-governmental organizations. Poverty reduction is a difficult and time-consuming process, which cannot be achieved either overnight or by a single strategy.

Notes

1. See the 1992 Constitution (Chapters 8 and 20); PNDC Law 207, 1988 which has been repealed by the Local Government Act (Act 462), 1993; the Civil Service Law (PNDC Law 327), 1993; Legislative Instrument (LI) 1514, 1991, which has been re-

pealed by LI 1589, 1994; District Assemblies Common Fund Act (Act 455), 1993; the National Development Planning Commission Act (Act 479), 1994; the National Development Planning (System) Act, (Act 480) and the legislative Instruments of 1988/89 that created the 110 District Assemblies (DAs). In addition to these, there are 8 administrative regulations, viz., the Financial Memorandum (Section 81) of the Local Government Act, (Act 54), 1961; Financial Administrative Decree (FAD), SMCD 221, 1979); the Financial Administration Regulation (FAR), LI 1234, 1979; bylaws of the 110 District Assemblies; Model Standing Orders for Municipal and District Assemblies, 1994; and Legislative Instruments of the Ministry of Local Government and Rural Development.

2. These responsibilities can be classified into three categories, namely, deconcentrated, delegated and devolved functions. For details see Ayee and Amponsah (2003).

3. This goal according to the Ghana Poverty Reduction Strategy, 2003–2005 will be achieved by (i) ensuring sound economic management for accelerated growth; (ii) increasing production and promoting sustainable livelihoods; (iii) direct support for human development and the provision of basis services; (iv) providing special programs in support of the vulnerable and excluded; (v) ensuring good governance and increased capacity of the public sector; and (vi) the active involvement of the private sector as the main engine of growth and partner in nation building.

4. The Poverty Alleviation Fund was created to remove the obstacle of lack of access to credit for self-employed, micro, small and medium scale entrepreneurs and to promote the development of micro, small and medium scale enterprises which have potential, but are constrained by lack of access to formal finance, to enhance productivity, create employment and improve incomes of the population.

5. This perception may be right or wrong. The Ministry of Local Government and Rural Development's paper on "Decentralization in Ghana: Implementation Status and Proposed Future Directions" published in March 2002 does not mention poverty reduction as an achievement or problem of decentralization This notwithstanding, one's view is that once the decentralization program was meant to give "power to the people" (empowerment) and redress the rural-urban drift, the element of poverty reduction is implicit implied in the objectives.

6. The PAMSCAD was implemented to take care of vulnerable groups who were affected by Structural Adjustment Program (SAP). For instance, the PAMSCAD credit line was to offer financial support for retrenched workers as a result of SAP to engage in small scale industries. For a review of the PAMSCAD, see Eboe Hutchful (2002).

7. Government of Ghana Budget Statement, 2003, 2005.

8. This section draws extensively on the following: J. R. A. Ayee (2003b) "Towards Effective and Accountable Local Government in Ghana," *Critical Perspectives No. 13*, Ghana Centre for Democratic Development (March): 1-27; J. R. A. and N. Amponsah, (2003c) "The District Assemblies and Local Governance: Reflections on the 2002 Local Elections" in Nicholas Amponsah & K. Boafo-Arthur (eds.) *Local Government in Ghana: Grassroots Participation in the 2002 Local Government Elections* (Accra: Department of Political Science), Chapter 3; J. R. A. Ayee (2004b) "Ghana: A Top-Down Initiative," in Dele Olowu & James Wunsch (eds.), *Local Governance in Africa: The Challenges of Democratic Decentralization* (Boulder, CO/London: Lynne Rienner), Chapter 6: 125–154.

9. The twelve districts are Bolgatanga, Bawku East, East Gonja, Wa, Kintampo, Nkoranza, Kwahu South, Akwapim North, Mfantsiman, Kommenda-Edina-Eguafo-Abirem, East Nzema and Kpandu. They were the study districts in which a pre- and post-district assemblies and unit committee elections surveys were conducted in July and August 2002. The surveys were conducted by the Department of Political Science, University of Ghana and covered 3,600 respondents in the twelve districts.

References

Alderman, H. *Social Assistance in Albania: Decentralization and Targeted Transfers.* Living Standards Measurement Study. Working Paper No. 134. The World Bank, Washington, D.C. 1998.

Amponsah, N. and Boafo-Arthur, K. "Ghana's Democratic Renaissance: An Overview." Pp. 1—18 in *Local Government in Ghana: Grassroots Participation in the 2002 Local Government Elections* edited by Nicholas Amponsah and K. Boafo-Arthur, (Accra: Department of Political Science),

Asante, F. A. *Economic Analysis of Decentralization in Rural Ghana.* (Germany: Peter Lang). 2003.

Asante, F. A. and Ayee, J. R. A. "Decentralization and Poverty Reduction.*"* A paper presented at the International Conference on *Ghana's Economy at the Half Century* organized by the Institute of Statistical, Social and Economic Research (ISSER) and Cornell University, (July 18—20, 2004), Accra.

Ayee, J. R. A. "Local Government, Decentralization and State Capacity." Pp. 45—81 in *Critical Perspectives on Politics and Socio-Economic Development in Ghana* edited by Wisdom Tettey, K.P. Puplampu & Bruce Berman. (Leiden: Brill). 2003a.

―――. *Towards Effective and Accountable Local Government in Ghana*, Critical Perspectives No. 13, Ghana Centre for Democratic Development (March): 1—27. 2003b.

―――. "Decentralized Governance and Poverty Reduction at the Local Level in Ghana." *Regional Development Dialogue*, Vol. 25, No. 1 (Spring): 71—86. 2004a

―――. "Ghana: A Top-Down Initiative." Pp. 125—154 in *Local Governance in Africa: The Challenges of Democratic Decentralization* edited by Dele Olowu and James Wunsch (Boulder, CO./London: Lynne Rienner), 2004b.

Ayee J. R. A. and Amponsah, N. "The District Assemblies and Local Governance: Reflections on the 2002 Local Elections." Pp 49-98 in *Local Government in Ghana: Grassroots Participation in the 2002 Local Government Elections* edited by Nicholas Amponsah & K. Boafo-Arthur. (Accra: Department of Political Science). 2003c.

Bird, R., Litvack, J. and Rao, M .G. *Intergovernmental Fiscal Relations and Poverty Alleviation in Vietnam*, Policy Research Working Paper 1430, East Asia and Pacific, Country Department 1, Country Operations Division (Washington, DC.: World Bank). 1995.

Bird, R. and Rodriquez, E. R. "Decentralization and Poverty Alleviation: International Experience and the Case of the Philippines.*"* *Public Administration and Development*, Vol. 19: 299—319. 1999.

Blackwood, D. L. and Lynch, R. G. *The Measurement of Inequality and Poverty: A Policy Maker's Guide to the Literature.* World Development, Vol. 22, No. 4. 1994.

Conyers, D. "The Management and Implementation of Decentralized Administration" in *Decentralized Administration in Africa: Policies and Training* (London: Commonwealth Secretariat). 1989.

Crook, R. C. and J. Manor *Democracy and Decentralization in South Asia and West Africa* (Cambridge: Cambridge University Press). 1998.

———. "Four Years of the Ghana District Assemblies in Operation: Decentralization, Democratization and Development," *Public Administration and Development,* Vol. 14, No. 3: 339—364. 1994.

———."Decentralization and Poverty Reduction in Africa: The Politics of Local-Central Relations." *Public Administration and Development,* Vol. 23: 77—88. 2003.

Crook, R. C. and Sverrisson, A. S. *Decentralization and Poverty Alleviation in Developing Countries: A Comparative Analysis or, is West Bengal Unique?* IDS Working Paper 130 (June 2001): 1—60.

Decentralization Secretariat, Ministry of Local Government and Rural Development. *National Decentralization Action Plan (NDAP): Towards a Sector-Wide Approach for Decentralization Implementation in Ghana (2003-2005)* (Accra: MLGRD) September (unpublished). 2003.

Demery, L. *Benefit Incidence: A Practitioner's Guide.* Poverty and Social Development Group, Africa Region. (The World Bank, Washington D.C). 2000.

Ellis, F. "Household Strategies and Rural Livelihood Diversification." *The Journal of Development Studies,* Vol. 35, No. 1. 1998.

Ekpo, A. H. and Ndebbio, J. E. U. *Local Government Fiscal Operations in Nigeria.* AERC Research Paper 73. African Economic Research Consortium, Nairobi. 1998.

De Tocqueville, A. *Democracy in America,* 1956 edition (Mentor Books: New York). 1835.

Government of Ghana, *Constitution of the Republic of Ghana, 1992* (Tema: Ghana Publishing Corporation). 1992.

———. *Local Government Act (Act 462)* (Tema: Ghana Publishing Corporation). 1993.

———. Ghana Poverty Reduction Strategy, 2002-2004): An Agenda for Growth and Prosperity–Analysis and Policy Statement. February 4, 2003.

Hutchful, E. *Ghana's Adjustment Experience: The Paradox of Reform* (UNRISD/Heinemann/James Currey: Oxford, Accra, 2002.

Jong, K. de, C. Loquai and I. Soiri. *Decentralization and Poverty Reduction: Exploring the Linkages.* IDS Policy Papers, 1/99. Institute of Development Studies, Helsinki and ECDPM, Maastricht. 1999.

Lipton, M. and van der Gaag, J. eds. *Including the Poor.* Proceedings of a Symposium Organised by the World Bank and the International Food Policy Research Institute, Washington, D.C. 1993.

Litvack, J., Ahmad, J. and Bird, R. *Rethinking Decentralization in Developing Countries.* Sector Studies Series. The World Bank, Washington, D.C. 1998.

Mill, J.S. *Considerations on Representative Government,* 1910 edition (J.M. Dent and Sons: London). 1861.

Ministry of Local Government and Rural Development. *Decentralization in Ghana: Implementation Status and Proposed Future Directions* (Accra: Ministry of Local Government and Rural Development), March: 1-28. 2002.

Olowu, Dele "Local Institutional and Political Structures and Processes: Recent Experience in Africa." *Public Administration and Development*, Vol. 23: 41—52. 2003.

————— and Wunsch, James eds. *Local Governance in Africa: The Challenges of Democratic Decentralization* (Boulder, CO./London: Lynne Rienner). 2004.

Rondinelli, D. A., McCullogh, J. S and Johnson, R. W. "Analyzing Decentralization Policies in Developing Countries: A Political Economy Framework", *Development and Change*, Vol. 20: 57—87. 1989.

Sen, Amartya *Development as Freedom* (New York: Knopf). 1999.

Shah, A. *The Reform of Intergovernmental Fiscal Relations in Developing Countries and Emerging Market Economies*, Policy and Research Series 23, (Washington, DC.: World Bank). 1994.

Smoke, P. "Decentralization in Africa: Goals, Dimensions, Myths and Challenges." *Public Administration and Development*, Vol. 23: 7—16. 2003.

World Bank *World Development Report, 2000-2001 Attacking Poverty* (Oxford: Oxford University Press). 2001.

10

Tackling Child Poverty in Ghana

Abena D. Oduro and Isaac Osei-Akoto

1. Introduction

In many African countries those aged under eighteen years make up between 40 and 50 percent of the total population. In Ghana, children make up about half of the population. Tackling child poverty is necessary because the deprivation that is usually associated with poverty during childhood increases the probability of becoming a poor adult. Childhood poverty is different from adult poverty. Severe childhood poverty can "cause children permanent damage (both physically and mentally) stunt and distort their development and destroy the opportunities of fulfillment, including the roles they are expected to play successively as they get older in the family, community and society."[1] It is not surprising therefore that UNICEF states that poverty reduction begins with improving the lives of children.

Reducing poverty amongst adults through, for example, education, skills training and income generating opportunities will not always result in a reduction in child poverty. A reduction in adult poverty is a necessary but not sufficient condition for the reduction of child poverty. Policy interventions must be designed to protect the rights of children and ensure that their basic needs are met. It cannot be assumed that the family unit or community will always ensure that the rights and the well-being of the child are protected and catered for. Protecting and ensuring the rights of children are required from a moral perspective. In addition, an improvement in the welfare of children will have positive development effects for society as a whole.

This chapter examines the extent to which the Ghana Poverty Reduction Strategy Paper (GPRS) for 2003—2005 identified child poverty as an issue and proposed strategies to protect the rights and ensure the well-being of children. The second section of the chapter provides a profile of child poverty in Ghana. An assessment of the extent to which the GPRS tackled issues of child poverty is conducted by providing answers to a number of questions. The first question asks whether the poverty profile contained in the GPRS adequately provides a situation analysis of child poverty. The second question is whether the growth strategy subscribed to in the GPRS is sufficiently pro-poor. The third question is whether social sector spending in the GPRS addresses the needs of children and the fourth question is whether child poverty is adequately prioritized in the GPRS. Section five concludes the chapter.

2. A Profile of Child Poverty in Ghana

Poverty has been traditionally measured using either income or consumption expenditure as the welfare measure. Thus individuals or households that have either income or consumption expenditure below a critical level, such as the poverty line, are identified as being poor. A rough and ready measure to identify poor children is to estimate the proportion of children who live in poor households. Using this measure it is estimated that approximately 44 percent of children lived in households with consumption expenditure per adult equivalent below the poverty line of 900,000 cedis in 1998/99.[2] The incidence of child poverty ranged from 6.4 percent in the Greater Accra Region to 40.2 percent in the Brong-Ahafo region and 89.6 percent in the Upper West region (Table 10.1). Approximately 30 percent of children lived in households in extreme poverty. They lived in households with consumption expenditure per adult equivalent below the lower poverty line of 700,000 cedis. Almost 54 percent of rural children lived in poor households. This finding is not surprising since in 1998/1999 almost half of the rural population was poor.

Counting the number of children living in poor households provides only a partial picture of the extent of child poverty. An underlying assumption of this method of identifying poor children is that the pattern of intra-household resource allocation is the same across households. It is therefore assumed that children in non-poor households must have higher consumption expenditures than children in poor households. If however, intra-household resource allocations vary across households, as they most certainly do, then it is possible that a child living in a non-poor household could have a level of consumption expenditure lower than that of a child living in a poor household.

Consumption expenditure or income provides an incomplete perspective of the nature, extent and depth of poverty. A child in poverty is most likely growing up without access to adequate nutritional resources needed for survival, has limited opportunities for human development, and is growing up without adequate family and community structures for nurturing and protection. Generally children in poverty do not have the opportunity to make their opinions heard.[3]

Thus as in the case of poverty in general, measuring and assessing the extent of child poverty should not be limited to the dimension of income or consumption poverty, but must also include non-income measures of poverty. Indeed the non-income dimensions reflect the very essence of child poverty.

Table 10.1 The Incidence of Consumption Poverty Amongst Children

Region	Children	Entire Population
Western	30.5	27.3
Central	54.9	48.4
Greater Accra	6.4	5.2
Eastern	45.8	43.7
Volta	42.7	37.7
Ashanti	33.0	27.7
Brong Ahafo	40.2	35.8
Northern	72.1	69.2
Upper East	86.1	83.9
Upper West	89.6	88.2
Locality		
Urban	22.0	19.4
Rural	53.7	49.5
Ghana	43.9	39.5

Source: Estimated by the authors using the fourth Ghana Living Standards Survey.

Child poverty will be discussed using the concept of absolute poverty that was adopted during the World Summit for Social Development in 1995. Absolute poverty is defined as "a condition characterized by severe deprivation of basic human needs including food, safe drinking water, sanitation facilities, health, shelter, education and information. It depends not only on income but also on access to social services."[4] These seven measures of absolute poverty will be used to present a profile of child poverty using non-income variables.[5]

2.1. The Seven Measures of Absolute Poverty amongst Children

Severe Food Deprivation
Children less than five years old who suffer severe food deprivation have weight to age ratios more than three standard deviations below the median of the international reference population. Approximately 16 percent of children less than five years old were severely food deprived in 1997 (Table 10.2). In 2003 the

Oduro and Osei-Akoto

Table 10.2 Incidence of Severe Deprivation among Children, 1997

	Food	Water	Sanitation	Shelter	Education
Western	13.3	59.7	16.8	16.6	7.4
Central	14.2	41.2	17.8	22.3	9.0
Greater Accra	8.2	12.8	9.0	13.8	8.0
Volta	12.7	63.4	6.0	12.6	8.5
Eastern	14.0	73.8	26.3	7.5	5.1
Ashanti	11.8	40.8	12.5	25.6	8.6
Brong Ahafo	11.3	60.4	13.5	17.6	5.6
Northern	28.6	75.0	80.4	1.8	50.8
Upper East	35.7	46.8	92.4	1.8	44.9
Upper West	30.8	35.1	85.5	0.4	51.3
Ghana	16.1	52.6	27.5	13.9	14.9

Source: Estimated using the Core Welfare Indicators Questionnaire Survey, 1997.

Table 10.3 Incidence of Severe Deprivation Among Children, 2003

	Food Deprivation	Water Deprivation	Health Deprivation	Sanitation Deprivation	Shelter Deprivation	Education Deprivation	Information Deprivation
Western	16.3	29.5	7.3	14.2	25.4	7.3	22.5
Central	15.2	17.9	7.4	21.3	25.5	6.2	29.4
Greater Accra	21.3	12.7	4.6	9.0	12.4	4.7	11.4
Volta	17.3	47.8	9.4	30.3	25.5	14.7	34.7
Eastern	14.2	34.8	8.1	7.4	27.3	6.7	21.7
Ashanti	21.6	17.8	6.8	9.6	27.2	5.3	18.9
Brong Ahafo	16.0	41.2	7.8	17.1	35.3	10.9	27.6
Northern	22.3	53.9	9.1	82.8	19.2	43.5	34.8
Upper East	16.2	31.8	9.9	90.5	48.2	34.3	37.0
Upper West	13.9	38.0	7.5	79.6	48.1	37.2	40.4
Ghana	18.3	30.9	7.6	27.5	26.5	13.4	25.3

Source: Estimated using the Core Welfare Indicators Questionnaire Survey, 2003.

proportion of severely food deprived children was higher at 18.1 percent (Table 10.3). Severe food deprivation amongst children was highest in the three northern and poorest regions, the Upper East, Upper West and Northern regions in 1997 (Table 10.2). However, in 2003 there was a significant decline in the proportion of children with severe food deprivation in these regions (Table 10.3). The southern regions, on the other hand, registered increases. In the Greater Accra region for example, the proportion of children who were severely food deprived more than doubled between 1997 and 2003 (Tables 10.2 and 10.3).

At the national level severe food deprivation was more likely amongst rural children in 1997. Approximately 18 percent of rural children were severely food deprived compared to 11 percent of urban children. However, the Central, Greater Accra, Volta, Brong-Ahafo and Upper West regions were the exceptions to this pattern. In these regions the incidence of severe food deprivation was higher amongst urban children. In 2003, there was no significant rural urban difference. The proportion of children suffering from severe food deprivation averaged approximately 18 percent in both urban and rural locations. In 1997, 15 percent of girls were severely food deprived compared to about 17 percent of boys. In 2003 the proportion of severely food deprived girls and boys was 17 percent and 20 percent respectively.

Severe Water Deprivation
Children suffer from severe water deprivation when the only source of drinking water is surface water or where the nearest water source is more than fifteen minutes away from the household. Approximately 53 percent of children suffered severe water deprivation in 1997. The proportion declined to about thirty-one percent in 2003 (Table 10.3).

In 1997, the highest proportion of severely water deprived children was to be found in the Northern, Eastern and Volta regions (Table 10.2). In 2003, although significantly lower, the Northern region still had the highest proportion of children experiencing severe water deprivation (Table 10.3). Approximately 65 percent (42 percent) of rural children were severely water deprived compared to 21 percent (13 percent) of urban children in 1997 and 2003 respectively. In none of the ten regions was the proportion of severely water deprived children in rural households lower than the proportion in urban households.

Severe Deprivation of Sanitation Facilities
Approximately 27 percent of children do not have access to toilet facilities of any kind in the vicinity of their dwelling. This is a particular problem in the three northern regions where the proportion of children do not have access to sanitation is almost three times the proportion of children in the other regions (Tables 10.2 and 10.3). In all regions of the country rural children are at a disadvantage with a greater proportion of them, compared to urban children, being without access to proper sanitation. The proportion of children experiencing severe sanitation deprivation is estimated to have remained at 27 percent in 2003 (Table 10.3).

Severe Health Deprivation
Severe health deprivation occurs when a child has not been vaccinated against any childhood diseases. About 8 percent of children in 2003 fell into this cate-

gory. The Upper East region had the highest proportion of children who had not been immunized against any of the childhood diseases (Table 10.3). In all regions, except for Greater Accra, the proportion of rural children that had been immunized was lower than the proportion of urban children.

Severe Shelter Deprivation
In 1997 and 2003 approximately 14 percent and 26 percent of children lived in dwellings with more than five people in a room (Tables 10.2 and 10.3). Rural children are more likely than urban children to be severely shelter deprived. The lack of privacy and exposure to infectious disease that is associated with overcrowding can have negative impacts on the well-being of children.

Severe Education Deprivation
Approximately 15 percent of children aged seven to seventeen years were severely education deprived in 1997. These are children who have never attended school. The three northern regions had the highest incidence of severe education deprivation amongst children. Rural children were more likely not to have attended school compared to urban children. However, in 1997 the incidence of severe education deprivation was higher amongst urban children in Ashanti, Brong-Ahafo and Eastern Regions. Overall, severe education deprivation declined in 2003 to 13.4 percent (Table 10.3). Even then, the proportion of rural children with severe deprivation was higher than the proportion of urban children. The Central Region was the exception because there was no significant difference between urban and rural children. A lower proportion of boys compared to girls were severely education deprived in 1997. The pattern was the same in 2003, with 12.5 percent of boys experiencing severe education deprivation compared to 14.3 percent of girls.

Severe Information Deprivation
Severe information deprivation is measured as the lack of access to television, radio, telephone or newspapers. Approximately a quarter of children aged three years and above in 2003 was severely information deprived (Table 10.3). The three northern regions and the Volta region had the highest proportions of severely information deprived children in 2003 (Table 10.3). Rural children were particularly disadvantaged in all regions. Thirty percent of rural children were severely information deprived compared to 18 percent of urban children.

2.2. Children in Absolute Poverty

Amongst the seven indicators of severe deprivation that have been examined water deprivation affected the highest proportion of children in 1997 and 2003 (Tables 10.2 and 10.3). Severe sanitation deprivation ranked second after water deprivation. Drinking unsafe water and having poor or non-existent sanitary facilities expose children to infections and diseases, some of which are life threatening if not diagnosed early and properly treated. Worm infestations can result in below average child health indicators and can adversely affect the child's attendance and performance in school.

A child may be described as living in absolute poverty if he or she suffers from severe deprivation with respect to more than one of the following five needs: food, water, sanitation, shelter, and education. Using this measure and the comparable datasets for 1997 and 2003,[6] about 29.3 percent of children were living in absolute poverty in 1997. In 2003 the proportion declined to 27.7 percent. However, five regions (Eastern, Volta, Brong Ahafo Upper East and Upper West regions) recorded increases in absolute poverty (Figure 10.1). The highest increase (a 10.2 percent rise) was observed in Upper East mainly due to an increase in the proportion of children experiencing shelter deprivation (see Tables 10.2 and 10.3).

Nearly 40 percent of rural children in 1997 and 2003 were living in absolute poverty compared to about 10 percent of urban children. This goes against the fact that significant progress was made between 1997 and 2003 in increasing access to basic services for children, in the three northern regions in particular.[7] At the start of the implementation of the GPRS in 2003 about 28 percent of children lived in absolute poverty. The proportion ranged from 7.5 percent in the Greater Accra Region to 69.2 percent in the Upper East region.

Figure 10.1 Proportion of Children Living in Absolute Poverty in 1997, 2003

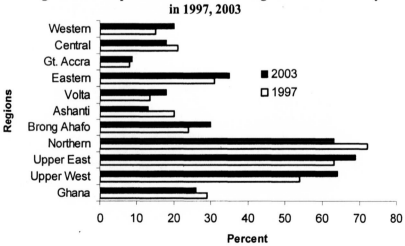

Source: Estimated by the authors using the Core Indicators Welfare Questionnaire, 1997 and 2003.

The focus of the discussion has been on children living under what may be considered as severe conditions. However, there are children who do not live in absolute poverty, but who also face the risk of developing into poor adults with limited options. Children less than five years old who suffer what may be described as moderate food deprivation have weight to age ratios more than two standard deviations below the median of the international reference population. In 1997 and 2003 approximately 10 percent and 7.5 percent of children suffered from moderate food deprivation.[8] The discussion on shelter deprivation has focused on children living in overcrowded conditions but is silent—because of insufficient data—on children living on the streets either with or without their families. In addition to children who have never attended school there are also those children who do not complete primary school or basic education and are therefore likely to face constrained options in the future. The measures of absolute poverty that have been discussed do not include evidence on child labor. For some children work substitutes for school and for others work substitutes for leisure. In 2003 about 6 percent of children aged between seven and fourteen years worked. The evidence provided here suggests that reducing severe deprivation and what is described as moderate deprivation amongst children is imperative if a sustained reduction in poverty is to be achieved.

3. Child Poverty in the GPRS

The main goal of the GPRS is to "ensure sustainable equitable growth, accelerated poverty reduction and the protection of the vulnerable and excluded within a decentralized democratic environment".[9] This goal is to be achieved through a number of objectives. Two of these objectives address the concerns of children. These are facilitating direct support for equitable human resource development and providing special programs in support of the vulnerable and excluded. A reading of the main GPRS document reveals that child poverty issues are dealt with, sometimes explicitly and sometimes implicitly. The authors of the strategy intended that an attempt would be made to exceed the Millennium Development Goals (MDGs). Three of the MDGs (See Annex.) directly address the well-being of children. These are achieving universal primary education, eliminating gender disparity in primary and secondary education, and reducing the under-five mortality rate by two-thirds by 2015. Thus even though reducing child poverty is not explicitly set out as a target, the process of attaining the Millennium Development Goals would result in some dimensions of child poverty being addressed.

Profile of Child Poverty in the GPRS

The third chapter of the GPRS contains a discussion on the dimensions of poverty in Ghana. The chapter presents a poverty profile based on income (and consumption expenditure) and non-income measures of poverty. The presentation of the poverty profile does not provide any information on the proportion of children living in households with consumption expenditure below the poverty line. It is in the discussion of the trends in the social dimensions of poverty that some evidence is provided on child poverty. The evidence provided is on education and health indicators. With respect to education, data is presented on the proportion of children aged six to fifteen years attending school and distance to the nearest primary school.

Evidence provided in the document shows that most children drop out of school because they have to work. Pregnancy and early marriage were other reasons why girls dropped out of school. The GPRS recognizes that "child labor breeds another cycle of people who most likely will be less well off or end up in poverty later."[10] The health statistics provides information on mortality rates of infants and children, malnutrition, the proportion of children less than eight years old who have been vaccinated against childhood killer diseases, and on distance to the nearest health facility. The link between malnutrition, abnormal growth, vulnerability to disease, and capacity to participate effectively in school, is noted.

In the participatory poverty assessments reported in the document, urban communities were concerned about the growing number of street children and rural communities were concerned about the increase in school drop out rates. During the discussions conducted as part of the participatory poverty assessments two of the family coping mechanisms identified included reducing food consumption and withdrawing children from school. These responses to poverty and welfare-reducing shocks contribute to deepening the deprivation of children.

Uneven growth in Ghana is because "development policies ... were not sufficiently guided by adequate data on the incidence and depth of poverty...."[11] A weakness of the GPRS with respect to child poverty is its failure to provide enough information on the incidence and depth of child poverty by gender and by location and the failure to provide an explicit analysis of the scope of child poverty. Nevertheless, the chapter on the dimensions of poverty does provide some information to inform policy design.

4. Strategies to Address Child Poverty in the GPRS

In designing strategies to reduce poverty amongst children it is important to remember that children are not always in a dependent relationship with adults, and even when they are, children are individuals in their own right. A three-pronged strategy must be pursued to reduce poverty amongst children. The first strategy must consist of measures to increase family incomes. The macroeconomic framework and sector policies are important in achieving this goal. The second prong of the strategy must consist of social policy interventions to improve the capacity of families, institutions and communities to ensure the welfare of children, particularly when the preferences of parents or guardians do not sufficiently protect the welfare of children. Under this prong of the strategy for example, access to, and the quality of basic social services for children must be enhanced. A policy of providing school children with a balanced school meal each day would ensure that children receive the necessary nutrients irrespective of the ability or willingness of the child's family to provide this. The third prong of the strategy involves the enactment and the enforcement of laws that protect the rights of children. Each of the three strategies on their own is necessary but not sufficient to reduce the incidence of poverty and deprivation amongst children.

4.1. The Macroeconomic Framework of the GPRS

The growth strategy in the GPRS is based on a combining of market-led resource allocation with state intervention. Poverty reduction is expected to occur as a result of both economic growth and the appropriate distribution of resources sectorally and geographically. Although the GPRS does not indicate explicitly where greater emphasis is to be placed, for example on market forces versus state intervention, this mix is generally preferable compared to dependence only on liberalization and market forces. "Without efforts to thin out disparities in the distribution of income and assets as well as specific policies to ensure access to basic social services . . . for all, economic growth cannot guarantee an overall improvement in the quality of life."[12]

A macroeconomic framework that is pro-children and anti-poverty should create conditions for increased adult employment and income. Adult employment is necessary because evidence from Ghana and elsewhere suggest that children are less likely to be involved in child labor if adult incomes are above a critical minimum. Adequate adult incomes should normally mean that the education of children would not be compromised because of their need to enter the labour force. Also their nutritional, medical, and leisure needs will be met. Studies in the United States show that parents who are poor are also prone to irritability and depressive symptoms and this can lead to less than satisfactory emotional, social and cognitive development of children.[13]

Second, the macroeconomic framework should generate sufficient growth to support spending on basic services and programs that are supportive of children. Adequate family or household income is not enough to ensure the well being of children. There is a role for the state to make sure that all children have access to adequate nutrition, basic education, shelter and health irrespective of the income or poverty status of their family.

The GPRS targets a growth rate of 5 percent during the period 2003—2005. It is expected that the fiscal deficit will be narrowed over that period with the revenue-GDP ratio rising faster than the expenditure-GDP ratio. The document discusses strategies to increase productivity, employment and incomes. The main challenge is whether the strategies proposed would yield growth that is employment and income-generating. Whilst an increase in the incomes of adults can reduce the incidence of child labor, there is the danger that increased income opportunities will increase the demand for labor and therefore increase the demand for child labor.

4.2. Social Policy Interventions in the GPRS

Social policy interventions in the GPRS are concentrated largely within the realms of health and education. The GPRS proposes that the sectoral composition of development costs should be in favor of the social sector. Within the social sector, it is expected that 60 percent of the spending will be earmarked for education.

Several of the education targets are specific to children. Targets were set for government spending on pre-school, primary, junior secondary and senior secondary schools, and special education. In addition targets were set for gross primary and junior secondary enrolment rates, drop out rates, transition rates between primary and junior secondary and between junior secondary and senior secondary and the proportion of primary schools that had pre-schools.

The emphasis of the strategy is on basic education and measures related to early child development are also mentioned. In addition, the Ministry responsible for education is expected to work with non-governmental organizations to develop alternative education programs for out of school children such as street children. Social investment projects are expected to be adapted to include alternative education programs.[14] Targets were set for reducing the drop-out rate amongst girls. However, there were no strategies set out in the main document to improve female enrolment. Using the 1997 Core Welfare Indicators Questionnaire Survey, the proportion of boys with severe education deprivation was 2.9 percentage points lower than that of girls. This difference is not large suggesting that in some districts and communities the proportion of boys severely education deprived is higher than the proportion of girls. In 2003 the proportion of girls that suffered severe education deprivation in the Upper East and Upper West regions was lower than the proportion of boys (34.6 percent and 35.3 percent in the Upper East region and 37.2 percent and 39.8 percent in the Upper West region). The absence of a profile of child poverty in the GPRS did not mask the emerging phenomenon of lower net enrolment rates amongst boys in some districts of the country. There is a need to increase enrolment and retention rates of all children, taking into account the possibility of having to develop different strategies encouraging enrolment and retention rates amongst different groups of children in different parts of the country.

Combating HIV/AIDS is one of the priorities under human resource development and basic services in the GPRS. The GPRS reports that in Ghana there are approximately 14,000 AIDS orphans in 2001. The GPRS proposes actions to reduce the incidence of HIV/AIDS in children through programs that reduce mother-to-child transmission. The strategy also proposes the development of programs targeted at youth to increase HIV/AIDS awareness.

Child health is an important component of the strategy for health. Interventions are aimed at reducing the under-five and maternal mortality rates and child malnutrition. Other child related targets set out in the document are antenatal care, post-natal care, DPT 3 coverage and increasing the proportion of supervised births.[15] As a short-term strategy the GPRS recommends that the health exemption policy cover amongst other things mortality due to childhood illness. Child related health targets are to be achieved primarily through food based approaches and increased immunization. The GPRS also identifies vulnerable and excluded children in difficult circumstances as a distinct group. This group is made up of malnourished children, underweight and wasted children, street children, working children and *kayaye,* children subject to abuse, and children not in school

4.3. Protecting the Rights of Children in the GPRS

State organizations such as the Ghana National Council on Children (now the Children's Department in the Ministry for Women and Children's Affairs) and the Women and Juvenile Unit are to be strengthened. The strategy recommends the development of programs to increase awareness of legal provisions that protect the rights of children such as the Convention on the Rights of the Child and the Children's Act. Other recommendations include advocacy against child betrothal and child abuse, enforcement of legislation that protects children, and the implementation of elements of the International Program on Elimination of Child Labor in major towns.

4.4. Is Child Poverty Adequately Prioritized in the GPRS?

The GPRS Priorities
The main GPRS document does not highlight either child poverty or the rights of children. The actions to attain the goals of the GPRS mention the attainment of gender equity, but no mention is made of improving the welfare of children. Despite this omission, in the section on the human dimensions of poverty, some aspects of child poverty are the focus of discussion and strategies are suggested

that are aimed at reducing deprivation amongst children in the areas of child mortality, malnutrition and illiteracy.

The cost of the proposed actions to achieve the objectives was monumental; hence there was a need to prioritize the strategy because of the low absorptive capacity even if there was no financial constraint. Programs were chosen with the objective of obtaining the right balance between growth and poverty reduction[16]. The Government's medium term priorities found on pages 143 to 148 of the GPRS deviated from the main document by not explicitly incorporating the section on the vulnerable and excluded. The medium term priority programs are infrastructure, modernized agriculture based on rural development, enhanced social services, good governance, and private sector development.

Some aspects of the Government's medium-term priority programs that may have a direct impact on the welfare of children are the emphasis on early childhood developments, basic education, alternative education for children out of school, and the establishment of a model health center in each district. Modernization of agriculture was to involve actions that would ensure food security and increased agricultural production, but incentives to increase agriculture production could act as two-edged sword if the increase in production is attained by making greater use of child labor.

The Costed GPRS Programs
Although the Government's medium-term priorities did not explicitly address the issue of vulnerability and exclusion, the costing exercise classified programs on the basis of the five themes of the main GPRS document. Approximately 57 percent of the costed programs are classified as programs to encourage production and gainful employment. Infrastructure development is expected to take up 90 percent of those expenditures. Improving upon infrastructure will help reduce the marketing constraints faced by most agricultural producers. However, there is no guarantee that these measures will improve the welfare of children.

Programs to improve human resource development and provide basic services accounted for approximately 30 percent of the total budget. Programs that will have a direct impact on child welfare make up approximately 66 percent of these programs. The emphasis on early child development and basic education to age seventeen is maintained and specific mention is made of programs to keep girls in school. However there was no mention of alternative education programs for out of school children in the costed program. Programs to support the vulnerable and the excluded make up approximately 5 percent of the costed program and all the interventions have either a direct or indirect impact on the welfare of children. These programs include increasing resources to protect the rights of children, enhancing the capacity of child-care providers, and supporting orphans and people living with HIV/AIDS.

Oduro and Osei-Akoto

Table 10.4 Child Welfare Indicators in the GPRS M & E Plan

Overaching Indicators	Baseline[1]	2003 [2]	2005 Target[3]
Child Malnutrition	25%[4]	35.80%	20%
Infant mortality rate	57/1000[4]	64/1000	50/1000

Outcome Indicators	Baseline[1]	2003 [2]	2005 Target[3]
Gross Enrolment ratio:			
Pre-school	not reported		not reported
Primary	77.6%[5]	81.10%	82%
Junior Secondary	61%[5]		65%
Survival rate to P6 and JSS 3	not reported		not reported
Reported cases of Guinea worm infection	3678	8000	0
Percent of households with access to safe water			
Rural	40%	46.40%	54%
Urban	70%		78%
HIV Prevalence[6]			24%[7]

Output Indicators	Baseline[1]	2003 [2]	2005 Target[3]
% of deprived basic schools improved, with emphasis on the three northern regions			
Percent of trained teachers in pre-schools and basic schools	68.6%[5,8]	73.5%	not reported
Proportion of supervised deliveries	49%	47.1%	55%
Immunisation coverage (DPT 3)	75%[1]	69.4%	90%
Adequate security and protection for women and children			
Cases Reported to Women and Child Juvenile Unit	not reported	6,298	not reported

Input Indicators	Baseline[1]	2003 [2]	2005 Target[3]
Budgets available to institutions caring for vulnerable and excluded	not reported	not reported	not reported

Notes

1 Baseline data is obtained from the GPRS and is for 2000 or most recent year.

2. Obtained from 2003 Annual Progress Report on Implementation of the GPRS

3. 2005 targets are obtained from the GPRS

4. Data is for 1998

5. Data is for 2001

6. HIV prevalence in the Monitoring and Evaluation Plan is defined as the number of pregnant women who are reported as zero-positive.

7. Target in the GPRS for 2005 measures reductions in new infections amongst 15-49 age-group.

8. Figure is for primary schools only

Source: Republic of Ghana, An Agenda for Growth and Prosperity. Ghana's Poverty Reduction Strategy 2003–2005. Monitoring and Evaluation Plan, Accra, March 2003.

Monitoring and Evaluation

Another indicator of the priorities of reducing child poverty is the extent to which progress in achieving this goal is monitored. A monitoring and evaluation plan has been developed for the GPRS. Thirteen out of the fifty-two indicators used to monitor implementation of the GPRS are child welfare indicators (Table 10.4). The targets of the indicators would not appear to be overly optimistic. Child malnutrition, infant mortality rates, immunization coverage and the reported cases of guinea worm infection were worse in 2003 compared to the base year (Table 10.4). No appreciable change was recorded in the proportion of supervised births between the baseline year and 2003. Assessing progress towards achieving these targets for each of the indicators is therefore a central policy issue that needs to be addressed. Achievement of these targets will reduce the incidence of severe deprivation amongst children.

5. Conclusion

In 2003, the year when implementation of the GPRS began, approximately 28 percent of children were living in absolute poverty. Given the significant proportion of children living in absolute poverty and that child poverty need to be distinguished from adult poverty, the GPRS did not adequately tackle the issue of child poverty. Furthermore, the reduction in child poverty is not an explicitly stated objective of the GPRS. The implicit assumption was that tackling adult poverty indirectly tackles the problem of child poverty. This is not unreasonable in so far as children are in family relationships. Nevertheless, the GPRS contains strategies that address some of the critical health and education needs of children, however, these were part of the strategy to dealing with poverty generally in Ghana and was not developed with the specific objective of reducing poverty amongst children.

If poverty and deprivation are to be reduced amongst children the updated poverty profile of the GPRS must highlight those aspects of the well-being of children that have registered slow progress if not deterioration. The worsening of child malnutrition and infant mortality indicators between 1998 and 2003 means these should be priority areas for action. It is important that a review contains a gender perspective because of the differences that have emerged between boys and girls with respect to some education and health indicators for example. The current thinking is that the female child is disadvantaged in terms of education. However, the national Core Welfare Indicators Questionnaire Survey of 2003 shows that in some districts net primary and junior secondary enrolment rates of boys is significantly lower than that of girls.

Explicit strategies must be developed to reduce child labor and the number of street children. Measures must be recommended to ensure the enforcement of laws that have been enacted to protect the rights of children.

Poverty can have long-term debilitating effects on children and undermine efforts to develop the human capital base of the economy. Studies from other African countries have shown that inadequate food intake due to droughts even for short periods can stunt the long-term development of children. It is imperative therefore that the living conditions of children and their health and nutrition status are regularly monitored to inform policy. For most of the indicators of deprivation amongst children, public sector organizations collect information on a fairly regular basis. For example, the Ministry of Health annually collects data on child malnutrition, reported cases of guinea worm infection, immunization coverage and the proportion of supervised deliveries. The Ministry of Education has been collecting data relating to basic education indicators and is currently strengthening its management information system. For information on sanitation and housing conditions however, nationally representative data is collected during the household surveys, which unfortunately are not conducted regularly. An organization such as the Ministry for Women and Children's Affairs should be given the responsibility of collecting information on developments relating to child indicators. These should be used to present an annual report on progress made in reducing poverty and deprivation amongst children. If the incidence of child poverty in Ghana is not reduced, the dynamics of poverty will be sustained and this will undermine the poverty reduction objectives of the GPRS and Ghana's ability to attain the Millennium Development Goals.

Notes

1. Gordon *et. al* (2003).
2. This estimate of the incidence of poverty amongst children was obtained using data from the fourth Ghana Living Standards Survey conducted in 1998/99. This is a nationally representative household survey.
3. CHIP, Children in Poverty: Some Questions Answered Briefing Paper 1 (2002)
4. United Nations, The Copenhagen Declaration and Program of Action: World Summit for Social Development 6-12 March1995, New York: UNDP.
5. Information on the non-income measures of child poverty was obtained from two nationally representative household surveys——Core Welfare Indicators Questionnaire Surveys conducted in 1997 and 2003.
6. For comparison purposes between 1997 and 2003 the measure of absolute poverty is based on the five indicators that are common across the two data sets in tables 9.2 and 9.3.
7. The proportion of children severely deprived of access to basic services declined from 42.3 percent to about 19.6 percent at the national level between 1997 and 2003. The proportion for rural areas dropped from 55.2 percent to 29.6 percent, while the three northern regions recorded an average decrease of 38.1 percent. The proportion of severe deprivation of access to basic services was measured as the proportion of children living

in an area where primary school, a clinic or a hospital is not within sixty minutes of reach with what ever means of travel available to them.

8. These figures are obtained by subtracting the proportion of children suffering severe food deprivation from the proportion of children whose weight to age ratio is two standard deviations below the median of an international reference population.

9. In 1997 and 2003 the proportion of children whose weight to age ratio was more than two standard deviations below the median was 26 percent and 25.8 percent respectively.

10. Republic of Ghana, Ghana Poverty Reduction Strategy 2003-2005. An Agenda for Growth and Prosperity, Vol. I (Accra, 2003), 30.

11. Republic of Ghana, "Ghana Poverty Reduction Strategy," 24.

12. Republic of Ghana, "Ghana Poverty Reduction Strategy," 29.

13. Santosh Mehrotra and Enrique Delamonica, "Public Spending for Children: An Empirical Note", *Journal of International Development* 14, (2002): 1106.

14. Jeanne Brooks-Gunn and Greg J. Duncan, "The Effects of Poverty on Children," *Children and Poverty* 7, no.2, (Summer/Fall 1997): 55-77.

15. Republic of Ghana, "Ghana Poverty Reduction Strategy," 104.

16. Republic of Ghana, "Ghana Poverty Reduction Strategy," 110.

References

Brooks-Gunn, J. and Greg J. Duncan. "The Effects of Poverty on Children," *Children and Poverty* 7, no.2, (Summer/Fall 1997): 55–77.

CHIP. *Children in Poverty: Some Questions Answered* Briefing Paper 1 (2002)

David Gordon, S. Nandy, C. Pantazis, S, Permberton and P. Townsend, *Child Poverty in the Developing World,* (Bristol: The Policy Press, 2003)

Republic of Ghana. *Ghana Poverty Reduction Strategy 2003–2005. An Agenda for Growth and Prosperity, Vol. I* (Accra, February 2003)

———. *Ghana's Poverty Reduction Strategy. Agenda for Growth and Prosperity, Vol. II.* (Accra, 2003)

———. *An Agenda for Growth and Prosperity. Ghana's Poverty Reduction Strategy 2003-2005. Monitoring and Evaluation Plan,* (Accra, March 2003).

Santosh M. and E. Delamonica. "Public Spending for Children: An Empirical Note," *Journal of International Development* 14, (2002): 1106.

United Nations. *The Copenhagen Declaration and Program of Action: World Summit for Social Development 6-12 March 1995,* New York: UNDP.

11

Employment Generation for Poverty Alleviation

William Baah-Boateng

1. Introduction

The shift in policy focus towards poverty alleviation in Ghana since 2001 suggests that stabilization and adjustment programs, the centerpiece of economic management in Ghana since 1983, fell short of achieving desired changes in the living standards of the majority of Ghanaians. By the mid-1990s, sluggish growth, persistent unemployment, and underemployment remained worrying features of the Ghanaian economy. The gradual drift of labour from the formal to the informal sector further decreased average household incomes. Critics point out that the lack of structural transformation of the economy constrained the development of new and better employment opportunities and more productive use of the labour force. As a result, employment opportunities remained largely in low income agriculture and informal sectors. The employment aspects of the reform measures were not explicitly incorporated into the design and implementation of the policy.

To reduce its debt burden, gain more fiscal resources, and help address the deteriorating living standards, in 2001 Ghana adopted the Highly Indebted Poor Country (HIPC) Initiative. In line with the major conditions of the initiative, the government developed the Ghana Poverty Reduction Strategy (GPRS). The main goal of the GPRS is "to ensure sustainable equitable growth, accelerated poverty reduction and the protection of the vulnerable and excluded within a decentralized, democratic environment" (Government of Ghana, 2003a: 30). This goal was to be achieved by pursuing six strategies: ensuring macroeconomic stability, increasing production and gainful employment, promoting human development, improving access to basic services, providing special programs for the vulnerable and the excluded, and promoting good governance. Generating gainful employment was seen as one of the key anchors to improving individual livelihoods.

This chapter assesses the employment content of the GPRS framework. A brief examination of the economic activities of the poor follows the introduction in section two. I review the overall employment trends in section three, followed in section four by a review of employment policies in a historical context. Section five assesses the design and implementation of the GPRS with special focus on the employment content, the opportunities for job creation and their links to poverty reduction. This is followed by remarks and suggestions to inform future national development plans.

2. The Economic Activities of the Poor

The decline in the overall incidence of poverty by 12 percentage points (Table 11.1) between 1991/1992 and 1998/1999 was unevenly distributed across different economic sectors. While poverty in Ghana generally remains a rural phenomenon, the incidence is highest among food crop and export farmers as well as the non-farm self employed. The drastic decline in incidence of poverty among export farmers in the 1990s is credited to the technical support and other export promotion packages the government continues to provide for export farmers. However, there are no such comparable schemes for food crop farmers making them vulnerable to low production and low incomes.

Table 11.1 Incidence of Poverty by Type of Employment (percent)

Type of Work	Incidence			Contribution to Aggregate Poverty		
	1991/1992	*1998/1999*	*Change*	*1991/1992*	*1998/1999*	*Change*
Paid Public Work	34.3	22.7	-11.6	9.1	6.2	-2.9
Paid Private Formal Work	30.3	11.3	-19.0	2.3	1.4	-0.9
Paid Informal Work	38.6	25.2	-13.4	2.3	1.9	-0.4
Export Farmer	64.0	38.7	-25.3	7.8	6.9	-0.9
Food Crop farmer	68.1	59.4	- 8.7	57.3	58.1	+0.8
Non-farm Self-employed	38.4	28.6	- 9.8	20.5	24.5	+4.0
Non-working & Others	18.8	20.4	+ 1.6	0.7	1.1	+0.4
National	51.7	39.5	-12.2	---	---	---

Source: Derived from Poverty Trends in Ghana in the 1990s Table A1.4, GSS

Although the legal backing of the minimum wage agreed upon by the Tripartite Committee was abandoned in 1991, wage employees are in the minority of the poor and also have relatively low incidence of poverty, particularly among those in the private sector. Public sector employees have also benefited from the implicit government policy of keeping minimum wage above the poverty threshold. In contrast, farm and non-farm self-employed hardly benefit from the minimum wage provisions. The absence of legal backing of the minimum wage law, means that many people in the informal sector are condemned to low pay activities thereby making them vulnerable to poverty.

3. Employment Trends

One of the fundamental changes experienced in the Ghanaian labour market over the last two decades is the shift of employment from formal to the informal sector. The public retrenchment exercise and privatization program pursued as part of the Structural Adjustment Program (SAP) significantly contributed to loss of employment in the formal sector of the labour market. This prompted a shift to the informal sector. The increasing size and the role of the informal sector and the rising unemployment and underemployment rates have been traced to the low absorption capacity of the economy against the backdrop of high growth of the labour force. The average annual GDP growth rate of about 5 percent throughout the 1990s fell short of the estimated labour force expansion rate of about 6 percent. This, coupled with the estimated 230,000 number of new labour market entrants and a formal sector absorption capacity of 2 percent, provide a recipe for high rate of joblessness and poverty incidence.

Table 11.2 Sectoral Composition of Employment and GDP: 1984-2000

(Percent)					
Sectors		1984	1992	1998	2000
Agriculture	Employment	61.1	62.2	55.0	50.7
	GDP	47.9	37.8	36.7	36.0
Industry	Employment	12.8	10.0	14.0	16.3
	GDP	19.6	25.0	25.1	25.2
Service	Employment	26.1	27.8	31.0	33.0
	GDP	22.1	27.0	29.1	29.7

Note: Real GDP values are measured at 1993 constant prices
Source: GLSS & National Population and Housing Census; GSS

The agricultural sector and related activities remain the major source of employment for the growing workforce despite the decline in this sector's total output by nearly 12 percentage points between 1984 and 2000 (Table 11.2). The average annual growth of the agricultural sector of 3 percent is below the 6.2 percent and 6.5 percent achieved by industry and service over the period 1984–2000. This translated into increased share of industry and service sectors in both production and employment with the service sector performing better overall.

The share of service sector in employment rose by 7 percentage points between 1984 and 2000 compared with 8 percentage points in total output. The marginal increase in employment share of the industry sector by 4.5 points as against six in total output could be traced to significant growth recorded in the mining sector where employment response to output expansion is very low due to the technological bias of mining activity in favor of capital.

3.1 Formal Sector Employment

Formal sector employment which is perceived to be relatively stable and the most remunerative experienced an annual average growth of 1.5 percent between 1960 and 1985, largely because of the rapid growth of public sector employment which averaged 4.5 percent annually over the period (Table 11.3). The public sector led policy pursued in the 1960s and 1970s contributed to the expansion of public sector employment faster than the growth of the labour force. In contrast, private sector employment declined by 2.1 percent on average. There was a reversal of the growth trend in public sector employment beginning in the late 1980s as a result of retrenchment and privatization. Public sector employment dropped by 59 percent between 1985 and 1991, resulting in the overall decline in formal sector jobs by nearly 60 percent (Table 11.3). The formal private sector also suffered a significant decline in employment of about 61 percent during the same period.

Table 11.3 Formal Sector Employment: 1960-1991 ('000)

Year	Public	Private	All
1960	184.0	149.0	333.0
1970	288.0	110.0	398.0
1975	318.0	137.0	455.0
1980	291.0	46.2	337.2
1985	397.1	67.2	464.3
1990	189.4	40.2	229.6
1991	159.8	26.5	186.3

Source: Quarterly Digest of Statistics: GSS

Since the mid-1990s the trend in formal sector employment has seen some improvements, particularly in the private sector as a result of government efforts to facilitate the growth of the sector. For example, the free zone enclave has, as of 2003, created 13,760 new jobs over a seven year period. Six divested companies also succeeded in generating 3,053 new jobs over an average of four years.[105] The number of companies registered by the Ghana Investment Promotion Centre (GIPC) between September 1994 and end of 2004 is estimated to have created about 98,311 new jobs. The public sector also recorded gains in employment after 1991 largely in the education and health sectors as a result of building more schools and health centers to meet the growing demand for health and education services.

3.2 Informal Sector Employment

The informal sector according to the International Labour Organization (ILO) refers to very small-scale units producing and distributing goods and services, and consisting largely of independent, self-employed producers, employing family labour and/or a few hired workers or apprentices. These enterprises generally employ low or unskilled labour, use low levels of technology, generally provide highly unstable employment at very low and irregular incomes.

Figure 11.1 The Share of Informal Sector Employment and the Official Unemployment Rate

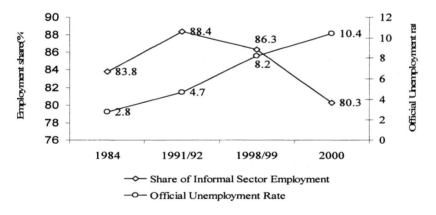

Source: GLSS and Population and Housing Census: Ghana Statistical Service

The expanded role and size of the informal sector matched the overall decline in the economy beginning in the mid-1970s and the rapid decline in formal sector employment in the mid-1980s. This confirms the assertion that the informal sector becomes the sector of last resort in times of economic downturns and in periods of economic adjustment and transition. The expansion of informal activity in many cases represents a willingness to accept extremely low quality employment as the only option available. The easy flow of labour from the formal sector to the informal sector is made possible by the lower job entry requirements with regard to education and capital requirements, and by the unregulated nature of the activities in the sector. The characteristics of the informal sector have prompted some analysts to describe the sector as dumping ground for unemployed labour, particularly in times of severe economic crisis (Ninsin, 1991). The shift of the labour force into the informal sector against the backdrop of low productivity further puts a downward pressure on the average earnings of participants. Data from the Ghana Living Standard Survey and the Population and Housing Census (Figure 11.1) suggest that the informal sector engages between 80 and 88 percent of the total employed. These numbers together with the official unemployment rate of about ten percent in 1998/1999 obscure the prevalence of unemployment and underemployment in the economy.

3.3 Unemployment and Underemployment

The high incidence of unemployment and underemployment reflects the low labour absorption capacity of the economy. The situation is not helped by the slow growth of formal sector employment due in part to the shrinking of the role of government in direct economic activity. For instance, under the on-going Public Sector Management Reform Program (PSMRP), about 20,000 public servants are to lose their jobs by the end of the exercise in 2011[106] (Boateng, 2002).

The economy has consistently recorded an increasing adult unemployment rate since 1988. From an estimated rate of about 2.8 percent in 1984, the unemployment rate rose to 10.4 percent in 2000 (Figure 11.1). It is estimated that the redeployment exercise in the public sector alone resulted in the loss of 49,873 jobs between 1987 and 1991. Many of these workers lacked the requisite skills that could make them employable in an alternative job other than in the informal sector (Aryeetey et al, 2004). The negative effects of the adjustment program such as the exposure of domestic enterprises to cheap imports, rapid depreciation of the cedi, rising interest rates and withdrawal of agricultural subsidies crippled many industrial and agricultural enterprises to a considerable extent causing a reduction in their workforce.

The unemployment rate is generally higher among females than males. The low educational attainment of women relative to men has been blamed for the relatively high rates of unemployment among women in Ghana. The incidence of unemployment is high among urban dwellers, high among youth and it declines with age. There is also a growing incidence of joblessness among university and polytechnic graduates. In its 1999 survey, the Ministry of Employment and Social Welfare observed that about 68 percent of graduates interviewed were unemployed. The inability of educational institutions to produce graduates with skills required by employers is a result of a lack of effective linkages between industry and educational institutions. This has contributed to a mismatch between demand for and supply of tertiary graduates in recent times.

There is a growing incidence of underemployment in Ghana in the midst of increasing unemployment. Underemployment is the extent to which people are employed but not as fully as desired. The overall adult underemployment rate increased from 8 percent in 1992 to 14 percent in 1998 with the rate relatively low among women (GLSS3 & GLSS4). The lower rate among women compared to men has been explained by the high domestic commitments of women which prevent them from accepting work for more hours when offered the opportunity.

4. Employment Policies

Public policies on employment are motivated by the failure of the labour market to achieve reasonable employment growth, partly the result of the presence of distortions and rigidities in the market, but largely the result of the overall slow growth of the economy. Effective employment policies involve measures to stimulate labour demand through growth and to enhance the productivity of labour supply through human resource development, removal of institutional rigidities, and population control. Ghana cannot boast of any comprehensive employment policy except the National Service Scheme. The program provides temporary jobs for tertiary school leavers as a way of ushering them into the labour market and given them experience in the work place. Development strategies so far pursued in Ghana rather treats employment as a residual of sectoral and macroeconomic policies.

Government policies prior to the economic reform of the mid-1980s were characterized by direct state involvement and control of economic activity and thus account for the expansion of public sector employment in the 1960s and 1970s. For example, a substantial increase in formal sector employment occurred during the first half of 1960s under the state enterprises regime and again in the mid 1970s, albeit temporarily, under the Operation Feed Yourself program. The economic downturn during the late 1970s and early 1980s prompted the birth of the IMF/World Bank sponsored economic reforms. The reforms saw first, a dramatic shift from direct state involvement in economic activities to private sector led economic strategies, and second, a shift of labour from the public sector to the informal sector. These measures were aimed at freeing the government from the trap of persistent fiscal deficits due to excessive recurrent expenditures especially the government wage bill. Although the reduction in the public sector workforce was accompanied by improvement in real wages for the remaining workers, many of those let go became poor.[3]

Some changes were also observed in the demand for labour in favor of skilled professionals and management personnel in the service sector in response to these reforms and to global technological changes. In addition, the service sector, particularly the commercial sub-sector, has become the major source of employment. Much of the increase in the service sector share of employment, however, has come from the hospitality subsectors.

Realizing the negative effect of the reform measures on the labour market, the government introduced the Program of Action to Mitigate the Social Cost of Adjustment (PAMSCAD). It established community projects to generate employment for rural households particularly in northern Ghana; these being largely low income, unemployed and underemployed urban households and retrenched workers. It was also meant to provide small enterprise credit for women and small scale miners, among others. The agricultural sector program was also initiated to achieve food security and to generate employment and income in the rural areas through increased agricultural research and extension, smallholder credits, and the provision of other services. The design and implementation of the ongoing Alternative Employment Program (AEP) is also meant to accommodate displaced public servants who are affected by the Public Sector Management Reform Program (PSMRP).

Several projects have also been undertaken at different times to enhance employment generation. These include the Labour Based Feeder Road Rehabilitation and Maintenance Project; Feeder Roads Project; Priority Public Works Projects; Food for Work Projects and Special Employment Schemes. However, the employment outcomes of these projects were largely limited to the life of each project and had little impact at the national level.

Ghana's Vision 2020, a blueprint to achieve a middle income status by the year 2020, also seeks to build employment promotion considerations into all macroeconomic and production policies in order to reduce high levels of unemployment and underemployment. The legal and regulatory framework governing economic activity was also expected to be reviewed to enhance employment creation particularly in the informal sector. Training, including apprenticeship schemes, was expected to be an important aspect of the employment strategy. However, the implementation of the first phase was described by critics as ad hoc. More attention was paid to macroeconomic stability to the neglect of growth of the real sector thereby diminishing the employment impact of the reforms.

5. Policy Assessment of the GPRS

5.1 Relevant Ingredients for Employment Growth and Poverty Reduction

The GPRS document provides a medium-term framework for addressing poverty in Ghana through accelerated economic growth and employment creation. The national employment policy agenda in the GPRS treats employment as the core objective of the policy framework for poverty reduction. Employment generation is expected to emanate primarily from economic growth through physical infrastructure development and the adoption of labour intensive technology. The key areas expected to be sources of employment growth were roads and highway construction, agricultural and non-traditional export development, promoting agro-processing and stimulating private sector activities in general.

The GPRS recognized the high incidence of poverty among food crop farmers and therefore outlined strategies to stimulate agricultural production. It emphasized commercial agriculture with some attention to small holder agriculture. Strategies to address low yields and post harvest losses in the food crop sector included providing adequate agricultural infrastructure such as irrigation and storage facilities as well as feeder roads to link the farms and marketing centers. The broad strategy for non-traditional exports was to increase production of handicrafts, salt, and processed gold as well as to increase productive capacity of exporters.

To promote production and employment in the agro-processing sector, the document outlined strategies to provide processing equipment, establish small business enterprise zones, and improve institutional support for industrial productivity. With the objective of enabling accelerated growth and employment, the national employment framework emphasized increasing micro and small-scale enterprises and employment opportunities for women.

For a more direct impact on poverty, the document proposed that measures put in place to support large-scale manufacturers should be complemented by strategies to enhance productivity of small-scale producers. This requires measures to strengthen institutions such as the National Board for Small Scale Industries (NBSSI) and the Management Development and Productivity Institute (MDPI). Also incorporated into these strategies are the establishment of a special micro finance fund to help female-owned enterprises to augment their earning from agricultural, processing and marketing activities and acquire resources for future investments.

The strategy on production and employment also sought to improve the efficiency of public sector programs and provide sufficient incentives to stimulate private sector entrepreneurial development. Key issues identified which facilitate private sector entrepreneurship include the promotion of land administration reforms, improved security of land tenure, and the need for incentives to attract entrepreneurs into agriculture and agro-industries. Finally, the GPRS recognized numerous problems in the urban informal sector that require urgent attention. Therefore, measures were proposed to equip the workforce in the informal sector with financial and management skills to improve their productivity.[4]

5.2 Assessment of Implementation of the Proposed Strategies

The implementation of job creation and poverty reduction measures was incorporated in the annual Budget Statement and Economic Policies for the period

2003-2005. Some activities have been undertaken since 2002 towards modernizing agriculture through farm mechanization, provision of irrigation facilities,
increased access to inputs, and the production of high valued crops. A number of
new irrigation dams and dugout wells have been constructed or rehabilitated
between 2002 and 2004. Some farmers have also benefited from access to improved breeds of livestock and seeds of various crops including cashews, cassava, cereals and legumes. The Ministry of Food and Agriculture also provided
funds to import spare parts for the repair of agricultural machinery and equipment. Efforts were made to provide credit to crop and livestock farmers and
fishermen. For instance, at least eighteen billion cedis of credit were advanced to
various groups of farmers in 2004.[5] To facilitate transportation of farm produce
to the market centers, a number of feeder roads and bridges were constructed or
repaired.

The cocoa sub-sector has also benefited from tremendous policy support in
the form of a higher producer price and mass spraying of cocoa farms. The producer price of cocoa to farmers rose from ¢3.87 million to ¢9 million per metric
ton between 2001 and 2004, an increase of 132 percent. In addition, the government paid about ¢428 billion to cocoa farmers as bonuses during the same
period. Some roads in cocoa growing areas also saw some rehabilitation. These
policy initiatives contributed significantly to about an 89 percent increase in
cocoa output between 2000/2001 and 2003/2004 to 736,911 metric tons.

Considerable efforts were made to support industrial enterprises in the form
of providing training and credit. Under various financial schemes of the National
Board for Small Scale Industries (NBSSI), a number of micro and small enterprises were supported with access to credit of about ¢4.8 billion between 2002
and 2003. In addition, various entrepreneurial training programs were organized
for industrial business operators. The Board also facilitated the establishment of
120 new businesses while 400 informal businesses were incorporated into the
formal sector in 2004.[6] Some gains in employment were also recorded under the
Presidential Special Initiatives (PSI) in the cassava and starch, garment and textile, oil palm and salt subsectors. For example, it is estimated that about 10,000
new jobs were created under the PSI on cassava between 2002 and 2004.

In the area of skill development a number of measures were initiated by the
Ministry of Manpower Development and Employment to facilitate various
forms of skills training. In 2003 and 2004,[7] under the Skills Training and Employment Placement (STEP) program, about 16,250 benefited from training in
different trade areas including "batik tie and dye," food processing, dressmak-
ing, hairdressing, masonry and carpentry. Others were also trained in agricultural vocations such as snail and mushroom farming, grass cutter and rabbit rear-
ing, bee-keeping, and leafy vegetable growing. A considerable number of job
seekers (20,371 of them in 2004) were placed in various jobs through Public
Employment Centers throughout the country. The government also established a
number of new training centers offering skills training for youth and organized
apprenticeship training programs under various master craftsmen. For example,

according to the 2005 National Budget, a total of 1,218 trainees completed training in employable, vocational/technical skills through a special outreach program in partnership with master craftsmen and women at the Opportunity Industrialization Centre (OIC). The National Vocational Training Institute (NVTI) was also given various forms of support to maximize their intake of students.

5.3 Missing Links

Whereas the link between economic growth and job creation depends on the extent to which growth generates employment, the impact of employment creation on poverty reduction depends on the extent to which poor workers benefit from their labour. The implementation of the programs and activities of the GPRS, incorporated in the Budget Statement of 2003, 2004, and 2005, has yielded some positive outcomes as outlined in the preceding section. However, there have been some obvious shortfalls in the design and implementation of the strategies which are examined below.

Weak integration of Employment Strategies
Even though employment creation remains one of the core elements of the strategy, there are shortcomings in the extent to which employment policies were integrated. For one thing, like previous development plans, employment was treated as a passive outcome of sectoral and macroeconomic policies. Even though the document highlighted some measures to enhance labour demand for poverty reduction, it failed to demonstrate explicitly how employment would be created. The document did not set any specific sectoral employment targets to be achieved within the plan period. It did not clearly show the number and nature of new jobs expected to be generated in agriculture, manufacturing, services, and the non-traditional export sectors. These shortcomings are not helped by the absence of reliable employment data in the country.

Lack of Labour Market Data
The absence of timely, consistent and coherent data on both formal and informal employment is a constraint on designing effective policies and monitoring outcomes. Lack of basic information on employment, incomes and the profile of the labour force limits the development of employment-oriented growth strategies within the context of poverty reduction measures. The national medium-term framework recognized these data limitations and proposed to develop labour market statistics. However, annual employment and poverty data are either unavailable or difficult to come by. The analysis of poverty and employment issues has always been based on GLSS, the Core Welfare Indicators Questionnaire (CWIQ) and the population census. However, these data sources are not easily comparable because the purpose for each of the surveys was different.

Skills Development

In human resource development, emphasis was placed on strengthening the traditional apprenticeship system, formal technical and vocational training, as well as reforming the formal education system. The training system, particularly the formal education system, so far seems not to have been demand driven which emphasizes the design of training to meet labour market requirements. On the contrary, supply driven approach to·training tends to create a situation where many people acquire skills but still find it difficult to get placed in the labour market.

The formal educational system especially at the tertiary level is dominated by courses and programs that turn out graduates who eventually become frustrated in the job market. The increasing unemployment and underemployment rates among university and polytechnic graduates, in recent times, have been linked to the limited relevance of their skills and training to the economy. Available data suggest that while 31 percent of the unemployed graduates had pursued courses in social sciences and/or arts, graduates in specialized programs such as business studies, medicine, computer science and engineering constituted less than 1 percent of the respondents (Ministry of Employment and Social Welfare, 1999). This revelation does not, however, discount the relevance of arts and social science programs offered in tertiary institutions. Rather, it points out that while there is excess supply of arts/social science graduates, there is a noticeable shortfall of graduates with skill most in demand in the emerging economy.

The lack of an effective link between research institutions and industry has contributed greatly to the widening gap between the relevance of programs in the tertiary institutions and what industry requires. The GPRS proposed the introduction of entrepreneurial training into the curricula of the universities, polytechnics, and agricultural colleges. However, apart from the University of Ghana which proposed to run a course in entrepreneurial training during the 2005/2006 academic year, the other tertiary institutions are yet to take up the challenge.

The success stories of programs and institutions involved in entrepreneurial, technical and vocational training including STEP, NBSSI, NVTI, and Integrated Community Centers for Employable Skills (ICCES) suggest that the country is making progress in this direction. However, the challenge is to ensure the beneficiaries of such training programs get placement in the labour market. The difficulty faced by trainees trying to survive in the labour market exposes the weaknesses in the overall policies of the government. For instance, most tie-and-dye trainees and apprentices in tailoring have difficulty surviving in the midst of international competition resulting in the influx of "second hand" clothing. These observations underscore the need to emphasize a demand driven approach in human capital development strategies.

Urban Informal Sector
Attention given to the informal sector in the policy document appears to be fragmented. The GPRS does not adequately analyze the dynamics of the informal economy or provide a well structured approach to poverty reduction for the working masses in the informal sector. The proposals to strengthen traditional apprenticeship, to promote technological proficiency of the informal sector workforce, and to develop mechanisms facilitating formal and informal sector vertical linkages are laudable. However, strategies to achieve these objectives were not explicitly spelt out in the document. This reflects in part on the failure of the Ministries, Departments and Agencies (MDAs) to translate the objectives and proposals of the GPRS into actions. The establishment of community based vocational apprenticeship schemes needs to be backed by a policy to set the trainees up after training. The proposal to provide support for craft villages has received little attention by way of implementation.

Agricultural Development
The implementation of agricultural development strategies in the national document appears to be weak. The sector still lacks irrigation dams and storage facilities necessary to address the high incidence of post harvest losses in the food crop sub-sector. There appears to be unevenness of sub-sector support in the sector. The policy of increasing the producer price of cocoa to farmers and absorbing price shocks on the world market is an incentive not yet available to the food crop sector. Lack of comparable "subsidies" and adequate support in the form of guaranteed prices and ready markets for farmers in the poultry and particularly food crop sectors has in part contributed to low production in these sectors. One could therefore expect that it would be difficult for poverty incidence among food crop farmers to decline by the predicted 13 percentage point by the end of 2005.

Institutional Rigidities
A key feature of the Ghanaian labour market is the strong influence of labour market institutions which tend to account for the wage rigidities in the market. It is estimated that over two-thirds of the formal sector jobs are subject to collective bargaining agreements confirming the high rate of unionization in the labour market. No concrete measures were incorporated in the formulation of strategies to minimize the institutional rigidities in the labour market. Nevertheless, the coming into force of the Labour Act of 2003 (Act 651) is expected to reduce the inherent rigidities in the Ghanaian labour market. The act introduces some flexibility in terms of union formation and in the settlement of industrial disputes, among others, into the industrial relations system.

Macroeconomic Stability Bias of Policies
The apparent over-concentration of the GPRS on achieving macroeconomic stability to the neglect of structural problems has raised doubts about the coun-

try's ability to generate the much needed employment for poverty reduction. The considerable attention devoted to the realization of macroeconomic stability is informed by its relevance to reducing risk associated with long-term investment in the real sector.

Macroeconomic stabilization through public expenditure-control measures has constrained government's effort to invest in infrastructure needed for productive activities. Tight monetary policy, adopted to control inflation, has evidently slowed down credit flow to the private sector including employment friendly sectors such as agriculture and small scale manufacturing. Real interest rates have remained at high levels in recent times in spite of declining inflationary trend. This is because commercial banks have been reluctant to reduce lending rates in response to declining rates of inflation and declining central bank rate. Evidence suggests that in spite of the decline in the bank rate from 38 percent to 18.5 percent between 2000 and 2004, in line with the declining inflationary trends, average lending rates of commercial banks remained at 29 percent in 2004 (Bank of Ghana, 2004). As a result, domestic credit expansion to the private sector has been very slow. According to ISSER (2005), the share of domestic credit to private enterprises including agriculture and manufacturing increased marginally from 46 percent to 49 percent between 2002 and 2004.

In addition, the structure of the financial system and the practices of financial institutions tend to favor large private companies, the public sector and importers. Agricultural and informal enterprises are normally denied access to formal finance despite their employment generating potential. The high rates of interest and collateral demands of formal financial institutions are two of the major factors that discourage agricultural and informal sector enterprises from accessing credit from formal financial institutions. Evidence shows that credit allocation to agriculture and manufacturing where the labour absorption rate is high declined from 9.6 percent and 28.1 percent in 2000 to 7.6 percent and 21.5 percent respectively in 2004 (ISSER, 2005). Clearly, the macroeconomic environment in terms of price stability with high interest rates and a slow rate of credit expansion to productive sectors as well as infrastructural and bureaucratic bottlenecks constrain employment-intensive economic activities. Thus, macroeconomic stability in Ghana can be seen as a necessary but not sufficient condition for growth, employment generation and poverty reduction.

Private Sector Development
The GPRS also sought to provide sufficient incentives to stimulate the private sector and enable it to play its role as the engine of growth and poverty reduction. However, after two years of implementation, the private sector is still struggling to overcome the numerous problems which tend to impede its growth and job creation potential. The high cost of credit, poor telecommunication services, high energy costs coupled with the erratic supply of power continue to constrain the operations of private enterprises. Bureaucratic practices in the public service remain unresolved while land acquisition continues to constrain pro-

spective investment. The government's commitment to good governance appears to have boosted investors' confidence in the economy but these infrastructure constraints continue to hamper private investment.

Donor Conditionalities as counterproductive
Incidentally, some of the IMF/World Bank conditionalities tend to conflict with employment and poverty reduction policy objectives. For example, all reform countries were compelled to withdraw agricultural subsidies as part of the conditions of IMF and World Bank stabilization and adjustment programs with the view to reducing fiscal deficits of these countries. In the 2003 budget, the government raised import duties on poultry as a strategy to minimize the external competition facing domestic poultry producers. However, disapproval by the IMF led to the suspension of the policy leaving domestic poultry producers to face stiff external competition. The withdrawal of subsidies has led to stagnation of the agricultural sector of reform countries including Ghana, particularly in the food crop sub-sector where poverty is pervasive. This suggests that poverty reduction within the agricultural sector may remain elusive if strategies adopted to improve growth ignore this need for some form of government support.

5.4 Opportunities for Job Creation and Poverty Reduction

The design of the national vision fell short of exploring deeply the opportunities available for the promotion of quality employment and poverty reduction. One key area that received limited policy attention is the informal sector despite its enormous potential for poverty reduction. The GPRS acknowledged problems facing the informal sector and proposed measures to deal with them. It was expected that implementation of these measures would lead to an increase in the sector's labour absorption capacity and improve incomes of participants. Progress, however, has been slow. The implementation of proposals, for example, to introduce entrepreneurial training into the curricula of tertiary institutions and to increase credit support at reasonable rates to encourage the youth to take active interest in self-employment, has been slow.

The informal sector is still confronted with limited demand for its products particularly by the formal sector due to low quality, poor packaging and a lack of publicity. A government role in providing training support to enhance production technology could help improve the quality of these products. The establishment of small business zones in urban centers can also contribute to expanding the demand for products from this sector. The government can also revise its procurement policies to breaking the bids into smaller units to enabling small enterprises to take part in the bidding process. This would enable the informal sector to benefit from public sector procurement programs.

The agricultural sector also possesses considerable potential for job creation and poverty reduction if the strategies outlined in the GPRS for modernization of the sector are seriously implemented. These measures include increasing irrigation and storage facilities, feeder roads and extension services. In addition, adequate support in the form of increased credit, restoration of subsidies, and guaranteed prices would boost agricultural production, create more jobs, and curb rural-urban migration. Efforts to facilitate the processing of agricultural produce would also provide ready markets for farmers and offer them opportunities to expand their farms.

The Presidential Special Initiative in cassava and oil palm production has spurred considerable interest in these areas. While some suggest that the initiatives should be expanded to cover many other crops or products and create more new jobs, others suggest caution. While Presidential Initiatives may fit the mood of the time, there are concerns about the sustainability of these initiatives. Those skeptical of new political initiatives believe that progress will come if policy focuses on some key drivers or "winners" and explore deeper the opportunities for growth through their backward and forward linkages. Judging by the record, policy makers are more adept at initiating than in carrying the initiatives through to their limits. The lessons learnt from one area can then be extended into other areas because there is no substitute for learning by doing.

In relation to the latter, enormous potential for employment expansion and poverty reduction exist in the industrial sector particularly in the area of agro-processing, salt mining, handicrafts including woodworking and textiles, especially African prints. The economy does not appear to have seriously considered agro-processing as a major avenue for generating quality jobs besides the additional value added to the product. Ghana currently processes only 18 percent of domestic cocoa (Government of Ghana, 2003a). The employment opportunities in the *kente* and woodworking sectors could be fully tapped through governmental support to boost production for export within the framework of AGOA. The establishment of textile and handicraft villages would contribute to the growth of the sector, expanding employment, and providing income for many people.

In the service sector, the hospitality, transportation and ICT industries possess opportunities for quality employment and income generation. The increase of 94 percent in hotel beds between 1989 and 1999 (Baah-Boateng, 2004) gives an indication of the rate at which the hospitality industry is expanding. The development of the tourism sector could boost the hospitality industry and create secondary job opportunities. The country can take advantage of the ICT industry to improve job creation by extending telecommunication facilities to rural areas opening them up for investment. Moreover, measures to construct and rehabilitate more feeder and trunk roads and revamp the railway system would not only facilitate the transportation of agricultural produce to market centers and create employment in the distribution sector. The employment potential in the agricultural, industrial and service sectors could best be tapped for poverty reduction through private sector initiatives with public sector playing a facilitating role.

6. Concluding Remarks

The GPRS outlined measures to stimulate production, gainful employment and enhance skill development. Even though some gains were made in the area of entrepreneurial, technical and vocational training, it appears the training was largely supply rather than demand driven. Institutions established to facilitate the operation of micro and small enterprises such as NBSSI are not sufficiently resourced in terms of human and material capital to effectively execute their mandate as envisaged in the GPRS.

Agricultural infrastructure, such as feeder roads, irrigation facilities, and credit advances continue to lag behind the demand for them. The withdrawal of agricultural subsidies, the absence of guaranteed prices for food crops, limited access to markets, and problems with land acquisition and land tenure system remain major constraints on growth of the agricultural sector. The prospects of job creation in the industrial sector rest largely in the area of agro-processing, and in the service sector largely in the hospitality and information technology areas.

The lack of consistent and timely labour market data continues to hinder effective monitoring and assessment of employment and poverty reduction outcomes relating to measures outlined in the document. The inability of the GPRS to set employment targets for the relevant sectors is explained by the lack of human resource data base in the economy. Measures to improve labour market information and to provide a regular set of employment indicators should be a priority. The Ghana Living Standard Survey and the Population Census need to be harmonized to generate the information needed for effective assessment of labour market indicators and for effective policy design. The Labour Ministry must be adequately equipped with human and material resources to effectively coordinate and monitor employment surveys on an annual basis.

Addressing the development of the informal sector through entrepreneurialship, access to land and affordable credit, and the strengthening of traditional apprenticeship and formal-informal sector linkages should graduate from the policy formulation level to actual implementation. Finally, the design of the national vision of employment generation fell short of exploring at length the opportunities for the promoting quality employment. One reason for this omission is the time constraint on putting together the strategy. The issue of time constrains was discussed at length in a previous chapter in this volume. It matters here again because the search for quality employment opportunities depends on the choice of the different pathways that the country wishes to take out of poverty. More immediate employment opportunities tend to require low skills and provide low earnings, often holding little prospects of upward mobility. As impressive as the breadth of the GPRS may have been in promoting production and gainful employment, the strategy still suffered from the structural bottlenecks of the economy and tended to favor opportunities that would increase immediate employment.

Notes

1. This implies that the attempt by an employer to pay his/her workers below the minimum wage possibly would not attract any prosecution.
2. The companies include Coca-Cola Bottling Company (264 jobs), Golden Tulip (231 jobs), Ghana Agro-Food Co (1074 jobs), West Africa Mills Company (280 jobs) all in 4 years; Ghana Rubber Estates Ltd (748 jobs) in two years; and Tema Steel Co Ltd (454 jobs) in six years,
3. However, through the envisaged Alternative Employment Program (AERP), the overall net benefit is expected to be positive.
4. However, the success stories of some six divested companies however presented a positive aspect of privatization with overall expansion of workforce by about 70 percent after divestiture. Nonetheless, the net effect of privatization in Ghana points to an obvious decline in formal sector employment.
5. The issue of urban informal sector employment is addressed more fully by Amoako-Tuffour and A. Sackey in the next chapter of this volume.
6. Government of Ghana Budget Statement, 2005.
7. Government of Ghana Budget Statement, 2005.

References

Aryeetey E.(ed.) *Globalisation, Employment and Poverty Reduction: A Case Study of Ghana.* Report of a Study commissioned by the International Labour Organisation (ILO), May 2004

Baah-Boateng, W. "Employment Policies and Sustainable Development: the Experience of Ghana." (mimeo), Department of Economics, University of Ghana, presented at the National Workshop on Employment Framework for Ghana's Poverty Reduction Strategy, Government of Ghana/UNDP/ILO (May 7, 2004), Accra

Bank of Ghana, "Annual Report 2004." Report for the Financial Year Ended 31st December, 2004

Boateng, K. "Impact of Structural Adjustment on Employment and Incomes." Pp. 14-33 in *The Social Dimension of Structural Adjustment in Ghana*, edited by Anthony Yaw Baah, TUC/ICFTU-AFRO, 2001.

————. "Public Policy and Public Investment for Poverty Reduction and Employment Generation in Ghana,." An ILO IPRE *Study on Jobs for AFRICA-PRESA Program* submitted to the Ministry of Manpower Development & Employment, May 2002.

————. "Economics of the Labour Market and the Ghanaian Experience." Department of Economics, University of Ghana, 2000.

————."Quality Jobs or Mass Employment: A Study of Some Impacts of the Structural Adjustment Program." *Ghana Economic Outlook* 3(1): 46-61, March 1998.

Ghana Statistical Service. *2000 Population and Housing Census, Summary Report of Final Results*, March, 2002
———. *Poverty Trends in Ghana in the 1990s*. October, 2000.
———. *Ghana Living Standards Survey*. Report of the Fourth Round (GLSS 4), October, 2000
———. *Ghana Living Standards Survey*. Report of the Third Round (GLSS 3), September 1991-September 1992, March 1995
———. *1984 Population Census of Ghana*. Demographic and Economic Characteristics, Total Country, 1987
Gockel A. F. "Structural Adjustment and the Informal Sector." Pp. 34-58 in *The Social Dimension of Structural Adjustment in Ghana* edited by Anthony Yaw Baah, TUC/ICFTU-AFRO, 2001.
Government of Ghana. *Ghana Poverty Reduction Strategy 2003-2005: An Agenda for Growth and Prosperity*, Vol. 1 Analysis and Policy Statement, February 19, 2003.
———. *The Coordinated Program for Economic and Social Development of Ghana (2003-2012)*, presented by the President of the Republic of Ghana to Parliament, 2002
———. *Ghana Vision 2020: The First Step: 1996–2000*, Presidential Report to Parliament on Coordinated Program of Economic and Social Development Policies, 1995.
———. *Labour Redeployment Program (July 1987–December 1990): Achievements, Problems and Prospects*, 1990.
———. *Annual Budget Statement and Economic Policy*, various issues, 1999 to 2005
International Labour. *"Organisation, Employability in the Global Economy, How Training Matters."* World Employment Report 1998-99, ILO Publication, 1998.
———. *The Dilemma of the Informal Sector*. Report of the Director-General (Part 1), International Labour Conference, 78th Session, Geneva, 1991
ILO/JASPA. *From Redeployment to Sustained Employment Generation: Challenges for Ghana's Program of Economic Recovery and Development*, ILO Publication, 1989.
ISSER. *The State of the Ghanaian Economy in 2004*, ISSER— University of Ghana, 2005.
———. *The State of the Ghanaian Economy in 2003*, ISSER —University of Ghana, 2004
———. *The State of the Ghanaian Economy in 1994*, ISSER— University of Ghana, 1995
Ministry of Employment and Social Welfare, *Report on Graduate Unemployment in Ghana*, Published by Ministry of Employment and Social Welfare, 1999.
Ninsin, Kwame A. *The Informal Sector in Ghana's Political Economy*, Freedom Publication, Accra, Ghana, 1991
Sudharshan Canagarajah and Saji Thomas. *Ghana's Labour Market (1987-92)*. Policy Research Working Paper 1752, The World Bank Africa Technical Families Human Development 3, 1997
World Bank. *Ghana International Competitiveness—Opportunities and Challenges Facing Non-Traditional Exports*, Washington D.C, 2001.
———. *World Development Report* Washington D.C., 1995.

Younger S. "Labour Market Consequences of Retrenchment for Civil Servants in Ghana" Chp. 6 in *Economic Reform and the Poor in Africa* edited by David E. Sahn. Oxford. Clarendon Press, 1996.

12

Informal Sector Activities and Urban Poverty in Ghana: Patterns and Poverty Policy Options

Joe Amoako-Tuffour and Harry A. Sackey

1. Introduction

While most of the poor in Ghana live in the rural areas, urban poverty is widespread, too. The World Bank estimates that nearly 30 percent of the world's poor live in the urban areas and it is projected that this figure may rise to 50 percent by the year 2035. Sub-Saharan Africa has some of the world's highest levels of urban poverty and the majority is engaged in some form of employment in the informal sector. In 1997, informal sector employment accounted for about 79 percent of total urban employment in Ghana (ILO data cited in Bhorat, 2005). According to Bhorat, Ghana ranked high as one of the countries in Africa where over 70 percent of urban workers engage in an assortment of informal sector employment.[1] A characteristic of urban poverty is that while most of the poor may consider themselves as working, they are not engaged in well-paying, steady jobs. As a result, the official urban unemployment rate in Ghana of 12 percent[2] in 1998/1999 grossly understates the level of underemployment in the informal sector.[3]

This chapter looks at urban informal sector employment and its place within the context of the Ghana's Poverty Reduction Strategy (GPRS). We examine the main economic activities in the urban informal sector in section two. This is followed in section three by an analysis of the incidence and depth of poverty of those engaged in informal sector activities across administrative regions. Using a probit model, we throw light on the economic and social characteristics of urban informal sector poverty in section four. We review the treatment of the informal sector in the GPRS in section five, followed in section six by some policy options.

Urban informal sector activities range from street vending to small garage shops, food kiosks, repair shops, barber shops, tailoring, beauty salons, market stalls and a wide assortment of micro-enterprises. The sector[4] generally comprises of low skill activities that typically have low capital intensity, low rates of productivity, long working hours, and low and elastic incomes. These characteristics, combined with the lack of labor rules or protection, suggest that those who work in the sector are vulnerable to high incidence of poverty (Rempel, 1996). While the urban informal sector may be seen as a "sector of hope" or a safety net for people who do not or cannot participate in the formal sector, its growth is a source of concern for several reasons.

Urban informal sector employment is the result of rural-urban migration and a symptom of an economy that cannot provide more and better jobs to absorb its growing labour force. Increasing informality of economic activities in general does not help growth. The larger the size of the informal sector the more persistent is unemployment and underemployment. Indeed, while informal sector enterprises in theory can deliver the same growth potential, in practice they seldom do. They tend to remain small or smaller, are less productive, and offer little or no scope and opportunities for upward mobility. Moreover, a large urban informal sector may not contribute enough taxes to finance spending on urban social services and public amenities that are critical to urban poverty reduction. Finally, and perhaps most worrisome, is the prospect that urban informal sector could become a "trap" for the youth and school drop-outs who prematurely enter the labor force. For the majority of this group, current income gains may be at the expense of their human capital formation and as a result limit future productivity and their hope to escape from poverty.

2. The Urban Informal Sector in Ghana

The labor market situation in Ghana varies by gender and by urban and rural areas (Table 12.1). According to the Ghana Living Standard Survey (GLSS) of 1998/99, formal sector employment accounted for only 13.7 percent of the working age population. The remaining 86 percent identified themselves as working in the informal sector and comprised of 52 percent in agricultural activities and the 34 percent in self-employment activities outside of agriculture. At the national level, a large percentage of the female (45.1 percent) and nearly one-fifth (21.4 percent) of the male working population were engaged in non-agricultural informal sector activities. The evidence suggests that the latter is essentially an urban phenomenon, providing nearly 55.3 percent of urban employment (nearly twice as much as in the rural areas) of which 71 percent were female.

For the purposes of this chapter, we define the urban informal sector as comprising of four groups: (a) the self-employed in non-agricultural activities and without employees (we will refer to this simply as "self-employment"); (b) the self-employed in non-agricultural activities with less than five employees (or simply "employers"); (c) paid employees in enterprises with less than five

Table 12.1 Employment and Unemployment in Ghana 1998/1999
(Percent)

	All	Urban	Rural	Male	Female
	Total population aged 15+				
Employed	82.1	78.3	84.0	84.0	80.7
Unemployed	6.7	11.9	4.3	7.2	6.4
	Employed population aged 15-64				
Formal private and public employment	13.7	25.9	8.1	22.7	6.2
Total informal employment	86.3	74.1	91.9	77.3	93.8
Private informal and non-agricultural self-employment	34.3	55.3	24.7	21.4	45.1
Self-employment (agriculture)	52.0	18.8	67.2	55.9	48.7
Unpaid family work	17.2	8.6	21.2	10.7	22.7

Source: Ghana Statistical Service GLSS 4 1998/1999

people (or simply, "paid employment"), and (d) unpaid family labour in non-agricultural activities. With this classification, the evidence suggests average probability of employment as follows: self-employment, 80 percent; employer, 3 percent; paid employment, 9 percent; and unpaid family labor, 8 percent. In the sub-sections to follow, we examine the distribution of workers among the various economic activities, and the proximate determinants of participation in the informal sector.

2.1 Employment Distribution and Educational Attainment

The major activities in the urban informal sector are shown in Table 12.2. Retail trade, manufacturing and personal services are the three most dominant informal sector economic activities in urban Ghana. About 61 percent of the self-employed are in retail trade. This predominance is not surprising since getting started in petty trading is often not too difficult, although in a typical market setting there are bound to be rivalries, competition, scramble for customers, and in some cases "quasi collusion" to drive away potential entrants. In terms of small enterprise employers in this sector, about 31 percent of them are found in retail trade. Over one-half of unpaid family labor is also found in retailing. Under manufacturing, the major activities are food manufacturing, wearing apparel, and furniture and fixtures. Manufacturing activities account for about 27 percent of self-employment, 10 percent of paid employment, about 24 percent of employers, and 32 percent of unpaid family labor.

Table 12.2 Distribution of Urban Informal Sector Workers by Economic Activities

	Self-Employment	Paid Employment	Employer	Unpaid Family Labor
Retail & Wholesale Trade	(percent)			
Retail trade	60.8	14.1	30.9	58.1
Wholesale trade	0.2	0.8	0.0	0.0
Manufacturing				
Food manufacturing	12.9	5.6	14.4	23.6
Wearing apparel	8.6	1.2	4.1	2.6
Furniture & fixtures	2.1	0.0	2.1	0.0
Beverage	1.1	0.0	0.0	0.9
Others	2.2	2.8	3.1	5.2
Personal & Social Services				
Repair services	1.5	5.6	8.2	1.3
Other personal	5.2	7.6	4.1	0.9
Education services	0.5	9.6	5.2	0.0
Others	1.2	16.9	1.0	0.4
Transport & Communication				
Land transport	1.0	19.7	5.2	4.8
Others	0.4	6.0	5.2	0.9
Construction	1.8	1.2	15.5	1.3
Other Activities	0.5	8.8	1.0	0.0
Total	100	100	100	100
No. of observations	2343	249	97	229

Notes: (i) Self-employment refers to working for one's self in non-agricultural activities in urban areas. Paid employment refers to working in a small enterprise for an employer. Employer refers to an owner of a small non-agricultural enterprise, employing less than five people. (ii) Values of zero should be interpreted as no observations found for that particular activity, and is driven by the characteristics of the sampled population.

Source: Calculations based on Ghana Living Standards Survey 4 (1998/1999) data from the Ghana Statistical Services.

Figure 12.1 Educational Status of Urban Informal Sector by Employment Status

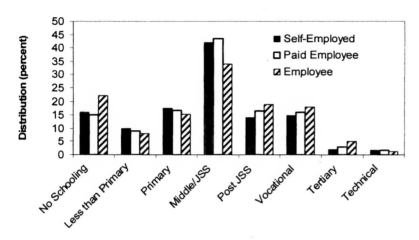

Source: Author's calculations based on 1998/99 survey data from the Ghana Statistical Services.

The educational status of workers in the urban informal sector is summarized in Figure 12.1. About 42 percent of the self-employed, 37 percent of the paid employees and 41 percent of employers have either no schooling, or less than primary schooling. These statistics are alarming since the lack of basic literacy can have negative repercussions on activities carried out by these workers in the labor market. Various studies have shown the importance of schooling not only in the area of earnings but also on an intergenerational level with parental education having a direct effect on the education of their children.

The evidence in Table 12.1 suggests that while there are more self-employed with only primary education than employers, there are more employers with post junior secondary school status than the self-employed. In addition, the level of vocational and technical education among urban informal sector workers is low. This shortcoming could be the direct result of the structure and content of the educational system in the country, which until the educational reform program of the late 1980s, had paid very little attention to "specific vocational or technical education."

Finally, the probability of being poor is related to the level of education. The poverty line used in our analysis is based on the upper poverty threshold of 900,000 cedis per adult, set by the Ghana Statistical Service (2000). Based on the 1998/1999 survey for urban workers, the observed correlation between poverty and the various educational status are as follows: poverty incidence and no schooling 0.132; poverty incidence and primary school attainment -0.004;

**Table 12.3 Main Sources of Set-up Capital for Urban Informal
Sector Workers: 1998/1999**

Sources of Start-up Capital	Self-employment (No employees)			Informal Sector Employers		
	Mfg. *	Retail Trade	Personal Services	Mfg	Retail Trade	Personal Services
Household savings	47.3	52.9	39.2	55.6	76.9	46.7
Loans from bank	1.1	0.8	1.1	0.0	0.0	0.0
Remittances from abroad	1.3	1.5	3.7	0.0	0.0	0.0
Family property income	1.9	1.2	0.0	0.0	3.9	0.0
NGO support	0.0	0.0	0.0	11.1	0.0	0.0
District Assembly	0.4	0.0	0.0	0.0	0.0	0.0
Church assistance	0.8	0.0	1.1	0.0	0.0	0.0
Relatives/Friends	33.5	33.7	37.6	27.8	19.2	53.3
Other source	13.8	10.0	17.5	5.6	0.0	0.0
Total	100	100	100	100	100	100

* *Manufacturing Activities*
Source: Calculations based on 1998/1999 survey data from the Ghana Statistical Services.

poverty incidence and middle school/junior secondary -0.091; poverty incidence
and post junior secondary -0.129.

2.2 Urban Informal Sector Activities and Finance

Table 12.3 lists the main sources of start-up capital for the urban informal sector. A major feature of is the near absence of institutional financial support for
start-up. Social networks are the prime source of mobilizing resources to launch
activities in this sector. Relatives or friends provide about one-third of the financial capital to support self-employment in manufacturing, retail trade and personal services. In retail trade which includes street vendors, household savings
constitute about 50 percent of start-up capital. Though the available data does
not provide the actual amounts associated with the various start-up capital
sources, prevailing patterns suggest that these are very small. The low levels of
financial resources mean that enterprises remain small, unable to grow, which in
turn makes it difficult to realize any economies of scale. This trend adversely
affects the profitability of such activities and increases the probability of falling
below the poverty threshold.

Table 12.4 Main Sources of Credit for Urban Informal Sector Workers 1998/1999

Credit sources (percent)	Self-Employment (No employees)			Informal Sector Employers		
	Manufacturing	Retail Trade	Personal Services	Manufacturing Activities	Retail Trade	Personal Services
No credit used	81.4	81.9	87.3	66.7	76.9	73.3
Chartered Bank	0.0	0.8	0.5	0.0	0.0	0.0
Other financial agencies	0.6	0.5	0.0	0.0	19.2	0.0
Co-operative	0.4	0.2	0.0	0.0	0.0	0.0
Money lender	1.7	1.7	1.1	0.0	0.0	0.0
Family/Friend	7.7	10.5	5.3	11.1	3.9	20.0
Retained earnings	7.3	4.2	5.8	22.2	0.0	6.7
Other	0.8	0.3	0.0	0.0	0.0	0.0
Total	100	100	100	100	100	100

Source: Calculations based on 1998/1999 survey data from the Ghana Statistical Services.

Table 12.5 Debt Indicators for Urban Informal Sector Workers

	Urban Self-Employment (No Employees)			Urban Informal Sector Employer		
	Amount borrowed ('000 cedis)	Amount Repaid ('000 cedis)	Debt Outstanding ('000 cedis)	Amount borrowed ('000 cedis)	Amount Repaid ('000 cedis)	Debt Outstanding ('000 cedis)
Manufacturing	426	268	158	467	333	133
Retail trade	491	293	198	32100	30000	2100
Personal services	143	78	65	98	98	0

	Urban Self-Employment (No Employees)			Urban Informal Sector Employer		
	Loan Repayment Rate (%)	Debt/Earnings Ratio (%)	Debt Per Capita ('000 cedis)	Loan Repayment Rate (%)	Debt/Earnings Ratio (%)	Debt Per Capita ('000 cedis)
Manufacturing	63.0	120.0	31.1	71.4	64.7	29.2
Retail trade	59.8	76.9	36.9	93.5	976.6	301.4
Personal services	54.6	47.8	14.9	100.0	0.0	0.0

Note: We have calculated debt outstanding as the difference between amount borrowed and amount repaid. The amount of interest payments charged on the loans has not been included since this information is not available from our database.

Source: Calculations based on 1998/1999 survey data from the Ghana Statistical Services.

The major sources of start-up capital for informal sector employers are similar to those of the self-employed (without employees). A major difference between these two groups is the role of non-governmental organizations (NGOs) in helping owners of manufacturing enterprises. About 11 percent of such manufacturing enterprises have received such from NGOs. Beyond start-up capital, it is observed that over 80 percent of the self-employed and about 70 percent of informal sector employers use no credit facilities whatsoever. About 22 percent of those in manufacturing enterprises depend on retained earnings from activities and 11 percent on family members or friends as credit sources. Only about one percent of the self-employed identified chartered banks as providing them with credit. Money lenders play a role in the provision of finance, though the percentage of urban informal sector workers benefiting from such credit facility is estimated to be no more than 2 percent (Table 12.4).

Table 12.5 gives the levels of outstanding debt as well as other debt ratios for urban workers who have taken credit to finance their activities. The loan repayment rate for the self-employed (without employees) is 63 percent for manufacturing workers, 60 percent for retailers, and 55 percent for personal service workers. These figures do not necessarily imply that the residuals constitute debt default. The calculations are based on the amount of debt paid expressed as a share of the amount borrowed. We have no information on when the loans were contracted, the repayment schedule or loan maturity period. What it does show is that there is a tendency on the part of workers in the informal sector to repay their loans. With the exception of the self-employed in manufacturing activities, the outstanding debt is lower than the average monthly earnings of workers.

Small scale employers, on the other hand, show very high debt/earnings ratio with regard to retail and wholesale trade. About 19 percent of those employers with access to credit took loans from other formal non-bank financial institutions. They are therefore more likely to obtain relatively higher amounts to finance their activities. The average monthly earnings are influenced by seasonal patterns in the economy. Larger loans in the context of relatively lower earnings could result in the observed higher debt/earnings ratio.

3. Spatial Aspects of Urban Poverty Characterization

3.1 Poverty Incidence and Depth

There is a wide spatial variation in the extent of urban poverty. Poverty is relatively lower among those in the major urbanized regions (i.e., Greater Accra, Ashanti and Western) as shown in Table 12.6. In the Accra Metropolis which has about 62 percent of the urban population in that region, about 7 percent of the informal sector workers are below the poverty line, with a welfare measure (real expenditures per adult equivalent) that is 1.3 percent below the poverty threshold. In contrast, urban informal sectors in the Tamale district have a poverty incidence of about 33 percent and a poverty depth of 8 percent. The variation in poverty among urban informal sector workers is not only inter-regional but also intra-regional. Some districts appear very vulnerable to poverty even though the overall regional poverty may be lower than other regions. For example, the poverty incidence of about 33 percent for the Dangbe West district of the Greater Accra Region is obscured by the overall regional average of 7 percent.

The relationship between specific informal sector activity and poverty is a mixed one. The degree of poverty incidence for specific economic activities appears to be region-specific. For some regions, poverty incidence is higher among retail workers than those engaged in manufacturing activities. For other regions it is the opposite. This phenomenon has implications for poverty reduction policies and tends to suggest that "across the board" policies without consideration of regional specifics could result in less than desirable outcomes.

3.2 Economic Indicators of Urban Poverty: Earnings, Assets, Labor Usage, Food Expenditures and Credit

At the national level, the average earnings of low income workers in the urban informal sector is about 71 percent of what is earned by all workers in that sector as shown in Table 12.6. The business assets of these workers are also worth 11 percent of their annual earnings, which is not unexpected since workers in this sector especially in retail trade have little working capital, and are frequently changing locations depending on the season of economic activities, particularly the case of street hawkers. Urban regional differences are also observed with the poor in Western Region earning about only 40 percent of the average informal sector earnings, while in northern Ghana the earnings ratio is not less than 90 percent. These patterns in earnings suggest that it is possible to have high poverty incidence but low poverty depth or poverty gap ratio in a particular region and vice versa. In terms of labout usage, the national average weekly hours of work of the urban poor falls short of the overall informal sector average by 4.3 hours (that is, an hours ratio of 90 percent). From a regional perspective, the hours gap is as low as 0.6 hours in the Greater Accra Region and as high as 8.3 hours in the Western Region. In terms of expenditure, the national urban food expenditure per capita for the poor is about 36 percent of the average for all workers in the informal sector. This shortfall in food expenditure has nutritional and health implications and is likely to have adverse effects on the long term status of the urban poor. In terms of credit, about 60 percent of the urban poor in the informal sector use no credit sources as means of finance with the result that

Table 12.6 Poverty Patterns among Urban Informal Sector Workers

	Urban Informal Sector Activities and Poverty Incidence and Depth (percent)						District's Share of Region's Urban Population
	Retail Trade		Manufacturing		All Urban Informal		
	Poverty Incidence	Poverty Depth	Poverty Incidence	Poverty Depth	Poverty Incidence	Poverty Depth	
Western Region							
Shama-Ahanta East	6.74	1.20	15.12	2.69	10.00	1.78	65.59
Central Region							
Cape Coast District	7.14	2.98	30.00	8.40	10.00	3.49	20.54
Agona District	46.43	14.14	-	-	40.00	12.29	27.84
Komenda-Edina	47.06	14.86	75.00	25.96	62.16	18.31	10.00
Greater Accra Region							
Accra Metropolis	7.48	1.37	4.76	0.91	7.25	1.34	62.15
Tema-Municipality	1.71	0.04	1.12	0.06	1.13	0.03	32.72
Dangbe West	-	-	57.14	7.89	33.33	4.60	1.18
Eastern Region							
West Akim District	54.55	18.46	83.33	43.19	51.43	20.05	29.95
Akwapim North	8.33	0.26	50.00	8.52	35.48	3.35	15.94
Manya Krobo District	36.84	5.96	58.33	30.79	44.12	14.90	15.46
Volta Region							
Keta District	20.00	6.22	7.69	4.39	11.11	2.57	18.04
Ho District	75.00	14.03	66.67	35.71	55.56	18.14	7.62
Kpandu District	22.86	5.12	21.43	8.68	18.75	5.21	17.84

Urban Informal Sector Activities and Poverty Incidence and Depth (percent)							District's Share of Region's Urban Population
	Retail Trade		Manufacturing		All Urban Informal		
	Poverty Incidence	Poverty Depth	Poverty Incidence	Poverty Depth	Poverty Incidence	Poverty Depth	
Ashanti Region							
Kumasi District	19.60	3.19	9.57	1.46	14.17	2.37	54.28
Sekyere West	36.00	12.90	72.73	22.19	78.13	24.69	6.83
Brong Ahafo Region							
Sunyani District	19.05	2.97	-	-	10.81	1.69	31.71
Atebubu District	26.32	9.35	-	-	21.74	7.72	14.98
Northern Region							
Tamale District	12.50	3.32	35.71	2.90	32.50	8.32	34.75
East Mamprusi	76.92	41.28	33.33	20.49	64.71	35.18	19.69
Upper East & West							
Jirapah-Lambussie	-	-	46.43	6.31	61.29	9.72	
Bawku East District	31.43	10.83	83.30	30.95	41.38	13.84	

Note: Poverty incidence is calculated using the national poverty threshold of annual consumption expenditures per adult equivalent of 900,000 cedis. The poverty depth (or poverty gap ratio) measures how far the poor are from the poverty threshold.

Source: Calculations based on 1998/1999 survey data from the Ghana Statistical Services

Table 12.7 Economic Indicators of Poverty Among Urban Informal Sector Workers

Urban Regions	Labor Usage [a]		Earnings & Assets [b]		Expenditures [c]		Credit [d]
	Weekly Work Gap (hours)	Hours Ratio (%)	Earnings Ratio (%)	Assets-to-Earnings Ratio	Food Expense Ratio (%)	Food Per Capita Ratio (%)	No Credit Incidence (%)
Western Region	8.3	79.1	40.0	7.7	50.9	38.7	53.6
Central Region	2.0	95.3	88.6	7.9	56.0	52.4	65.1
Greater Accra	0.6	98.8	79.4	3.2	56.3	34.7	77.6
Eastern	3.3	92.5	47.3	8.4	59.2	57.1	87.0
Volta	6.1	85.4	61.4	6.9	53.5	38.6	65.7
Ashanti	7.6	84.1	44.4	3.5	48.9	32.8	37.2
Brong Ahafo	3.2	93.1	93.8	5.8	57.4	32.4	66.7
Northern	5.8	87.4	90.9	7.7	60.7	51.8	43.2
Upper East & West	2.0	94.8	93.9	11.7	64.6	75.3	34.5
National	*4.3*	*90.1*	*71.1*	*10.8*	*55.2*	*35.7*	*59.9*

Notes: *a.* Weekly hours of work gap equals the average weekly hours of work by all workers in the urban informal sector minus the hours of work by 'the poor'. The hours of work ratio is the average hours of work by the poor divided by the average hours of work by all urban informal sector workers (expressed as a percentage). *b.* The earnings ratio is the ratio of average earnings by the poor informal sector workers to that of average earnings of all workers in that sector. The assets-to-earnings ratio is the value of business assets of poor workers in the urban informal sector divided by their average annual earnings. *c.* Food expense ratio is the annual food expenditures of poor urban informal sector workers as shares of total household expenditures. The food per capita ratio expresses the per capita food expenditure of the urban poor as a share of the average for all urban informal sector workers. *d.* The no credit incidence is the proportion of urban informal sector who are poor and do not use any credit facility to finance their enterprises.

Source: Calculations based on 1998/1999 survey data from the Ghana Statistical Services.

children. At the same time growth and upward mobility are key to making informal sector employment viable alternatives to formal sector employment.

3.3 Social Indicators of Urban Poverty: Education, Child Survival Rates, Health, Child Labor and Schooling

Table 12.7 shows the educational status of the urban poor by administrative region. At the national level about 24 percent of low income workers in the urban informal sector who fall below the poverty line have had no schooling. An additional 14 percent have pre-school status. Thus, over one-third of such workers have less than primary schooling. Compared with the average school attainment for urban informal sector workers, we observe that the poor "exceed" the urban average at relatively lower levels of schooling (that is, no school, less than primary, and primary categories) but fall behind at higher levels of education (that is, middle or junior secondary, and post junior secondary), as is evident in the last column of Table 12.7. There is also regional variation in educational endowment of the "urban poor." Generally, urban regions with relatively high poverty incidence tend to be associated with lower educational status (as is the case of Northern Region and the Upper East and West Regions) and vice versa. A notable exception to this generalization is the Central Region.

Table 12.8 shows the survival rates of children among informal sector workers. The survival rates are generally higher in urban than rural areas, and there are also marked differences between the urban poor and the non-poor. Overall, the survival rates of children among those who are poor are between 71 and 95 percent as compared to between 79 and 96 percent for the non-poor. Moreover, as expected, more impoverished urban regions have relatively lower survival rates of children than is the case of urban regions with better infrastructure. The irony is that in the more urbanized regions where poverty incidence is lowest, children's involvement in informal sector activities is relatively high, perhaps an indication of the greater opportunities for children to work. In the Greater Accra and Western Regions where more children from poor homes are seen to be working, a relatively high percentage of these children have stopped schooling with ominous implications for the dynamics of inter-generation poverty pattern.

The percentage of the urban poor nationwide, who declared they were ill and had to stop working, is lower than that for the urban average. Most worrisome, the urban poor are less likely to consult a health practitioner when ill than the poor in general. Unlike the rural poor, affordability rather than proximity is often a decisive factor for the urban poor.

Table 12.8 Educational Attainment of Poor Workers in the Urban Informal Sector

Educational Status of the 'The Poor' in the Urban Informal Sector (percent)

	Western Region	Central Region	Greater Accra	Eastern Region	Volta Region	Ashanti Region	Brong Ahafo	Northern Region	Upper East & West	National
No school	17.9	20.8	24.6	21.2	15.4	22.5	33.3	40.5	34.5	23.6
Less than primary	7.1	17.9	15.8	8.2	15.4	9.8	0.0	21.6	17.2	13.8
Primary	25.0	14.2	17.5	21.2	21.5	25.5	44.4	8.1	24.1	20.4
Middle/JSS	46.4	38.7	35.1	28.2	40.0	33.3	22.2	13.5	20.7	33.6
Post JSS	3.6	8.5	7.0	21.2	7.7	8.8	0.0	16.2	3.4	8.6
Total	100.0	100.0	100.0	100.0	100.0	100.0	100.0	100.0	100.0	100.0

Education Gap: 'Education Status of The Poor' minus Average Urban Informal Sector Performance (percent)

	Western Region	Central Region	Greater Accra	Eastern Region	Volta Region	Ashanti Region	Brong Ahafo	Northern Region	Upper East & West	National
No school	1.0	1.7	11.1	1.9	6.3	11.2	6.4	-1.8	-5.8	7.4
Less than primary	0.1	2.5	9.9	-1.9	8.3	-2.0	-9.9	6.2	6.8	4.8
Primary	6.5	-2.4	2.4	0.5	5.4	6.6	30.3	-3.4	10.7	3.8
Middle/JSS	6.0	1.0	-7.2	-4.8	-10.4	-10.8	-13.9	-3.8	-4.7	-6.9
Post JSS	-13.6	-2.8	-16.1	4.2	-9.6	-5.0	-12.8	2.8	-7.0	-9.1

Note: Education gap is calculated as follows: Using the Western Region as an example, we calculate the distribution of all urban informal educational categories and compare this with that of 'the poor' workers in the urban informal sector. The difference between the latter and the former is what we have used as proxy for the education gap. Thus, the gap is not measured in years. A positive value means that, there are more 'poor' urban informal sector workers in that educational category than the average for all urban informal sector workers. Source: Calculations based on 1998/99 survey data from the Ghana Statistical Services.

Table 12.9 Social Indicators of Poverty for Urban Informal Sector Workers 1998/1999

Urban Regions	Child Survival Rate [a]		Illness and Activity Stoppage [b]		Doctor Consultation		Children not schooling	Children working [c]
	"The Poor"	All Urban Informal	"The Poor"	All Urban Informal	"The Poor"	All Urban Informal	Urban Poor	Urban Poor
			percent					
Western	88.6	92.1	32.1	18.3	14.3	16.0	5.9	73.3
Central	88.0	89.9	8.5	14.9	4.7	11.3	3.1	80.9
Greater Accra	94.9	95.7	8.6	11.5	5.2	11.9	5.9	76.5
Eastern	89.8	92.6	7.8	6.7	7.8	7.6	2.2	56.1
Volta	93.4	94.2	7.5	11.3	4.5	8.2	3.3	48.9
Ashanti	88.0	90.4	13.3	13.9	8.0	12.7	2.1	61.6
Brong Ahafo	93.1	90.1	6.7	23.6	22.2	16.7	5.6	38.9
Northern	81.8	92.2	10.8	10.3	8.1	9.3	2.4	28.6
Upper East & West	70.5	79.0	13.8	16.4	3.4	10.4	3.6	29.2
National	88.8	92.7	10.9	13.2	6.9	11.9	3.3	58.8

Notes: (a) We measure child survival rate simply as the number of children still alive divided by the number of children born by a given woman. (b) Illness and activity stoppage is measured by the proportion of workers who reported being ill and had to stop working in the last two weeks prior to the household survey. (c) The percentage of children working is measured by children aged between 8 and 14 years who are self-employed and on average work between 30 and 49 hours a week.
Source: Calculations based on 1998/1999 survey data from the Ghana Statistical Services.

4. Determinants of Participation in Urban Informal Sector Activities

The preceding discussion motivates the statistical estimation to follow. We use a choice probability model to explain and to predict the choices that are made, voluntarily or otherwise, to participate in the informal sector. The model assumes that individuals derive some utility from the observed labor market choices. The decision to participate in any of the range of activities in the urban areas is assumed to depend on an unobservable utility index, I_i, that is itself determined by a set of explanatory variables X's in such a way that the larger the influence and the larger the value of the index, the greater is the pull towards participation in the urban informal sector. In a regression setting, the utility index of the i-th individual is

$$I_i = X_i' \beta$$

where the vectors of covariates and parameters of influence to be estimated are $X_i' = (1, X_{i2}, X_{i3}, \ldots X_{ik})$ and $\beta = (\beta_1, \beta_2, \beta_3 \ldots \beta_k)'$. β_1 is a constant. The probit specification represents the probability of choosing P_i as $P_i = F(I_i) = F(X_i'\beta)$. Where $F(I_i)$ is the cumulative distribution function of the standard normal.[5] The sign of β indicates the direction of the relationship between the explanatory variable and the probability of working in the urban informal sector. The X's represent three broad categories of influencing variables—educational status, demography and household characteristics, and geographical region. The results based on maximum likelihood estimation are reported in Table 12.10. Specifically, the effects of education, demographic and household characteristics and regions of residence on (1) informal sector participation in general and (2) self-employment in particular are estimated using probit technique. Although some urban workers choose the informal sector for the freedom and flexibility of work it offers, the weight of the evidence suggests that this may not be the case for the majority. The negative values of the estimates of the constant in Table 12.10 suggest that individuals exhibit a negative bias towards participation in the urban informal sector. This observation partly supports an earlier study by Ninsin (1991). He remarked that the informal sector in general is a haven for people seeking desperately to eke out a living because they are unable to secure wage or salaried employment in the formal sector, or unable to make a living in the rural areas.

Table 12.10 Probit Estimates of the Determinants of Urban Informal Sector Participation

	Urban Informal Sector (Pooled)		Self-Employment (Without employees)		Marginal Impact	
	Coef.	z-value	Coef.	z-value	Urban informal	Self-employment
Educational Status [a]						
No schooling	0.221	3.17*	0.188	2.75*	0.079	0.074
Basic education	0.263	5.29*	0.273	5.60*	0.097	0.108
Vocational school	0.192	1.48	0.127	1.01	0.069	0.050
Technical school	0.238	1.74***	0.235	1.77***	0.084	0.092
Demographic & Household Characteristics						
Household assets (x10^{-2})	0.025	2.87*	0.025	3.28*	0.009	0.010
Age	-0.001	-0.10	0.031	2.46**	0.001	0.013
Age squared (x10^{-2})	-0.011	-0.65	-0.053	-3.09*	-0.004	-0.021
Migrant status (migrant=1)	-0.026	-0.61	-0.060	-1.43	-0.010	-0.024
Household head (head=1)	0.109	2.02**	0.122	2.35**	0.040	0.049
Young children (<5 years)	0.167	2.94*	0.208	3.74*	0.063	0.083
Gender (female=1)	0.193	4.04*	0.176	3.80*	0.072	0.070
Regions [b]						
Central	0.441	3.96*	0.367	3.34*	0.149	0.143
Western	0.512	4.74*	0.402	3.78*	0.170	0.156
Greater Accra	0.603	6.64*	0.351	3.90*	0.211	0.139
Eastern	0.107	0.99	-0.010	-0.09	0.039	-0.004
Volta	0.081	0.78	0.065	0.63	0.030	0.026

	Urban Informal Sector (Pooled)		Self-Employment (Without employees)		Marginal Impact	
	Coef.	z-value	Coef.	z-value	Urban informal	Self-employment
Ashanti	0.449	4.71*	0.171	1.81***	0.155	0.068
Northern	-0.282	-2.32**	-0.228	- 1.86***	-0.108	-0.090
Upper East & West	0.146	0.95	-0.074	-0.48	0.052	-0.030
Constant	-0.280	-1.21	-1.053	-4.64*		
LR chi^2	246.9		180.9			
Log likelihood	-2482		-2676			
Pseudo R^2	0.047		0.033			
No. of observations	3992					
Observed probability					0.641	0.511
Predicted probability					0.649	0.513

Notes: *, ** and *** indicate statistical significance at the 1 percent, 5 percent and 10 percent levels respectively.
a. The educational status variables are dummy variables with a value of 1 if relevant status is applicable, and zero if otherwise. The reference level is post basic education. b. The regional variables are dummy variables with values of 1 if relevant region is applicable, and zero if not applicable.

The results show that, relative to post basic education (i.e., senior secondary education and above), workers with no schooling or basic education are more likely to opt for urban informal sector work, holding other factors constant. This is not surprising because of the higher educational prerequisites for most formal sector jobs. Specific education in the form of vocational and technical training are also positively associated with informal sector work choices. Those with technical training (mostly male) appear more likely to end up in the urban informal sector. Most female with vocational training exit the labor force early because of marriage and child-bearing only to re-enter later when children are of school-going age. In the case of self-employment, the marginal impact of the different levels of education show that, relative to higher levels of education, basic education increases the probability of being self-employed by about 11 percent, *ceteris paribus*. For the most part, those with technical and vocational education reconcile themselves with employment in the informal sector in the hope of either getting themselves a formal sector employment or setting themselves up as owners of some enterprise also in the informal sector as self-employment.

Age plays an important role in self-employment more so than it does for the general urban informal sector because of the precarious nature of the array of economic activities. Age therefore shows a non-linear effect on the probability of being self-employed in the informal sector. The coefficient of the age variable bears a positive sign, while the age-squared variable bears a negative sign. Participation rises initially with age and then falls later in life. Household headship, relative to otherwise, increases the probability of participating in the informal sector. This result is largely due to the responsibilities associated with such a status. The need to earn income to meet the basic needs (i.e., food, clothing and shelter) of household members becomes urgent with such a status. It appears the presence of young children (under five years) in the household does not hinder informal sector activities.

To a large extent, the urban informal sector (especially self-employment in retail trade) could be said to be a "territory" for females, while the formal sector has more male participants. This result is upheld by the positive coefficient on the gender variable. Women are more likely to work in the urban informal sector than in the formal sector as a result of their household responsibilities, particularly their responsibilities for the care of children. In their study of informal sector employment in Indonesia, Gallaway and Bernasek (2002) noted that the presence of infants in the household have different effects on the employment of men and women. While infants in the home may have no effect on men's labor force participation, they decrease the odds that a female will participate in the formal sector. Those who take a positive view of informal sector employment would argue that it is better suited to allowing women to combine household work with income generating activities that can be undertaken from the home. Public policy that recognizes and encourages this option will improve the opportunities of women in the informal sector. In terms of the regional dummy variables, we observe that relative to the reference region (i.e., Brong Ahafo Region), the three most urbanized regions in the country (i.e., Greater Accra, Ashanti and Western Regions) are all positively associated with urban informal sector participation. What policy options are available to address poverty in the urban informal sector? We review the problems of urban informal sector in the context of the GPRS in the next section.

5. Informal Sector Employment in the Ghana Poverty Reduction Strategy

The perception of the informal sector as stated in the poverty reduction strategy document is that:

> the informal sector provides other potential economic and social benefits in Ghana's development efforts. These include the production of goods and services, the creation of activities that maximize both forward and backward linkages between economically and socially diverse sectors. Its flexible adaptations to labor market fluctuations providing alternative employment opportunities for alleviating the negative consequences of the structural adjustment policies make the informal sector one of the most crucial in Ghana's development efforts. *(Government of Ghana, 2003, 73)*

The policy goal is to transform the nature of the economy to achieve growth, accelerated poverty reduction and the protection of the vulnerable and excluded. The category of people classified as being "vulnerable" and "excluded" include not only rural agricultural producers but also children in difficult circumstances (e.g., street children which is more of an urban phenomenon and school drop-outs), disadvantaged women, and residents of urban slums.

As impressive as the policy goal is, there are obvious weaknesses in the key areas of employment generation in general, as discussed by Baah Boateng in the preceding chapter, and also in dealing with the urban informal sector in particular. First, although employment in general featured prominently in much of the discussion on growth and poverty alleviation, it was noticeably absent from the medium-term priorities. It must have been assumed that employment was an integral part of all the priority areas—infrastructure development, modernization of agriculture, provision of social services, good governance and private sector development. For example, the construction of three major highways, the rehabilitation or development of roads to open up the country, the policy to encourage the production of cash crops and support further processing of traditional crops were all expected to have strong employment components in the medium to long term.

It is reasonable to assume that the production and employment objectives were to be achieved directly through these means and indirectly through support for private sector development. The long-term human development goal was expected to be achieved through changes to the educational system that will ensure uninterrupted education from pre-school to age seventeen. While job creation and employment objectives may have been implicit in the priority areas, immediate human resource development concerns did not receive as much prominence despite the policy intent to formulate a manpower plan for the country.

Moreover, the GPRS recognized the general features of urban informal sector that needed to be addressed, including, the low levels of education and skills, the limited access to credit, the lack of institutional framework, the lack of effective contract enforcement, low levels of technology use, and the limited vertical integration with the formal sector of the economy. These features, however, did not emerge from any careful analysis of the dynamics of the informal economy as we have attempted to do in this chapter. The poverty problem of the urban informal sector was assumed to be all too known as manifested by the ubiquitous street venders and *"kayayie"* — teenage girls who work as head porters. By this assumption, the GPRS proceeded with a generic picture of the urban informal sector in mind.

But, however common the circumstances of the participants of the informal sector may be, the motivations for the teenage boys and girls and the adults, in the rural and urban areas, may be dissimilar. For example, women's preferences to combine household work with income generating activities that can be undertaken from the home or close to home call for public policy that supports them in this choice. For the youth, it is not sufficient to assume that those who join the urban informal sector do so because the formal sector fails to accommodate them. It is conceivable that they represent a workforce with limited habits of work or no skills of work. As a result, they are more vulnerable to inferior employment arrangements than adults in the informal sector. Moreover, the position of boys and girls in the urban informal sector may be distinct, arguably to the disadvantage of girls. Most girls in the urban informal sector are uneducated, school dropouts, more likely to be exploited, more vulnerable to sexually transmitted diseases, and are more likely to remain in the permanent underclass. Most boys are school leavers with unemployable skills, more prone to underground and criminal activities than girls, yet more likely to want higher skills training to improve their earnings prospects and to accommodate their future household responsibilities.

By failing to analyze the dynamics of the urban informal sector, the motivations of the participants, the hierarchies and the level of informality, the GPRS fell short in its public policy focus. For example, the goal to improve the international competitiveness of the workforce in the urban informal sector[6] was too ambitious for a medium-term strategy. This is a less pertinent goal, especially if we consider the pressing problems of the urban informal sector, the social ills, and the crime associated with poverty in the urban areas.

The attention given to the informal sector in the strategy appeared fragmented. The proposals to strengthen skills and entrepreneurial development for the youth, strengthen traditional apprenticeship, promote technological proficiency of the urban informal sector workforce, and develop mechanisms to facilitate formal and informal sector linkages are laudable. However, the steps to achieve these objectives were not spelt out in the document. Some would argue that the GPRS was only a strategy document and that it was left to the Ministries, Departments and Agencies (MDAs) to translate the broad goals into concrete policies, programs and activities. They may be right.

Considering that the majority of the youth engaged in the urban informal sector migrate from the rural areas, establishing community-based vocational apprenticeship schemes, and providing technology upgrading training through the use of master craftsmen were the most direct policy attempts to addressing the urban challenge of youth unemployment. The coordination task of the specific programs and activities to achieve the goals of the GPRS was left to the National Development Planning Commission (NDPC) working with the MDAs, especially Ministry of Manpower Development and Employment, Ministry of Education, Ministry of Finance and Economic Planning (MoFEP) and Department of Social Welfare.

Like many aspects of the GPRS, we have to place enormous trust in the capacity of the MDAs to identify the specific cross-cutting issues in urban unemployment and to transform the issues into policy initiatives. We are left to trust the readiness of the MDAs to cooperate and the ability of the NDPC and MoFEP to coordinate initiatives to ensure effective implementation. Historically, poor organizational structures, overlapping mandates, ineffective coordination among the Ministries of Education, Health, Manpower Development and Employment and other relevant departments and agencies have been major weaknesses in human resource planning and training. Moreover, it is plausible to argue that the weak capacity of the NDPC has in the past not helped in coordinating the design and execution of multi-sector programs.

6. Policy Options

It is much easier to diagnose the problems of urban informal sector employment than to propose solutions. The following proposals are intended to promote the positive and to minimize the potential negative aspects of the urban informal sector.

First, where possible, public policy should seek to move individuals engaged in informal work into licensed micro-enterprises. The immediate goals of this policy should not be merely for taxation purposes or to eliminate the informal sector. The former may be premature. The latter is neither desirable nor feasible. Rather voluntary registration and licensing are essential first steps towards any policy initiative to improve the employment and earning capacity of informal sector participants, and to expand their access to credit, skill and entrepreneurial development in any systematic way.

Second, the informal sector may serve as an entry point into the formal sector and as an incubating stage of many small enterprises. To this end, public policy needs to address issues of training and apprenticeship with greater vigor. The urgency of training is underscored by the fact that over 20 percent of small scale employers in our study have never been to school and that nearly 60 percent of the graduates from the first cycle institutions (the equivalent of nine years of basic schooling) tend to join the ranks of the unemployed youth in the urban areas.[7] This tends to affect their skills development, managerial capabilities in future self-employment, overall profitability of their enterprises, and upward mobility out of poverty. Government efforts to provide skill-upgrading have culminated in the establishment of Integrated Community Centers for Employable Skills (ICCES). As of 2002, a total of thirty-five new ICCES had been established and these had begun training in various skills. Apart from these, the National Vocational Training Institute, which provides training over a wide range of competencies such as computer technology and hairdressing, opened ten new centers throughout the country under the government's community-based vocational and technical training initiative.

Beyond community initiatives, apprenticeship must be encouraged as a route to paying jobs in the formal sector, to a self-employed career, or to building the industrial labor force with employable skills. The challenge is how to design a nation-wide apprenticeship program with the maximum human development outcomes at the least cost. In the absence of any institutional mechanisms of welfare assistance, income transfers or negative income tax policies, any wholesale subsidized apprenticeship program is likely to be fraught with abuse.

One option will be to give priority to employers with apprenticeship schemes for government contracts. However, such a policy measure risks compromising value for money in government contracting and procurement. Unless standards of apprenticeships are set, enforced, and monitored there is always the risk of corruption and makeshift apprenticeship programs. In the long run, it is better if structured apprenticeship is promoted and encouraged through tax incentives to succeed on its own, offering an attractive option for employers to build up their own labor force, as opposed to making it a bureaucratic requirement. The apprenticeship program must proceed in a step-by-step basis guided at each stage by research to inform the designing of the programs, the monitoring and evaluation of their effects, and identifying the areas where apprenticeship programs are most likely to succeed. The role of the private sector is in its response to incentives to promote the apprenticeship program.

Optimists may argue that the motivation for the youth who engage in street vending is to generate cash and build capital to engage in other entrepreneurial activities with higher earning potential. If that is the case, then the scope for public policy will be to organize the youth into cooperatives to make it possible to gain access to credit. Critics argue that access to credit, however, must be preceded by an opportunity for the youth to learn good habits of work through specific vocational and skills training side by side with entrepreneurial training.

On access to credit, there are various policy options. One such option is to consider the creation of parallel structures or mechanisms for credit delivery to the informal sector.[8] While this has the merit of reaching specific targets, such as the urban poor, this could lead to what Heintz (2004) refers to as 'dichotomization of markets and/or institutions' with potential market segmentation problems. An alternative is to use existing structures and work towards integrating formal and informal financial institutions through specific linkages as proposed by Amoako-Tuffour (2002) and Aryeetey (2003). Even in the era of financial sector liberalization, informal finance has grown rapidly. In part because informal financial institutions have emerged in response to the unmet needs of a large segment of the informal sector activities. The reliance on informal sources of credit is evident in Table 12.4. Banks operating in the formal sector can channel financial resources to informal sector workers through informal credit mechanisms that already exist such as "susu groups", credit unions, and cooperatives organized at the community level.

On the issue of vulnerability, the fact is that there are seasonal patterns to urban informal sector activities and earnings. The challenge is how to minimize the degree of inter-temporal deprivation in the absence of welfare or income transfer programs. Our knowledge of the coping mechanisms of informal sector participants to seasonal variations in income is limited. Do they migrate from urban to rural areas temporarily, change or diversify their activities, or do they simple remain idle?

To a large extent, child labor is the clearest manifestation of poverty especially in the urban areas, as we saw in Table 12.9. The obvious prescription is that economic growth and a rise in per capita income, which reduces the absolute number of those at the tail end of the income distribution, will more likely reduce the incidence of child labor and encourage school attendance by children. But the lure of young people to the urban informal sector is as much a survival necessity for some as it is a reflection of the lack of hope and opportunities in the educational system, particularly in the rural areas where the majority of the urban informal labour force comes from. Children despair in school when there is inadequate teaching, and when the learning environment does not signal hope and opportunities. In the rural areas, it is the quality of instruction and the opportunities for greater learning, perhaps more than any direct incentives to go to school, that must become a matter of greater concern. On cost-benefit basis, improvements in children's learning environment might just be the best antidote to school dropout rates.

Urban health issues and workplace safety are important sources of risk and vulnerabilities of the urban poor and cannot be overlooked. In fact, poor sanitation and unsafe work environments pose greater dangers in the urban areas than in rural areas. Unlike the rural areas, the urban poor often work long hours and in dangerous and insecure conditions. Lack of access to basic amenities and garbage accumulation tend to occur in urban markets and workplaces where traders, carpenters, car repair mechanics (or "fitting shops") and those engaged in personal services ply their trade. These outcomes are often the result of coordination problems among the large number of individual participants and the lack of attention of local authorities to these work environment hazards. Matters are not helped by the fact that the local authorities are often unable to collect enough tolls and fees from the vendors and artisans to finance the supply of the needed basic amenities. The need to ensure healthy work environment and basic standards of safety especially in food stalls for urban informal sector workers is vital for public health and safety. In this regard the metropolitan assemblies need to sustain the gains realized from the various urban environmental sanitation projects.[9] This calls for allocating budgetary resources towards such social-oriented activities and at the same time involving market groups in urban environmental health programs. Educational campaigns on maintaining clean environment will also be helpful.

7. Conclusion

While the GPRS acknowledged the potential role of the informal sector in dealing with poverty in general and urban poverty in particular, the poverty diagnosis that informed the strategy was very superficial in this regard. We have argued that the dimensions of the urban informal sector are many.

First, many female-dominated activities are in personal services, food production and the distributive trade. These activities are likely to have problems with initial capital, food safety and personal hygiene standards. Second, male-dominated activities are in machinery, automobile and footwear repairs, masonry, plumbing, electrical, carpentry, painting and repair shops. In addition to sanitation, these activities are prone to problems of occupational safety and labor law violations and "sweatshops." Third, while the youth supply labor services in all these areas, they also tend to dominate street vending. Much of the latter is subordinated to micro-enterprises who contract out merchandise for a commission. The youth in these enterprises are also more likely to be victims of informal labor and market practices. More worrisome, their participation in urban street vending has increased in recent years even when the opportunities for skill-building and upward mobility are limited to nil.

These observations notwithstanding, our knowledge of urban informal sector activities is still limited. Further research is needed to provide an accurate picture of the participants, the range of motivations, the accurate typologies of the range of activities, the hierarchies or level of informality as well as the prospects of linkages with the formal sector. Understanding these issues is central to public policy effort to tackling urban poverty. Failing that, there will always be anecdotes indicating opportunities or hardships for the informal sector. But the variation around the mean of anecdotes is likely to be large and thus not a reliable guide to policy-making. Research should throw light on the capacities of the urban informal sector and on the perceptions about (a) whether it is a "liberating," "entrepreneurial" alternative to formal sector employment, (b) whether it is an incubating stage to more dynamic entrepreneurial activities, or (c) whether it is simply a poverty trap, especially for the youth.

Notes

1. The role played by the informal sector in job creation, income generation and poverty alleviation is recognized worldwide. As a source of employment, the informal sector is estimated to have accounted for over 90 percent of all new jobs in Africa in the 1990s (ILO, 2005).
2. Ghana Living Standards Survey, 1998/1999.
3. Losby et. al (2002) provide a comprehensive review of the literature.
4. The concept of the informal sector according to the literature was first coined in an International Labour Organization (ILO) study of urban labor markets in Ghana (Hart, 1973).
5. Gujarati (1995).
6. Government of Ghana, Ghana Poverty Reduction Strategy, February 19, 2003, p.74.
7. Government of Ghana Budget Statement, 2003. p. 87.
8. A notable example is the establishment of a Women's Development Fund, under the management of the Ministry of Women and Children's Affairs, which seeks to improve accessibility to and control of productive resources by women. In 2002, women's group across the country benefited from 250 machines for the processing of gari, shea butter and groundnut oil. 7000 women in trading related activities also benefited from this scheme.
9. An evaluation of the 1996 Urban Environment Sanitation Project (which targeted seven communities in the cities of Accra, Kumasi and Secondi-Takoradi) by the World Bank's staff, Banes *et al.* (2000), suggests that the provision of improved drainage has reduced the incidence of flooding in these communities, while solid waste collection has decreased garbage accumulation to some extent, though more needs to be done to provide a healthy environment. Targeted urban poverty reduction interventions in recent times included the Urban V Project (2000), under which 25 towns were to benefit from rehabilitation of basic municipal services, notably slaughterhouses, public toilets and markets. As of 2002 the work completion rate was 38 percent (Ministry of Finance, 2003).

References

Amoako-Tuffour, J. "Forging Links between Formal and Informal Financial Sectors: Emerging Practices in Ghana." *The African Finance Journal* 4(1) (2002): 1-31.

Aryeetey, E. "Recent Developments in African Financial Markets: Agenda for Further Research." *Journal of African Economies* 12(2) (2003): 111-152.

Banes, C., R. Huque, and M. Zipperer. "Towards a National Slum Upgrading Program for Ghana." Pp. 1-8 in *Urban Notes 22023: Thematic Group on Services to the Urban Poor*. The World Bank, Washington D.C. 2000.

Bhorat, H. "Poverty, Inequality and Labour Markets in Africa: A Descriptive Overview." Development Policy Research Unit, Working Paper 05/92. March 2005.

Bivens, J. L., Sarah Gammage, "Will Better Workers Lead to Better Jobs in the Developing World?" in *Good Jobs, Bad Jobs, No Jobs: Labor Markets and Informal Work in Egypt, El Salvador, India, Russia and South Africa*, edited by Tony Avirgan, L. Josh Bivens, and Sarah Gammage. Global Policy Network, Economic Development Institute, Washington, D.C. 2005

Cross, J. C. "The Informal Sector." in *Encyclopedia of Political Economy* edited by P. O'Hare. London: Routledge, 1998.

Gallaway, J. and A. Bernasek. "Gender and Informal Sector Employment in Indonesia." *Journal of Economic Issues*, 36,2 (2002):313-21.

Ghana Government. *Ghana Poverty Reduction Strategy 2003-2005: An Agenda for Growth and Prosperity*. Accra, Ghana. February 2003.

Ghana Statistical Service. *Poverty Trends in Ghana in the 1990s*. Accra, Ghana. October 2000.

Gujarati, D. N. *Basic Econometrics*, Third ed. McGraw-Hill, Inc. 1995.

Hart K. "The informal income opportunities and urban employment in Ghana." *Journal of Modern African Studies* 11 (1973):61-89.

Heintz, J. *Elements of an Employment Framework for Poverty Reduction in Ghana*. Report of a joint ILO/UNDP Mission. 2004.

International Labor Organization. *Global Employment Trends Brief*. Geneva: Switzerland. 2005: 1-8.

Losby J. L, Else, J. F., Kingslow M. E., Edgcomb, E. L., Malm, E. T. and Kao.V. "Informal Economy Literature Review," ISED Consulting and Research (Newark) and the Aspen Institute (Washington). December 2002.

Ministry of Finance. *The 2003 Budget Statement*, Accra, Ghana 2003

Ninsin, K. N. *The Informal Sector in Ghana's Political Economy*. Freedom Publications, Accra, Ghana, 1991.

Rempel, H. Rural-to-Urban Migration and Urban Informal Activities. *Regional Development Dialogue* 17(1) 1996: 37-51.

Sackey, H. A. "Modelling Poverty in Sub-Saharan Africa and Policy Implications for Poverty Reduction: Evidence from Ghana". *Canadian Journal of Development Studies* 25,5 (2004): 609-624.

Sethuraman, S. V. *Urban Poverty and the Informal Sector: A Critical Assessment of Current Strategies*. Geneva: International Labor Organization. 1997.

13

Achieving Gender Equity in Ghana: How Useful is the Ghana Poverty Reduction Strategy?

Abena D. Oduro

1. Introduction

The UN Office of the Special Advisor on Gender Issues and Advancement of Women defines gender as "the social attributes and opportunities associated with being male and female and the relationships between women and men, and girls and boys, as well as the relationships between women and those between men" (2001:1). Gender has been defined by the World Bank as "socially constructed roles and the socially learned behaviors and expectations associated with females and males" (World Bank, 2001:2). It has also been defined as "how a person's biology is culturally valued and interpreted into locally accepted ideas of what it is to be a woman or man." (Reeves and Baden, 2000:30). In all societies these social attributes and roles often result in different treatment, roles and inequities between females and males that often place women and girls at a disadvantage with respect to men and boys. Gender inequality not only has an adverse impact on the well-being of individuals, but it can also have a dampening effect on the progress and development of communities and nations. Economic and social policies, often thought of as gender neutral, can have differing impacts on men and women precisely because of the different roles and functions they perform in society, their differential access to and control of resources, and guaranteed rights. It is for these reasons that a poverty reduction strategy must take into account the different circumstances of different categories of men and women and must define strategies that have the explicit objective of improving the welfare of these different groups.

The main goal of Ghana's Poverty Reduction Strategy (GPRS) is "to ensure sustainable equitable growth, accelerated poverty reduction and the protection of the vulnerable and excluded within a decentralized, democratic environment." (Government of Ghana, 2003a:30). This goal cannot be achieved if issues relating to gender equality are not an integral part of the strategy. Gender equity is one of the objectives to be achieved in order to attain the overarching goal of the GPRS (Government of Ghana, 2003a: 30). The GPRS does not expound on its concept of gender equity but the literature suggests "gender equity denotes the equivalence in life outcomes for women and men, recognizing their different needs and interests, and requiring a redistribution of power and resources (Reeves and Baden, 2000: 10). The goal of gender equity, sometimes called substantive equality, goes beyond the objective of equality of opportunity by requiring transformative change. Thus it is expected that the GPRS to address gender equity will be sensitive to the different circumstances and needs of men and women. It will also involve changes in structures and institutions to ensure equality of outcomes for women and men.

My objective is to assess the extent to which the strategies of the GPRS contribute to achieving gender equity in Ghana. Many African poverty reduction strategy papers have been criticized for either not tackling gender issues at all, or when they are raised they are not a priority. A women in development approach is often used (Whitehead, 2003 and Zuckerman and Garret, 2003). This approach is not considered adequate because it focuses on women's problems without adequately addressing the issues of inequality and inequity between women and men. As noted by the Office of the Special Advisor on Gender Issues and the Advancement of Women of the United Nations "the concept of gender is not interchangeable with women. Gender refers to both men and women." (2001b: 2). Sometimes social rules and norms can have negative effects on men as well as on women—for example forcing men to behave in narrowly defined ways. Indeed if the objective is to reduce gender inequity then gender mainstreaming is the preferred approach since it is

> the process of assessing the implications for women and men of any planned action, including legislation, policies or programs, in all areas and at all levels. It is a strategy for making women's as well as men's concerns and experiences an integral dimension of the design, implementation, monitoring and evaluation of policies and programs in all political, economic and social spheres so that women and men benefit equally and inequality is not perpetuated. The ultimate goal is to achieve gender equality[1]

Another criticism of poverty reduction strategy papers is that even when gender issues are raised there is an "evaporation" of the issues between the development of the strategy to implementation and to monitoring. Policy evaporation occurs, for example, when commitments made by high-level government officials are not reflected in sectoral policies. It is also manifested when "attention to gender equity is not systematic in policy-making, planning, implementation and evaluation." (Derbyshire, 2002: 31).

To assess the effectiveness of the GPRS in achieving the objective of gender equity, I evaluate the approach that was taken by the architects of the strategy; that is, whether a gender and development or women in development approach was adopted and whether gender was effectively mainstreamed. I will also consider whether there has been policy evaporation. A brief background of poverty and gender in Ghana follows in section two. The assessment of how adequately the poverty analysis of the GPRS identified issues of gender inequality is presented in section three. The extent to which strategies were developed to reduce the identified inequalities is assessed in section four, followed in section five by an assessment of whether the GPRS contained gender-sensitive indicators to effectively monitor progress in gender equity.[2] The lessons for future poverty reduction strategy papers are summarized in the concluding section.

2. Some Dimensions of Poverty and Gender in Ghana

The poverty indicator normally used in Ghana is the real consumption expenditure per adult equivalent. This indicator is usually estimated at the level of the household. As a result, inequality within the household is not captured in such data. This is a major weakness for analyzing the gender dimensions of poverty since what is needed is information on the relative well-being of women and men within the household as well as outside of it. However, the sex of the head of the household is a popular, though not always an adequate basis of classification to reveal gender inequality. The rising incidence of households headed by women has been used as evidence to support the thesis of the feminization of poverty (Chant, 2003).

In Ghana, however, female headship is not always associated with a higher incidence of poverty. In both the national household surveys of 1991/1992 and 1998/1999, the incidence of poverty amongst households headed by women was lower than the incidence of poverty amongst households headed by men (Table 13.1). The data in this table suggests that households headed by women are not always poorer than those headed by men when using consumption expenditure per adult equivalent as the poverty measure. Households headed by women and men experienced declines in the incidence of poverty in the 1990s. However, the reduction in the incidence of poverty amongst households headed by men was larger than amongst households headed by women (Table 13.1).

There is a substantial amount of heterogeneity within the two groups of households (Table 13.2). Both categories of households in the coastal and forest zones have lower poverty headcounts compared to households in the savannah zone. Interestingly, the incidence of poverty amongst households headed by women in the poorest ecological zone, i.e. the savannah zone, is lower than for households headed by men in that ecological zone in both 1991/1992 and 1998/1999. This is a particularly interesting finding since many of the non-income indicators for women in this ecological zone suggest that they are worse off than men. This raises questions about the factors that cause the formation of

Abena Oduro

Table 13.1 The Incidence of Poverty by Gender of Household Head

	% Very Poor[1]	%Poor[2]	% Non-Poor
1991/1992			
Households headed by women	29.15	13.96	56.89
Households headed by men	39.24	15.65	45.15
1998/1999			
Households headed by women	23.68	11.52	64.79
Households headed by men	28.04	13.01	58.95

Notes
(1). Households with real consumption expenditure per adult equivalent below the lower poverty line of 700,000 cedis.
(2). Households with real consumption expenditure per adult equivalent below the upper poverty line of 900,000 cedis and above the lower poverty line of 700,000 cedis.

Source: Calculated by the author using Ghana Living Standards Surveys 1991/92 and 1998/99.

households headed by women. An investigation into the determinants of welfare finds that the marital status of the household head is significant in explaining welfare. Households headed by married women do not have significantly different levels of welfare than do households headed by married men (Oduro, unpublished).

2.1 Gender, Poverty and Education

For both boys and girls the net primary and secondary school enrolment rates of the very poor are lower than that of the poor, and these in turn are lower than the non-poor (Table 13.3). Net primary and net secondary enrolment rates for boys and girls increased between 1991/1992 and 1998/1999 (Table 13.3). In both years however the net enrolment rates of boys was higher than that of girls. The gap between net primary enrolment rates of boys and girls was reduced between 1991/1992 and 1998/1999 by two percentage points. In 1998/1999 the gender was highest amongst the very poor. Policy interventions, such as the establishment of the Girls Education Unit in the education ministry and improvements in income can explain the reduction of the gender gap in net primary enrolment rates over time.

Table 13.2 Spatial Patterns of Poverty and Gender of Household Head

	% Very Poor[1]	%Poor[2]	% Non-Poor
1991/1992			
Rural Households			
Households headed by women	40.50	15.83	43.67
Households headed by men	49.21	16.66	34.13
Urban Households			
Households headed by women	13.18	11.33	75.49
Households headed by men	16.05	13.30	70.65
Ecological zone: Coastal			
Households headed by women	19.25	11.83	68.91
Households headed by men	23.36	18.32	58.33
Ecological zone: Forest			
Households headed by women	34.47	15.72	49.81
Households headed by men	38.20	14.57	47.23
Ecological zone: Savannah			
Households headed by women	41.63	13.98	44.39
Households headed by men	53.00	14.71	32.30
1998/1999			
Rural Households			
Households headed by women	30.74	14.72	54.54
Households headed by men	35.66	15.10	49.24
Urban Households			
Households headed by women	12.91	6.65	80.44
Households headed by men	10.97	8.33	80.70
Ecological zone: Coastal			
Households headed by women	20.04	10.76	69.19
Households headed by men	15.98	11.06	72.95
Ecological zone: Forest			
Households headed by women	21.15	11.41	67.43
Households headed by men	16.99	15.63	67.37

Table 13.2 Continued

	% Very Poor[1]	%Poor[2]	% Non-Poor
Ecological zone: Savannah			
Households headed by women	40.77	13.69	45.53
Households headed by men	55.57	11.34	33.09

Notes
1. Households with real consumption expenditure per adult equivalent below the lower poverty line of 700,000 cedis.
2. Households with real consumption expenditure per adult equivalent below the upper poverty line of 900,000 cedis and above the lower poverty line of 700,000 cedis.

Source: Calculated by the author using Ghana Living Standards Surveys 1991/1992 and 1998/1999.

Table 13.3 Gender, Poverty and net Enrolment Rates

	% Very Poor[1]	%Poor[2]	% Non-Poor	All
1991/1992				
Net enrolment in primary school				
Girls	62.4	68.9	81.1	71.50
Boys	68.2	76.2	85.7	76.50
Net enrolment in secondary school				
Girls	27.6	34.8	37.6	33.70
Boys	35.6	42.1	46.3	40.90
1998/1999				
Net enrolment in primary school				
Girls	69.6	85.9	87.2	81.9
Boys	75.1	86.7	90.6	84.9
Net enrolment in secondary school				
Girls	27.5	37.6	44.0	39.0
Boys	30.5	45.6	48.4	42.4

Notes
1. Households with real consumption expenditure per adult equivalent below the lower poverty line of 700,000 cedis.
2. Households with real consumption expenditure per adult equivalent below the upper poverty line of 900,000 and above the lower poverty line of 700,000.

Source: Ghana Statistical Service, Poverty Trends in Ghana in the 1990s. (Accra: 2000).

Table 13.4 Educational Attainment of Persons Aged 15 Years and Over

	1991/1992	1998/1999
Never been to school		
Women	49.8	41.0
Men	29.1	21.1
Less than Middle School Leaving Certificate		
Women	26.6	25.6
Men	29.2	24.6
Middle School Leaving Certificate		
Women	20.3	27.8
Men	32.6	38.6
Secondary or Higher		
Women	3.3	5.7
Men	9.1	15.8

Source: Ghana Statistical Service, Ghana Living Standards Surveys, 1991/92 and 1998/1999.

There was not much improvement in the net secondary enrolment rate for boys between the two periods. There was a decline in the net secondary enrolment rates of boys from very poor households whilst that of girls from very poor households remained the same (Table 13.3). The improvement in the net secondary enrolment rate amongst girls at the national level is largely because of increased enrolment of girls in non-poor households.

Over time the educational attainment of the adult population has improved but the inequality between women and men remains (Table 13.4). The proportion of women aged fifteen years and above who have never attended school was double that of men in 1998/1999. The proportion of men with secondary education or higher was almost three times that of women in both 1991/1992 and 1998/1999. Thus even though progress has been made in increasing the proportion of both boys and girls that attend school, a lot remains to be done to reduce the drop-out rate of girls in particular, and to encourage girls to continue to higher levels of education once a level has been completed. The decline in the net secondary enrolment of boys from very poor households suggests that measures need to be implemented to encourage the boys to continue their education.[3]

2.2 Gender, Poverty and Employment

Agriculture is the largest sector of employment for both men and women, although its relative importance is declining over time (Table 13.5). The proportion of women employed in agriculture is lower than that of men, but women dominate the trading sector and their presence in this sector has increased over time (Table 13.5). The lower incidence of poverty amongst households headed by women in 1991/1992 has been explained by the greater involvement of women in nonfarm activities compared to men (Newman and Canagarajah, 2000). Occupational segregation by gender is evident in both 1991/1992 and 1998/1999 (Table 13.6). Women are under-represented in the mining and utilities sectors of the economy as well as in the professional/technical, managerial/administrative and clerical occupations. Since most women have less formal education compared to their male counterparts, they are likely to be under-represented in those sectors that require formal training. This under-representation can also be attributed to the responsibilities of women in the care economy as well as the traditional perceptions which do not support the role of women as paid workers in the economy.

Table 13. 5 Employment of Adult Men and Women by Sector

	1991/1992[1]			1998/1999[2]		
	Men	Women	All	Men	Women	All
Agriculture/Forestry	66.2	58.9	62.2	59.8	51.1	55.0
Miining and Quarrying	1.0	0.1	0.5	1.4	0.1	0.7
Manufacturing	6.7	9.4	8.2	8.9	13.9	11.7
Construction	2.5	0.1	1.2	2.8	0.2	1.4
Transportation	4.5	0.2	2.2	4.6	0.1	2.2
Trading	4.7	25.0	15.8	7.4	27.4	18.3
Finance	0.9	0.2	0.5	1.7	0.1	0.8
Utilities	0.2	0.0	0.1	0.4	0.1	0.2
Community /Social Services	13.3	6.0	9.3	13.0	7.1	9.8

Notes:
1. Population aged fifteen years and above.
2. Population aged 15—64 years.
Source: Ghana Statistical Service, Ghana Living Standards Surveys, 1991/1992 and 1998/99.

Table 13. 6 Occupation of Adults by Gender

	1991/1992[1]			1998/1999[2]		
	Men	Women	All	Men	Women	All
Professional/Technical	5.5	3.2	4.2	5.7	2.7	4.1
Administrative/Managerial	0.5	.	0.2	0.4	0.1	0.2
Clerical	3.6	1.6	2.5	3.7	1.2	2.3
Sales or Commercial	4.4	23.9	15.1	7.8	27.3	18.5
Service	3.4	2.2	2.8	5.5	4.0	4.7
Agricultural	64.3	58.6	61.1	59	50.3	54.3
Production	18.4	10.4	14	17.9	14.4	16.0

Notes:
1. Population aged fifteen years and above
2. Population aged 15–64 years.
Source: Ghana Statistical Service, Ghana Living Standards Surveys, 1991/1992 and 1998/1999.

Table 13.7 Basic Hourly Earnings by Gender, by Occupation

	1991/1992[1]		1998/1999[2]	
	Ratio of mean earnings of men to women	Mean Earnings (nominal)	Ratio of mean earnings of men to women	Mean Earnings (nominal)
Professional/Technical	0.97	782	1.11	1339
Administrative/Managerial	.	775	0.75	2694
Clerical	0.87	256	2.85	2859
Sales or Commercial	1.75	178	2.56	1427
Service	0.73	168	1.45	805
Agricultural	1.67	100	1.61	519
Production	0.96	167	1.33	889
All workers	1.14	176	1.43	918

Notes:
1. Population aged fifteen years and above.
2. Population aged 15–64 years.
Source: Ghana Statistical Service, Ghana Living Standards Surveys, 1991/1992 and 1998/1999.

Labor laws in Ghana protect women against wage discrimination. The laws also protect women against being sacked or being paid reduced wages during pregnancy and after childbirth. However, the ratio of the mean basic hourly wage of men to women exceeds unity in most occupations (Table 13.7) and between 1991/1992 and 1998/1999 this wage gap widened (Table 13.7). This could be explained by a number of factors. Despite the improvement in educational attainment of women they are not able to get placements in higher paid jobs because of the biased perceptions of employers. Second, wage discrimination may be practiced despite the existence of laws against it. Finally, with the structural changes that are occurring, such as the rapid expansion of information technology, not enough women may be acquiring the needed skills to fill these jobs.

Most people who identify themselves as employed are paid. The major exception is in agriculture where there is a substantial amount of unpaid family work. In 1991/92 it was estimated that 42 percent of women were paid for their work in agriculture compared to 81 percent of men (Ghana Statistical Service, 1995). In 1998/99 about 23 percent of women were unpaid family workers with most of them involved in agriculture; compared to 11 percent of men. A typical characteristic of unpaid family workers in agriculture is that they have never been to school, and approximately 60 percent of the female unpaid family workers in agriculture had never been to school (Ghana Statistical Service, 2000). Often girls are not sent to school because they are needed on the farm and at home for home-based production activities. This unpaid family work can perpetuate dependency reducing development potential of the individual.

2.3. Gender and Unemployment

The unemployment rate amongst women was higher than amongst men in both 1991/1992 and 1998/1999 (Table 13.8). This is particularly so for women in the 15–24 year age group. Ideally most of the young women and men in this age group should be attending secondary school or possibly tertiary institutions. Women in this age group are particularly disadvantaged since they are less likely to be in school compared to boys and are less likely to be employed. Therefore, there is a need to understand why women in this age group are unlikely to be in any form of employment.

2.4. Gender and the Reproductive Economy

A greater proportion of women and girls spend more time on household related activities than men do (Table 13.9). Over time there has been a decline in the proportion of men and women involved in activities such as collecting wood and fetching water. The increase in access to pipe borne water and wells and the reduction in the use of wood for cooking may explain this.

Table 13. 8 Unemployment Amongst Men and Women: 1991/1992 and 1998/1999

Unemployment	1991/1992 Men	1991/1992 Women	1998/1999 Men	1998/1999 Women
15-24	15.1	18.7	12.7	18.7
25-44	3.3	5.1	7.3	7.5
45-59	1.8	3.5		
45-64			4.8	4.5
60+	2.5	2.3		
All	3.7	5.4	7.5	8.7

Source: Ghana Statistical Service, Ghana Living Standards Survey. Report on the Third Round (GLSS3), (Accra: 1995). Ghana Statistical Service, Ghana Living Standards Survey. Report of the Fourth Round (GLSS4), (Accra: 2000).

Table 13. 9 Time Spent on Housekeeping Activities by men and Women

		1991/1992 Proportion doing that Activity (%)	1991/1992 Mean time spent (mins)	1998/1999 Proportion doing that Activity (%)	1998/1999 Mean time spent (mins)
Collecting Wood	Male	24	38	16	30
	Female	43	52	34.6	37
Fetching Water	Male	45	48	37.7	33
	Female	68	60	60.2	41
Child Care	Male			12.5	108
	Female			41.3	204
Cooking	Male			12.3	55
	Female			64.7	107

Source: Ghana Statistical Service, Ghana Living Standards Survey. Report on the Third Round (GLSS3), (Accra: 1995). Ghana Statistical Service, Ghana Living Standards Survey. Report of the Fourth Round (GLSS4), (Accra: 2000).

Responsibilities in the reproductive economy can compromise the participation of girls in formal education and the participation of women in directly productive activities. It can also affect their choice of the type of employment they would like to have (i.e. wage earning versus self-employment), whether or not to participate in the market economy and how many hours a day or week they should be involved in market based activities. A significantly lower proportion of women (24 percent) compared to men (35 percent) worked more than forty hours a week in their main job in 1998/1999 (Ghana Statistical Service, 2000). Amongst those who worked forty hours or less in their main job, a higher proportion of women (43 percent) compared to men (35 percent) indicated that they did not want to work additional hours. Approximately 52 percent of rural women did not want to work more hours in their main job. There may be two reasons why women are less likely to want to work more hours. Women may prefer to spend more time at a second job that may provide them with more income. Another reason may be that the time required for their domestic responsibilities makes it difficult to work extra hours to earn more income.

Table 13.10 Gender of Household Head and Access to Basic Utilities: 1998/1999

	Men	Women
Source of Drinking Water		
Inside Plumbing/Standpipe	12.45	14.87
Other source of safe drinking water	56.76	64.89
Unsafe drinking water	30.80	20.24
Fuel Used for Cooking		
Wood Fuel	92.50	96.16
Non-wood Fuel	7.50	3.84
Sanitation		
Safe sanitation e.g. flush toilet/KVIP/pit látrine	65.60	77.04
No latrine/pan or bucket	34.40	22.96

Source: Estimated by the author using data from the fourth Ghana Living Standards Survey, 1998/1999.

Strategies must be developed to reduce the burden the care economy places on women and improve the demand for their labor in the labor market. Yet, the responsibilities of women within the household economy must be viewed positively because these activities sustain the market economy. They do so by providing for the needs of current workers as well as nurturing and developing the invaluable human qualities and work ethic of future entrants into the labor market.

2.5. Gender and Access to Basic Utilities

Judging by access to safe drinking water and safe sanitation (Table 13.10), households headed by women are not necessarily at a disadvantage compared to households headed by men. Therefore, children living in households headed by women are no more likely to be exposed to the risk of contracting diseases caused by drinking unsafe water than those in male headed households.

2.6. Gender, Poverty and Landownership

Table 13. 11 Gender, Poverty and Landownership, 1998/1999

	% Very Poor[1]	%Poor[2]	% Non-Poor	All
All Households	33.9	42.9	44.6	40.6
Households headed by women	36.0	48.6	46.2	43.1
Households headed by men	33.3	41.4	44.0	39.9
All Rural Households	34.3	41.9	46.9	41.5
Households headed by women	35.9	50.1	49.8	44.9
Households headed by men	33.9	39.8	46.0	40.5
By Ecological Zone				
Coastal				
Households headed by women	20.8	60.6	42.0	36.4
Households headed by men	31.7	34.7	40.9	37.2
Forest				
Households headed by women	45.5	51.2	52.0	50.0
Households headed by men	41.9	43.2	51.6	48.2
Savannah				
Households headed by women	33.9	28.1	28.2	30.9
Households headed by men	30.1	43.8	28.5	31.2

Notes:
1. Population aged fifteen years and above.
2. Population aged 15–64 years.
Source: Ghana Statistical Service, Ghana Living Standards Surveys, 1991/1992 and 1998/1999.

Although land is critical for agricultural production, a minority of households have members who own land. This can be explained largely by the fact that in many communities ownership of the land rests with the community as a whole, the chieftaincy, the extended family or with the traditional religious leaders. Very poor households are less likely to contain members that own land whilst non-poor households are more likely to have members that own land (Table 13.11). The proportion of households headed by women having members that own land is higher than the proportion of households headed by men irrespective of the poverty status of the household. This pattern also exists amongst rural households.

However, a classification of households by ecological zones reveals heterogeneity amongst households. Land ownership is less prevalent amongst households in the savannah. Non-poor households in the savannah zone are less likely to own land compared to poor households. In the northern part of the country land is owned largely by priests. Amongst the non-poor households in the savannah there is no significant difference between households headed by women and those headed by men in terms of land ownership. Amongst poor households in the coastal and forest zones the proportion of households headed by women that own land is significantly larger than the national average (Table 13.11). That a greater proportion of households headed by women have members that own land, compared to households headed by men, provides little information about the proportion of women or men that own land. The fact that less than half of households have members that own land also suggests that the concerns from a policy framework should not be focused only on land ownership per se. Participatory poverty assessments highlight issues such as soil fertility and erratic rainfall patterns for example as major concerns of rural people with respect to their livelihoods (Kunfaa, 1999). What really would appear to be the issue would be equal access to good quality land and security of tenure.[4]

3. Poverty and Gender Inequality in the GPRS

The GPRS analysis of the dimensions of poverty did not present a comprehensive perspective and analysis on gender and poverty even though it contained a section entitled "Disparities by Gender," Sex-disaggregated data was provided for some education and employment indicators. In the table containing information on the dimensions of poverty in Ghana the data is not classified using the gender of household head, the popular dimension in the discussions on gender and poverty. The failure to provide more extensive data disaggregated by sex is not because the data was unavailable. In failing to conduct a careful gender analysis with respect to poverty runs the risk of making statements and assertions that are inaccurate. The data in Table 13.11 shows that such an analysis was possible.

This shortcoming notwithstanding, the GPRS recognizes that women have greater demands on their time and that gender disparities exist with respect to access to and control of a range of productive assets, including land and credit, human capital, and social capital. The document also notes gender disparities with respect to HIV prevalence, legal status and rights and protection under the law. These disparities are attributed to socio-cultural factors. The analysis however does not identify the reasons for the greater demands on women's time nor does it explicitly discuss the link between women's responsibilities in the care economy and the implications this has for their participation in income generating activities. There is no discussion of the gender dimensions of labor market participation and poverty nor is there a discussion of the existence of gender wage gaps.

The participatory poverty assessments reveal that there "was noticeable gender differentiation in relation to poverty. Men gave priority to the need to support agriculture . . . Women stressed the importance of being able to support the family by provision of basic needs . . ." (Government of Ghana, 2003a: 27).[5] The participatory poverty assessments provided much more information on the perceived causes of poverty and the strategies to reduce poverty recommended by men and women than was reported in the GPRS. The implementation of measures to ensure equal rights to women was one of the priority interventions that emerged from the participatory poverty assessments (Government of Ghana, 2003a: 29). The poverty analysis of the GPRS addressed some aspects of the gender dimensions of poverty. In particular it assessed in some detail gender inequality in educational attainment, the incidence of HIV/AIDS, and the less favorable nutrition indicators amongst boys compared to girls. Also, it made mention of gender inequality in the access to and control of assets and services.

Despite identifying gender equity as a means to achieving the overall goal of the GPRS, the poverty reduction targets set out in Table 4.4 of the GPRS document suffers from a dearth of gender-sensitive indicators. The gender-sensitive indicators are limited to the school enrolment rate of girls and the HIV/AIDS prevalence. However baseline sex-disaggregated data is available for underweight children under-five years, the proportion of children that achieved mastery in the Criterion Referenced Test, gross junior secondary enrolment rate, the incidence of poverty amongst households and the incidence of poverty amongst households headed by food crop farmers. The failure to provide gender-sensitive indicators for these targets cannot be attributed to the absence of baseline data.

4. Measures to Achieve Gender Equity in the GPRS

The GPRS sees gender as a crosscutting issue relevant to these four broad themes: production and gainful employment, human resource development, special programs for the vulnerable and excluded, and governance. The overview section of the chapter on production and gainful employment contains a subsection on "Gender equity for increasing production." The section identifies access to land, marketing constraints due to lack of bargaining power and lack of access to credit as constraints on women's productive activities. The strategy to relax these constraints involves providing women with support programs including credit, improved technological services and facilities and skills upgrading in management and finance. In the sub-sections of the chapter on production and gainful employment there is further discussion of the issues raised in the overview section. Support for agro-processing is to be "particularly targeted toward women" although it is not clear whether all such support will go to women and if not, what proportion will be targeted at women (Government of Ghana, 2003a: 86). It is proposed that the agro-processing strategy will favor labor-intensive technologies. Considering that women have greater time commitments than men and may not always be able to hire labor, a labor-intensive strategy may not be the most appropriate. Fortunately the strategy with respect to energy provision in rural areas aims at promoting the use of energy resources that will reduce the time burden of women. If this is effectively implemented, some women may be able to participate in labor-intensive production strategies. The GPRS also sets out measures to address the credit constraint facing women. Although women are to be supported through the provision of skills upgrading in management and finance, these implementation measures are not developed in the document.

In the GPRS, human development is captured under five themes: education, skills and entrepreneurship development, HIV/AIDS, population management and health care. Under education the only gender-sensitive indicators that are provided are for the gross primary enrolment rate and the primary school drop out rate. It is not clear how the strategy of school improvement would increase girls' primary school enrolment rates and reduce drop out rates of boys and girls. The discussion on youth skills and entrepreneurialship development did not take into consideration the differences in endowment of formal education and skills training between the sexes as well as the tendency to gender-stereotype the skills acquisition process. Some of the strategies to deal with HIV/AIDS address the disadvantaged position of women. Under population management, gender-sensitive targets were set for the use of modern contraceptive methods and the proportion of the population that would be exposed to family planning messages.

Three categories of women are identified as vulnerable and excluded. These are disadvantaged women including single mothers and malnourished rural pregnant women; victims of abuse, particularly women and their children and women suffer from sexual abuse and battery; and victims of harmful traditional practices such as widowhood rites and early marriage. No categories of men are explicitly identified as being amongst the vulnerable and excluded. The programs for the vulnerable and excluded are expected to "develop systems that enforce the rights on protection, especially for children and women" (Government of Ghana, 2003a: 116). One of these programs is the expansion of social security coverage by 100,000 people. This will have a limited impact on poverty in general and on women in particular if an effort is not made to target them since more than 90 percent of working women are self-employed in the informal sector. Unfortunately there are no targets for the number of women and men who are expected to be part of these schemes. Gender discrimination is identified as a key issue with respect to governance and poverty reduction. However, apart from land administration reform and recruitment into the police service, gender equity does not feature much in the strategies outlined in the section on governance.

The GPRS has two parts: the main document and the medium-term priorities. The main document contains a wide range of measures under the five different themes- macroeconomic stability, production and gainful employment, human resource development, special programs for the vulnerable and excluded, and governance. There was a need to prioritize largely because of financing constraints and the low administrative capacity to absorb high amounts of funding (Government of Ghana, 2003a: 143).[6] Examining the costed program of the medium term priorities provides an indication of the extent to which gender issues remained an integral part of the implementation of the GPRS. A reading of the second volume of the GPRS, which contains the costing and financing of programs and projects reveals that many of the strategies aimed at targeting women were maintained. Whereas in the main document it is not clear that the strategies adopted would reduce the gender gap in education, in the costed program the mainstreaming of pre-education for all schools in Ghana is considered an initiative that would "reduce gender gaps in enrolment" (Government of Ghana, 2003b: 9).

5. Monitoring Progress towards Gender Equity in the GPRS

The main GPRS document did not always contain gender-sensitive targets even when baseline data was available. This omission raises concerns about whether progress in achieving gender equity would be tracked. However, a monitoring and evaluation plan was developed to track progress in implementation, outputs and outcomes. Several principles were used to determine the indicators. Three of these principles were availability, measurability and the requirement that the indicators "should be disaggregated to enhance usability: to the district level, by the level of poverty/well-being, and by gender" (Republic of Ghana, 2003:39).

All the thematic areas had at least one gender-sensitive indicator (Table 13.12) with the exception of the Production and Gainful Employment theme. The Monitoring and Evaluation Plan addressed some of the gaps that exist in the main document, where gender-sensitive targets could have been set but were not provided. However, the Monitoring and Evaluation Plan also contained some indicators where the requirement for gender-sensitive indicators was not met, but which could have been provided. For example, under the Production and

Abena Oduro

Table 13.12 Gender Disaggregated Indicators in the Monitoring and Evaluation Plan

Indicators	Category of Disaggregation
Overaching Indicators	
Child malnutrition	Sex
Infant Mortality Rate	Sex
Accessibility of Services	Sex of household head
Accessibility of Extreme Poor to services	Sex of household head
Parliamentary Committee on Poverty Reduction Established	Balance of membership by gender
Macro-Stability	
Growth of credit to agriculture	Sex of borrower
Human Resource Development	
Gross Enrolment Rate in pre-school and basic education	Sex
Survival Rate to Primary 6 and Junior Secondary School 3	Sex
Percent of households with access to safe water	Sex of the household head
Percent of households with access to adequate toilet facilities	Sex of the household head
Vulnerable and Excluded	
Drug based treatment available for people with AIDS	Sex
HIV Prevalence	Sex
Adequate security and protection of women and children	Measured by number of cases reported to WAJU, CHRAJ, NADMO, Department of Social Welfafe.
Budget avaiable for institutions caring for the vulnerable and excluded.	
Governance	
Utilisation of legal aid services	Sex of the client

Source: Republic of Ghana, An Agenda for Action. Ghana's Poverty Reduction Strategy 2003-2005. Monitoring and Evaluation Plan (Accra:2003).

Gainful Employment section of the plan, some indicators, such as the number of small-scale agro-processing firms, could have been made gender-sensitive. This information could be provided not only for regions, as required in the Monitoring and Evaluation plan, but also by the sex of the firm owner(s).

Even though the choice of indicators was based on availability, the Monitoring and Evaluation plan could have required sex-disaggregated data as part of the monitoring process. This requirement would have put pressure on the Ghana Statistical Service and the research and policy, planning and monitoring units of the various ministries, departments and agencies to begin collecting sex-disaggregated data, or systematically store and publish the sex-disaggregated data that is already being collected.

An evaluation of the annual progress reports on the implementation of the GPRS finds that the monitoring process did not always follow the requirements of the monitoring and evaluation plan. The reports of progress in 2002 and 2003 did not provide gender-sensitive data on child malnutrition and infant mortality rates, access to services, growth of credit in agriculture, the proportion of trained teachers in pre-schools and basic schools, and the utilization of legal aid services. Some indicators were not reported on at all, for example, survival rate to Primary Six and Junior Secondary School and the accessibility of the extreme poor to basic services. Failure to provide gender-sensitive indicators cannot be attributed only to a lack of data. The annual progress reports provided information on additional indicators that were not required by the monitoring and evaluation plan and which could have been presented in a gender-sensitive format. Examples of these are households that faced difficulty with food needs, the farmer-tractor ratio, the proportion of households using non-wood fuel and farmers benefiting from several programs such as the Smallholder Credit Supply and Marketing Project and the Food Crop Development Project. The progress report of 2003 was able to report on how many people had benefited from these and other projects. With a little extra effort these beneficiaries could have easily been classified by their sex. The Core Welfare Indicators Questionnaire Survey of 2003 that collected data on food security and source of energy allows for the classification of these indicators on the basis of the sex of the household head.

6. Conclusion

The GPRS is not silent on gender. Achieving gender equity is one of the objectives through which the overall goal of poverty reduction could be attained. However, gender was not adequately mainstreamed into the thematic areas. This is partly because in the preparation of early drafts of the GPRS gender was not adequately addressed. Appendix J of the GPRS contains comments on various drafts of the GPRS. Some of the comments were "coverage of gender issues needs to be improved," "further work on gender and poverty required" and "strategy must address gender inequality and promote women's advancement." These suggest that initially gender was not adequately incorporated into the GPRS. The final version is an attempt by the architects of the strategy to respond to such comments made.

The GPRS approach is the women in development approach. The bias of the approach is towards targeting women without presenting a comparative framework which would bring out clearly the issues of gender inequality and gender equity. The approach adopted in the GPRS also presents women as a homogenous group. However, for effective targeting it is important to take into consideration the heterogeneity amongst women and amongst men and looking into the causes of this heterogeneity.

The GPRS did not suffer entirely from policy evaporation. Some issues that were identified during the poverty analysis stage, for example, gender inequality in education and access to credit were followed through to the policy and strategy stage, and were included in the Monitoring and Evaluation plan. However, reporting on these and several other gender-sensitive indicators in the annual progress reports has been inadequate.

Reaching the objective of gender equity, as set out in the GPRS, requires "transformative change." The social attributes and roles that define the parameters of gender in any society are determined by cultural, religious, political, economic and legal factors. Transformative change is possible only when there are changes in these dimensions of society. The strategies of the GPRS made some contribution towards bringing about this change. Including pre-school as part of the basic education system and the training of caregivers in the strategy could contribute to increasing the participation of women in the market economy. Effective implementation of the proposed national campaign on fertility regulation could strengthen women's ability to control their sexuality. The GPRS proposes that "the legal system will be streamlined to more effectively address gender-based violence, violations of freedoms and to protect property rights of spouses and protection of children, the elderly and disabled. In addition, the repeal of laws that are discriminatory against women will be undertaken" (Government of Ghana, 2003a: 117). Changes in legislation are important first steps towards bringing about change in societal rules and norms. The next major challenge is the enforcement of the law. This requires political commitment at all levels of government, education, sensitization and the creation of incentives to encourage change. However, meaningful transformative change cannot be completed within the three year life of the GPRS. The GPRS therefore provides a limited foundation from which this change can begin.

Lessons for the Future

The implementation period of the GPRS ends in 2005 and then a new poverty reduction strategy is to be developed for the next three years. If progress is to be made towards achieving gender equity then gender equity must be a priority in subsequent attempts at poverty reduction. Three pre-requisites must be met if this is to happen. The first is commitment from all political levels. Without the necessary commitment to achieve gender equity at all levels of government, it will be difficult to propose, implement and monitor the legal, institutional and other changes that are required.

The second prerequisite is having the capacity to undertake the preparation, implementation and monitoring of a poverty reduction strategy that mainstreams gender. This requires the capacity to conduct a gender analysis, to develop strategies to improve the well-being of both men and women; to develop gender-sensitive indicators, and to effectively track progress in implementation with respect to achieving gender equity. The lack of sufficient expertise to conduct a gender analysis on all aspects of economic, social and political life that was covered by the original GPRS may explain some of the weaknesses that have been identified here.

The third pre-requisite is the timing of the process of mainstreaming gender. Gender considerations were not an integral part of the initial design of the strategy. During the participatory poverty assessments consultations, the opinions of youth, women and men were sought. The outputs of these assessments were to inform the development of the policy framework and the strategies. A one-day seminar was held with women's groups during which dissatisfaction with the draft document was expressed. The women's groups proposed improvements to the document and a consultant was engaged by one of the women's groups to facilitate this process. It is critical that gender analysts, with expertise in economic, social and political issues, are employed to ensure that gender is mainstreamed. These analysts must be an integral part of the process of developing the GPRS and must be involved from the initial stages.

Incorporating gender considerations into poverty analysis brings to the fore the issue of new data requirements. Traditionally living standard surveys have collected data on expenditure and income using the household as the unit of analysis. However, gender analysis requires information about individuals. Information on intra-household resource allocations is critical if an assessment is to be made, for example, on the proportion of men and women that have income or consumption expenditure levels below the poverty line. This is also the case if an analysis is to be conducted on the causes of malnutrition amongst boys and girls. Thus changes will have to be made to the format of the living standards surveys to obtain information on intra-household resource allocations. Living standards surveys must also aim at capturing spatial diversity by collecting data that is national but also representative at the district level. The results from the

2003 Core Welfare Indicators Questionnaire Survey show quite dramatically the disparities that exist in the country and the danger that national aggregates can masking deviations from the average that are significant with respect to their impacts on human development and poverty. Time use data is also important to assess the time commitments of women and men. Greater effort must be made to collect and publish micro data disaggregated by sex where possible. Examples of such data are average wages, employment, credit to individuals, credit to enterprises. Indeed it should be a requirement that where feasible data should always be presented not only by region and district, but also by sex. Participatory poverty assessments can also provide additional information that can be used to understand patterns observed from quantitative data.

Notes

1. Office of the Special Advisor on Gender Issues and Advancement of Women "Gender Mainstreaming: Strategy for Promoting Gender Equity," 2001, http://www.un.org/womenwatch/osagi/pdf/factsheet1.pdf
2. "A gender-sensitive indicator can be defined as an indicator that captures gender-related changes in society over time. Thus whereas a gender statistic provides factual information abut the status of women, a gender-sensitive indicator provides direct evidence of the status of women, relative to some agreed normative standard or explicit reference group." (Beck, 1999: 3).
3. Preliminary findings from the nationally representative household survey (Core Welfare Indicators Questionnaire Survey) conducted in 2003 indicate that the net secondary enrolment rate of girls slightly exceeds that of boys, i.e. 38.4 percent as against 37.9 percent.
4. In the participatory poverty assessments conducted in communities in the Northern region it was found that there was the tendency to exclude women and non-indigenous groups when improvements were made to resources (Amadu and Atua-Ntow, 2000).
5. The preparation of the GPRS involved the conduct of participatory poverty assessments in 36 communities located in 14 districts and 6 regions.
6. The total cost of the GPRS was estimated at US$5,283 million. The medium-term priorities programs were estimated to cost US$2,515 million.

References

Amadu, M. B. and K. Atua-Ntow. *Regional and District Level Consultations on Poverty Reduction: Northern Region.* (Accra: GOG/UNICEF) 2000.
Beck, T. *Using Gender-Sensitive Indicators* (London: Commonwealth Secretariat) 1999.
Chant, S. *New Contributions to the Analysis of Poverty: Methodological and Conceptual Challenges to Understanding Poverty from a Gender Perspective* (Santiago: CEPAL) 2003.

Derbyshire, H. *Gender Manual: A Practical Guide for Policy Makers and Practitioners* (London: Dfid,). 2002.

Kunfaa, E. Y. *Consultations with the Poor. Ghana Country Synthesis Report* (Washington D.C: World Bank) 1999.

Ghana Statistical Service. *Poverty Trends in Ghana in the 1990s.*(Accra. 2000.

Government of Ghana. *Ghana Poverty Reduction Strategy 2003-2005. An Agenda for Growth and Prosperity, Vol. I*(Accra: Government of Ghana, 2003a.

———. *Ghana's Poverty Reduction Strategy. Agenda for Growth and Poverty, Vol. II* Accra: Government of Ghana, 2003b.

Newman, C. and S. Canagarajah. *Gender, Poverty and Nonfarm Employment in Ghana and Uganda*, Policy Research Working Paper, Washington D.C: The World Bank, 2000.

Oduro, A. D. *Poverty in Ghana: An Analysis of Trends in the 1990s* (Accra: unpublished manuscript, undated).

Office of the Special Advisor on Gender Issues and Advancement of Women "Gender Mainstreaming: Strategy for Achieving Gender Equality," 2001a http://www.un.org/womenwatch/osagi/pdf/factsheet1.pdf

———. "Important Concepts Underlying Gender Mainstreaming", 2001b http://www.un.org/womenwatch/osagi/pdf.factsheet2.pdf

Reeves, H. and S. Baden. "Gender and Development: Concepts and Definitions." *Bridge Report No. 55.* February 2000.

Republic of Ghana. *An Agenda for Growth and Prosperity. Ghana's Poverty Reduction Strategy 2003-2005. Monitoring and Evaluation Plan*, (Accra: Republic of Ghana) 2003.

Whitehead, A. *Failing Women, Sustaining Poverty: Gender in Poverty Reduction Strategy Papers,*(U.K: Christian Aid, 2003.

World Bank. *Engender Development: Through Gender Development in Rights, Resources and Voice*, Policy Research Report No. 21492 Washington D.C: The World Bank, 2001.

Zuckerman, E. and A. Garret. *Do Poverty Reduction Strategy Papers (PRSP) Address Gender? A Gender Audit of 2002 PRSPs.* A Gender Action Publication. 2003.

14

Environmental Sustainability and Poverty Reduction in Ghana

Daniel K. Twerefou and Eric Osei-Assibey

We recognize that poverty, environmental degradation and population growth are inextricably related and that none of these fundamental problems can be successfully addressed in isolation. We will succeed or fail together.

— *"Making Common Cause"*
U.S. Based Development, Environment, Population NGOs
WCED Public Hearing, Ottawa, 26-27 May 1986.

1. Introduction

Issues about the environment have in recent years gained prominence in development literature because of their potential effects on development and growth. The environment provides some basic, yet essential functions to sustain human existence and development. De Groot (1992) sets out the role of the environment in human development. The environment, according to De Groot, provides four basic functions. The *regulatory or stabilization function* involves the ability of the environment to sustain the human community and to regulate basic ecological processes. In its *production function* role, the environment provides resources that can be harvested directly or transformed through human work. In its *carrier function the environment* provides geological stability and space, and in the *information function* provides a cognitive and information framework used by human communities to organize social relations. Quite often, however, in our search for rapid economic growth and poverty reduction, environmental concerns are not given the attention that they deserve or are neglected completely. The *World Development Report 1999/2000* points out that protecting the environment is often viewed as a peripheral issue in poverty alleviation, perhaps even a luxury. It does not feature at the very centre of rural livelihoods, nor as a means of pulling individuals and rural communities out of poverty.

Ghana has made some strides in reducing poverty through reforms and sustainable development of some sort. Notable reforms are the Economic Recovery Program (ERP) and the Structural Adjustment Program (SAP) launched in 1983, as blueprints for economic recovery, to halt decades of economic decline and the descent into poverty of the majority of the Ghanaian population. Government programs with respect to the environment and natural resource management are represented by a series of action plans and policies that aim to protect, rehabilitate and sustainably manage land, forest and wildlife resources (Government of Ghana, 2003). The country is currently a signatory to almost all the international agreements on the environment.[1] Despite these efforts environmental concerns remain. This chapter reviews Ghana's experience in integrating environmental issues into its poverty reduction and development programs. We examine the extent to which issues of natural resource use, management and conservation, environmental amenities and sustainability were dealt with in the Ghana Poverty Reduction Strategy (GPRS). We discuss in section two the link between poverty and the environment. In section three we examine the extent to which sustainable development issues were incorporated into the key thematic areas of the GPRS. We assess the policies of the GPRS and their potential impact on the environment in section four, followed in section five with concluding observations.

2. The Link between Poverty and the Environment

To understand the potential links between poverty and the environment we must understand the two terminologies as used in development literature. Past efforts in fighting poverty focused on income/consumption poverty. The World Bank *(2000)* defines absolute poverty as the state of an individual/household in comparison with a "food poverty" line, indicating the level below which a person does not normally acquire enough dietary energy. Complementary to the income/consumption-based measure of poverty is the United Nations Development Program's (UNDP) Human Poverty Index (HPI). The HPI concentrates on deprivation in three areas of human well-being: longevity, knowledge, and standard of living. Longevity is represented by the percentage of people not expected to live past age forty. Knowledge is represented by the percentage of adults who are illiterate. Decent standard of living depends on three variables – the percentage of people without access to safe water, the percentage of people without access to health services and the percentage of moderately and severely under-weight children under age five. It is now universally acknowledged that poverty is a state of pronounced deprivation in "well-being." Poverty is multi-faceted and should be looked at from all sectors of human development. The different dimensions of poverty suggest a multi-pronged approach in poverty reduction. While there is a consensus that economic growth is necessary for poverty reduction, research on the growth-poverty link highlights that the link may be tenuous, especially in many developing countries due to policy, market and institutional failures. In addition to targeted policies, addressing poverty requires changing the means and processes by which groups gain and hold control over all productive assets including that of the environment.

Sustainable development is one of the oldest development doctrines though perceived today as a new development strategy. Ancient societies employed sustainable development strategies to guide their economic and societal activities.[2] The term "sustainable development" appeared much earlier in the *World Conservation Strategy* (IUCN 1980), but the basic ideas and concept of "Ecologically Sustainable Development" was popularized by the Brundtland report - *Our Common Future* (WCED, 1987). According to this report, sustainable development is "development that meets the needs of the present without compromising the ability of future generations to meet their own needs" (p. 43).

The definition of sustainable development implies that there should be intra- and inter-generational equity as elaborated by Sen (2000).[3] Moreover, the ability of generations to meet their needs as highlighted by the Brundtland report should be taken into account. To this end, development policies must seek to eliminate the causes of natural resource depletion and environmental degradation. "It also requires securing those public goods that are essential for economic development to last, such as those provided by well-functioning ecosystems..." (OECD, 2001, p.2). Conceptualizing sustainable development has not posed many challenges. The challenge today is how to construct a practical methodology to achieve the desired vision. Certainly, concerns about sustainable development will be meaningless if the practical steps to that end remain elusive. One major constraint in the search for practical measures is the lack of information on the value of the asset base with respect to the four pillars of sustainable development—social, economic, institutional, and environmental. Correct asset values include not only the produced capital with market values but also the non-marketed natural value. The latter is often assigned a zero weight in the national accounts.

There are many direct and indirect links between the environment and poverty. For example, inadequate access to land limits the ability of the poor to produce food for sustenance and income to maintain livelihoods. There are also negative externalities of the environment on the poor. Land degradation, often the result of improper farming, logging and mining practices, could lead to the depletion of micro-organisms and destruction of protective cover and watersheds. These in turn destroy the protective functions of natural ecosystems. Poverty reduction and improvement in natural resource use and management are therefore vital for the attainment of sustainable development.

The "vicious cycle" argument of the relationship between poverty and the environment suggests that poverty alleviation is likely to reduce environmental degradation in the long-run, and arresting and reversing environmental decline is likely to help the poor (Leonard, 1989). In many parts of the world the poor usually depend directly on natural resource use, such as agriculture, livestock, fisheries, and firewood, for their livelihood and survival. Overexploitation of natural resources coupled with degradation of the environment weakens the productive base and life support systems of the poor. The negative externalities of degraded soils, depleted forests, water shortages and biodiversity loss further intensify poverty. In all these areas, the risks of reaching critical thresholds in the regenerative capacity of renewable resources and overlooking the absorptive functions of the environment pose real threats to the long-term sustainability of the environment (OECD, 2001). According to Leonard (1989), poverty alleviation measures that focus on arresting and reversing environmental decline will be most beneficial to the poor.

Concerned about the threats of environmental damage, health hazards and other visible economic costs, policy makers gave some attention to the environment in the 1980s through investments in environmental activities. Due to the growing inequalities, the focus of the 1990s was on poverty reduction. At the beginning of this millennium, one can generally conclude that sustainable development concepts have not been adequately taken into consideration in designing poverty reduction policies and knowledge of the concept has not seriously been put into practice. For example, poverty-focused policy measures in the forestry and mining sectors rarely incorporate or support good environmental practices. And policies on environmental sustainability usually have weak links with poverty reduction. Critics argue that in many developing countries, the integration of environmental issues with poverty reduction measures remains at the rhetorical level. Perhaps, this rhetoric is only meant to persuade concerned citizens that policy makers are aware of the problem and are ready to act. The fact, however, is that even in developed countries, pressing problems of social exclusion, growing poverty, and unemployment tamper to some extent the attention paid to environmental problems.

3. Ghana's Experience in Environmental Sustainability

Natural resource extraction has long been the basis of Ghana's development. At least 50 percent of the goods and services produced in the country are derived from natural resources-related activities in agriculture, forestry, fishing, wildlife, mining, electricity generation, water management and tourism. Ghana's natural resource base, therefore, accounts for a vast portion of the country's economic activity and provides goods and services that are fundamental to rural and urban households. This substantial contribution notwithstanding, there is presently no law which mandates the government of Ghana to implement sustainable development programs. The 1992 Constitution of Ghana (the Directive Principles of State Policy) indirectly covers issues pertaining to economic, social, environmental and institutional development. Specific articles that indirectly touch on sustainable development include articles 36 (1) and 36 (9). Article 36(1) states:

the state shall take all necessary action to ensure that the national economy is managed in such a manner as to maximize the rate of economic development and to secure the maximum welfare, freedom and happiness of every person in Ghana and to provide adequate means of livelihood and suitable employment and public assistance.

Article 36(9) states

The State shall take appropriate measures needed to protect and safeguard the national environment for posterity; and shall seek co-operation with other states and bodies for purposes of protecting the wider international environment for mankind.

After independence in 1957, the leaders were occupied with problems other than environmental conservation. Besides traditional conservation practices, very little was done in terms of policies to conserve and maintain natural resources. Moreover, environmental issues were not a priority then, even in the international arena.

The United Nations Conference on the Human Environment, held in Stockholm in 1972, provided the impetus for developing environmental conservation measures. Subsequently, many governments initiated various programs for the conservation of forests, soil, water, and wildlife. In response to the global call for environmental conservation, Ghana created the Environmental Protection Council (EPC) in 1973 with the responsibility to manage the environment. However, the EPC remained largely dormant failing to implement any program of environmental sustainability till the 1980s.

The dry weather and bushfires in 1982/1983 kindled public concerns about environmental degradation and provided a practical basis for a national concerted effort in environmental management (EPC, 1994). A national Oil Spill Contingency Plan was put in place in 1985 and a National Plan of Action to Combat Desertification followed in 1986. Ghana drafted a National Environmental Protection Program (NEPP) in 1987 aimed at (a) the maintenance of ecosystems and ecological processes for the functioning of the biosphere (b) the sound management of natural resources and the environment (c) the protection of humans, animals and plants and their habitats (d) promoting healthy environmental practices in the national development effort, (e) integrating environmental considerations in sectoral, structural and socio-economic planning at all levels and (f) developing a common approach to regional and global environmental issues. Tutu and Convery (1988) estimated an annual environmental degradation of about 4 percent of the total GDP. This result justified the need for an integrated national environmental policy strategy to curtail such a level of degradation. Unfortunately, progress has been slow.

The economic reform measures initiated in the early 1980s paid little attention to environmental issues and arguably discouraged sustainable management of resources. Growth in export income and improvement in trade balance of the late 1980s and early 1990s were largely the results of increases in exports of primary commodities from agriculture, mining and forestry as well as the promotion of non-traditional exports.[4] Mostly resource-based, increased economic activities in these areas invariably meant increased resource depletion. The economic reform program implicitly provided the basis for diminished state control in the use of natural resources. Though diminished state control in resource exploitation may be a welcome change from the inefficiencies of state enterprises in the past, the ability to establish and enforce regulatory standards and to provide opportunities for the poor should not be underestimated. The weaknesses of institutions mandated to check the rational use of natural resources led to unregulated resource exploitation, especially by mostly foreign owned timber and mining companies.

The mining sector provides a good example. Under the economic reform program, specific sectoral policies were instituted in mid-1980 to revamp the mining sector. Unfortunately, the Environmental Assessment Regulations and Guidelines, aimed at streamlining the activities of mining industry with regards to environmental degradation were not published until 1994. The promulgation of these guidelines was in response to the environmental, cultural and social effects of mining and the international calls for sustainable development and biodiversity conservation. It is worth noting that these guidelines came late compared to the other sectoral policies that were instituted to revamp the mining sector. The basic aim of the government at that time was to encourage investment in the sector and tying mining investment to environmental protection could discourage investments in the sector. Pollution control and abatement controls were seen as additional costs to investors. The spate of confrontations between local communities and mining companies are indicative of the burdens imposed on the former by the latter, all made possible by policy neglect.

Although reforms in the mining sector have led to an increase in production, the neglected environmental effects could have a long-term deleterious effect on the people and needs critical consideration. An approach to development, which consistently fails to internalize the social and environmental costs, but rather places the burden on vulnerable communities and on future generations is contrary to the notion of sustainable development. Inherent in mining practices is limited concern about the welfare implications of their actions.

An Environmental Action Plan (EAP) was formulated and published by the Environmental Protection Council (EPC) in 1991. The aim of the EAP was to identify specific actions needed to protect the environment and to ensure the better management of the country's natural resources. Following the publication of the EAP, the National Environmental Policy (NEP) was adopted to provide the framework for the realization of the goals of the EAP. The NEP seeks to: improve the quality of life of all Ghanaians; promote sustainable development through sound management and use of natural, human and cultural resources; and to ensure the exploitation of resources in a manner that is consistent with sound environmental practices (EPC, 1994).

A major element in Ghana's environmental policy is the requirement of an Environmental Impact Assessment (EIA) for proposed development projects. PNDC Law 116 established the Ghana Investment Code. The code requires that the Ghana Investment Promotion Centre, the state agency for promoting and coordinating private investments (except for mining, petroleum and cottage industries), must in its appraisal of enterprises, pay regard to any adverse effects the enterprise is likely to have on the environment. The EPC took over this responsibility in 1988. It issued a "certificate of clearance" stating that no environmental damage will result from the implementation of a project or that adequate provisions have been made in the project proposals to contain potential adverse environmental impacts, before the project is implemented. The establishment of an effective EIA received further formal support when the Environmental Protection Agency Act 490 was passed in December 1994. Act 490 replaced the Environmental Protection Council with the Environmental Protection Agency (EPA) and mandated the agency to protect and enhance the country's environment as well as resolve common global environmental problems. Its provisions also gave further legal boost to the institutionalization of EIA as an important management tool for the environment. However, Salami (2001) argues that in spite of the claims to scoping in many available EIA reports, the socio-economic, cultural and environmental problems that were meant to be addressed through scoping still persist, especially in mining projects.

In addition to the Ministry of Science and Environment which has an overall executive responsibility for the environment, other public institutions in environmental management include the Ministry of Lands and Forestry (Forestry Commission, Wildlife Division and Forestry Services Division), the Minerals Commission, the Town and Country Planning Department, the Energy Commission, the Department of Parks and Gardens, the Survey Department, the Mines Department, and the Water Resources Commission. Furthermore, development partners and NGOs have played a large role in environmental management.

These institutions especially the EPA have played their facilitating and regulatory roles to some extent by ensuring that different development actors comply with the laws, policies and guidelines of environmental sustainability. Through the EPA and other stakeholders, various legislation, regulations, education and awareness creation programs have been developed to enhance the effective management of the environment, though much needs to be done to make them effective in the control of environmental degradation. Weaknesses of the EPA can be attributed to the lack of coordination, inadequate capacity and the weak EIA process. In general, the problem is not the lack of laws and regulations. The problem rather lies in the weak implementation of these laws and guidelines. The capacity of the institutions both in terms of personnel and resources is woefully inadequate to perform their duties efficiently. For example, in the Mining Department of the EPA, there are only six experts overseeing all mining[5] activities in the country. The department is not adequately funded to undertake the monitoring and evaluation of environmental degradation and to subject environmental reports from companies to critical scrutiny. Also, penalties for non-compliance under Act 490 and its legislative instruments are too mild to deter companies. For example, Executive Instrument 9 (1999) on public prosecutions under which non-compliance is judged is limited to the lower courts where the minimum fine does not exceed 200 thousand cedis ($ 23 in 2003). This figure is too low to deter non-compliance. The only option left to the EPA is the threat of the withdrawal of license. Similar situations can be found in almost all the institutions.

Inter-sectoral coordination in developing and implementing policies, programs and plans, as well as coordination between governmental and non-governmental institutions also poses a major problem. Vordzorgbe (2004) argues that the integration or coherence of economic, social, environmental and institutional objectives across sectors, territories and generations in development planning in Ghana is weak. Ineffective coordination between organizations sometimes results in development plans of various districts being at variance with national objectives.

At the end of the twentieth century, the government strategy to address the challenges in resource management was largely embodied in the National Environmental Action Plan (1990-2000), the 1994 Forest and Wildlife Policy, the Forest Development Master Plan (1996-2000), the 1997 Timber Resources Management Act (Act 547), the 1997 National Land Policy, the Science and Technology Policy (2000), and the Action Plan for Science and Technology Management. The Forest and Wildlife Policy focuses on conservation and sustainable development of forest and wildlife resources. The Timber Resource Management Act compelled companies to use the forest with the understanding that they also manage the forest in a sustainable manner (Donkor, 2001). In the next section we assess the extent to which the programs of the GPRS contribute to achieving environmental sustainability.

4. Environmental Sustainability and the GPRS

As part of the Heavily Indebted Poor Countries (HIPC) initiative, eligible countries were expected to prepare a Poverty Reduction Strategy Paper (PRSP) as a broad policy framework for the eradication of poverty. PRSPs were to be the basis for all donor supported programs and were expected to establish standards of good governance and identify specific outputs and timetables for their achievement. As discussed in earlier chapters in this volume, the GPRS identified five main thematic areas of government policy: enhanced infrastructure development, rural development based on modernized agriculture, enhanced social services, good governance, and private sector development. Strategies to sustain macroeconomic growth, develop special programs for the vulnerable, increase production and gainful employment, enhance good governance, accelerate human resource development and improve access to and delivery of basic social services formed the heart of the poverty reduction efforts.

Generally the GPRS recognized the inextricable link between poverty and the environment. The poverty diagnosis behind the strategy recognized poverty as a multi-faceted phenomenon with different and complex linkages.[6] The document defined poverty on the basis of income or consumption capabilities as well as nutrition deprivation, health, illiteracy, access to safe water and sanitation, and general insecurity. The GPRS I recognized that government expenditure on poverty reduction had not only been inadequate but also did not always benefit the poor, with limited emphasis on social services, particularly in health and education.

The broad impacts of environmental degradation on poverty are recognized by the GPRS and environmental conservation is regarded as one of the important conditions for sustainable development.[7] The decision to incorporate environmental conservation in poverty reduction is based on the understanding that maintaining natural capital is imperative for the long–term growth and sustainability of the economy. In this regard, the enforcement of Environmental Impact Assessment and the prevention of activities that damage the environment are the main tools for ensuring environmental sustainability. However, on environmental issues, the poverty diagnosis of the GPRS was weak. As impressive as later discussions of the government's commitment to environmental sustainability may have been, the issues of water scarcity, soil degradation, deforestation, poor agricultural and forest management practices and their effect on rural economies received little attention. The analysis failed to identify the specific dimensions of environmental problems and their links to poverty, as was done for health and education. As a result, GPRS I did not prioritize environmental issues as in the case of health and education. Environmental issues were scantly treated and in isolation without providing the necessary linkages that were required. This neglect made it difficult to coordinate and provide the linkages that were needed to integrate the four pillars of sustainability——economic, social, environmental and institutional (Vordzorgbe and Caiquo, 2001).

Missing in the analysis of the institutional and environmental causes of poverty is the weakness of the private sector, particularly the informal sector. Ghana's private sector is largely made up of small-scale informal businesses. Though this sector plays a significant role in terms of employment and contribution to GDP, many of these small-scale businesses do not meet any environmental and health standards. They pollute the environment in many diverse ways through chemical and solid waste disposal into open waters and sewage, noise pollution, indoor air pollution, and deforestation. These practices contribute to ill-health and reduce people's quality of life.

The major targets of environmental protection were to reduce degradation arising from agricultural production by 20 percent, forest loss by 10 percent and degradation from mining by 20 percent (Government of Ghana, 2003, p. 90). Evidently, these targets were vaguely set and therefore difficult to measure. Data limitations make it difficult to assess the meaning of these targets. There being no baseline, it is difficult to know the basis of these numbers and even how to monitor the outcomes. Although the GPRS developed sixty core indicators in various thematic areas, several of the indicators were developed without attention to cost, relevance, data availability and the capacity to track the indicators. The 2003 annual implementation report of the GPRS attests to these measurement problems. Although the report provided some information on the selected indicators, which showed improvements over the previous year, it cautioned that there are problems with availability and consistency of the data. Perhaps it would have been much easier to link the more focused but expanded set of sustainable development indicators, selected by the Ministry of Environment and Science, to the five thematic areas.

It is difficult to determine the impacts of the policy measures described in GPRS on environmental sustainability and poverty reduction. This is in part because the policy measures were cast in broad terms. Their impact will depend on commitments in the GPRS to provide more concrete and specific policy actions that recognize fundamental environmental and poverty issues. These are the number of people involved, the sensitivity of the local environment, the trickle down effects, the appropriate budget support and the mode of implementation of the policy measures. For example, the policy to "improve export competitiveness" could help the poor, yet harm the environment. The question is what concrete measures are being taking to ensure the implementation of this policy? There are many statements of intent which did not figure in later policy actions. For example, the GPRS emphasized the importance of land administration reform and stressed that land tenure security is pivotal for the development of rural areas and the transformation of the economy as a whole (Government of Ghana, 2003, 9.1). However, there seem to be no directions to guide the ministries, departments and agencies in developing concrete instruments to guide such reform efforts. The extent of environmental considerations in four of the five thematic areas of the GPRS follows in the next sub-sections.

4.1 Macroeconomic Policy and the Environment

The objective of macroeconomic policies in the GPRS is to reduce inflation and set the basis for sustained macroeconomic growth through prudent fiscal, monetary and trade policies. These short-term macro-economic policies have both positive and negative environmental implications, the scale and magnitude of which will depend on the type of policy and the nature of its implementation. While the various macroeconomic policies have the potential to generate positive economic benefits such as increased employment, foreign exchange, and private investments, they could pose a risk to the natural resource base through over exploitation. For example, while measures that achieve competitive interest rates and exchange rates are incentives to domestic production, increase exports and job creation, they can potentially accelerate resource extraction when the complementary institutions are not in place to enforce regulatory measures.

The development literature establishes a positive link between macroeconomic policies and the environment based on the environmental Kuznets-Curve (Bartone et. al., 1994, 16). Macroeconomic stability and income growth are expected to enhance incentives to preserve the environment (Gandhi and McMorran, 1996, 30) as part of improvements in the standard of living. Good as the argument is, what is needed with such macroeconomic policies are complementary environmental, resource management and intervention policies that can mitigate the adverse impacts of increased economic activities on the environment.

4.2 Production and Gainful Employment

In Ghana, about 50 percent of GDP is derived from the exploitation of resources in the agriculture, fisheries, forestry and mining sectors. The GPRS aims to consolidate this growth through private sector-led agro-based industrial production propelled by the application of science and technology. The specific pathways identified in the strategy include improving environmental and natural resource management, modernizing agriculture and increasing agricultural productivity, promoting manpower development, creating the institutional environment for entrepreneurialship and enterprise development, improving productivity in the industrial and service sectors, providing infrastructure and increasing the production and export of non-traditional exports (Government of Ghana, 2003 p 157-160). Most of these pathways have implications for the environment which were not adequately explored in the strategy. In the agricultural sector, the focus on increasing mechanization stopped short of identifying complementary practices to minimize soil degradation and erosion. Moreover, while increased mechanization may favor large scale commercial agriculture, rural farming is predominantly undertaken by small holders operating at a subsistence level. Paying more attention to subsistence farming through policy actions that improve soil quality and reduce exposure of farmers to hazards will be of great help to the majority of poor farmers.

While the strategy sought to encourage mining and forestry activities, it failed to suggest measures to accelerate the capacity of the Environmental Protection Agency to monitor environmental problems. Akabzaa (2000) argues that the benefits to rural communities from mining activities are often low compared to the environmental problems created as a result of mining and logging. Nonexistent or improperly defined property rights remain as one of the key causes of environmental conflicts. The issues of the state having vested rights and offering extractive rights to mining and logging companies, which often usurp the custo-dial and land use rights of rural communities, the ineffective role of the Lands Commission, the Forestry Commission and the Minerals Commission and the weak legal system could adversely affect agriculture, land use, atmospheric and water pollution and employment in general. Other problems related to mining that need critical attention include use of explosives, conflicts in mining com-munities and water and soil pollution resulting from use of mercury and cyanide in mining.

4.3 Human Resource Development and Basic Services

The focus of policies in this thematic area is on improving the standard of living of average Ghanaians through increased education, skills and entrepreneurship, population management, improved health, safe water, and environmental sanita-tion. The GPRS identifies challenges to the delivery of these services. These include spatial and financial access, utilization, geographical disparity, poor targeting of policies, inefficiency, financing among others. The GPRS provides strategies to effectively overcome them.[8]

The GPRS recognizes that poor access to environment based amenities such as safe water, sanitation systems, sewage facilities, and exposure to pollution could result in ill health through water-borne diseases, river blindness, bilharzia, guinea worm infestation, malaria, and cholera, among others. These have both direct and indirect effects on poverty.[9] Therefore, preventive measures such as access to improved waste management, water and food supplies, health informa-tion and medical facilities, housing and sewage facilities, and environmental pollution prevention were to be taken. Placing more emphasis on the prevention of prevalent diseases such as malaria, diarrhoea, and upper respiratory diseases as well as the development of traditional medicine will greatly help to reduce mortality and morbidity among the poor. Emphasizing the development of tradi-tional medicine mostly used by the poor will greatly reduce the huge health care cost for these marginalized groups.

A notable feature of human resource development and basic services poli-cies is that, none of the policies focused on improving natural resource man-agement. This neglect suggests that the causal links between providing basic amenities and environment use have not been adequately explored. Strengthen-ing the capacity to manage water catchment areas will be imperative to solve health problems in areas prone to water-borne diseases. Also, planned skills de-velopment curricula should include basic environmental management modules to ensure that trainees manage their businesses with environmental sustainability in mind.

Noticeably missing in the poverty reduction policies is a focus on liquid and solid waste management. This is an emerging problem in urban areas, with ad-verse environmental health effects, especially on the poor who live in the periphery of urban communities. Developing sustainable waste management projects that restore degraded lands, produce organic fertilizers, and convert waste to energy becomes imperative since waste generation is bound to increase with economic growth and development.

4.4 Good Governance

Good governance is one of the key pre-requisites for sound environmental management. It establishes an effective legal, regulatory and institutional framework for sustainable development and ensures accountability in resource use. Bad governance, resulting from weaknesses in the civil service, compromises the actions civil servants in designing, administering, and enforcing compliance to rules and regulations. This could affect public financial management and indirectly deepen poverty and environmental degradation.

The GPRS recognizes weaknesses in these areas and recommends capacity building in the public sector, especially in the judicial services. Governance policies focus on increasing enforcement, strengthening leadership and capacity of District Assemblies (DAs), deepening DAs association with civil society, and institutionalizing public access to government business. Better management of public policy and decentralization is envisaged through the empowerment of civil society groups enabling them to participate in discussions on critical environmental issues, about developing minimum environmental standards, and about enforcement of various laws and by-laws on bush fires, illegal mining, and chainsaw activities. Most of the policies target institutional reforms and therefore have wider spatial implications and present environmental opportunities.

It is important to create new laws, establish environmental courts, and enable the legal sector to better deal with environmental issues, and encourage greater public involvement in governance processes. Increasing public awareness, increasing opportunities for individuals to express their views on governance reform, and critically considering such views will help improve public policy formulation. Also, giving traditional authorities an enhanced role in arbitration could provide an alternative resolution mechanism and thereby reduce pressure on the courts.

Policies to improve on governance through decentralization are certainly in-line with modern conservation practices, which require community involvement in the management of natural resources. However, the weak environmental management capacity of local governments, the lack of expertise in environmental management, as well as the lack of consideration of environmental issues by many districts can lead to unsustainable use of natural resources. Also, financial constraints can cause many decentralized governments to focus their attention on recurrent expenditure rather than on capital expenditures that go to improving on the environment.

4.5 Strategic Environmental Assessment of the GPRS

In principle, the government of Ghana is committed to sustainable development. Despite this commitment, critics, including the World Bank and other bilateral development partners, have argued that environmental issues have not been taken seriously enough. In response, a post Strategic Environmental Assessment (SEA) of the GPRS was undertaken by an independent consultant with the support of the Environmental Protection Agency (EPA) and the National Development Planning Commission (NDPC). The objective of the SEA was to ensure that the environmental concerns of plans and programs listed in the GPRS are clearly identified, assessed and given attention through a broad participatory based consultation. Largely donor-driven, SEA is process-oriented and provides space for some level of involvement by stakeholders, policy makers and the wider public in environmental issues. To a large extent the SEA has improved the environmental policy debate in Ghana and has increased government's understanding of the wider impacts of policies and programs on the environment, economic growth and poverty reduction. In all, twenty-five MDAs, 108 District Assemblies and representatives from parliament, civil society, NGOs, and business community have endorsed the SEA document (NDPC & EPA, 2004). It has also been accepted by the NDPC as the basis of future updates of the GPRS. However, there are some risks. Because the whole process appears to be donor-driven, there is the risk that politicians may not make it a political priority. Implementation may be set back whenever environmental assessments constrain political choices.

5. Conclusions

Sustainable development involves a process of reorientation of political, economic and social behavior in order to safeguard the interest of future generations in the use and management of natural resources. When this reorientation has implications for how economies grow, how wealth is created, and how the pathways out of poverty are identified, it bears heavily on public policy. It urges policy-makers to take on the challenge of sustainable development. Ghana has made some strides in reducing poverty through sustainable development. In fact, Ghana is signatory to almost all the international agreements on the environment. These efforts notwithstanding, environmental problems persist largely as a result of institutional failures and challenges in policy implementation. As impressive as the government's commitment may have been, most of the GPRS strategies focused on satisfying the economic, social and institutional dimensions of sustainable development but placed little emphasis on preventing or addressing the environmental consequences of the policies contained in the strategy.

Key setbacks include the limited diagnosis of the links between poverty and resource depletion, polluted rivers, air pollution, and soil and forest degradation associated with logging and mining in particular. Environmental problems were treated as cross-cutting and therefore were not given a specific home in the government institutional machinery. Environmental issues once again suffered the classic problem of the commons. What is considered as everybody's problem ultimately is no one's problem. This is manifested in weak inter-sectoral coordination and linkages in the development and implementation of those aspects of the strategy that relate to the environment. The difficult trade-off is the additional cost that is needed to mainstream environmental issues into development programs. The good news, however, is that the cost of sustainable development could be recouped if policies are carefully designed and implemented.

The cost of sustainability and the policy instruments to achieve sustainability should not be seen as a burden on the economy. Such perceptions will be tempered if there is widespread acceptance by citizens of the benefits of sustainable development. To this end, public education becomes a crucial tool.

The way forward is to look for win-win policies that will accelerate poverty reduction and at the same time maintain the environment. In the agricultural sector, conservation agriculture provides a better option and market based regulatory policies would help in the sustainable use of natural resources, which remain the primary drivers of growth. It is imperative to develop the capacities and the institutions, particularly at the local level, to better manage the process of environmental mainstreaming. In addition, measures that promote participatory risk reduction, disaster preparedness, reduction in environment related conflicts, and the assignment of clear property rights as well as environment education are key to the achievement of sustainable development.

Notes

1. These include the Stockholm Convention on Persistent Organic Pollutants; the Basel Convention on the Control of the Trans-boundary Movements of Hazardous Waste and their disposal; the Kyoto Protocol of the United Nations Convention on Climate Change; International Convention on Oil Pollution Preparedness, Response and Cooperation; Montreal and Beijing amendments to the Montreal Protocol on Substances that Deplete the Ozone Layer; the Cartegena Protocol on Biosafety; the Rotterdam Convention on Prior Informed Consent Procedure for Hazardous Chemicals and Pesticides in the International Trade; Tropical Timber 81 and 94 among others.
2. In Ghana for example, prior to the 1920s, communities managed their wildlife resources sustainably through traditional rules that protected some species and regulated exploitation. Hunters needed to obtain the consent of the chiefs before hunting and the community prohibited hunters from hunting certain animals because they were 'totem' animals (Wildlife Division, 1997)

3. Nobel Laureate Amartya Sen made this interpretation in his keynote address at the International Conference on "Transition to sustainability" held in Tokyo in May 2000
4. See the collection of papers by Asa, Donkor and Anyinam in Konadu Agyeman (2001)
5. Mining here includes all minerals.
6. Government of Ghana, 2003, 19-24.
7. Government of Ghana, 2003, 39, 74-75.
8. Government of Ghana, 2003, 161-165.
9. Government of Ghana, 2003, 19.

References

Akabzaa, T. *Boom and Dislocation: Environmental Impacts of Mining in Wassa West District of Ghana*. Third World Network, Accra, Ghana, 2000.
Anyinam C. "Structural Adjustment Programs and the Mortgaging of Africa's Ecosystems: The case of Mineral Development in Ghana." Pp. 197-218 in *IMF and World Bank Sponsored Structural Adjustment Ptograms in Africa: Ghana's Experience, 1983-1999* edited by Konadu-Agyeman, K., Ashgate Bulington USA. 2001
Asa, E. "Structural Adjustment Programs and Ghana's Mineral Industry," Pp. 157-180 in *IMF and World Bank Sponsored Structural Adjustment Programs in Africa: Ghana's Experience, 1983-1999* edited by Konadu-Agyeman, K., Ashgate Bulington USA. 2001
Bartone, C., J. Berstein, J. Leitman, and J. Eigen. "Toward Environmental Strategies for Cities: Policy Considerations for Urban Environmental Management in Developing Countries," Pp. 16 *in Urban management Program 18*. Washington D.C. The World Bank, 1994.
De Groot, R. S. *Functions of Nature: Evaluation of Nature in Environmental Planning, Management and Decision Making,* Wolters Noordhoff BV, Groningen, 1992.
Donkor N. T. "Impact of Structural Adjustment Policies on Forest and Natural Resource Management," Pp. 181-196 in *IMF and World Bank Sponsored Structural Adjustment Ptograms in Africa: Ghana's Experience, 1983-1999* edited by Konadu-Agyeman, K., Ashgate Bulington USA. 2001
Environmental Protection Council (EPC). *Ghana Environmental Action Plan*, Volume 1, 1994.
Gandhi, Ved P., and R. T. McMorran. "How Macroeconomic Policies Affect the Environment: What Do We Know?" Pp. 30 in *Macroeconomics and the Environment*, edited by V. P. Gandhi. Washington, DC: International Monetary Fund, 1996.
Government of Ghana, *Ghana Poverty Reduction Strategy Paper, 2003-2005, An Agenda for Growth*. Vol 1. February 2003.
Hardoy, J. E., D. Mitlin, and D. Satterthwaite. *Environmental Problems in Third World Cities*. London: IIED, 1992.
IUCN (International Union for the Conservation of Nature). *World Conservation Strategy: Living Resource Conservation for Sustainable Development*, International Un-

ion for the Conservation of Nature, United Nations Environment Program and World Wildlife Fund, Gland, 1980.

Konadu-Agyeman K. ed., *IMF and World Bank Sponsored Structural Adjustment Ptograms in Africa: Ghana's Experience, 1983-1999.* Ashgate Burlington USA. 2001.

Lele, S. M. "Sustainable development: A critical review." *World Development* 19 (6):607-621, 1991.

Leonard, H. J. "Environment and the Poor: Development Strategies for a Common Agenda." Pp. 112-135 in *Environment and the poor: development strategies for a common agenda*, edited by H. Jeffrey, M. Yudelmen, J. D. Strycker, J. O. Browder, J. J. de Boer, T. Campbell and A. Jolly. Washington: Overseas Development Council, 1989.

Munasinghe, M. and W. Cruz. "Economy-Wide Policies and the Environment: Developing Countries." Pp. 30 in *Macroeconomics and the Environment*, edited by V. P. Gandhi. Washington, D.C.: International Monetary Fund, 1996.

National Development Planning Commission (NDPC). Implementation of the Ghana Poverty Reduction Strategy, 2003 annual progress report, March 31, 2004.

————.National Development Planning Commission (NDPC) and Environmental protection Agency (NDPC & EPA). Strategic Environmental Assessment of the Ghana Poverty Reduction Strategy Paper, NDPC and EPA, Accra, Ghana, 2004

Organization for Economic Co-operation and Development, "Sustainable Development: critical issues," *Policy Brief, OECD Observer*, September 2001.

Salami, M. B. "Environmental Impact Assessment Policies, their Effectiveness or Otherwise for Mining Sector Environmental Management in Africa." Pp. 50-65 in *Mining Development and Social Conflicts in Africa*, The Third Work Network, Africa, 2001.

Sen, A. Keynote Address at the International Conference on *Transition to Sustainability*. Tokyo May 2000.

Tutu, K. A. and F. Convery. *The Economic Cost of Environmental Degradation in Ghana*, A Technical Report submitted to the Environmental Protection Council, 1988.

Vordzorgbe, S. D. and Caiquo B. OECD/DAC Dialogues with Development Countries on National Strategies on Sustainable Development: reports on Status Review in Ghana submitted to the international Institute for Sustainable Development, London, UK and the National Development Planning Commission, Accra, Ghana, (2001)

Vordzorgbe, S. D. *Environment Sector in Ghana's Development – A human rights-based assessment, Common Country Assessment*, United Nations Development Program and Government of Ghana. July 2004.

World Bank. *World Development Report 2003: Sustainable Development With a Dynamic Economy*, Public Review copy, April 3, 2002, The World Bank, Washington, 2002,

————. *World Development Report 1999/2000*, Oxford University Press, New York, 2000.

World Commission on Environment and Development (WCED). *Our Common Future*, World Commission on Environment and Development and Oxford University Press, Oxford, 1987.

Wildlife Division, Ecotourism Development Strategy of Ghana, Wildlife Division, Accra, Ghana. 1997.

Williams, S. W. 1997. "The Brown Agenda——Urban Environmental Problems and Policies in the Developing-World." *Geography* 82 (354):17-26.

PART 4

Lessons and the Way Forward

15

Conclusions and Policy Lessons: The Next Generation of Poverty Reduction Strategies

Bartholomew Armah and Joe Amoako-Tuffour

1. Introduction

The chapters in this book provide some perspectives of the poverty problems in Ghana and the comprehensive attempt to address these problems within the framework of the country's first Ghana Poverty Reduction Strategy (GPRS I). As we stated at the outset, our focus was not to assess the impacts and outcomes of the implementation of the strategy. Our modest objective was to examine how the strategy was formulated, the implicit assumptions, the content of the strategy, the missing pieces, the prospective challenges in implementing the strategy, and, finally, to evaluate the overall prospects that the strategy puts Ghana on the right path on the war on poverty. As the first cycle of Poverty Reduction Strategies (PRSs) nears completion for several countries, reflections on Ghana's experiences provide a useful roadmap for the new generation of PRSs.[1]

In this context, the year 2005 was a watershed as several African countries, including Ghana, began the process of formulating and in some cases implementing a new generation of PRSs hereafter referred to as Second Generation PRSs (SGPRSs). Dubbed the year of Africa, we witnessed in 2005 several international initiatives and commitments to address poverty on the continent. These include the findings of the United Nations Millennium Project and the Commission for Africa Report led by Jeffery Sachs and Tony Blair respectively. The findings of both reports underpin the commitments by the Group of eight (G8) in Gleneagles to double aid to Africa. These commitments were subsequently endorsed by the 2005 UN General Assembly Summit.

The renewed commitments by the international community to address poverty in Africa were spurred by the realization that despite attempts by several African countries to address the problem through the implementation of PRSPs and the adoption of the Millennium Development Goals (MDGs), the poverty incidence, particularly in sub-Saharan Africa (SSA), ranks highest in the world

315

and, unlike most other regions, is rising. Furthermore, most African countries are off-track with respect to achieving the MDGs.[2] Indeed, by 2005, five years after the MDGs were set, only eight SSA countries were on track to eradicate extreme poverty and hunger (MDG1). Ten were on track to promote gender equality and empower women (MDG3). Progress on several of the remaining goals is even more discouraging. In particular, SSA is unlikely to meet, by 2015, the goal of reducing child mortality (MDG4), improving maternal health (MGD5) or combating HIV and other diseases (MDG6). In contrast, North Africa has made remarkable progress in reducing maternal and child mortality and already achieved gender equality in secondary education (Economic Commission for Africa, 2005). In fairness, the SSA performance masks some country-level successes. For instance, Botswana, Cape Verde and Mauritius are on track to improve maternal health by three-quarters by 2015, while Gambia, Swaziland and Cape Verde are on track to ensure environmental sustainability. Since PRSs are central to the implementation of national policy priorities, not least in achieving the MDGs, policymakers in Africa must take stock of the first generation PRSs and share their experiences in order to improve their effectiveness in achieving national development objectives.

This chapter is a synthesis of the lessons from Ghana's experiences. Drawing on the preceding chapters, the next section puts Ghana's PRS experience in the context of Africa-wide experiences by drawing on the findings of the UN Economic Commission for Africa's PRSP-Learning Group (a knowledge sharing network of PRSP experiences in Africa) and country studies undertaken by the World Bank, IMF and other organizations. Section three distills lessons from Ghana's PRSP experience for policymakers. The fourth section examines the way forward with special reference to the implications for increased resources for accelerated growth. What will it take for the so called "big push" to jump start the economies of low-income countries in SSA?

2. Ghana's Experience in Context

Ghana's poverty-reduction experiences add value to the stock of knowledge about PRSPs. To be sure, Ghana's experiences reveal similarities and differences from the experiences of other African countries and some broad cross-country similarities. Invariably, assessments of PRS experiences in Africa[3] suggest that the poverty reduction exercises have indeed been associated with several positive results. More than ever before, PRSs improved the focus on poverty, especially through the allocation and the incidence of spending on priority areas. "Pro-poor" sectors received on average 2 percent of GDP higher allocations in twenty countries over the period 1999—2003. PRSs engaged stakeholders more actively, especially in the preparation of the strategies, and helped to focus attention on governance issues, especially in terms of budgeting and expenditure management as well as monitoring and evaluation. They also provided an opportunity to explore a new framework for aid delivery through direct budget support. And, finally, they were consistent with, and reinforced by, the New Partnership for Africa's Development.

However, the studies also found weaknesses in the content. The key findings include: the lack of micro and sectoral level data for planning; insufficient attention to growth and employment relative to social sectors; weaknesses in prioritization and sequencing of policies; insufficient analysis especially of the sources of growth and their distributional impact; inadequate response by external partners especially in terms of resource alignment with the PRSP; and the limited attention to gender issues and the environment.

The process of formulating the poverty reduction strategies also had its shortcomings. Often cited are the time constraints, the failure to explore different pathways out of poverty, and the general failure to integrate the PRSs into broader national processes. While the process of PRSP formulation may have benefited from reasonably wide public consultation in several countries, the same cannot be said of the formulation of the macro-economic framework and structural policies which matter most for poverty outcomes. In particular, stakeholders were typically left out of PRSP monitoring. Furthermore, legislators were invariably excluded from the PRSP process in several countries, or their involvement was at best superficial. Issues of capacity building were also generally under-emphasized by most PRSs. Although donor coordination, harmonization and alignment with national priorities generally improved in the context of the Multi-Donor Budgetary Support program, for some major donors, the PRSs made no difference in their approaches to dealing with country governments. Finally, PRS processes were driven in large part by the need for IMF and World Bank endorsement.

With respect to content and antipoverty policy tools, the PRSs of various countries shared many features. The war on poverty was to be fought through conventional macroeconomic policies to maintain macro stability, through expenditure re-allocations and anti-poverty public sector spending, and through human development. The premise was that it is improvements in these non-income correlates of poverty (such as, greater and more equitable access to health and basic education facilities, better sanitation and improved public amenities) that are within the immediate realm of public policy, and, therefore could be more effectively tackled in the short term. The PRSs were particularly weak in addressing issues of growth even when governments wanted to do more in this direction. The differences in perspectives between governments and development partners about the dimensions of poverty, the spatial distribution of the poor, the pathways out of poverty, the planning horizon, and the political-economy no doubt influenced the content of the PRSs in a way that puts the spotlight on the ownership of the strategy and on the limits of development partnership.

3. Key Lessons from Ghana's Experience

Despite the similarities with other African countries, Ghana's PRS experiences offer several important lessons for policymakers particularly with respect to: growth and spatial inequality; gender, child poverty; decentralization; the environment; linking PRSs to the budget and expenditure frameworks; monitoring and evaluation; participation and ownership, external aid; and job creation.

3.1 Lessons based on PRS Content

Growth, Inequality and Demographic Transition
The causes of national poverty are many (Chapter 2) and knowledge about the dominant causal factors and their interactions is necessary to guide policy options and sequencing. Implicit in the first generation PRSP is that causes of poverty are the same everywhere. However, the multiplicity of causes, which are not likely to be of the same ranking in different economic and social contexts, suggest that the template of PRSP is not likely to achieve poverty reduction everywhere. For Ghana, bad public policies and the disintegration of the public sector capacities to perform the basic functions of governing contributed to the persistence of overall poverty. Although demographic transitions did not feature prominently in our analysis, the limited evidence suggests that sustainable growth must be supported by demographic transitions that reduce dependency ratios and manage population growth. Both issues deserve more attention in PRSs. After all poverty is about people and their numbers relative to the capacity of the economy to provide for their primary and demographic needs matter. Ghana's experience in this context is instructive since efforts to address poverty were rendered more difficult by trends in population growth.

Also relevant from the Ghanaian perspective is the significance of embedding social welfare initiatives in broad developmental strategies. Although governments have always professed to be pro-poor, past efforts, for the most part, suffered from poor program design, poor targeting, poor coordination and weak monitoring and evaluation of policies that had potential poverty reducing impacts. The experience with anti-poverty and social welfare programs such as Ghana's PAMSCAD suggests that treating poverty issues as an add-on is unlikely to yield sustained success (Chapter 2).

Both income and spatial inequality are recurring themes in Ghana's experience, even during periods of rapid economic growth. Inequality in Ghana, increased by 22 percent, between 1988 and 1999, driven largely by spatial differences in income and resources, differences that policymakers should not underplay (Chapter 3). There is therefore the need for spatial targeting of resources and infrastructure to address the problem.

Child Poverty

The analysis of child poverty (Chapter 10) highlighted three important issues and lessons for policymakers. First, addressing child poverty must constitute an explicit policy objective. Merely reducing the incidence of adult poverty will not always result in a reduction in child poverty since children are not always in a dependency relationship with respect to adults. In effect, a reduction in adult poverty is a necessary but not sufficient condition for the reduction of child poverty. Secondly, since child poverty is closely linked to key MDG indicators such as the incidence of under-five mortality and primary enrollment and completion rates, addressing child poverty is vital for the realization of the MDGs. Third, policy interventions designed to protect the rights of children and ensure that their basic needs are met requires age disaggregated poverty data and information on health and education trends for children. For timely public policy intervention, such data should be compiled and analyzed at shorter time intervals than would normally be done for overall poverty indicators.

Job Creation, Training and Skills Development

Ghana's PRSP was not devoid of measures to create jobs, improve training and facilitate skills development (Chapters 11 and 12). The Ghanaian experience, however, shows that addressing the employment and poverty reduction link requires a good diagnostic analysis of the informal sector given its role as a refuge for unemployed formal sector workers. It also requires a transformation of the economic structure towards high-productivity activities that guarantee high real wages and earnings.

The analysis identifies low educational attainment as a specific driver of informality; the educated are less likely to participate in the informal sector. But even the educated must find jobs. Hence, Ghana's experience also highlights the need to improve synergies between skills training programs or human capital improvement initiatives and employment opportunities. It cannot be assumed that "if you train them, they will find jobs." Skills training must be demand driven and underpinned by robust economic growth.

The disconnect between the greater part of programs in tertiary educational institutions and the practical skill-needs of the economy remains a concern Ghana can ill-afford to downplay. The GPRS was weak in its support for institutions involved in entrepreneurial, technical and vocational training. A more concerted effort is needed to develop apprenticeship programs by trade, vocation and industry. Moreover, our knowledge of informal sector activities is limited and public policy is heavily reliant on anecdotal evidence. It is extremely challenging to develop appropriate employment policy tools and to assess their effectiveness when labour market data is weak or nonexistence and when employment targets are set without the benefit of baseline data.

Gender

Ghana's experience (Chapter 13) with gender issues in the context of the PRS suggests that gender-mainstreaming is not a well-understood concept. Developing capacity in this area is therefore vital to improving the gender dimension of PRSs. Furthermore, monitoring the implementation of gender-focused policies requires the collection of more gender disaggregated data as a basis for designing gender indicators, benchmarks and targets.

The case study of Ghana also reveals that treating women as a homogeneous group could result in a misrepresentation of their economic conditions. For instance, although women are generally perceived as poor and asset-deprived, female headed households in Ghana have a lower incidence of poverty than male headed households and are more likely to contain members with access to land. This, however, is not to deny the fact that the hardcore poor in Ghana are rural, female-headed households with high dependency ratios, little or no education and engaged in food crop farming.

The Environment

Sustaining and improving the quality of the environment in developing countries, a key component of the MDGs, requires data on relevant environmental indicators. Ghana's experience (Chapter 14) highlights the need for improved data collection for effective monitoring of the environmental impact of poverty reduction. In the absence of benchmark data, targets will tend to be vague and hence virtually impossible to monitor. For instance, Ghana's PRS aimed to reduce environmental degradation arising from agricultural production by 20 percent, forest loss by 10 percent and degradation arising from mining by 20 percent (Government of Ghana, 2003). These targets, however, are of limited use since no benchmarks are specified. Improving data collection and publication in these vital areas of concern is critical in assessing and monitoring progress towards the achievement of the MDGs.

Any useful analysis of environmental implications of policy measures requires specific knowledge of the policies in question. Since PRSs tend to be restricted to broad strategic policy frameworks, comprehensive environmental assessments must be based on PRSs *Action Plans* as opposed to PRS strategic frameworks; *Action Plans* are by nature more specific than frameworks. The implicit lesson here is that countries need to complement their PRSs, or broad policy frameworks, with *Action Plans* that spell out more precisely the programs and projects that underpin the policy frameworks.

3.2 Lessons based on PRS Processes

Participation and Ownership
Ghana has been cited as one of the few countries where the GPRS brought some vibrancy to public consultation and stakeholder involvement in policy-making (Chapter 5). Despite the time constraints, it is difficult to draw the conclusion that the process had no influence on content. For one thing, the process of open consultation in policy-making was new to both the government and the governed. Both were on a learning curve. On this count, the GPRS was precedent setting because it opened spaces for policy dialogue, and provided civil service organizations with the opportunity to deepen and to widen their role in policy-making. The buy-in by civil servants early in the design and costing of the programs and activities would have helped not least in the coherence of content, in maximizing synergies between programs and activities across ministries, in linking the strategy to the budget, in the implementation, monitoring and in the evaluation of the programs.

Technically, Ghana's legislators were involved in the poverty reduction strategy process on account of the establishment of a Parliamentary Sub-Committee on poverty. However, substantively, their involvement occurred late in the process: well after the strategy paper had undergone several drafts. *De facto*, the parliamentary sub-committee was not a major player in the PRS formulation and consultative process. In part, this was due to omission but more importantly it emanated from the fact that parliament itself, weak in its capacity to engage in meaningful public consultations, was a passive player in the process.

The lesson is that the effectiveness of parliament's involvement may depend largely on its role, status and assertiveness within the country's political system. Parliaments vary in relation to both decision-making power and popular perception of their importance. There are parliaments that play a very active role in the formulation and enactment of legislation and those that endorse decisions made elsewhere. Others fall midway. Some legislatures are highly regarded by the citizenry and some are not, depending on the balance of power between the executive, the judiciary and parliament. Parliaments are more likely to be relevant to the PRS process if they are assertive, active in the formulation and enactment of legislation, and have the capacity and the instruments to engage in own consultative process.

Linking PRSs to the Budget and Expenditure Frameworks
Linking the programs and activities outlined in the poverty reduction strategy to the national budget and expenditure framework is critical for implementation (Chapter 6). The key lesson from Ghana's experience is that institutional dynamics are central to the success or failure of this process. For instance, where the Planning and Finance ministries constitute separate entities there is a ten-

dency for asymmetries between national priorities, as reflected in the PRS, and budget priorities. Unlike ministries of Planning, Finance Ministries tend to be preoccupied with the imperatives of short- to medium-term fiscal management. Besides, Ghana's experience shows that the relationship between the Finance ministry and Economic Planning ministry was not necessarily harmonious. Indeed, several countries have struggled with this issue, resulting now and then in mergers and separations of the two entities. Countries that have opted for a merger, as Ghana subsequently did, however, face the challenge of ensuring that the priorities of long term planning are not sacrificed in the newly created institution. This possibility is real given the relative power of the Finance ministry.

The Aid Architecture
Ghana's relationship with donors has evolved over time as have the modalities of aid delivery. While project aid still dominates aid delivery, general budgetary support is gaining prominence as the preferred aid modality (Chapter 7). However, Ghana's experience reveals that narrow interests of ministries, departments, and government agencies may work against the need for consensus and better intra-government coordination that are so crucial for budget support to work as expected. Indeed, some line ministries prefer project aid because of the direct benefits it confers to them. Hence, heterogeneity in the aid preference set within recipient countries may prevent them from speaking with one voice in their dialogue with donors. Where such discordant views converge with donor preferences for more "visible project aid" the push for general budget support is less likely to achieve wide support. Moreover, the tendency for "off budget" allocations is likely to continue, made possible by the complicity of donors, non-governmental organization, line ministries and other narrow interest groups. Aid that continues to work outside of and parallel to government systems ultimately undermines the coherence of the development efforts by governments.

Monitoring Performance
Effective monitoring and evaluation requires the capacity to collect, analyze and disseminate data (Chapter 8). It also requires recognition of the importance of monitoring processes as well as outputs, outcomes and impacts. Most importantly, to be sustainable, monitoring and evaluation (M&E) must be demand driven or underpinned by an appreciation of its relevance for improved policy formulation. One way to nurture appreciation of such processes is to ensure that the findings of M&E reports visibly and credibly influence or inform policy making. The link between M&E outcomes and policy direction and reform is therefore vital.

Decentralization and Capacity
As policy implementers in priority sectors such as health, education water and sanitation, the institutional and managerial capacity at the sub-national level is vital for pro-poor service delivery. However, many local governing bodies lack

capacity to efficiently manage the resources allocated to them. Ghana's decentralization experience has exposed weaknesses in local capacity to implement development plans through sub-national structures. It has shed light on the importance of factoring capacity building into strategic planning systems and embedding them in national processes (Chapter 9).

Furthermore, although the Ghana poverty Reduction Strategy (GPRS) was greatly informed by the consultative process, overall, poverty programs were designed at the centre and subsequently reinforced by decentralizing provisions to ensure effective implementation at the local levels. Thus, for the most part, the role of decentralized agencies was limited to the implementation of the PRS, rather than being involved as partners in its design. This tended to undermine sub-national ownership of the PRS in spite of the fact that decentralized agencies designed their own development plans. Indeed, local development plans should not be substitutes for sub-national involvement in PRS design since these plans must take their cue from the overarching national poverty reduction strategy. Furthermore, due to limited capacity, district or local plans are in practice often formulated by consultants with limited local input. Capacity building, particularly at the sub-national level, must be an explicit strategic policy objective. To be successful, however, capacity building strategies must be supportive of national priorities, coherent and not dictated by the directives of donor partners.

Improvements in Data
Effective monitoring requires reliable data that is readily accessible and routinely updated. Even with improvements in Ghana's household survey since 1987, our knowledge of the incidence and depth of poverty remains partial. Seeking improvements in child poverty statistics, gender disaggregated data, and employment data are but small aspects of improving the overall statistical system. Such improvements are needed so that policy making is informed by recent knowledge not by anecdotes about what is happening with regards to poverty. More needs to be done to improve the information content of household survey. This effort must be complemented by a comprehensive population census to know how the numbers, composition, and spatial distribution may be changing over time to improve planning.

3.3 Operationalizing the Lessons

Lessons learned from experiences are useful frameworks for improving existing processes. But understanding how these lessons operationally inform policies is even more vital. In theory, incorporating all these lessons outlined above in the new generation of PRSs is likely to make them more comprehensive documents, but at the same time they may overburden and confuse the policy implementation agenda which indeed has been the bane of most African countries. The question that needs to be addressed from the outset is, is everything equally important? The additional questions that arise include the following. How do we prioritize or sequence these lessons in terms of implementation modalities? Are there synergies among these lessons such that internalizing one may in reality have a positive domino effect in addressing other concerns?

Unfortunately, these are country specific issues that depend in part on the initial conditions such as availability of capacity, the quality of existing institutions and the prevailing growth rate. Highlighting these lessons and concerns, however, provides a rich menu for debate during the PRS consultative process.

4. Second Generation PRSs: The Need for Growth

Despite improvements in Africa's growth record since 2002, only five African countries sustained growth at the estimated 7 percent rate required to halve poverty by 2015. Moreover, in countries where growth has been rapid and sustained, it has not been broad-based but largely concentrated in capital-intensive extractive sectors.

Informed by these developments, the emerging consensus in the PRS debate is that the absence of sustained and robust broad-based growth constitutes a key constraint to reducing poverty and achieving the MDGs particularly in low-income sub-Saharan Africa. In the middle-income countries the concern is less with growth but more with the distribution of the benefits of growth.

Indeed, at the 2005 ECA Conference in Abuja, the African Ministers of Finance, Planning and Economic Development affirmed that, "it is clear that Africa's progress towards significantly reducing poverty and achieving the MDGs has been hampered by insufficient economic growth, and because the benefits of the growth achieved have not, for the most part, been shared broadly across society". Ironically, these trends of inadequate growth and re-distribution have occurred even as Africa embraced, formulated and implemented poverty reduction strategies.

There are, however, indications that the new generation of PRSs is giving greater prominence to growth. For instance, Tanzania's "Mkutuka" or National Strategy for Growth and Reduction of Poverty (NSGRP), Uganda's most recent Poverty Eradication Action Plan (PEAP), Ethiopia's Plan for Accelerated and Sustainable Development to End Poverty (PASDEP) and Ghana's GPRS II (Growth and Poverty Reduction Strategy) have all revisited their growth strategies. Ethiopia's PASDEP targets an average yearly growth rate of about 8 percent to halve poverty by 2015. This is considerably higher than the 5 percent growth target adopted during its first generation PRSP (i.e. the Sustainable Development and Poverty Reduction Program). PASDEP also highlights the need to minimize volatility in growth.

GPRS II: Ghana's Response to the Growth Challenge

In recognition of the importance of growth to poverty reduction, Ghana has re-named its second generation PRS the Growth and Poverty Reduction Strategy (GPRS II) and recalibrated its growth targets and expenditure allocations to reflect this new emphasis. Compared to GPRS I, GPRS II targets a higher growth rate (6-8 percent versus 5 percent) and devotes more (10 percentage points) resources to growth.[4] The challenge for GPRS II will be to maintain this progress while also reinforcing efforts to address inequalities and the pro-poor focus of the growth agenda.

GPRS II is organized around three pillars: growth; human resource development; and governance. This is in contrast to GPRS I, which was organized around five thematic areas: Macro-economic Stability; Production and Gainful Employment; Human Resource and Social Development; Governance and Special Programs for the Vulnerable and Excluded.

Notwithstanding the reorganization of the GPRS II, agriculture remains the focal growth sector and the private sector maintains its designated role as the key driver of the growth process. The substantive differences between GPRS I and GPRS II center on emphasis, prioritization and resource allocation across the PRS pillars. The growth emphasis is reiterated in the GPRS II executive summary: *"While GPRS I emphasized poverty reduction programs and projects, the GPRS II emphasizes growth-inducing policies and programs as a means to wealth creation and poverty reduction."*

The growth focus of GPRS II cannot, however, be inferred from the costed resource needs of the strategy. A comparison of GPRS I with GPRS II reveals that the social sectors of the economy still account for the bulk of the total cost of implementing GPRS II even though the estimated resource needs for growth are greater in GPRS II than in GPRS I. The government's explanation is that, the cost of GPRS II only reflects public sector programs and projects. Since the public sector is directly involved in providing social services and not directly engaged in productive activities, costed public sector activities will invariably reflect a bias towards the social sector.[5]

Arguably, the costed resource needs of the GPRS II "growth pillar" could likely have been higher if the strategy had taken into account public-private partnerships projects in the sensitive area of energy and other government funded programs to cushion the vulnerable from potential economic shocks including energy price hikes. Furthermore, it is debatable whether, in the absence of scaled-up government interventions, particularly in the high risk agricultural sector, the private sector will respond appropriately to the policy incentives and objectives of GPRS II.

Perhaps in recognition of this fact Ghana's 2006 budget allocates the largest share of resources (45 percent) to activities identified to promote growth. Furthermore, donor resource commitments are aligned to the priorities of GPRS II.

Donor alignment is underpinned by a surge in resource commitments to the agricultural sector in 2006, and a relative decline in commitments to health and education. Over the period 2005-2006 the share of donor resources committed to the human resources pillar is projected to decline from 58 to 36 percent while the share of resources devoted to the priority area of growth is projected to rise from 37 percent to 58 percent.

The macro-economic framework of poverty reduction strategies has traditionally raised concerns about transparency and more recently about the need to expand the fiscal space for growth oriented initiatives. In Ghana, transparency of the discussions around the macro-economic framework continued to be a problem even during the formulation of GPRS II. The basis of formulating macro-economic projections remains weak and ad hoc, and so is the internal capacity of the relevant economic management institutions. As a result, many fear a continued dependence on the multilateral institutions for macro-economic policy directions. There is currently no institutional mechanism for engaging all stakeholders in a debate on the macro-economic framework. This is particularly important given the current focus on increasing the growth focus of second generation PRSs, and the constraints that fiscal and monetary restraint, the hallmarks of most macro-economic frameworks, tend to place on growth.

Preliminary estimates put the resource gap for full implementation of the poverty reduction strategy at approximately $1.2 billion. A relevant question emanating from the Ghana experience is: *What scope does the macro-framework provide for financing resource gaps through domestic and or additional foreign borrowing?* GPRS II indicates that the gap is likely to be financed through borrowing from the capital market. However, given the fact that the mechanisms for formulating the GPRS and the crafting of the macro-economic framework are carried out through parallel processes, it is uncertain whether the GPRS II document has the final say about the financing options for the macro-framework.

In sum, it appears that more work needs to be done to improve the effectiveness of Ghana's second generation PRS in achieving broad based growth. Notwithstanding obvious improvements, GPRS II is still bedeviled by some of the constraints of GPRS I. In particular, ownership of the macro-economic framework remains illusive and rests largely within the domain of the IMF and World Bank. Yet, national leadership in the design and implementation of the macro-framework is vital to creating the fiscal space necessary to achieve GPRS II's optimistic growth targets. Tackling this issue must therefore be a national priority.

The Way Forward

The prospect of additional aid from the G8 countries opens up both opportunities and challenges for the implementation of the second generation of PRSs. On the one hand it creates possibilities for financing growth initiatives without necessarily compromising investments in social services. On the other hand it raises several concerns about the effectiveness of aid which need to be addressed if such large resource inflows are to be justified, notably macroeconomic concerns about possible "Dutch Disease" effects, and the two main components of "absorptive capacity" (i.e. overall governance, especially public finance and expenditure management, and availability and motivation of skilled and trained manpower to deliver services and manage the key institutions).

The relevant question therefore is whether second generation PRSs have the requisite strategies to make optimal use of the expected resources. The foregoing analysis reveals that positioning second generation PRSs for accelerated growth will require more flexibility and innovativeness in the design of macroeconomic frameworks, greater attention to employment, the spatial and income distributional effects of growth, and credible systems of economic and political governance.

Thus, additional resources for the proposed "Big Push" are not a sufficient condition for poverty reducing growth. The "Big Push" should be understood to comprise not only additional foreign resources but a concerted effort to put in place appropriate national policies and programs that ensure widespread ownership, and address implementation and capacity issues. These are the elements of the *"Capable State."* A well-governed state should be capable of delivering services effectively, managing funds transparently and respecting the rule of law so that businesses thrive and deliver growth, jobs and income.

But achieving all these can hardly be the end of poverty. In the *Affluent Society*, John Kenneth Galbraith reminds us that growth is only for those who can take advantage of it. Poverty and inequality therefore can survive growth. Growth alone can hardly eliminate the vulnerabilities of the handicapped, the elderly and the children of poor families. Their specific afflictions and circumstances may preclude them from participating in the opportunities of growth. For example, when elderly women become poor it is likely that they will remain chronically poor because marriage and employment may no longer be options out of poverty. While we can point to informal social networks and the extended family system as the traditional means to tackling elderly income poverty, public policy cannot be oblivious to what may be an emerging socio-economic problem. What is needed is a re-examination of how social institutions can be used as primary social safety nets to address some aspects of the poverty problem. Research needs to be done to ascertain the trends in intra-household support, the emerging challenges, and how public policy can be used to complement or to strengthen that support. In short, a policy of social development is needed to go hand-in-hand with the push for growth which no doubt is needed as well.

In the end, poverty reduction will remain a work-in-progress. The GPRS is simply a step forward. The GPRS forced Ghanaians into open conversations about the poverty problem. It brought out quite dramatically the dangers that national aggregate data on poverty can create by masking sectoral, spatial, gender and age differences that are not inconsequential for human development. It provided a framework, even if imperfectly built, to address the problem. It challenged citizens to examine constantly, through monitoring and evaluation, the scope and effectiveness of public spending, the tools of taxation (both in raising revenue and as redistributive device), the performance of the institutions as well as the processes of economic management in ensuring equitable growth and development.

Notes

1. Poverty Reduction Strategies refer to the national development programs in general while Poverty Reduction Strategy Papers (PRSPs) relate to IMF/World Bank specific programs to address poverty. In this context PRSP are a subset of PRSs in general.
2. North Africa is performing relatively better than sub-Saharan Africa in meeting the MDGs. Ghana's progress towards achieving the MDGs as of 2004 is reported in the Annex.
3. These include the findings of the UN Economic Commission for Africa's PRSP Learning Group, the Overseas Development Institute (ODI) on behalf of the Strategic Partnership for Africa (SPA) budget support working group, the World Bank's Operations Evaluations Department (OED) and the International Monetary Fund's (IMF) Independent Evaluation Office (IEO).
4. GPRS I and II are not strictly comparable because of differences in the composition of the thematic areas or pillars.
5. There is no standard methodology for costing PRS. Hence inter country comparisons of PRS resource needs is problematic.

References

Armah B. Links Between the Budget and the GPRS in *Implementation of the Ghana Poverty Reduction Strategy: Annual Progress Report 2002,* May 2003.
Arne B. and A. Shimeles. *Policies for Growth and Poverty Reduction in Africa: How to Reach the Millennium Development Goals,* Department of Economics Göteborg University. Paper Presented at the Expert Group Meeting on "Second Generation Poverty Reduction Strategy" for Africa. UNECA March 24-25, 2005 Addis Ababa Ethiopia.
Commission for Africa. *Our Common Interest.* Report of the Commission for Africa, March 2005.
Government of Ethiopia. *Plan for Accelerated and Sustainable Development to End Poverty (PASDEP),* Draft. 2005.
IMF Independent Evaluation Office, "Evaluation of the IMF's Role in Poverty Reduction Strategy Papers and the Poverty Reduction and Growth Facility", Washington DC. 2004.

Republic of Ghana. *Ghana Poverty Reduction Strategy 2003-2005. An Agenda for Growth and Prosperity, Vol. I* (Accra, February 2003).

————. Growth and Poverty Reduction Strategy (GPRS). Draft. National Development Planning Commission. 2005

Rwekaza S. M. Ownership, Leadership, And Accountability For Poverty Reduction, Issues Paper United Nations Economic Commission for Africa 2004.

United Nations Millennium Project, *Investing in Development. A Practical Plan to Achieve the Millennium Development Goals* Report to the UN Secretary General, New York 2005.

United Nations Economic Commission for Africa. *Economic Report for Africa, 2005.*

United Republic of Tanzania, National Strategy for Growth and Reduction of Poverty (NSGRP), Vice President's Office, June, 2005.

World Bank. *The Quality of Growth.* Oxford University Press, 2000.

Appendix: Ghana's Progress towards Achieving the MDGs (2004)

GOALS	WILL GOAL BE REACHED?			STATE OF SUPPORTIVE ENVIRON-MENT			
Extreme poverty and hunger 1. Halve the proportion of people below the national poverty line by 2015	Probably	Potentially Unlikely	Lack of data	Strong	Fair	Weak but Improving	Weak
2. Halve the proportion of people who suffer from hunger	Probably	Potentially Unlikely	Lack of data	Strong	Fair	Weak but improving	Weak
Universal primary education 3. Achieve universal access to primary education by 2015	Probably	Potentially Unlikely	Lack of data	Strong	Fair	Weak but improving	Weak
Gender equality 4. Eliminate gender disparity in primary and junior secondary education by 2005	Probably	Potentially Unlikely	Lack of Data	Strong	Fair	Weak but Improving	Weak
5. Achieve equal access for boys and girls to senior secondary by 2005	Probably	Potentially Unlikely	Lack of data	Strong	Fair	Weak but improving	Weak
Under-five mortality 6. Reduce under-five mortality ratio by three-quarters by 2015	Probably	Potentially Unlikely	Lack of data	Strong	Fair	Weak but improving	Weak
Maternal Mortality 7. Reduce maternal mortality ratio by three-quarters by 2015	Probably	Potentially Unlikely	Lack of data	Strong	Fair	Weak but improving	Weak
HIV/AIDS & Malaria							

GOALS	WILL GOAL BE REACHED?				STATE OF SUPPORTIVE ENVIRONMENT			
	Probably	Potentially	Unlikely	Lack of data	Strong	Fair	Weak but Improving	Weak
8. Halt and reverse the spread of HIV/AIDS by 2015	Probably	Potentially	Unlikely	Lack of data	Strong	Fair	Weak but Improving	Weak
9. Halt and reverse the incidence of malaria	Probably	Potentially	Unlikely	Lack of data	Strong	Fair	Weak but improving	Weak
Ensure Environmental Sustainability								
10. Integrate the principles of sustainable development into country policies and programs and reverse loss of environmental resources	Probably	Potentially	Unlikely	Lack of data	Strong	Fair	Weak but Improving	Weak
11. Halve the proportion of people without access to safe drinking water by 2015	Probably	Potentially	Unlikely	Lack of data	Strong	Fair	Weak but Improving	Weak
Global Partnership for development								
12. Deal comprehensively with debt and make debt sustainable in the long term	Probably	Potentially	Unlikely	Lack of data	Strong	Fair	Weak but improving	Weak

Source: Government of Ghana, National Development Planning Commission, 2004 and published in GPRS II.
* Lack of data implies inability to score appropriately

Index

About the Contributors

Joe Amoako-Tuffour is an associate professor of economics at St. Francis Xavier University (Canada) and research associate of Centre for Policy Analysis (CEPA, Ghana). He holds a Ph.D in economics from the University of Alberta (Canada). He has published in the American Journal of Agricultural Economics, the Review of Economics and Statistics, Water Resources Journal, Tourism Economics, Journal of African Finance, Journal of Environmental Management, Journal of Human Factor Review, and the Journal of African Economies and served as sub-editor of Journal of African Finance. In 2001—2003 he served as senior economist in the Ministry of Finance and Economic Planning (Ghana) and concurrently was the Coordinator of the joint Secretariat of the Consultative Group and the Multi-Donor Budget Support. At the request of the United Nations Industrial Development Organization (UNIDO), he coauthored the Annual Reviews of Ghana's Industrial Performance for 2002 and 2003. In 2004-2005 he coordinated the Economic Governance & Management Review technical team under the auspices of CEPA for the African Peer Review Mechanism of Ghana under NEPAD.

Felix Ankomah Asante has been a research fellow of the Institute of Statistical, Social and Economic Research (ISSER) of the University of Ghana since January 1996. He holds MPhil in agricultural economics from the University of Ghana, Legon, and a Doktor Agrarwissenschaften at the University of Bonn, Germany. His current research focuses on development issues relating to poverty, household food and water security, and decentralization. His work includes *Economic Analysis of Decentralization in Rural Ghana*. He also teaches Policy Analysis in the Master of Arts Development Studies program at the University of Ghana.

Bartholomew Armah is a senior policy advisor at the United Nations Economic Commission of Africa in Addis Ababa. He holds Ph.D from the University of Notre Dame and specializes in development and international economics. Dr. Armah spent the periods August 1998—August 1999 and again from August 2000 to 2003 on leave-of-absence from University of Wisconsin—Milwaukee and worked as a policy research analyst at the Institute of Economic Affairs (Ghana). He was subsequently invited by the government of Ghana to assist in the drafting and monitoring of Ghana's Poverty Reduction Strategy Paper. At the request of the United Nations Development Program (UNDP) and United Nations Industrial Development Organization (UNIDO) respectively, Dr Armah played a lead-role in drafting the first Millennium Development Goals (MDG) Report for Ghana and the Annual Reviews of Ghana's Industrial Performance.

Joseph R. A. Ayee is professor of political science and dean of the faculty of Social Studies, University of Ghana, Legon. He holds Ph.D from the Hebrew University of Jerusalem, Israel. He was a commonwealth scholar at the University of Glasgow from 1993—1994 and held the chair of the UNESCO/United National University Leadership Academy at the University of Jordan from February 2000 to December 2000. He was also the head, Department of Political Science, University of Ghana from 1995—January 2000. He has published extensively in the areas of decentralization, public policy, elections, leadership, public finance, public sector reform and human resource development. His current research interests include managing public toilets in Ghana, organizational culture of street-level bureaucrats in Ghana, financing democracy, and local conflicts in Africa.

William Baah-Boateng is a lecturer of economics at the University of Ghana. He is currently a doctoral candidate in the Harvard University and University of Ghana split Ph.D program in economics. His interest is in the area of Labor Economics, Industrial Economics, Public Economics and Macroeconomics. He has publications on "Trade Unions," "Small Manufacturing Firms," "Poverty, Informality and Employment," and "Demand for Carbonated Soft Drinks". He has consulted for ILO, UNDP and UNECA. He was a member of the Economic Governance & Management Technical team of the Centre for Policy Analysis (CEPA) for the African Peer Review Mechanism under NEPAD.

Abena D. Oduro is a research fellow at the Centre for Policy Analysis, Accra. She holds an M.Litt in Political Economy, from the University of Glasgow, Scotland. She participated in the preparation of the first Ghana Poverty Reduction Strategy and has been a resource person in several poverty analysis training workshops. In addition to her work in poverty analysis, Ms. Oduro has published work on trade policy, agriculture trade and the WTO. She was a member of the Economic Governance & Management Technical team of the Centre for Policy Analysis (CEPA) for the African Peer Review Mechanism under NEPAD.

Isaac Osei-Akoto is a research fellow at the Institute of Statistical, Social and Economic Research (ISSER), University of Ghana. He holds a B.A. and MPhil from the University of Ghana and Ph.D (Boon) in agricultural economics. His interest include issues relating to poverty and provision of public goods and services, and the health care.

Eric Osei-Assibey is a lecturer at the Department of Economics, University of Ghana and a part-time lecturer at the Institute of Professional Studies (IPS). His areas of interest include Environment and Natural Resource Economics, Econometrics Theory and Practice, and Monetary Economics. He has undertaken a number of environment related research including a review of Sustainable Development Strategy in Ghana and Energy Balance for Ghana. Mr. Osei-Assibey is a member of Economy of Ghana Network on Development Economics and Macroeconomics segments and a former member of OIKOS (Organization for International Resource Management).

Harry A. Sackey is an assistant professor of economics at the Malaspina University-College, British Columbia. He holds a Ph.D from the University of Manitoba, Canada, and an M.A. from the Institute of Social Studies in The Hague, The Netherlands. His research work on labour market issues, demography, community development, poverty, foreign aid effectiveness, and gender equity have revolved around the role of education, training and skills provision.

Daniel K. Twerefou is a lecturer at the Department of Economics, University of Ghana. He has consulted for the National Institutional Renewal Programme on the Social Impact Assessment of public sector reforms. He was also a member of an expert group constituted by the United Nations Economic Commission for Africa on the Sustainable Development Report for Africa under the theme "Managing Land-based Resources for Sustainable Development." He served as the dean of the School of Applied Sciences, Accra Polytechnic and the Policy Seminar Coordinator of the Economic Policy Management Program of the Department of Economics. Dr. Twerefou is a member of the Economy of Ghana Network—Development Economics and the Economic Society of Ghana.

Jacqueline Vanderpuye-Orgle is a doctoral candidate at the Department of Policy Analysis and Management at Cornell University. She graduated from the University of Ghana in 1999, with a bachelor of science degree in agricultural economics and was a recipient of the African University pre-doctoral fellowship in economics award. She spent a year at Yale University and went on to work as an intern with the macroeconomics and public policy divisions of the Development Research Group at the World Bank. She proceeded to Cornell University, where she earned a masters degree in applied economics and management.